OXFORD MONOGRAPHS ON
LABOUR LAW

General Editors: Paul Davies,
Keith Ewing, Mark Freedland

PENSIONS, EMPLOYMENT, AND THE LAW

Oxford Monographs on Labour Law

General Editors: Paul Davies, Fellow of Balliol College, Oxford and Reader in Law at Oxford University; Keith Ewing, Professor of Public Law at King's College, London; and Mark Freedland, Fellow and Tutor in Law at St John's College, Oxford.

This series is the first new development in the literature dealing with labour law for many years. The series recognizes the arrival not only of a renewed interest in labour law generally, but also the need for a fresh approach to the study of labour law following a decade of momentous change in the UK and Europe. The series is concerned with all aspects of labour law, including traditional subjects of study such as industrial relations law and individual employment law, but it will also include books which exmaine the law and economics of the labour market and the impact of social security law upon patterns of employment and the employment contract.

Titles already published in this series

The Right to Strike
K. D. EWING

Legislating for Conflict
SIMON AUERBACH

Justice in Dismissal
HUGH COLLINS

Pensions, Employment, and the Law

RICHARD NOBLES

CLARENDON PRESS · OXFORD
1993

Oxford University Press, Walton Street, Oxford OX2 6DP
Oxford New York Toronto
Delhi Bombay Calcutta Madras Karachi
Kuala Lumpur Singapore Hong Kong Tokyo
Nairobi Dar es Salaam Cape Town
Melbourne Auckland Madrid
and associated companies in
Berlin Ibadan

Oxford is a trade mark of Oxford University Press

Published in the United States
by Oxford University Press Inc., New York

British Library Cataloguing in Publication Data
Data available

Library of Congress Cataloging in Publication Data
Nobles, Richard.
Pensions, employment, and the law/Richard Nobles.
p. cm.—(Oxford monographs on labour law)
Includes index.
1. Pension trusts—Law and legislation—Great Britain. I. Title.
II. Series.
KD3132.N63 1993
344.41'01252—dc20
[344.1041252] 93–14379
ISBN 0–19–825448–2

1 3 5 7 9 10 8 6 4 2

Typeset by Cambrian Typesetters
Frimley, Surrey
Printed in Great Britain
on acid-free paper by
Biddles Ltd., Guildford and Kings Lynn

To Mary
and my parents

Editors' Preface

It is our aim as editors of this series to promote the publication of books which will make a distinctive contribution to the study of labour law. For this purpose, we have adopted a deliberately open-ended view of the subject. Consequently we expect to deal with topics which straddle the frontiers between labour law and other areas of law, whether it be social security law, pensions law, or company law. We expect that books in the series will not necessarily adopt a formal or legalistic approach, for we would wish to encourage authors to draw upon the contributions made by other disciplines, whether it be industrial relations, political science, or economics. And we expect, finally, that books in the series will not concentrate exclusively on legal developments in Britain. We are conscious of the importance of EEC law, and aware of the growing interest in the labour laws of EEC member states, as well as in comparative labour law generally.

This fourth title to appear in the series will, we hope, combine the virtues of fitting in extremely well with the theoretical aims and ambitions of the series as a whole and of contributing to a current practical debate about the state of the law relating to occupational pension schemes. So topical is this subject that we expect that the publication of this book will virtually coincide with the publication of the Report of the Pension Law Review Committee, to the proceedings of which Richard Nobles addressed a significant contribution. In one sense it was no accident that Richard Nobles' private project should converge upon the public view of pension law, for the Editors of the series had recognized that the inquiry which Richard Nobles was engaged upon was very necessary, and that he was singularly well qualified to develop such a project, significantly before Mr Robert Maxwell turned the issue into one of public investigation. His particular aim has been to relate pensions law to employment, and to the situation of the individual employee or pension scheme member. The central unifying theme which he has used to make this link is the idea of pensions as deferred pay. We commend to our readers the way in which Richard Nobles has built up that discussion on a sub-structure of more traditional trusts law.

P.L.D.
K.D.E.
11 July 1993   M.R.F.

Preface

The single good deed Robert Maxwell has done for pensioners generally is to ensure that the ownership and control of pension schemes is now high up on the political agenda[1]

By the time this book is published, the Pension Law Review Committee, chaired by Professor Goode, may well have reported. The committee was asked to 'review the framework of law and regulations within which occupational pension schemes operate'. The committee was formed in response to the scandal which accompanied the discovery that Robert Maxwell had removed some £420 million from pension schemes under his control. Its terms of reference, which go far beyond the prevention of fraud or the compensation of victims,[2] are a consequence of the attitude adopted by the House of Commons Social Security Select Committee.[3] For them, the scandal went beyond what Maxwell had taken illegally. It included learning that employers were able to benefit from their pension schemes, quite legally, through their general powers of control.[4] This book, which I began well before the Maxwell scandal broke, will, I hope, contribute to the debate, which that affair has generated, on the need to reform the law of occupational pensions.

Most of the book addresses the question of whether the current legal framework for private occupational pension schemes, based upon the law of trusts, is adequate to the task. A number of factors combine to make this a difficult question. First, there is no general agreement on what is promised to employees when they become members of an occupational pension scheme, or the basis on which those premises are made. In particular, there is a fundamental difference of opinion as to whether the pension scheme should operate entirely independently from the employer, or should be under its control. Second, the law of trusts is not easily stated. In the context of family trusts, where it originated, this body of law represents an extremely flexible

---

[1] Social Security Select Committee, Second Report, *The Operation of Pension Funds*, HC 61-II 1991/2 para. 13.

[2] Its full terms are to 'review the framework of law and regulations within which occupational pension schemes operate, taking into account the rights and interests of scheme members, pensioners and employers; to consider in particular the status and ownership of occupational pension funds and the accountability and roles of trustees, fund managers, auditors and pension scheme advisers and to make recommendations'. Pension Law Reform Committee, 'Consultation Document on the Law and Regulation of Occupational Pension Schemes', September 1992, para. 1.1.

[3] N. 1 above.

[4] Section 5 of the report gave examples of actions by employers where 'All too often there was nothing in law that could be done.'

form of regulation. This flexibility derives from the freedom of settlors, within broad limits, to draft their trusts in whatever terms they like; and from the ability of the courts, again within limits, to decide how those express terms relate to a broad selection of standards and principles. Third, the court's perspective on what the rights of pension scheme members ought to be, alters what those rights are. The view that pensions are deferred pay affects the process of interpreting the members' rights under the pension scheme. The express rules of a pension scheme, and the relationship between those rules and the general law of trusts, will be different if pensions are seen as part of deferred pay from what they will be if they are not.

Chapter 1 opens with a brief history of pension schemes, tracing how the legitimacy of employer control as been eroded with the increasing acceptance that pension schemes form part of the employees' pay. This is followed by a description of the main types of scheme, their benefit structures, and the most important of their rules. Chapter 2 introduces the problems of interpreting these rules, and the general law of trusts, and looks at the range of perspectives which can be brought to bear when interpreting pension schemes. Chapter 3 begins by looking at the manner in which trust law operates in the context of family trusts, concentrating on the duties of trustees. Chapter 3 will show that the general law of trusts is largely determined by judicial interpretation in the circumstances of the particular trust. Therefore, standards which appear to offer considerable protection of beneficiaries, such as duties to act in their best interests and not to have conflicting interests, are not automatically and inevitably applied. It continues with an analysis of the general duties of pension scheme trustees. Chapter 4 looks at the legal duties of employers under their pension schemes. Chapter 5 looks at the practical ability of members to enforce trust law duties.

Having introduced and analysed the general legal framework, the book proceeds to consider whether this framework serves to provide members and their dependants with sufficient protection in three crucial areas: funding (Chapter 6), the treatment of surpluses (Chapter 7), and decisions on investments (Chapter 8). These issues are linked by a common perspective: the claim that pensions are part of employees' pay, and as such, should not be open to exploitation by the employer. If one accepts this perspective, the employer's ability to control funding and investments and to benefit from surpluses is simply unacceptable.

Chapter 9 deals with sex discrimination. Here also, the perspective adopted by the courts affects the legal rights of members. In this section, the principal legal provision is Article 119 of the Treaty of Rome which, following the European Court's confirmation in *Barber* v. *Guardian Royal Exchange Group*[5] that pension benefits are pay within Article 119, gives members a directly enforceable right to equal benefits. This chapter

---

[5] [1990] IRLR 240.

examines the implications of European law for pension schemes, and contains little of the analysis of trust law which makes up the rest of the book. It has been included because of the importance of the issue of equality in pension provision, and because European law is based upon the acceptance of pension schemes as the employees' deferred pay, a perspective which UK employees hope their courts and government will come to share.

The final chapter sets out the legal reforms which need to be made in order to ensure that pension schemes operate in accordance with their members' legitimate expectations.

The book is concerned with private occupational pension schemes. As such it has little to say about those schemes within the public sector which are not based upon the law of trusts but upon statute, and which are unfunded. It also does not address the benefits paid to employees under the basic state pension scheme, since these are not paid by, or through, occupational schemes. Benefits paid under the State Earnings Related Pension Scheme (SERPS) are relevant since, unlike the basic state pension, benefits under this scheme can be provided by an employer through its occupational pension scheme. The rights given to employees and to the Occupational Pensions Board to protect benefits under SERPS have implications for the other benefits paid by private occupational schemes. The book does not consider the law surrounding the provision of individual or 'personal' pension schemes.

I should like to thank Mark Freedland, Paul Davies, Keith Ewing, Ruth Goldman, and Nicola Sheldon for reading and commenting upon drafts of this book, Erika Szyszczak and John Mesher for performing a similar service with respect to Chapter 9, and Graham Moffat for his assistance with Chapters 1 and 3. Bryn Davies's help with actuarial matters has been invaluable.

Contents

Table of Cases

Table of United Kingdom Statutes

Legislation from Other Jurisdictions

Table of Statutory Instruments

Table of European Community Secondary Legislation

[1]
Introducing Occupational Pension Schemes

In order to understand the law relating to occupational pension schemes, one needs to understand the schemes themselves: how they have come about; what benefits they offer; how they are administered; what rules they contain, etc. I have therefore chosen to start with a chapter which provides, in a condensed form, a lot of introductory material. It begins with a historical introduction to occupational pension schemes which maps out the evolution of pensions from *ex gratia* benefits to benefits as deferred pay. It then deals with some of the terminology of pensions (a more detailed glossary is to be found at the end of the book). The next section introduces the central features of the law of trusts (some of my readers will not be lawyers, and those who are may well have forgotten their trust law). The last part of the chapter sets out the most important provisions of pension schemes.

I. A BRIEF HISTORY OF OCCUPATIONAL PENSION SCHEMES: FROM GRATUITY TOWARDS DEFERRED PAY

Before the introduction of occupational pension schemes, the pensions paid by private employers were entirely *ex gratia* in nature. Old employees who were too sick to work would ask their employer to make some provision for their retirement. By the end of the nineteenth century, such ad hoc discretionary arrangements began to give way, especially within larger companies, to formal schemes. But although pensions had ceased to be ad hoc, they still had a large gratuitous element. Employers' contributions and the benefits which they provided were not seen as part of the employee's pay but, like the gratuities they replaced, were viewed as a reward for long service with one employer and something which the employer could legitimately control.[1] By contrast, employees' contributions were viewed as part of the

---

[1] This is not to say that employees never made claims against the employer's contribution at this time. At the turn of the century, civil servants organized the 'Deferred Pay Movement' to lobby for widows' pensions, arguing that their non-contributory scheme should pay death-in-service benefits that were equal to the returned contributions enjoyed by the widows of members of contributory schemes. But this movement did not survive its own success, and therefore

employees' pay, a form of enforced personal saving, and were generally returned to employees, with interest, if they should leave service, or given to their surviving dependents if they died before retirement.[2]

Occupational pension schemes were at first based upon private statute, or friendly societies' legislation but, by the beginning of the twentieth century, increasingly took the form of a trust. A trust was inexpensive, and it allowed the employer to set up its pension scheme on whatever terms suited it. The use of a trust established a separate fund to meet the cost of pensions, which thereby increased the employees' certainty that the pensions promised would in fact be paid, without the employer relinquishing control of the assets within that account. Hannah, in his book, *Inventing Retirement*, describes the early attractions of the trust as follows:

Initially, the concept of a 'trust' had an emotional appeal for those who were trying to create more harmonious relations between masters and men; it was especially favoured by liberal employers anxious to share the administration with employees, as had been traditional in most earlier statutory or friendly society schemes. . . . It was cheaper to establish than a statutory fund, and it was agreeably flexible since creative lawyers could draw up a trust deed with virtually any characteristic the employer chose. Those who wished to retain control of the funds themselves found, for example, that they could do so *de facto* by appointing all the trustees themselves, and many schemes of this nature were founded. Often these were non-contributory (i.e. entirely financed by the employer), so that all rights to pensions or refunds were lost by employees who left the firm.[3]

After 1921, the trust form became the universal basis for private occupational pension schemes. This was the result of the introduction, in that year, of tax reliefs which were conditional upon the schemes being trusts. Tax reliefs were justified by the 1920 Royal Commission on the basis that pension schemes represented the savings of employees, the majority of whom would *at that time* not pay tax. The Commission had recommended that tax reliefs be granted when 'an employer makes an irrecoverable contribution to a recognised fund for the benefit of his workforce.'[4] The Finance Act 1921 gave reliefs to pension schemes which took the form of 'irrevocable trusts',[5] a condition re-enacted in all subsequent legislation.[6]

In order to obtain tax reliefs, employers had not only to use a trust, but to relinquish their right to draft trusts in whatever form they saw fit. However,

sprawned no general recognition that the employer's contribution was as much earned as the employee's. See Leslie Hannah, *Inventing Retirement: The Development of Occupational Pensions in Britain* (Cambridge University Press, 1986), p. 116.

[2] In the case of manual workers, such practices were also mandated by the Truck Acts 1831–1940, repealed by the Wages Act 1986. Pension schemes were exempted from the Truck Acts by the Social Security Act 1973, s. 70(2).

[3] Hannah (n. 1 above), p. 19.

[4] Report of the Royal Commission on Income Tax (1920). Cmd. 615, para. 319.

[5] Finance Act 1921, s. 32 (3)(a).

[6] Now Income and Corporation Taxes Act 1988, s. 592 (1)(a).

since the Inland Revenue's conditions were the result of a concern to prevent tax abuse, their restrictions did not lead to the employees gaining many rights. The Inland Revenue have limited the maximum levels of benefit, ensured that these benefits are not taken prior to retirement, and have prevented overfunding.[7] They have not concerned themselves with minimum benefits or inadequate security. However, before 1970, the Inland Revenue insisted that schemes contain a rule prohibiting refunds to the employer, and prohibiting amendments which could lead to them.[8] This practice, which was not universally followed,[9] seems to have been based upon the Royal Commission's original recommendation that the employer's contribution should be 'irrecoverable'.[10] In 1970, the Inland Revenue introduced a requirement that all new schemes seeking tax reliefs should include a rule specifically providing that any surplus arising on winding up was to be returned to the employer. Whilst the reason for the 1970 change is unclear, it has had the effect of exposing schemes to the threat of being wound up for the purposes of asset stripping.

Aside from the Inland Revenue's interest in preventing tax abuse, employers were subject to little restriction in design and control of pension schemes during the first half of the twentieth century.[11] Occupational schemes continued, throughout this period, to be regarded as a reward for long service, offered to a privileged few. But the expansion of occupational pension scheme coverage amongst the workforce led to this view being challenged. With the growth in personal taxation that followed the Second World War, pension schemes offered a tax-efficient way of rewarding the ever-increasing proportion of the workforce who paid tax. Whereas the proportion of the workforce covered by pensions was 13 per cent in 1936, by 1956 it had risen to 33 per cent.[12]

The expansion of occupational pensions led indirectly to increased government regulation through the need to integrate them with the state pension scheme. The National Insurance Act 1959, which introduced graduated state benefits to supplement the basic flat-rate state pension, allowed employers to substitute their occupational schemes' benefits for the

[7] These restrictions are now to be found in Income and Corporation Taxes Act 1988 ss. 590–612; *Notes on Approval under the Finance Act 1970 as Amended by the Finance Act 1971*, issued by the Inland Revenue Superannuation Funds Office, IR 12 (1991); and various memoranda issued by the Superannuation Funds Office.

[8] Some Schedule D tax inspectors insisted that the scheme rules prohibit both a return of monies to the employer on winding up, and any amendment that could result in such a refund. See D. Bates, 'Payments to the Employer', in *Pensions World*, February 1984, p. 88; and the letter from the Controller of the Superannuation Funds Office to D. Bates, 13 May 1984, reprinted in *Pensions World*, July 1984, p. 408.

[9] In their evidence to the Millner Tucker Committee on Retirement Provision, the Inland Revenue stated that they allowed such clauses, but did not insist upon them. Report of the Committee on the Taxation Treatment of Provision for Retirement, Cmnd. 9063 1954, para. 72.38.   [10] Note 4 above, at para. 319.

[11] See Moffat and Ward, 'Occupational Pensions' in Lewis (ed.), *Labour Law in Britain*, p. 389.   [12] Hannah (n. 1 above) p. 40 and table 3.1.

new state benefit. Employers who did this paid a lower rate of national insurance contribution. This system, known as 'contracting out', represented a large state investment in the private pension sector. In order to protect this investment, the government created the Registrar of Non-Participating Employments to monitor schemes whose employers paid the lower national insurance contribution (a role now undertaken by the Occupational Pensions Board). The government's protection of its own investment has led to demands that all benefits offered by private schemes should receive scrutiny and protection.[13]

Expansion also meant that what had previously been seen as a privilege became a common term of employment. This focused public attention on the macro-economic effect of pension scheme provisions, particularly the practice of offering diminished pension rights to employees who left their employment before retirement. This came to be seen as an unaccaptable restriction on the mobility of labour, prompting government to legislate on the preservation of pension rights. The Social Security Act 1973[14] provided that employees who were over 26 years of age, with five years[15] membership of a pension scheme, who changed jobs, could no longer be offered a return of their own contributions plus interest. Instead, they had to be offered a deferred pension calculated on the same basis as that of members who remained with the employer. Following preservation, pensions could no longer be seen solely as a reward for long service, since members could now expect to accrue pension rights for each year of service once the five-year period has passed. With employees earning non-forfeitable pension benefits throughout their service with the employer, it was easier to see pensions as deferred pay.

Prior to the 1970s, unions had not sought pension schemes for their members. This may have been partly due to the concentration of early pension schemes on sectors of the workforce which were less likely to be unionized and, after the war, to the Trade Union movement's general commitment to the state pensions and the welfare state.[16] But the 1970s saw

---

[13] In response, the Occupational Pensions Board has produced reports on the security of scheme members' expectations (Greater security for the Rights and Expectations of Members of Occupational Pension Schemes. Cmnd. 8649 HMSO 1982); the position of women members (Equal Status for Men and Women in Occupational Pension Schemes. Cmnd. 6599 HMSO 1976); the treatment of early leavers (Improved Protection for the Occupational Rights and Expectations of Early Leavers. Cmnd. 8271 HMSO); and the extent of members' participation (Solvency, Disclosure of Information and Member Participation in Occupational Pension Schemes. Cmnd. 5904 HMSO 1975). Much of the content of these reports has been put into legislation with increased preservation of members' benefits, requirements for transferability of benefits, disclosure, and equality of access for male and female employees.

[14] Section 63, brought into effect 5 September 1973. Social Security Act 1973 (Commencement) Order. SI 1973, No. 1219.

[15] The age-limit was removed by the Social Security Act 1985, s. 1; and the five-year preservation limit reduced to two years by the Social Security Act 1986, s. 10.

[16] See T. Schuller, *Age, Capital and Democracy: Member Participation in Pension Scheme Management* (Gower, 1986), p. 39. Manual workers' unions were also more concerned to

trade unions becoming increasingly involved in the negotiation of pension rights. These negotiations were prompted by the introduction of statutory wage controls[17] which, since they did not cover the introduction or improvement of pension benefits, gave impetus to the spread of pension schemes and, for the first time, made union negotiation part of the process of introduction.[18] Another stimulus was the Conservative government's proposal for a new state pension scheme, the State Reserve Scheme, for all workers who did not have adequate occupational scheme benefits.[19] The Reserve Scheme's benefits were not generous, prompting unions to seek substitute occupational scheme benefits.[20]

Union involvement in pension negotiation has increased awareness of the importance of pensions as a form of remuneration, and reduced the ability of employers to present it as an *ex gratia* provision. The recognition that pensions are pay has in turn prompted calls for greater involvement for employees in the administration of their scheme, and increased protection for employees against the ability of employers to manipulate the scheme to their own advantage.[21] But, despite the greater willingness of unions and employees to describe pensions as pay, their commitment to restraining employer control of pension schemes is extremely weak.

Pensions are not negotiated at local level, being usually organized on a companywide basis. They also appear, to all but the older workers, as a topic of no immediate interest.[22] These two factors combine to make pensions a subject which few workforces are prepared to take industrial action over, a fact not lost on management.[23] Such pension bargaining as does take place concentrates upon the value of the benefits offered. Management does not negotiate over the scheme's administrative provisions and, once the scheme is up and running, the employer's contribution does not form part of the annual pay-round, but is calculated by the employer in consultation with the scheme actuary.

In 1977, the Labour government produced a White Paper[24] which

---

equalize the respective take-home pay of white- and blue-collar workers than to pursue equal pensions. H. Lucas, *Pensions and Industrial Relations* (Pergamon Press, 1977), p. 5.

[17] The Counter Inflation (Temporary Provisions) Act 1972.

[18] See H. Lucas (n. 16 above), p. 5.

[19] *Strategy for Pensions*. Cmnd. 4755.

[20] The General and Municipal Workers Union at its 1973 Congress recognized that its officers and members should take a much greater interest in the occupational pensions movement and confirmed that the union had a duty to prevent members from being 'consigned' to the State Reserve Scheme. H. Lucas (n. 16 above), p. 5.

[21] See *Pension Fund Investment and Trusteeship* (Trades Union Congress, July 1983).

[22] Schuller (n. 16 above), p. 41.

[23] 'Members won't take industrial action. I know they won't take industrial action. The employers know they won't take industrial action, and worst of all they know that I know they won't.' Union negotiator, quoted in Schuller, ibid.

[24] Occupational Pension Schemes: The Role of Members in the Running of Schemes. Cmnd. 6514 HMSO (1976).

proposed to make 50 per cent member-representation on pension fund boards of trustees mandatory, with the appointment of member trustees arranged through recognized trade unions. The White Paper formed part of the Labour government's commitment to industrial democracy.[25] The White Paper justified equal representation on trustee boards on the basis that:

Their distinctive feature, not shared by other elements of the programme, is they deal with the management of resources which comprise the *deferred pay* of the workers concerned and with schemes set up and administered under trust law as separate institutions solely concerned with promoting the interests of their members.[26]

The White Paper's proposals were never enacted, but the threat of them did result in an increase in the number of schemes which had member trustees.[27]

By the 1980s, concern about the performance of the UK economy focused attention on the ownership and control of pension funds, which by then were the largest investment medium in the United Kingdom.[28] Pension funds had been criticized for their investment policies which, it had been argued, starved industry of venture capital whilst pursuing short-term gains.[29] The TUC proposed that British pension funds should reduce overseas investment in favour of long-term investment in the British economy. Lacking government support for investment controls, the TUC tried to implement these policies through increased worker-control of pension fund investment, justifying that control on the basis that the funds were the workers' 'deferred pay'.[30]

Whilst the idea that pension funds are members' pay has gradually taken hold, this has not prevented employers from designing and administering pension schemes as they see fit. The legal framework of pension schemes, based on the law of trusts has, until fairly recently, hidden the conflict between the competing claims of management and employees. Placing pension scheme assets in a trust has encouraged employees to think of the pension fund as their property, held on their behalf although not controlled by them. But the public perception of a trust is not that of the lawyer, and it is the lawyer who advises the employer. As Hannah noted above, a trust can be drafted to include whatever terms the employer wishes. To quote the words of one pension lawyer:

There is nothing in the overriding legislation which prevents an employer from setting up a balance of power in his scheme in any way he sees fit . . . It is one of the last

---

[25] It was followed, a year later, by the proposal to put employee representatives on the boards of companies—the famous Bullock Report. 'Industrial Democracy', Cmnd. 6706, HMSO (1977).

[26] Note 24 above, at para. 26. Emphasis added.

[27] See Schuller (n. 16 above), p. 78.

[28] J. Gower, 'Review of Investor Protector' (HMSO, 1982); H. Wilson, 'Committee to Review the Functioning of Financial Institutions', Report. Cmnd. 7937 (1980).

[29] See R. Minns, *Pension Funds and British Capitalism: The Ownership and Control of Shareholdings* (Heinemann, 1980). [30] Note 21 above.

strongholds where we have seen very little government intevervention in the freedom to contract.[31]

Whilst employees have relied upon what might be called the ideology of trusts—the idea that the trust would operate as an independent entity, with trustees acting solely in the best interests of the members—lawyers have been drafting trusts which employers can control.

Recent events have highlighted the gap between this ideology and reality. Funding levels have risen, leading scheme actuaries to declare that schemes are overfunded, with more assets than are needed to secure current liabilities ('surpluses'). This has led to lower employer contributions and even, on occasions, refunds. The issue of 'who owns the surplus', which boils down, in legal terms, to who has power, under the scheme's rules, to benefit from the surplus, has focused public attention on the legal framework of pension schemes and, in particular, on the powers of administration. The discovery that the late Robert Maxwell had removed £420 million from the pension funds under his control and the investigation and report by the House of Commons Select Committee on Social Security which followed it,[32] highlighted the gap between the members' view of pension fund money as their 'pay', and the view of many employers that it was simply part of their commercial operations. The fact that so much money could be removed from a pension scheme in breach of trust, cast doubt on the protections offered by trust law. But it also focused attention on the ability of employers to manipulate pension schemes and benefit from their assets without committing breaches of trust. The first shock to the public arising from the Maxwell scandal was to learn that £420 million had been removed illegally, the second was to discover that a determined Maxwell could have removed similar sums from his pension schemes quite legally by, for example, taking pension refunds such as those granted to Lucas Industries by the Occupational Pensions Board (£90 million after tax),[33] or by introducing a broad self-investment clause and then carrying out large amounts of self-investment, like the manufacturer which loaned 30 per cent of its pension scheme to its parent company at 2 per cent interest, with security of only a second charge on its freehold properties.[34]

In light of the Maxwell scandal and the Social Security Committee's report, there is reason to hope that the law of pensions may be reformed. But this does not make it any less important to review the workings of the existing legal framework. There is no panacea in moving from the general law of trusts to a Pensions Act, unless we know the content of that Act. To

---

[31] Sean Hand, quoted in 'The Operation of Pension Funds', Second Report of the Social Security Committee. 4 March 1992 HC Papers 61–II 1991/2 HMSO, para. 42.

[32] Ibid.

[33] See 'Lucas Pension Trustees Attacked', *Financial Times* 2 September 1992, p. 6.

[34] See 'Clouds on the Retirement Horizon', *Financial Times*, 7 March 1992. This may have been a breach of trust, but what would amaze most members of the general public is that it may *not*.

understand what needs to be reformed, and how, you need to understand the workings of the existing system. The rest of this book, will, I hope, provide part of that understanding.

II. TERMINOLOGY

A. TYPES OF SCHEME

This book is concerned with the pensions offered to employees by their employers: 'occupational pension schemes'. The benefits offered by these schemes are either calculated by reference to the amount of contributions paid by, or on behalf of, an employee, or fixed by reference to that employee's salary. In the first type of scheme, known as a 'defined contribution' or 'money purchase' scheme, the accumulated contributions, plus the return on their investment, are used to purchase an annuity. The second type of scheme offers benefits fixed by reference to some formula, and the employer undertakes to fund those benefits. Such schemes are called 'defined benefit schemes'. In the past, the benefit promise has been fixed in nominal terms: a pension of £x per week. But more recently, the benefits have been fixed by reference to the employees' salaries. 'Average salary schemes', as the name suggests, offer benefits that are fixed by reference to the employees' average salary during their membership of the scheme. But the dominant form of occupational pension provision is fixed by reference not to average salary, but to the salary at, or shortly before, the member leaves the scheme. These are called 'final salary schemes'.

Occupational pension schemes can offer their benefits as substitutes for those paid under the State Earnings Related Pension Scheme (SERPS), and in return, the employer and employees pay a lower rate of national insurance contribution. Such schemes are known as 'contracted-out schemes'. By contrast, schemes which offer benefits only as additions to SERPS, where the employer and employees pay the full national insurance rate, are called 'contracted-in schemes'. Until 1988, only average or final salary occupational pension schemes could be contracted out. Since then, money purchase schemes have also been allowed to contract out of SERPS.[35]

A large number of schemes reduce the benefits which they pay in order to take account of the state's basic (flat-rate) retirement pension ('integrated schemes').

Occupational schemes which require employee contributions are called 'contributory schemes', and those that do not are 'non-contributory schemes'.[36] Occupational schemes which pay benefits out of current revenue

---

[35] Social Security Act 1986, s. 8.
[36] The National Association of Pension Funds (NAPF) found in 1991 that 75% of schemes, covering 89% of members, required members to make contributions. National Association of Pension Funds Annual Survey 1991, para. 2.26 ('NAPF 1991').

are called 'unfunded' schemes. Those which pay for pensions using a separate fund of assets which have been previously set aside for this purpose are called 'funded' pension schemes.

Where an employee's occupational scheme offers benefits that are below the Inland Revenue maximum, employees may make individual payments to the scheme to increase their own pension provision. These arrangements are called 'additional voluntary contributions schemes' (AVCs). Some AVCs credit members with extra years of pensionable service, whilst others offer money purchase benefits.[37]

B. SCHEME MEMBERSHIP

Employees gain their pension benefits through being 'members' of the pension scheme. Some schemes require employees to reach a certain age or to have served a period of employment with the scheme employer before they can be admitted to membership. The period during which benefits are accrued is known as 'pensionable service'. A member who has two years' pensionable service and who leaves the scheme before her retirement must be offered a pension, payable on retirement. This pension is called a 'deferred pension' and the ex-scheme members who are entitled to it are called 'deferred pensioners'. Persons in receipt of pensions are called, as one might expect, 'pensioners'. Deferred pensioners can have the value of their deferred pension transferred into another pension scheme, or to their own individual pension scheme (a 'personal pension scheme'). This payment, called a 'transfer payment', extinguishes the transferring scheme's liability to pay the deferred pension it represents. Membership of an occupational pension scheme cannot be compulsory,[38] so employees may leave the pension scheme without changing employment. Such employees are entitled to a deferred pension or, if they prefer, a transfer payment.

In this book, 'members' refers to all persons who are currently in pensionable service and to ex-employees, whether the latter are deferred or actual pensioners. When there has been any necessity to be more specific, I have referred to 'current members', to distinguish those who are in pensionable service from those who have, for whatever reason, left the scheme.

C. THE TRUST DEED AND RULES

The provisions of an occupational pension scheme are found in its 'Trust Deed and Rules'. Generally, the trust deed will establish the scheme and will

---

[37] The NAPF found that 8% of scheme members were paying AVCs'. 75% of schemes offered money purchase benefits, 5% offered additional years of pensionable service, and 16% offered more than one type of benefit. Ibid., para. 2.3.4.
[38] Social Security Act 1986, s. 15.

often contain powers to appoint trustees and make amendments, whilst the rules cover the contributions to be paid and the benefits to be provided. The rest of the scheme's provisions can, depending on the practice of the drafting solicitors, be found in either document.[39] In this book, references to a scheme's 'rules' are intended to encompass both documents.

D. FUNDING

Scheme benefits are funded from a number of sources. In a contributory scheme, members will contribute a fixed percentage of their salary. Any assets not currently required to meet pensions in payment are invested in order to earn income and capital gains. New members may bring transfer payments with them. Any deficit between these sums and the full cost of the promised benefits is met by the employer. The employer is thus said to pay 'the balance of cost'.

III. INTRODUCING THE PENSION TRUST

WHY HAVE TRUSTS?

Occupational pension schemes within the public sector are usually constituted by statue. Often they are unfunded. Whilst their administration may involve fiduciary duties, they do not take the form of a trust. By contrast, within the private sector, the trust is almost universal. This is a result of the structure of tax reliefs. The Income and Corporation Taxes Act 1988, section 592, provides that for an approved pension scheme to have exempt status, it must be established under 'irrevocable trusts'.[40] The benefits of having 'exempt' status are that the income and capital gains which accrue to the scheme's investments are not subject to tax. Aside from tax relief, the greatest advantage of using a trust is the ability to put the assets securing pensions beyond the reach of the employer's creditors. In addition, using a trust overcomes the problems of privity which may arise when a dependant of a former employee seeks to enforce the pension promise. Historically, using a trust allowed employers to operate pension schemes on behalf of their manual workers with less risk of infringing the Truck Acts 1831–1940[41] (which prohibited the employer from making deductions from wages for its own benefit).[42] These advantages have determined that *funded* pension schemes

---

[39] B. Escolme, D. Hudson, and P. Greenwood, *Hoskings Pension Schemes and Retirement Benefits*, 6th edn. (Sweet & Maxwell, 1991), 3.01.

[40] An identical provision was included in the Finance Act 1921, when special tax reliefs were first granted to private superannuation funds.

[41] Repealed by the Wages Act 1986.

[42] Employers who made deductions on behalf of a third party were less likely to fall foul of the Truck Acts, contrast *Hewlett* v. *Allen* [1891–4] All ER 1024 with *Kenyon* v. *Parwen Cotton Manufacturing Co. Ltd.* [1936] 1 All ER 310. The Social Security Act 1970, s. 70(2) provided that the Truck Acts should no longer apply to occupational pension schemes.

should take the form of a trust. Private occupational pension schemes in the UK are almost all funded schemes.[43]

B. WHAT IS A TRUST?

Lewin on Trusts[44] states that:

The word 'trust' refers to the duty or aggregate accumulation of obligations that rest upon a person described as trustee. The responsibilities are in relation to property held by him or under his control. That property he will be compelled by a court in its equitable jurisdiction to administer in the manner lawfully prescribed by the trust instrument . . . As a consequence the administration will be in such a manner that *the consequential benefits and advantages accrue, not to the trustee, but to the persons called the cestui que trust, or beneficiaries.*[45]

The central concept of a trust is the idea of a trustee as a fiduciary: one who holds property on behalf of others, and acts in their interests rather than the trustee's own.[46] It is an idea that explains many of the general principles of the law of trusts such as, for example, the rule that trustees must act in their beneficiaries' best interests; must not put themselves in a position where their personal interests conflict with their duties as trustee;[47] must not act for their own benefit or for the benefit or any third party; must treat beneficiaries of the same class equally and the beneficiaries of different classes fairly; and must not act capriciously or unreasonably.[48]

The central idea of what it means to be a trustee locates trustees at the pinnacle of those who hold duties towards others, above strangers, bailees, or agents. Indeed, when discussing the obligations which people hold towards each other, 'trustee' is often used in substitution for the word 'fiduciary'.[49]

By drafting a trust, a lawyer intends to make use of the concept of a fiduciary relationship, and the law of trusts: the body of statute and case law which has grown up around earlier uses of the trust. The law of trusts fleshes out the fiduciary relationship, reducing the need for the trust to be a long and

---

[43] Of the 19 million people in the UK in 1987 with pension rights, 14 million were in schemes where there was an accumulated fund from which pensions were paid. Occupational Pension Schemes 1987: Eighth Survey by the Government Actuary HMSO (1991), para. 1.4.

[44] 16th edn. (1964), p. 3.   [45] Emphasis added.

[46] 'Let us begin with what is generally agreed. First, but by no means uniquely, fiduciary law's concern is to impose standards of acceptable conduct on one party to a relationship for the benefit of the other where the one has responsibility for the preservation of the other's interests. Secondly . . . it does this by proscribing one party's possible use of power and of the opportunities his position gives, or has given, him to act inconsistently with that responsibility.' P. D. Finn, 'The Fiduciary Principle', in T. Youdan (ed.), *Equity, Fiduciaries and Trusts*, (Carswell, Canada, 1989), p. 2. See also F. W. Maitland, *Equity*, 2nd edn. (1936), p. 44.

[47] See *Bray* v. *Ford* [1896] AC 44; and the discussion of trustees' duties in Chapter 3.

[48] See generally P. D. Finn, *Fiduciary Obligations*, (1977), ch. 10.

[49] A practice which led Westbury LJ to complain: 'Another source of error in this matter is the looseness with which the word "trustee" is frequently used . . .'. *Knox* v. *Gye* (1872) LR 5 HL 656 at pp. 656–6.

complicated document. As well as the general duties just mentioned, it also contains specific rules about the administration of a trust, such as when trustees can be replaced and what investments are acceptable.[50] These duties and rules operate as a useful set of implied terms. A trust which set out in detail everything that a trustee should do would be extraordinarily long and complex. The draftsman can use general words, but these may open the scheme to novel interpretations. Alternatively, the draftsman can rely on the rules which have been developed in the law of trusts. Where these rules accord with what the trust draftsman requires, there is no need to state them in the trust deed. Thus, for example, the statement that an employer is to be one of the trustees means that the powers which it exercises in this capacity must be carried out in accordance with the general duties of trustees and cannot simply reflect the employer's self-interest. Where the law of trusts does not suit the draftsman's purposes, it can usually be amended or supplemented by the express rules of the trust.

C. THE FLEXIBILITY OF TRUSTS

Whilst the general public may not know the law of trusts, they do understand that a trust involves assets being held by persons in a fiduciary position, and that this requires those persons to act not for themselves but for others. What they may not realize is the extent to which this central idea can be diluted by the express rules of a particular trust. The fiduciary relationship which is central to the trust can be combined with specific rules which make the particular trust operate in quite unexpected ways. To illustrate, consider the duty of the trustees to act in the beneficiaries' best interests. This duty can be circumvented by reducing the number of discretions left to the trustees, and allocating them instead to someone who is specifically excused from acting as a fiduciary.

The ability to exclude the Law of trusts, and to dilute or supplement the fiduciary relationship which lies at the heart of trust law, is part of the reason why the trust is said to be such a flexible legal form.[51] Whether this flexibility is to be applauded[52] depends upon what one seeks from a trust. If you want the trust to provide strong protections for the beneficiaries, its flexibility may be something to be deplored.

The law of trusts is not static. It develops over time. Because trusts are

---

[50] With pension schemes, the specific rules are less important than the general duties, since the deed (which is usually long and complicated) often replaces such implied rules with express provisions.

[51] F. W. Maitland described the trust as ' "an institute" of great elasticity and generality; as elastic, as general as contract'. *Equity*, 2nd edn. (1936), p. 23.

[52] Maitland certainly felt it was, calling it the 'greatest and most distinctive achievement performed by Englishmen in the field of jurisprudence'. *Selected Historical Essays* (1936), p. 129.

usually long-term arrangements, they can easily give rise to rights which were not within the contemplation of the draftsman at the time when they were drafted.[53] Again, this could be applauded as part of the flexibility of the law of trusts. Situations which were not envisaged at the time of drafting can be dealt with by changes in the law of trusts. But whether such flexibility is actually to be celebrated, at least within the context of pensions, depends on the view one takes of the entitlements of the parties before and after the legal development. For example, developments in the law of trusts which increase the employer's control over pension fund assets may, from the perspective of those who accept that the control of the fund has nothing to do with the benefits promised to members, be perfectly reasonable. For those who believe that the trust was intended to secure the independence of pension assets from the employer, such developments will be regarded as unfortunate.

Where new trusts are being set up, unwelcome changes in the general law of trusts can be quickly remedied through the flexibility afforded to the draftsman. Subject only to the limits of what can constitute a valid trust, an express clause can be introduced to nullify the judicial decision in question. With existing trusts, the position is very different. The ability to amend an existing trust depends on the power of amendment. In the absence of a suitable power, the trust assets will need to be transferred from an existing trust to a new one with suitable terms.

The ability to exclude or supplement most of the law of trusts by the express words of a particular trust means that the fact that pension schemes are trusts tells us very little about what the employee is likely to receive. The benefit formula, the level of contribution or solvency, the risk of the erosion of benefits due to inflation or poor investment returns, the ability to invest in the employer, the ability to return assets to the employer, the identity of the trustees, and power to amend the scheme itself are all things which may be stipulated in the trust deed and rules. All one can know from the fact that pension schemes are trusts is that they involve a fiduciary relationship. But this could be a very minimal relationship, with express rules creating such exceptions to the idea of trusteeship as to leave the trustee being hardly less than an absolute owner. For example, a trustee can be given power to terminate a trust by giving ('appointing') the trust property to herself. In these circumstances, the trust will exist only for so long as the trustee fails to make the necessary appointment. Whilst the pension trust is not so minimal as this, it does fall short of the kind of independence which the central idea of trust would seem to suggest.

To find out what the pension trust is, and how independent it is from the employer, one must ask what rules it has.

---

[53] Consider, for example, the development of investment duties described in M.R. Chesterman, 'Family Settlements on Trust: Landowners and the Rising Bourgeoisie', in G. R. Rubin and D. Sugarman (eds.), *Law, Economy and Society, 1750–1914: Essays in the History of English Law* (1984).

D. THE PROBLEM OF EMPIRICAL EVIDENCE

There is a lack of empirical evidence as to scheme rules. There are more than 80,000 different schemes in the UK.[54] Because public schemes tend to cover a very large number of employees, the vast majority of these 80,000 are private sector schemes, set up not under a statute, but as trusts. Whilst copies of scheme rules are available to the Inland Revenue, Occupational Pensions Board and scheme members, there is no central registry where scheme rules can be inspected by members of the public. Even if there were, those rules would have to be accompanied by a statement of current scheme membership before a researcher could gain a clear picture of the importance of any particular rule.

The only major empirical surveys are those conducted every four years by the Government Actuary, and the annual survey conducted amongst its members by the National Association of Pension Funds (NAPF). These surveys concentrate on the benefits offered by schemes rather than the rules which determine the basis upon which schemes are administered and controlled. With respect to the latter type of rule, the author has had to rely heavily on the experience of pension lawyers, as expressed in their pension journals and other publications, to gain a sense of the type and prevalence of different rules. The other useful guide has been the Inland Revenue's practice notes. Since all employers are presumed to want their schemes to operate in a tax-efficient manner, scheme rules can be generally assumed to comply with the Inland Revenue's requirements. With these caveats on the problems of evidence, we turn to look at scheme rules. The first rules examined are those which determine who trustees are. This will be followed by a consideration of the benefits offered, the contributions, investment powers, provisions for winding up, membership, and the power to make transfer payments from one scheme to another. The chapter ends by considering the general question of the different balances of power which result from different arrangements of these rules.

E. SCHEME RULES

1. Types of Trustees

The scheme rules may stipulate that the employer is also the scheme's trustee. It is also common for a subsidiary of the employer to act as a corporate trustee. But the most common form of trusteeship involves the

---

[54] Note 43 above, para. 5.3. The Superannuation Funds Office estimated the number as 130,000, but this included 30,000 schemes with less than twelve members. See 'Study of Self-Investment by Pension Funds: A Report to the Department of Social Security by Ernst & Young' (1991) HMSO.

appointment of individuals to a trustee board. The current use of each form of trustee is shown in Table 1, taken from the NAPF's 1991 Survey.

The scheme rules usually provide for trustees to be appointed[55] by the employer or, where it is a group pension scheme, by the principal employer.[56] As a result of this, a majority (if not all) of a scheme's trustees will be persons expected to have regard to the interests of the employer. The majority of the individual trustees or directors of the trustee company will be directors or senior employees of the employer. Following the threat in 1976 of legislation requiring a majority of employee-appointed trustees,[57] the number of employee trustees has increased.[58] The current level of member-representation is indicated in Table 2, taken from the same 1991 survey.

TABLE 1. *Types of trustees* (%)

	Private	Public	All schemes
Individual trustees (independent)	14	24	14
Individual trustees (not independent)	44	48	44
Corporate trustee (independent)	13	5	13
Corporate trustee (not independent)	40	19	40
The employer	12	19	12
Sample size	828	21	849

Source: National Association of Pension Funds Annual Survey 1991, table 32.

TABLE 2. *Schemes with employees other than management as trustees* (%)

	Private	Public	All schemes
Include employees other than management	59	76	59
Not included	41	24	41
Sample size	783	17	800

Source: National Association of Pension Funds Survey 1991, table 33.

[55] The 'statutory powers of appointment [of trustees] are, in the usual case, unlikely to be of importance in connection with large schemes because wide express powers of appointment are likely to be contained in the trust deed or rules of the scheme.' N. Inglis-Jones, *The Law of Occupational Pension Schemes* (Sweet & Maxwell, 1989), p. 39.

[56] Ibid., p. 42. 'The [trust] deed will usually provide for the holding company in the group to be the principal party to the deed and responsible for the appointment of the trustees and similar matters.' Escolme (n. 39 above), para. 3.06.

[57] Note 24.

[58] Whilst 57% of schemes have no member trustees, 62.2% of members are in schemes which have member trustees. See GAD 1991 (n. 43 above), p. 63, table 12.1. The NAPF found a

Even where employee trustees are appointed, their selection often remains with the management, without any democratic process. And even then, the employee trustees are unlikely to exceed 50 per cent of the total number of trustees.[59] Since scheme rules usually provide for decisions to be made by a majority of the trustees,[60] with the chair of the trustees having a second or casting vote in the event of disagreement,[61] the employee trustees can, if necessary, be overruled. In the words of one convenor and trustee: 'Our problem is that no matter how well or how long I argue, the chair's vote carries the day.'[62]

2. The Benefit Levels

The employer is under no obligation to provide his workforce with an occupational pension scheme and, unless the scheme is contracted out, need not provide any minimum level of benefits. The Inland Revenue have only been concerned with maximum levels of benefit. The employer must contribute to the scheme as a condition of receiving tax relief,[63] but the type and level of benefits that contribution is to fund, and the timing and adequacy of those contributions,[64] is left to be determined by the employer at the time of setting up the scheme.

The overwhelming number of occupational schemes offer defined benefits.[65] The most common such benefit is the right to a fraction of final salary of either 1/80th or 1/60th for each year of service.[66] The maximum benefit

somewhat higher percentage of schemes with member trustees: 59%, NAPF 1991 (n. 36 above), para. 2.2.5., and a more recent survey confined to larger company schemes found member-representation in 75% of schemes. Income Data Services Pensions Service Bulletin, September 1992. However, the definition of a member trustee is not exact: 'We have seen Lord Hanson on television telling us that he is an employee representative, which is not what most people mean.' Bryn Davies, independent actuary, quoted in 'Leading Company Pension Schemes Have Workforce Representatives on Trustee Board', *Financial Times*, 18 September 1992, p. 14.

[59] A survey of personnel managers, carried out in 1982/3, found that member trustees were in the minority in 95% of schemes. See T. Schuller (n. 16 above), p. 71.

[60] ESee Excolme (n. 39 above), 3–13. Such rules exclude the general Law of trust's rule that trustees must be unanimous. See *Luke* v. *South Kensington Hotel Co.* (1879) 11 Ch.D 121.

[61] Escolme (n. 39 above), 3–13.

[62] Labour Research Department's report on Surpluses, 1 September 1990, p. 4.

[63] 'The Board will not exercise their discretion to approve a scheme if the employer's contributions appear to be mere token contributions of insignificant amounts, i.e. of less than 10% of total contributions.' IR 12 (1991), para. 5.1 (n. 7 above).

[64] Ibid., para. 5.3.

[65] Private sector pensions are for over 90% of members calculated on a 'final salary' basis, i.e. based on salary at retirement or averaged over the final years or months of service. Schemes based on average salaries, and those based on a flat sum per year of service have virtually disappeared. GAD 1991, (n. 43 above), paras. 7.6 and 7.7. See also NAPF 1991 (n. 36, above), para. 2.4.2.: 87% of schemes, representing 94% of scheme members, provided benefits related to final salary.

[66] 'Nearly 90 per cent of the 10½ million members were contracted out of the earnings related additional pension under the state scheme, mostly with pensions based on 1/60th of their final salaries or, in the public sector, a pension based on 1/80th together with a lump sum on retirement.' GAD 1991, para. 1.5 and p. 38, table 7.7. The NAPF found that 69% of schemes

which the Inland Revenue will allow within a defined benefit scheme is two-thirds of final salary which, with a 1/60th scheme, ordinarily accrues over forty years.[67] A large number of schemes reduce the benefits which they pay in order to take account of the state's basic (flat-rate) retirement pension ('integrated schemes').

Within money purchase schemes, the maximum contribution is 17½% of salary p.a.[68] In 1989, the Revenue placed an upper limit of £60,000 p.a.[69] on the salary which may be taken into account when calculating the contributions payable under money purchase schemes, or the benefits payable under defined benefit schemes.[70]

The majority of the members of private sector schemes have an option to exchange part of their pension benefits for a lump sum at retirement.[71] The Inland Revenue limit lump sums to 3/80ths of final salary for each year's pensionable service, with a maximum of one-and-a-half times final salary after forty years. Members may take lump sums equal to two-and-a-quarter times the annual pension if this produces a higher figure.[72]

The Inland Revenue do not require occupational schemes to offer benefits to the spouse, offspring or dependants of a member. In practice, 85% per cent of married male members of private sector schemes are promised a widow's pension,[73] with most widows' pensions at least half the pension which was being paid to the member.[74] For most members in private sector schemes this pension is calculated using the spouse's full potential service, i.e. on all the years that he would have been a member if he had lived

had an accrual rate of 1/60th or its equivalent (1/80th plus a lump sum paid without commutation of pension). NAPF 1991, para. 2.4.3.

[67] IR 12 (n. 7 above), para. 7.3. Although the Inland Revenue will allow this maximum to be accrued over less than forty years, (ibid., para. 7.4). Where benefits are deferred beyond the scheme's normal retirement date, further accrual is possible up to 45/60ths of final salary. Ibid., para. 7.34.

[68] This is the limit for simplified, defined contribution schemes. See IR12 (ibid.) part 22. With these schemes the Inland Revenue do not limit the total value of the benefits which may be paid. Defined contribution schemes which do not qualify under part 22 are treated, for *revenue purposes*, as defined benefit schemes, i.e. their maximum benefits are 2/3rds final salary.

[69] Supposedly to be indexed to price inflation.

[70] Finance Act 1989, Schedule 6, para. 4; Income and Corporation Taxes Act 1988, s. 590c. There are complicated transition requirements. See generally *Simon's Taxes*, 3rd edn. Butterworths, 1985), E212–15B.

[71] GAD 1991 (n. 43 above), para. 7.2. In the public sector a lump sum is provided automatically.

[72] IR 12 (n. 7. above), para. 8.6. The option is popular with members. It represents a large cash payment which can be used for immediate consumption. It is untaxed, whereas the pension itself is taxed as earned income. It also represents a sum which can be invested to produce an income, and if not exhausted during retirement, can then be bequeathed to the member's relatives.

[73] Again the practice is almost universal in the public sector, raising the combined percentage to 94%. GAD 1991 (n. 43 above), para. 10.6.

[74] 77% of widows' pensions are based on 1/120th or better. GAD 1991 p. 52. The NAPF found that 78% of schemes paid a widow/er's pension of half the member's pension. NAPF 1991 (n. 36 above), p. 44, table 77.

through to retirement.[75] Widowers' pensions are offered to 67 per cent of the female members of private sector schemes.[76] Lump sums are often paid in addition to spouses' pensions,[77] and many schemes which do not pay spouses' pensions will still pay a lump sum.[78]

The Inland Revenue will not allow the payment of pension benefits to commence later than a member's 75th birthday.[79] Except on grounds of ill health, the earliest age that they will allow members to receive their pensions is 50.[80] In practice, the overwhelming majority of schemes have adopted at least one of the state pension ages as their normal retirement age,[81] and nearly all schemes pay a pension commencing immediately on premature retirement on grounds of ill health.[82] Where a scheme allows its members to take retirement early, the pension is often reduced to take account of the increased cost of providing it.[83]

Deferred Benefits and Preservation requirements   The benefits of deferred pensioners are inferior to those paid to member who stay with the scheme until retirement. Before 1973, there was no requirement to pay any pension to a member who had left a scheme before normal retirement date. The Social Security Act 1973[84] introduced a requirement that persons who leave an occupational pension scheme prior to their retirement be offered a deferred pension ('preservation'). This requirement currently applies to any member with at least two years' pensionable service.[85] The deferred pension has to be offered to those who leave on the same terms as those who remain.[86] Thus,

[75] Estimated as 2/3rds. GAD 1991, p. 52.

[76] Ibid., p. 53. A further 6% offer pensions to widowers on proof of their dependence on the member.

[77] 'The general pattern of benefits on death in service is for a lump sum to be paid with, in most cases, provision for a widows, widower's or dependant's pension.' Ibid., para. 4.

[78] The proportion of male members of pension schemes where a lump sum (other than a return of the member's own contributions) was provided for on the death in service of a married man was 94%. Ibid., para. 10.1.

[79] Income and Corporation Taxes Act 1988, s. 590 (3)(4). IR12 (n. 7 above), para. 6.1. This is the requirement for new schemes and new members. Earlier schemes are allowed to delay payment until after 75 (ibid.) but this would be extremely rare in practice.

[80] Earlier payment is allowed when a member retires due to ill health (ibid., para. 6.2). Certain occupational groups may have earlier retirement ages negotiated on a case-by-case basis (ibid., para 6.6).

[81] GAD 1991 (n. 43 above), p. 31. The NAPF found that 75% of schemes have the same pension age for men and women, with the majority of these choosing either 65 or 60. NAPF 1991 (n. 36 above), para. 2.4.1.   [82] GAD 1991, p. 39.

[83] 30% of the members of private sector schemes would have their pension calculated on the basis of their accrued service. Of these, 60% (i.e. 17% of total membership) would have this pension further reduced to take account of the fact that it was being paid from an earlier age. This reduction can be as much as one half. GAD 1991, p. 39. The NAPF found more generous treatment amongst its members: 57% of schemes, representing 44% of members, apply either no reduction or actually augment a pension where retirement is due to ill health. NAPF 1991 (n. 36 above), para. 2.4.4.   [84] Schedule 16, paras. 6(1) and (7).

[85] Social Security Act 1986, s. 10.

[86] Social Security Act 1973, S. 63, Schedule 16, paras. 8 and 10.

for example, if it is a 1/60th scheme, deferred pensioners and current members must both earn 1/60th of final salary for each years of pensionable service.

The protection offered by preservation is undermined by inflation. A final salary scheme fixes benefits by reference to the member's salary at the date on which that member leaves the scheme. The accrued rights of a current member are effectively indexed as long as the scheme is ongoing. The value of the benefits accrued by each year's pensionable service (1/60th, 1/80th etc.) is increased each time that their salary goes up. As earning inflation is usually greater than price inflation, the member's accrued rights are likely to increase in value in real terms. If the member expects to be promoted, she will expect the value of accrued benefits to increase by even more than earnings inflation. By contrast, the accrued benefits of deferred pensioners are fixed by reference to their salaries at the date of leaving service. They do not only lose the benefits which result from earnings inflation or promotion but, unless the deferred pension is increased in line with price inflation, they will see their accrued benefits fall in value in real terms. The combined effect of failing to increase accrued benefits in line with inflation and promotion is well demonstrated by the following example given in a 1981 report by the Occupational Pensions Board: under normal assumptions of earnings growth, the effect of just one job change at age 45 was to reduce an occupational pension to 60 per cent of that received by someone who stayed with the same employer throughout his working life.[87]

Continued concern over the plight of the early leaver has prompted improved protection for deferred pensions. The Social Security Act 1985 introduced a requirement to index deferred pensions up to the date of a member's retirement by the lower of the retail price index or a 5 per cent per annum.[88] The 1985 Act only required such indexation in respect of benefits accruing after 1 January 1985. For those leaving a scheme after 1 January 1991, all of their deferred pension must be indexed in this way.[89]

Pensions in Payment   When current members or deferred pensioners retire, and become eligible to draw their pension, they become pensioners. Because of inflation, pensioners cannot maintain their standard of living in retirement without the benefit of discretionary increases in their pension. The power to make them is sometimes held by the trustees alone, and more commonly

[87] Occupational Pensions Board, 'Improved Protection for the Occupational Pension Rights and Expectations of Early Leavers. Cmnd. 8271, HMSO London 1981, para. 5.10. Earnings inflation was 7½%, and indexation zero. Similar erosion is produced under the present legislation if earnings inflation is 12½%.

[88] Social Security Act 1985, s. 2, Schedule 1, para. 3. The NAPF found that 73% of private sector schemes, representing 53% of members, paid deferred pensioners no more than their statutory entitlement. NAPF 1991 (n. 36 above), para. 7.6.2.

[89] Social Security Act 1990, Schedule 4, para. 4.

shared between the employer and the trustees. Even where the fund has sufficient assets to increase pensions to offset the effects of inflation, there is no guarantee that such increases will occur. Any survivor's pension will likewise be devalued in real terms from the date it commences, until the survivor dies.

Whilst half of the schemes guarantee some increase to the pension in order to offset the effects of inflation,[90] these guarantees rarely exceed 5 per cent.[91] The Social Security Act 1990 will bring all schemes up to this level of protection and require all benefits accruing after the 'appointed day' to be indexed to price inflation up to 5 per cent,[92] and benefits accruing with respect to earlier service to be similarly indexed to the extent that this can be funded from actuarial surpluses.[93] There is no requirement to increase the pensions paid by money purchase schemes (except where the scheme is contracted out, and only then with respect to the benefits offered in lieu of SERPS.)[94]

Contracted-out Schemes   Nearly 80 per cent of scheme members in the private sector and virtually all scheme members in the public sector are in schemes which are contracted out.[95] These are the only schemes which are legally required to offer minimum levels of benefit.

Contracted-out defined benefit schemes are required to offer a benefit known as a Guaranteed Minimum Pension (GMP) which is intended to replace the benefit offered under SERPS. The accrual rate for a GMP is about 1/100th or earnings per annum. The GMP must be paid at state pension age: 65 for men, 60 for women. The GMP must be properly funded.[96]

Within contracted-out money purchase schemes, the minimum benefit is defined by reference to the financial advantage which the state provides to a contracted-out schemes: the lower rate of national insurance paid by the employer (the national insurance rebate). This rebate must be invested, and the accumulated sum which results from such investments must be used to buy the member an annuity on her reaching state pension age.

---

[90] GAD 1991 (n. 43 above), para. 9.5. Amongst NAPF schemes, the level of protection is somewhat better. The NAPF found that 70% of schemes representing 63% of members guaranteed some form of increase to pensions in payment under their rules. NAPF 1991 (n. 36 above), para. 2.6.1.

[91] GAD, ibid. NAPF, ibid.

[92] Social Security Act 1990, s. 11, Schedule 2, paras. 1 and 2.

[93] Ibid. para. 3. As at 4 April 1993, this provision was not in force.

[94] The benefit offered in lieu of SERPS must be indexed up to 3% RPI p.a. Social Security and Pensions Act 1975, s. 37A (introduced by the Social Security Act 1986, s. 9 (7)).

[95] GAD 1991 (n. 43 above), para. 5.5. The NAPF found that 87% of schemes, representing 94% of members, were contracted out. NAPF 1991 (n. 36 above), para. 2.4.2.

[96] Social Security and Pensions Act 1975, s. 41, Occupational Pension Schemes (Contracting-out) Regulations 1984, SI 1984/380, reg. 27; OPB, 'Contracted-out Salary Related Schemes Supervision of Scheme Resources', Memorandum No. 76.

A contracted-out scheme must provide a pension to the member's surviving spouse equivalent to half the GMP (or half the annuity purchased with the rebate in the case of defined contribution schemes).[97] The employer decides whether or not a scheme shall be contracted out, although there is a duty to consult with employees and trade unions before taking that decision.[98]

The GMP of deferred pensioners is indexed to earnings inflation, though this need not be undertaken by the scheme itself. If the scheme ceases to be contracted out, the members can be bought back into the state scheme by the payment of an Accrued Rights Premium. Otherwise, the scheme must preserve deferred pensions in one of three ways. It can increase them at a fixed rate;[99] or increase them in line with inflation;[100] or increase them in line with price inflation up to a maximum of 5 per cent p.a., on payment of a limited revaluation premium.[101] These options do not affect the amount which a member receives on retirement, only the form in which it is received: as a GMP paid by the scheme, or as an increased state pension ('additional component'). The GMP in payment is indexed by the scheme to the lower of 3 per cent or price inflation.[102] Where inflation exceeds 3 per cent, the state undertakes to maintain the real value of the GMP by increasing the pensioner's additional component.

The member is guaranteed to receive the GMP or its equivalent, whatever the solvency of the scheme.[103]

Discretionary Increases to Benefits The scheme will usually contain a power to increase the benefits; a power typically exercisable by the trustees, but requiring the employer's consent. In the absence of such power, benefits can be increased by using the power of amendment. Amendments have to be approved by the Inland Revenue as a condition of the scheme's continuing to

[97] Social Security and Pensions Act 1975, s. 36.

[98] Occupational Pension Schemes (Contracting-out) Regulations 1984, reg. 4. And to consult on variation of the contracting-out status, ibid., reg. 10(4).

[99] Currently 8.5% compound where contracted-out employment terminated before 6 April 1988, and 7.5% where it terminated on or after that date. Social Security and Pensions Act 1975, s. 35(7), Joint Office Memoranda 77, pp. 351–382.

[100] Social Security and Pensions Act 1975, s. 27.

[101] The NAPF found that 70% of schemes in the private sector, representing 63% of members, use the fixed revaluation basis, whilst 20% pay limited revaluation premiums. NAPF 1991 (n. 36 above), para. 7.6.2.

[102] The Social Security Act 1986, s. 9 (7), introduced a new Social Security and Pensions Act s. 37A, which requires GMPs accruing in the tax year 1988–9 and after to be indexed in this way.

[103] On a scheme ceasing to be contracted out, unless the Board approves arrangements for providing a preserved GMP, an accrued rights premium becomes payable, in return for which the employer is no longer liable for the GMP. If the scheme has insufficient funds to pay that premium, then, unless the default is due to that employee's connivance or negligence, the unpaid portion of the accrued rights premium will be waived. Occupational Pension Scheme (Contracting-out) Regulations 1984, SI 1984/380, regs. 23(1) 3(b), (5).

enjoy exempt approved status.[104] Contracted-out schemes must seek the OPB's consent to amendments, or risk losing contracted-out status.[105]

Contingent Benefits vs. Immediate Entitlements   All the members of a pension scheme are beneficiaries, and therefore have the right to insist that the trust be administered in accordance with its terms. In this sense, they all have entitlements. But only the current pensioners have a present right to payment. Current members only become entitled to demand payment from the trust when they retire and become pensioners, or where they leave the scheme before retirement and ask for a sum representing their prospective benefits under the scheme to be paid to another scheme or to a personal pension (a transfer payment). Thus, pensions in payment and requests for transfer payments represent the only current legal liabilities of a scheme; all the other liabilities are future or contingent liabilities, and the rights to them are future or contingent benefits. The only circumstance in which all the beneficiaries of a scheme gain a current entitlement to some part of the scheme's assets is on a winding-up.

3. *The Contribution Rate and the Level of Solvency*

The major advantage claimed for funded pension schemes is the greater security which this gives to the promised benefits. But the level of funding, and therefore that of security, is not laid down by statute. Instead, it depends on the rules of the scheme and the practices of professional actuaries.

The contributions of members do not vary from year to year. In non-contributory schemes, the members pay nothing. About 13 per cent of members belong to these kinds of schemes.[106] The rest are in what are known as contributory schemes. Here the members have to pay a fixed percentage of their salary. The most usual contribution rate for members within private sector schemes is 5 per cent.[107]

The balance of the cost of funding benefits over and above the members' contributions is met, within defined benefit schemes, by the employer. The employer contributes whatever sum the scheme actuary considers necessary to fund the promised benefits. Existing schemes will typically require the employer to make such contributions as the actuary decides.[108] Here, formally at least, the employer's contribution rate is set by the actuary. In more recent pension scheme rules, the employer may be expressly authorized to deviate from the actuary's recommendation. Here the employer may covenant to pay such contributions as the employer, having considered the

---

[104] Income and Corporations Act 1988, s. 590 (6). IR 12 (n. 7 above), paras. 16.5 and 18.3.
[105] Social Security and Pensions Act 1975, s. 50, unless the amendment is required in order to comply with Social Security Acts.
[106] GAD 1991 (n. 43 above), p. 28, table 6.2.
[107] Ibid., para. 6.4. Within public schemes the most common rate is 6%.
[108] Escolme (n. 39 above), ch. 10, para. 3.07.

advice of the actuary, decides.[109] There is considerable scope for the employer to influence the actuary's decision in order to weaken, or strengthen, solvency according to the employer's current financial needs and industrial relations strategy. (The limits of this influence are considered in Chapter 6.)

Schemes provide for the employer to terminate its contributions upon giving prior notice, with the usual period of notice being six months.[110] This means that the employer is never bound to continue with the scheme. If the scheme actuary indicates that next year's contributions will need to be greater than the employer is prepared to make, the employer can avoid this liability by giving notice. Any claim by employers that they 'guarantee' to pay the balance of cost of their pension scheme's liabilities, has to be seen in the context of this power to give notice, and thereby avoid the scheme's liabilities. Thus, all employers' contributions are voluntary payments, undertaken on the basis of a decision made, at least six months before, to continue with the scheme.

If employers' contributions are not paid, they remain a debt due to the trust, and enforceable by the trustees. In the event of the employer becoming insolvent, with employee contributions deducted but unpaid, up to four months of those contributions represent a priority debt. With contracted-out schemes, up to twelve months' employer contributions towards GMPs have priority.[111]

4. Investment Power

Under the terms of pension trust deeds, investment is the responsibility of the scheme's trustees. Employers do not reserve the right to tell the trustees how to manage the scheme's assets. The trustees' power of investment is usually in very wide terms.[112] Typically, the power will authorize them to invest in any type of investment that would be open to persons who were investing their own money.[113] The trustees will also have wide powers to delegate investment to fund managers.[114]

---

[109] This was the form of words in the current precedent of one firm of commercial solicitors.

[110] 'It is undesirable that the employer should be absolutely bound to continue contributions to the pension fund in all circumstances, and it is usual to add a proviso somewhat on the following lines: "Provided always that the company may at any time reduce, suspend or terminate its contributions by giving six months previous notice in writing to the trustee." ' Escolme (n. 39 above), para. 3.08.

[111] Social Security Act 1975, Schedule 3, paras. 2(3) and 2(4). The contributions are assumed to be 4½% of reckonable earnings in a contributory scheme, and 7% in a non-contributory one.

[112] Pension funds very rarely rely on the powers of investment set out in the Trustee Investment Act 1961. See J. Quarrell, *The Law of Pension Fund Investment* (Butterworths, 1990), p. 1.

[113] See e.g. W. Phillips, *Pension Scheme Precedents* (Sweet & Maxwell, 1957), para. 911.

[114] All but a few modern pension funds contain wider powers to delegate than the statutory ones set out in the Trustee Act 1925. See Quarrell, (n. 112 above) p. 27.

5. *The Winding-up Clause*

A full winding up is usually triggered by the employer being unable to continue contributing. The winding-up clause will require the trustees to convert the assets of the trust into cash, and use this to purchase annuities which offer identical benefits to those promised in the scheme.[115] Where the assets of the scheme are insufficient to purchase annuities for all classes of beneficiary, the winding-up clause will provide for certain classes to receive no annuities, or reduced ones. The benefits of existing pensioners and their survivors are usually the first to be secured.[116] Benefits earned by the members' additional voluntary contributions are usually the next order of priority.[117] If the scheme is contracted out, the next group of benefits to be secured must be those promised as a substitute for the state scheme benefits.[118] The benefits of deferred pensioners and curent members must be given the same priority on winding up.[119]

The benefits of current members on winding up are usually calculated on the same basis as if those members had left the scheme voluntarily, i.e. by reference to their actual salary at the date the winding up commenced. As with the benefits of those who change jobs, this has the effect of devaluing their benefits. They expected to receive benefits that were calculated by reference to a salary which would have risen in line with the general rise in earnings in the economy, and in some cases, would have risen even higher due to promotion or salary increments. Now they will receive benefits which will be calculated by reference to their current salary, and will only be increased up to their retirement by the lesser of price inflation or 5 per cent.[120]

The devaluation of current members' benefits which follows winding up makes the power to wind up, when held by the employer, a powerful weapon with which to influence even the most independent of trustees. It also further erodes the truth of any claim by the employer to 'guarantee', through balance of cost funding, the pension scheme's liabilities.

Where a scheme is insolvent on winding up, then, until recently, the

---

[115] Trustees may not always have to sell investments in order to purchase annuities. Insurance companies can simply take over the investments in exchange for providing annuities. Where the stock market is temporarily depressed, this may result in more of the scheme's liabilities being met than would otherwise be possible.

[116] See 'Greater Security for the Rights and Expectations of Members of Occupational Pension Schemes', report by Occupational Pensions Board, Cmnd. 8649 (1982), p. 95.

[117] Ibid.

[118] Social Security and Pensions Act 1975, s. 40 (3). Occupational Pensions Scheme (Contracting-out) Regulations 1984, regs. 40(1), (2), (3).

[119] Occupational Pension Schemes (Peservation of Benefit) Regulations 1984, SI 1984 No. 614, regs. 10, 12; Social Security Act 1973, Schedule 16, para. 9.

[120] Social Security and Pensions Act 1975, s. 52B, Schedule 1A; Social Security Act 1990, s. 14.

employer had no liability to make up the deficit. Since 1 July 1992 such deficits have become unsecured debts, enforceable against the employer.[121] Whilst such unsecured debts are unlikely to provide any great additional protection for members where the winding-up results from the employer's insolvency, the existence of such a statutory provision will increase the employer's willingness to claim that it underwrites the scheme's liabilities. When assessing such a claim, one must take account of the employer's ability, described in the last paragraph, to reduce the value of the current members' benefits.

Following the Finance Act 1970, the Inland Revenue introduced a requirement that the winding-up clause in all new schemes should provide for the employer to receive any surplus arising on winding up.[122] Whatever the Inland Revenue's intention in introducing this requirement, it has had the unfortunate effect of making all new pension schemes liable to pension asset-stripping. Although winding up is usually associated with a scheme's inability to meet its liabilities, the employer's right to receive surpluses on winding up provides it with an incentive to wind up solvent pension schemes.

The winding-up clause is likely to contain a power for the trustees to increase benefits, at least up to Inland Revenue maximum.[123] This power may be held by the trustees alone,[124] or held by them subject to the employer's consent, or held by the employer alone. Where the surplus would otherwise return to the employer under the clause described above, the power to augment benefits creates an extreme conflict of interest. Every £1 used to augment benefits is £1 less available to be returned to the employer. In the event of a winding up triggered by the employer's insolvency, the Social Security Act 1990 provides that the power to increase benefits will be exercised by an independent trustee.[125] This provision goes some way to prevent receivers or liquidators using the employer's powers under the scheme, and their own influence on the trustees, to veto benefit increases and thereby maximize the surplus which can be extracted from the scheme to pay creditors. In the event of winding up instigated by the management of a solvent employer, there is no such protection.

For schemes first approved by the Inland Revenue before 1970, the right of the employer to benefit from a surplus is less certain than in post-1970

---

[121] Social Security Act 1990, Schedule 4, para. 2; Occupational Pension Schemes (Deficiency on Winding Up etc.) Regulations 1992, SI 1992/1555.

[122] Occupational Pension Schemes, *Notes on Approval under the Finance Act 1970 as Amended by the Finance Act 1971*, IR 12 (1979) at para. 15.4. (IR 12 1991, n. 7 above, paras. 13.32 and 14.6).

[123] Benefits may also be increased by using the power of amendment, although there is a danger that this power will not be considered to survive the commencement of winding up. See e.g. *Re ABC Television, Goodblatte* et al. v. *John et al.* 22 May 1973, reported in R. Ellison, *Private Occupational Pension Schemes* (Oyez, 1979), p. 347.

[124] According to N. Inglis-Jones QC, scheme rules commonly allow trustees to increase benefits on winding up without the employer's consent. See Inglis-Jones (n. 55 above), p. 101.

[125] Social Security Act 1990, Schedule 4, para. 1.

schemes. Some of these schemes will have a similar clause to post-1970 schemes, and can be expected to operate in the same way. Others will contain a rule which prohibits any return of money to the employer or the adoption of any amendment which would have this effect.[126] These schemes usually make no provision for an eventual surplus.

As an alternative to winding up, trustees may be given discretion to close the scheme to new members. This allows the existing members to continue to accrue benefits.

6. *Membership*

Employees can only join an occupational pension scheme if they are employed by companies who are parties to that scheme.[127] The scheme may be a single-company scheme, or a group scheme. Companies owned by, or associated with, the principal companies of a group scheme can usually admit their employees to the group pension scheme. Conversely, where subsidiaries or associated companies leave the group scheme, their employees must, after a transitional period, cease to belong to the group scheme.[128]

Persons who cease to be employees of the companies covered by the scheme can no longer be members of the scheme.[129] This means that employees become early leavers, with benefits fixed by reference to current salaries, when they are made redundant or change jobs. They also have to leave the pension scheme if the company which employs them ceases to participate. This commonly occurs when subsidiaries are sold. The benefits received in these circumstances depend upon the circumstances of the sale and the scheme's rules regarding transfer payments.

When companies leave or join a group scheme, the accrued benefits of their employees are usually secured through a transfer payment. Schemes usually have power to make transfer payments to scheme which undertake to provide members' accrued benefits. Payments made on behalf of whole groups of transferring employees are called 'bulk transfer payments'.[130] The power to make a bulk transfer payment is used, following take-overs, mergers, and group reorganizations, to divide or consolidate the pension fund, and ensure that the members of the transferring scheme have adequate

---

[126] See e.g. the schemes in *Re ABC Television* (n. 123 above) and *Palmer* v. *Abney Park Cemetery Co. Ltd.* 4 July 1985, unreported but discussed in *Davis* v. *Richards & Wallington Industries* [1991] 2 ALL ER 563 at 590. The inconsistency of the Inland Revenue's approach is noted above at n. 8, 9.

[127] IR 12 (1991) (n. 7 above), para. 3.1.

[128] The usual transitional period is six months, though the Superannuation Funds Office will usually extend it to the end of the tax year following the tax year in which the change occurs. See R. Ellison, *Pensions: Law and Practice* (Longman, 1992), 8.021.

[129] 'The Inland Revenue, so far as is known, does not permit persons employed by companies other than companies participating in the scheme to continue to be contributing members.' Inglis-Jones (n. 55 above), p. 4 n. 3.

[130] The relevant rule usually forms part of the winding-up provisions, and is often referred to as 'partial winding up'.

security for their benefits in the new scheme. Where a new company joins the scheme, there is usually power to grant accrued benefits to the employees of that company in exchange for a transfer payment. Transfer payments have an immediate effect upon the solvency of the respective schemes involved, diluting one and increasing the other. Reaching agreement on transfer payments is extremely difficult in view of the different rules and standards of solvency which exist.[131]

Employees may lose their scheme membership when their business is sold, even though their company continues to participate in the scheme. This is a result of the Transfer of Undertakings Regulations,[132] whereby they become employees of the purchasing company. The regulations provide that the transferring employees receive identical contracts with the purchaser, except for the provision of retirement benefits.[133]

The scheme rules may contain preconditions to membership, thereby restricting membership to persons above a certain age, or to those who have been employees for some minimum period, or excluding certain classes or workers such as manual-trades or part-time workers.

Membership of an occupational scheme is voluntary, and any term purporting to require employees to join a scheme is void.[134] New employees are commonly admitted to the pension scheme without their consent, which puts the onus on them to 'opt out' if they do not wish to be members. Individuals who are entitled to deferred pensions can surrender those

---

[131] A problem often solved by letting the individual members choose for themselves whether to transfer or not. Then the transferring scheme only need to say what it will pay, and the receiving scheme what it will give in exchange. No agreement is then required on the 'fairness' of either scheme's proposals.

[132] Transfer of Undertakings (Protection of Employment) Regulations 1981 (SI 1981/1974) Ibid., regs. 3, 5.

[133] The regulations do not apply 'to so much of a contract of employment . . . as relates to an occupational pension scheme . . . [or] to any rights powers duties or liabilities under or in connection with any such contract . . . relating to such a scheme'. Ibid., reg. 7. However, because these regulations fail fully to implement the EEC Acquired Rights Directive, 77/187, industrial tribunals may be prepared to find that employees have rights when they are transferred to or from public sector employers, or perhaps even private sector ones. Article 3(3) provides that pension rights shall not automatically transfer to the purchaser, but then goes on to state that 'Member States shall adopt the measures necessary to protect the interests of employees . . . in respect of rights conferring on them immediate or prospective entitlement to old-age benefits including survivors' benefits under supplmentary schemes . . .'. In *Perry* v. *Intec Colleges Ltd.* [1993] IRLR 56, the Bristol Industrial Tribunal decided that Article 3 of the Directive could be added to the Transfer of Undertakings Regulations, and thereby create pension rights against acquiring employers in the private sector. The tribunal relied upon *Lister* v. *Forth Dry Dock & Engineering Co. Ltd.* [1989] IRLR 161, in which the House of Lords implied an additional clause into these regulations for a similar purpose.

The complexity and discretionary nature of the remedy offered by the tribunal illustrates why the Directive did not create automatic transfer of pension rights. It also shows why the ECJ is unlikely to find that this part of the Directive has direct effect, even against a public sector employer, let alone a private sector one. But the UK government may be liable for its failure to implement this part of the Directive. See *Francovitch* v. *Italian Republic* [1992] IRLR 84.

[134] Social Security Act 1986, s. 15.

pensions and demand a transfer payment into a new occupational pension scheme or personal pensions scheme.[135] There is no requirement for schemes to accept transfer payments (whether made on behalf of individuals or groups), but the overwhelming majority of schemes do accept them.[136]

7. *Powers of Amendment*

The power of amendment usually requires that amendments proposed by the trustees be agreed by the employer, or vice versa.[137] The power is often hedged about with restrictions which exclude amendments that are contrary to the scheme's main purpose (the payment of retirement benefits), and disallows changes which would have a detrimental effect on the existing rights of members.[138] In pre-1970 schemes it also typically prohibits amendments which will allow the employer to receive a refund from the scheme. Some older scheme will not allow amendments unless they are first approved by the majority of the members.[139] By contrast, new pension schemes are likely to place no restrictions upon the power of amendment.[140]

Schemes also have power to make transfer payments into a scheme which takes over the liabilities of members who transfer to that scheme. Such a power can be used to effect an amendment which would be contrary to the power of amendment. Where the employer does not like the rules which govern the fund, it may arrange for the fund to be transferred to a scheme whose rules suit its purposes.[141]

F. THE BALANCE OF POWER

Members have certain statutory rights, but they do not exercise any of the discretionary powers contained within the scheme.[142] Discretionary powers are allocated between the trustees and the employer. The division of these discretions varies widely between different schemes. At one extreme are trusts in which all the discretions are left to the trustees. They have power to increase benefits during the life of the scheme or on winding up, without the consent of the employer. They have a free hand in deciding the investment policy. They appoint their own financial advisers and pay these out of the trust fund. The employer is not entitled to a refund of contributions from the scheme. Winding up is a matter for the trustees to instigate. The trustees appoint the actuary, pay him out of the trust fund, and set the contribution

---

[135] Social Security and Pensions Act 1975, s. 52B, Schedule 1A, part 11.

[136] The NAPF found that 97% of schemes will accept transfer payments. The principle benefit granted by the receiving scheme is additional pensionable service (46% of private sector schemes). 20% offer fixed pensions. NAPF 1991, (n. 36 above), paras. 2.7.1.)

[137] Escolme (n. 39 above), at para. 3.18.   [138] Ibid. 3.19.

[139] Ibid. 3.18.   [140] Ibid. 3.22.

[141] See e.g. the transfer in *Re Vauxhall Motor Pension Fund* [1989] 1 PLR 49.

[142] Some older schemes give members collectively control over the power of amendment. See Hannah, (n. 1 above), p. 98.

rate themselves. In such a scheme the major element of formal and direct control retained by the employer is the ability to give notice discontinuing its liability to contribute to the scheme. Indirect control is maintained by the employer's power to appoint and/or dismiss the trustees, and thereby choose persons likely to be sympathetic to its point of view.[143] Where trustees are required to be employees of the company, the employer can also control the identity of the trustees through its contractual power of dismissal.[144] There is no statutory provision which affects the identity of the trustees so long as the employer remains solvent. Once the employer goes into receivership or liquidiation, the trustees' discretionary powers may be exercised only by an independent trustee.[145]

At the other extreme is the type of scheme in which the employer may unilaterally: decide upon the contribution rate; exercise the power of winding up (and enjoy any surplus on winding up); amend the scheme; decide whether to pay ill-health benefits; and require a refund to be made to itself without winding up the scheme provided this will not prejudice Inland Revenue approval.[146]

In between these extremes are schemes which have a mixture of powers. Some may be exercisable by the trustees acting alone, whilst others are exercisable by the employer. There may be powers which are given to the trustees but whose exercise requires the consent of the employer, and vice versa. This dual control, or veto, is quite usual with respect to at least two of the most important powers: the power to increase benefits, and the power of amendment. As was described above, the power of amendment may be further restricted by stipulating restrictions on the use to which it may be put.

The formal division of power is affected by the role assigned to the actuary. Some schemes make the taking of advice a precondition for the exercise of powers such as the fixing of a contribution rate, the calculation of a transfer payment, or a change in the benefit structure. Others allow the actuary to

---

[143] On the authority of *Re Skeats Settlement* (1889) 42Ch.D 522, this is a fiduciary power. But the practical limitation which this places on the employer will be slight. Trusteeship cannot be sold by the employer, nor can the employer appoint trustees who have agreed to exercise their powers in the employer's interest. These are somewhat extreme situations. The employer is not prevented from appointing trustees who can be expected to serve its interests. The fiduciary nature of the power is only likely to result in a challenge where the trustees find themselves in confrontation with the employer, and are then threatened with replacement. But this is unlikely except where control of the employer changes, and trustees who were chosen by one management find themselves facing a new one—for example, after a take-over.

[144] 'There is at least one case in which on one view of the facts trustees of a scheme who were unwilling to fall in with the employer's wishes lost their jobs and thereby automatically ceased to be trustees.' Browne-Wilkinson LJ, 'Equity and its Relevance to Superannuation Today', p. 9. Paper given at Superannuation 1992: A National Conference for Lawyers.

[145] Social Security and Pensions Act 1975, ss. 57C, 57D; Occupational Pension Schemes (Independent Trustee) Regulations 1990, SI 1990/2075.

[146] This summary is based on the precedent used by the pensions department of a large firm of commercial solicitors.

exercise these powers alone, or after consulting the trustees and/or the employer. But the actuary will be consulted in connection with the most important powers within a scheme even if the scheme makes no reference to the actuary. It is simply not possible to exercise powers which have implications for the scheme's assets or liabilities in a responsible manner without taking actuarial advice. Whether one is an employer acting in self-interest or a trustee acting prudently, decisions which affect the solvency of the fund require some actuarial guidance.

Whatever the formal balance of power within a scheme, the trustees cannot ignore the fact that the interests of the members and those of the employer are interdependent. The most obvious interdependence is the interest of the current members in their continued employment. For most members, a good pension is poor compensation for a long period of unemployment. In *Cowan* v. *Scargill*[147] Megarry VC held that it was wrong for the trustees to have regard to the members' interest in their jobs when exercising their investment powers.[148] Whatever the status of this decision in law,[149] it is hard for trustees to ignore the current members' important and obvious interest in continued employment.

The interdependence of current members and their employer is not limited to the need for continued employment, but extends to their interest in good pensions. The welfare of the current members, as future pensioners, is dependent upon the employer's willingness and ability to contribute to the pension scheme. Current members can only accrue benefits whilst the scheme continues and so, if the scheme is a good one, it can hardly be in the members' interests for it to be wound up. Further, once a scheme is wound up, all of its current members are treated as deferred pensioners, with the result that their accrued benefits are no longer increased as their salaries rise. Instead they are eroded by inflation.[150]

Pensioners no longer accrue fixed benefits and, since they are a priority group on winding up, they can expect their benefits to be adequately secured by the scheme's existing assets. To that extent, they are no longer dependent upon the employer's willingness to contribute. However, their welfare in retirement is usually dependent upon discretionary increases to offset the effects of inflation. The likelihood that they will receive such increases depends upon the current value of the scheme's assets, and the employer's willingness to continue contributing. But even if the scheme had more than

---

[147] [1985] Ch. 270.

[148] 'I can see no justification for holding that the benefits to [the pensioners] should run the risk of being lessened because the trustees were pursuing an investment policy intended to assist the industry that the pensioners have left, or their union.' Ibid., p. 290. The case involved trustees' investment powers, but the reasoning can be applied to other power. See R. Nobles, 'Who is Entitled to the Pension Fund Surplus?', 3 ILJ (1987) 164, 173.

[149] For criticisms, see R. Nobles, '*Cowan* v. *Scargill*', 13 ILJ (1984) 167; H. Rajak, 'Trade Unions, Trustees and Public Policy', 1 Haldane Law Journal (1985) 39.

[150] See 'Deferred Benefits and Preservation Requirements', Part III E.

enough assets to meet the cost of such discretionary increases, this would not guarantee that the pensioners received them, since the employer usually has power to veto such increases. The presence of this veto ensures that the pensioners's standard of living cannot be maintained without the employer's continued goodwill.

In summary, trust law allows the rules of a pension scheme to be drafted in such a way as to maximize the employer's control of a pension scheme. But, even where all of these mechanisms for control of the trustees are eliminated, this does not create a trust in which the trustees can reasonably be expected to ignore the interests of the employer. The welfare of the members as employees and present or future pensioners is dependent on the willingness and ability of the employer to continue to contribute to the scheme. As such, it is wholly unrealistic to expect employers to exercise no influence over the administration of pension schemes. The question which remains is, how much influence should they exercise, and in what form? But identifying the ability of an employer to influence the administration of a pension is made difficult by the need for the powers and duties of the trust to be interpreted. Interpretation is, as we shall see in the next chapter, a controversial and indeterminate process.

[2]
Interpreting the Provisions of a Pension Scheme

Although the variety of clauses referred to in the last chapter represent different opinions amongst employers and their lawyers about where the balance of power should lie, the allocation of power does not stop with the drafting of rules. These rules have to be interpreted, and the immediate background for that interpretation is the general law of trusts. Of primary importance is the question of whether a particular power has, or has not, been allocated to the trustees, or to the employer, or to both. Once one has decided who has the power, one then has to decide how that power may be exercised. In particular, which of the various standards or duties available within the law of trusts apply to the power in question?

The thesis of this chapter, and much of the rest of the book, is that this process is not straightforward. Interpreting scheme rules, and deciding which duties attach to them, requires the interpreter to have regard to consideration of reasonableness. But, in the context of pension schemes, as in other aspects of the employment relationship, there is not simply one view of what is reasonable. Interpreting occupational pension schemes requires judges to have regard to two opposing perspectives for interpretation: the view that pensions are an important element in an employer's labour costs and should be left within the control of management; and the view that pensions represent the members' pay, and should be outside management's control.

The first part of this chapter seeks to demonstrate this process of construction, and show that the rights under an occupational pension scheme cannot be determined without reference to ideas of what those rights ought to be. It uses the example of two cases and a rule from the law of trusts. The two cases are *Re Courage Group's Pension Schemes, Ryan* v. *Imperial Brewing and Leisure Ltd.*[1] and *Imperial Group Pension Trust Ltd.* v. *Imperial Tobacco Limited.*[2] Both of these show the importance of interpretation in deciding the balance of power within a scheme, and the difficulties of resolving questions of interpretation by reference to the text alone. The trust rule then

---

[1] *Re Courage Group's Pension Schemes; Ryan* et al. v. *Imperial Brewing and Leisure Ltd.* et al. [1987] 1 All ER 528; [1987] 1 WLR 495.
[2] (Ch. D) [1991] 2 All ER 597; [1991] 1 WLR 589.

considered is the duty to act in the best interests of the beneficiaries. This gives rise to similar ambiguities which can only be resolved by a similar process of construction: one influenced, if not determined, by judicial views of what is reasonable.[3]

The rest of the chapter looks in detail at the perspectives which inform the interpretation of occupational pension schemes.

I. EXAMPLES OF INTERPRETATION

A. RE COURAGE GROUP'S PENSION SCHEMES, *RYAN* V. *IMPERIAL BREWING AND LEISURE LTD.*[4]

The court had to decide whether a particular clause gave the power of amendment to the employer, with the trustees being required to concur, or whether the power was joint, with the trustees having the right to withhold consent. The relevant clause stated that:

> The company may at any time . . . add to, delete or vary all or any of the provisions of this Deed or the rules and the [trustees] *shall* concur in executing any such deed Provided that no deletion or alteration shall be made which would (a) have the effect of altering the main purpose of the Fund namely the provision of pensions . . .[5]

Without further knowledge of pension schemes, one might be inclined to interpret the word 'shall' in this clause as a mandatory provision, meaning 'must'. The provision anticipates that the trustees might take a different view from the company, but provides that their opposition shall be overridden. Yet Millett J held that the trustees not only had a right to refuse to execute a deed of amendment, but in the particular circumstances of the case he felt that they were under a duty to refuse. He interpreted the word 'shall' to mean that amendments would not be valid unless the trustees complied.

Although Millett J claimed that his interpretation was the more 'natural', he admitted that this was only a 'peripheral' reason for his interpretation.[6] What was decisive was his view that:

> to exclude any discretion in the [trustees] would not only deny any effective protection to the members, but would make nonsense of the careful allocation found elsewhere in the trust deed and rules. What is the point of conferring a power on the [trustees] or

---

[3] 'Very often their choice is guided by an assumption that the purpose of the rules which they are interpreting is a reasonable one, so that the rules are not intended to work injustice or offend settled moral principles'. H. L. A. Hart, *Concept of Law* (Oxford University Press, 1961), p. 200.   [4] See n. 1 above.   [5] [1987] 1 All ER 528, p. 535.

[6] He had to choose between two interpretations of this inelegant clause in the knowledge that either interpretation could have been more clearly expressed through a different form of words. The interpretation sought by the company could be achieved by simply giving the company power to make amendments, without referring to the trustees. The interpretation sought by the members could have been better achieved by stating that 'the company may *with the consent of the trustees* . . . at any time add . . .'. Ibid., p. 536.

requiring the [trustees] consent to be obtained, if the power can be assumed by the committee, or the trustees' consent can be dispensed with by an amendment made by the company alone in which the [trustees are] bound to concur?[7]

Whilst members' may applaud his reasoning, the point' from the employer's perspective is that ultimate control remains with the company. Millett J is not denying that this could be desired by an employer, or that, with a different form of words, it could be achieved. He was simply unwilling, in the face of these words, in this scheme, to grant the employer such overriding control.

B. *IMPERIAL GROUP PENSION TRUST LTD.* V. *IMPERIAL TOBACCO LIMITED*[8]

This case arose because Hanson Trust PLC ('Hansons') wanted members to transfer from a scheme which had a large surplus, was closed to new members, and did not allow refunds, into a scheme which was open to new members, and which allowed refunds to go to the employer on winding up. If the members transferred, the surplus could be transferred with them as part of a bulk transfer payment. The members wanted to know if there was any way to ensure that the surplus in the first scheme was used to increase their benefits under that scheme. If there was, they would be ill advised to accept the transfer, since they could do better in the first scheme. If there was not, they might as well transfer.

The court was asked to construe two words: 'at least'. These occurred in a rule introduced two days before Hansons announced a take-over bid for the Imperial Group. The rule provided that pensioners would have their benefits increased by 'at least the minimum of 5 per cent or RPI'.

The pensioners argued[9] that the words 'at least' represented a power to give more than the required minimum, and that it was a fiduciary power exercisable by the committee of management alone. They claimed that this was the most reasonable explanation of such a provision within a scheme whose benefits were being eroded in value by inflation. Their interpretation would not place an unreasonable funding burden upon the employer, since the employer was able to give notice discontinuing its contributions. Even if such a power was unlikely to be introduced by an employer in a scheme under ordinary conditions, it was quite understandable in the context of a hostile take-over, where the existing management might be concerned that their replacements would cease to grant *ex gratia* increases to pensions in payment.

The employer offered a completely different interpretation. It argued that the words 'at least' constituted no more than a 'signal' to the committee of management to consider whether to grant increased benefits under the other

[7] [1987] 1 All ER 528, p. 536.   [8] Note 2 above.
[9] Transcripts of the argument were kindly supplied to the author by John Quarrell of Messrs. Nabarro Nathanson.

provisions of the scheme, i.e. that 'at least' meant that awards under this rule did not prevent the members from receiving further increases under other rules (the other rules gave the employer a veto over benefit increases). Because the employer paid the balance of cost, it was only right that it had control over all powers that could result in it losing the benefit of a surplus. A sensible employer was most unlikely to give the trustees powers which could result in it having to pay increased contributions without its consent. The words in question could not be seen to create an independent power because, unlike every other provision which set out a power, the clause did not specify who was to exercise it. If it were a power, then it was most unlikely, in light of the other powers set out in the scheme, that it could be exercised without the consent of the company.

Browne-Wilkinson VC came down on the employer's side on this point. He found it inconceivable that the draftsman would have intended these words to create an independent power without identifying the party to exercise it, and felt it was improbable that a company would wish to hand *this much control* to trustees.

These two cases not only demonstrate that ambiguities in the division of power are possible, they also provide examples of the ways in which those ambiguities are resolved, and indicate the importance within that resolution of judicial perspectives on what the entitlements of the various parties ought to be. Words are interpreted by reference to considerations of reasonableness. The judge looks to the words to find the intention of the drafting parties, and looks for an intention which is judged to be reasonable and probable. In forming a view as to what is reasonable, the judge looks at the implications of different interpretations. Reasonable parties are assumed to intend reasonable consequences. Such reasoning may appear circular: one has to form a view on what the balance of power within a scheme ought to be, in order to find out from the rules of the particular scheme what that balance is.[10] But this description is too crude. Judges do not simply start with a moral view of what they think the legal duties in a trust ought to be, and then announce what they are. Judges search amongst possible meanings, for one that seems most probable and reasonable. Ideally, the interpretation given to a form of words will be an acceptable interpretation in terms of syntax, a reasonable provision to find alongside the other rules of the scheme, and represent a reasonable intention of the parties which produces just results. Within this process, the judge's perspective on what the entitlements of the parties ought to be forms a crucial background matrix to the interpretation of the words in dispute. Such perspectives do not determine the outcome, in the sense that they overwhelm all forms of words and all arrangements of rules. But they do influence the outcome, in the sense that the duties, powers, and consequent

---

[10] See R. Nobles, 'Don't Trust the Trustee', 53 MLR (1990) 377.

balance of power found within pension schemes will be affected by the judicial view of what entitlements the parties can reasonably expect to enjoy.

C. THE DUTY TO ACT IN THE BENEFICIARIES' BEST INTERESTS

The importance of judicial perspectives is not limited to the interpretation of particular rules. It also affects the relationship between such rules and the general law of trusts. Deciding upon the duties of pension trustees, scheme actuaries, or employers cannot be the result of some kind of straightforward or automatic application of the law of trusts, as developed in the context of family settlements, to pension schemes. (Indeed, as will be shown in Chapter 3, the duties of trustees, even within family trusts, are quite flexible.) Instead, judges have to decide which of the many standards contained within the law of trusts should be applied to pension schemes, and how those standards should be given effect.

To illustrate the importance of perspectives to the general law of trusts, let us consider the question of what duties, if any, the trustees owe to the employer. One of the duties of trustees is to act in the best interests of their beneficiaries, but is the employer one of those beneficiaries? Within post-1970 schemes, the employer is entitled to the benefit of any residuary surplus arising on winding up. In an ordinary family trust, such a provision would make the party in question into a beneficiary. It would be one of the parties whose interests the trustees should protect. Apply this logic to a pension scheme and the conclusion is that the trustees are under a duty to act in the best interests of the employer as well as those of the members. Where these interests conflict, the trustees are under a duty to act impartially as between these two types of beneficiary. But this is not the view of the Occupational Pensions Board, nor of one of the leading Queen's Counsels in this area of law. The Occupational Pensions Board seems to regard the employer's right on winding up as an isolated right which does not convert it into a proper beneficiary. In its 1989 report it stated that although the 'trustees must act in the best interests of the beneficiaries, and impartially between all the categories':[11]

The trustees have only limited obligations towards the employer unless such an obligation is specifically created in the trust deed and rules.[12]

Inglis-Jones QC thinks that employers are beneficiaries for some purposes but not for others. Thus, in his book on the law of occupational pensions,[13] he states that trustees have to consider the position of employers 'as residuary *beneficiaries* of the scheme' when disposing of a surplus on winding up; whilst

---

[11] OPB, 'Protecting Pensions: Safeguarding Benefits in a Changing Environment', CM 573, para. 4.4.   [12] Ibid.
[13] N. Inglis-Jones, *The Law of Occupational Pension Schemes* (Sweet & Maxwell, 1989), p. 236.

generally they must 'ignore the well-being of [the] employers except in so far as this promotes the interests of the beneficiaries under the scheme . . .'[14] and that this 'must be particularly so if the scheme in question is in substantial surplus'.[15]

So how are we to choose between these interpretations of the trustees' duties to the employer? The starting-point must be to understand why it might not be appropriate to treat the employer as a beneficiary for all, or perhaps any, of the trustees' powers under the scheme. This is part of a much larger question: why can't one interpret pension scheme provisions in the same manner as one would a family trust? The answer to this question lies in the different context of a pension scheme and a family trust, and the different perspectives which this gives to any consideration of what the members and the employer may legitimately expect from the pension arrangement.

II. FAMILY TRUSTS AND PENSION TRUSTS

Family trusts involve someone, called the settlor, putting capital into a settlement for the benefit of other family members: the beneficiaries. It is primarily a device for the orderly transmission of wealth from one generation of a family to another.[16] The beneficiaries receive gratuitous benefits, and the settlor is presumed to be giving effect to his duties as head of the family. The primary maxim of construction—the need to give effect to the intention of the settlor—is a mixture of deference to an individual's right to dispose of property, and concern that members of a family should receive appropriate treatment.[17] The settlement is a one-off arrangement, with no further contributions from the settlor. The beneficiaries' interests are usually defined as a given share of income or capital, the quantum of which is fixed by the size of the original settlement and the consequences of investment. The settlor appoints trustees who can be expected to give effect to the settlement, and act independently of any outside pressure or interest.

This description of a trust is not true of all family trusts. It represents an ideal type. A similar description often appears at the beginning of a book on the law of trusts, usually followed by a discussion of the many ways in which a particular trust can vary from this ideal.[18] The function of such a description is, like the fiduciary relationship described in the last chapter, to

---

[14] Ibid., p. 103.   [15] Ibid.

[16] 'Most of the principles governing the creation, duration and administration of express trusts have been developed in this context of family wealth holding.' Moffat and Chesterman, *Trust Law: Text and Materials* (Weidenfeld and Nicolson, 1988) p. 23.

[17] See S. Gardner, *An Introduction to the Law of Trusts* (Oxford University Press, 1990), Chapter 2.

[18] See Moffat and Chesterman (n. 17 above), pp. 3–4; Gardner (n. 17), 1–9.

make sense of the rules which surround the trust. And, like the fiduciary relationship, express rules can be used to supplement or subtract from the general understanding of what a trust entails.

One modification of the ideal family trust is particularly important. This is the assumption that beneficiaries are entitled to definitive shares of the trust's capital or income. This assumption has been threatened by the increasing use of trusts as tax-planning devices. Tax planning has generated trusts, called discretionary trusts, in which the beneficiaries have no fixed entitlements, but receive whatever income or capital the trustees decide to give them. Trusts which continue to offer the beneficiaries definite shares of income or capital are now called, in contrast to the discretionary trusts, fixed trusts.

Pension trusts are certainly different from family trusts. With a pension trust, the members provide services in exchange for the benefits which they receive from the pension scheme and may also contribute from their own salaries. The size of the trust fund is not determined by the initial settlement plus investment, but is the result also of a continuous process of contribution; transfer payments in and out of the fund following take-overs and mergers; and, somewhat less often, refunds to the employer. The members' benefits are not fixed by reference to the size of the fund, but by their current salaries at the date of leaving the scheme.

III. PERSPECTIVES FOR PENSION SCHEME INTERPRETATION

There are obvious and important differences between a pension trust and a family trust, but what are the consequences of this for the interpretation of their respective rules? Differences do not, of themselves, make the trust an inappropriate legal form for pension schemes. It all depends upon how one views those differences: upon one's perspective. The rest of this chapter examines the perspectives which enable one to make sense of these differences. It will show that, from the employer's perspective, there is good reason to believe that the trust is an appropriate legal form for a pension scheme, especialy when one takes into account not only the traditional fixed trust, but the more recent discretionary trust.

There are three perspectives which can be expected to influence the interpretation of pension schemes: 1. the employer's general right to control the costs of employing its workforce; 2. pensions as dererred pay; and 3. pensions as contractual rights. The first two of these perspectives operate in opposition, providing reasons to interpret schemes in the interests of the employer or the members respectively. Neither of them provides an automatic and obvious answer to the interpretation of pension schemes. Each of them may nevertheless influence a judge's approach to the interpretation of scheme rules, and the relationship between a scheme's rules and the general law of trusts.[19]

The consequence of viewing pension schemes as contractual arrangements is that they can give rise to rights in contract as well as trust, and can be construed by reference to contractual rules of construction as well as trust ones. But the law of contract is as open to contrary applications and interpretations as the law of trusts. As such, it will not, by itself, provide reasons for interpreting pension schemes in favour of members rather than employers, or vice versa. Its importance lies in providing a mechanism through which to give effect to conclusions already reached on the basis of the employer's general right to manage or deferred pay considerations.

A. THE EMPLOYER'S RIGHT TO 'MANAGE' PENSION SCHEMES

If one accepts that occupational pension scheme members are in receipt of *ex gratia* benefits, they have much in common with the beneficiaries of family trusts. The Occupational Pensions Board, in its 1982 report, put it thus:

In the days when pension schemes were looked upon as a form of employer benevolence it may have been easier to equate the employer with a *paterfamilias* endowing his infant successors with an inheritance held in trust, but the notion now seems increasingly incongruous . . . Under trust law the employer is considered to be the 'settlor' who endows the trust from which the members or 'beneficiaries' draw their pensions, overlooking the fact that the members, as well as the employer often contribute to the scheme and the employer's contributions can scarcely be considered as an act of unilateral benevolence.[20]

But, despite the comments of the Occupational Pensions Board, recognizing that pensions are part of the cost of employing labour does not, by itself, make the trust form inappropriate. Although employers had little choice as to the legal form of their pension arrangements, given the tax legislation, there is every reason to believe that trust law has suited their purposes very well. Let us first consider why employers offer pension schemes, and then examine how the trust can be tailored to their needs.

Employers offer pensions as part of their industrial relations policy on the assumption that, like other aspects of industrial relations, this will result in

---

[19] In *Re Courage Group's Pension Schemes* [1987] 1 All ER 528, Millett J denied that the circumstances of pension schemes required any special approach to construction other than the need to ensure that interpretation did not frustrate the commercial purposes of the schemes. However, one can agree with this statement and still recognize that pension schemes are likely to be interpreted in a different manner from other trusts. As Warner J observed in *Mettoy Pension Trustees Limited* v. *Evans* [1991] 2 All ER 513 at 537, [1990] 1 WLR 1587 at 1610, even if the rules of construction are the same, the background *'matrix of fact'* against which they have to be construed is different. Identifying the likely commercial purpose of a pension scheme, and making sense of the scheme's provisions, requires a court to take note of factors which affect the reasonableness of any interpretation.

[20] 'Greater Security for the Rights and Expectations of Members of Occupational Pension Schemes', report by Occupational Pensions Board, Cmnd. 8649 (1982), para. 4.10.

greater efficiency (and profitability) from the workforce.[21] Pension benefits are part of the cost of employing the workforce, part of the reward which it receives for its services, and part of what motivates it to labour. Pensions provide an efficient means to secure enforced retirement of the workforce at normal retirement age or, where this suits the employer's purposes, even earlier. They attract, and retain, employees. (Their ability to retain labour is enhanced by the relatively poor benefits paid to early leavers.) They may also suit the employer's financial policy, since they provide a tax-efficient method of sheltering profits during periods of high tax rates, or low investment reliefs.[22]

The trust offers an employer a tremendously flexible instrument with which to pursue its management policy. Part of the pension promise can take the form of fixed benefits, whilst the rest of the arrangement (funding, solvency, access to scheme membership, discretionary pension increases), can remain within the employer's control.

With a new scheme, the employer can attempt to secure such flexibility and control by the use of express terms which seek to retain power with the employer instead of giving it to, or sharing it with, the trustees. But the need for such terms depends largely on the view which the courts adopt towards the role of trustees. If the trustees were left to make such decisions as they saw fit, with no interference from the courts unless they acted in a manner which was outside of any sensible intention that the employer might have intended, the employer could control the exercise of discretions through its control over who may be a trustee.

The type of family settlement which comes closest to giving settlors this type of contol is the modern discretionary trust. Under this form of trust, the beneficiaries are not entitled to a definite sum of money, but only receive such amounts as the trustees decide to give ('appoint') to them. (The relevant power is known as a 'power of appointment'.) The courts' attitude to the exercise of a trustee's power of appointment is captured in the words of Templeman J in *Re Manisty's Settlement*:[23]

---

[21] Some employers offer pension benefits instead of higher current wages because they wish to protect their workforce against the likelihood that, left to themselves, they will make insufficient provision for their retirement. Whilst this may be a paternalistic attitude it is not, as the Occupational Pensions Board rightly observed, entirely altruistic or gratuitous.

[22] This is not to say that every management has a rational understanding of the purposes which underlie the introduction or maintenance of its pension scheme. Some schemes were introduced without full consideration of their costs or what they might achieve. There are also divisions within management as to what they seek from pension schemes. Managers from the personnel department may see pensions as part of the management of human resources, whilst those from finance and production may see pensions as an unfortunate addition to labour costs. See T. Schuller, *Age, Capital and Democracy: Member Participation in Pension Schemes* (Gower, 1986), pp. 43–4. But interpretation requires one to attribute a unitary and rational intention to the employer, as part of the process of seeking the intention expressed in the trust.

[23] [1974] 1 Ch. 17.

The court may be also persuaded to intervene if the trustees act 'capriciously', that is to say, act for any reasons which I apprehend could be said to be irrational, perverse, or irrelevant to any sensible expectation of the settlor . . . the trustees have an absolute discretion and cannot be obliged to take any form of action save to consider the exercise of the power and a request from a person who is within the ambit of the power.[24]

In a large discretionary trust there is no question of the trustees having to exercise their discretionary power over benefits in the interests of all the eligible beneficiaries, or of having their impartiality questioned when they choose to exercise their discretion in favour of one beneficiary instead of another. The court's control is minimal, for it recognizes and accepts the settlor's desire to pursue her own interests with maximum flexibility and minimum interference from the court. Trustees can be trusted to exercise such uncontrolled discretions because they have been chosen by the settlor, and 'the settlor has no doubt good reason to trust the persons whom he appoints trustees'.[25]

There is a lot in common between pension schemes and the type of trust discussed in *Re Manisty's Settlement*. Both can be interpreted as part of a settlor's desire to secure maximum advantage from the trust form, with least loss of control, and with maximum tax efficiency. With both types of trust, the class of beneficiaries is often large and fluctuating. This is particularly the case with group pension schemes, when membership expands every time that a new subsidiary company joins the parent group, and contracts again each time a subsidiary is sold.

In *Icarus (Hertford) Limited* v. *Driscoll*,[26] the court treated a pension trustee's discretion to increase benefits on winding up a pension scheme in the same manner as a power to appoint income under a modern discretionary trust. The members were only acknowledged to have a right to be 'considered' for benefit increases. Aldous J interpreted this right as an essentially procedural question.

That task involves three stages: first, a decision to exercise the discretion; second, ascertainment of relevant facts to enable the discretion to be exercised; and, third, a decision to be made in good faith whether to apply the whole or part of the surplus to augment the entitlements of any of them. Provided that the trustee does that in good faith in the sense that he does not act for reasons which are irrational or perverse, then a court will not intervene.[27]

Provided that the trustee had assembled sufficient facts to enable her to form a view as to how to exercise discretion, the court would not interfere. In gathering these facts, there was no need to make inquiries as to the position of each individual member, but only to assess the position of each of the general categories of membership. Aldous J was not concerned by the fact that the

[24] Ibid., at 26.
[26] 4 December 1989. [1990] 1 PLR 1.
[25] Note 3 above.
[27] Ibid., at 6.

trustee, who was the scheme employer, was in liquidation, and that the liquidator was under a conflicting duty to act in the interests of the creditors, nor by the fact that she had stated her intention to act in the creditors' interests.

Aldous J's approach represents a straightforward application of the approach in *Re Manisty* to a pension scheme. There is no suggestion that the right to be considered was to have any substance, or that the trustees could be challenged unless they acted in a manner which no sensible employer could have intended. Thus the knowledge that pension benefits are not gratuitous does not necessarily dictate that they be interpreted in a different manner from family trusts. If the starting-point for their interpretation is a desire to fulfil the settlor's intention, the settlor is taken to be the employer, and the employer is understood to have wanted an industrial relations tool which gave it maximum flexibility with minimum loss of control, then there is every reason to interpret the two sorts of trusts in the same way. The fixed benefits can be interpreted in accordance with a fixed trust, whilst the discretionary benefits are interpreted in accordance with principles applied to powers of appointment within large discretionary trusts. On this basis, the members get exactly the same treatment as volunteers: they are given their fixed benefits, in so far as these are adequately funded, and they have no more than a somehwat vague 'right to be considered', with respect to any additional benefit. The fact that the benefits were earned makes no difference to the *employer's* intention.

Whilst the modern discretionary trust provides employers with an instrument which frees their trustees from close supervision by the courts, the same result can also be achieved through another interpretation of the pension scheme. There is no need for the employer to rely on case law generated by the modern discretionary trust, provided that the employer's right to the eventual surplus on winding up is treated as sufficient to make it into a beneficiary. If the employer is a beneficiary, then the trustees are free to consider its interests alongside those of the members when deciding how to exercise their discretions. In family trusts, the person who is entitled to property when the trustees fail to exercise a power is known as the 'object in default of appointment'. At the beginning of the twentieth century, the courts felt that the primary purpose of a settlement was to benefit the object in default, and there could be no challenge where property went to this party. According to Lord Parker of Waddington of the Privy Council in *Vatcher* v. *Paul*,[28] there can be nothing wrong with failing to exercise a power where this leads to the property in question going to the object in default of appointment:

Nor is there any case in which a bargain to allow funds to go in default of appointment . . . has been successfully impeached. *The limitation in default of appointment may be*

---

[28] [1915] AC 372.

looked upon as embodying the primary intention of the donor of the power . . . A bargain or condition which leads to the fund going in default of appointment can never defeat the donor's primary intention.[29]

A modern court may not be prepared to go this far when interpreting a pension scheme. But from the point of view of the employer's control, it does not have to. As long as the courts accept that a decision to prefer the employer is acceptable within a scheme in which the employer is a beneficiary, the employer can control the scheme by controlling who may be trustees.

1. Legitimizing the Employer's Control

Employers have not relied on the law of family trusts being applied to pension schemes just because the schemes share the fact of being trusts. They have not, therefore, expected that their intentions should provide the dominant basis for interpretation just because they could be described as settlor. Nor have they asserted their right to be considered or preferred by the trustees simply because they have an interest in default. Instead, employers have accepted the need to legitimize their control of pension schemes.

The Unitarist Approach   When seeking to justify their control over issues such as manning, current wages, training, etc., employers sometimes argue that the interests of management and those of the workforce are one and the same. E. Batstone, in *Working Order*,[30] calls this the 'unitarist' perspective. Within the unitarist perspective, the welfare of the workforce depends wholly upon the skill of the management, to whom it should defer.[31] If one accepted the legitimacy of the unitarist perspective of industrial relations, the pension scheme ought to be interpreted in whatever manner best enabled the employers to achieve their objectives. The employer is 'father to the workforce'[32] and, as such, can readily be compared to the settlor of a family trust. The purposes of the employer are the same as those of the workforce. There is no conflict of interest.

Within the unitarist perspective, as described by Batstone, the absence of conflicting interests is a product of the efficiency of market forces: the continued survival of the firm in a competitive world depends upon the ability of management to achieve its objectives. By asserting a contrary

---

[29] Ibid., at 3 79, emphasis added.

[30] E. Batstone, *Working Order* (Blackwell, 1984).

[31] 'Put at its most simple, unitarists believe that workers' interests are compatible with, and dependent upon, the achievement of employers' interests. If the latter are endangered—as with reform—then so are the former.' Ibid., p. 26. On the influence of the unitary perspective on labour law, see B. Napier, 'Judicial Attitudes towards the Employment Relationship—Some Recent Developments', 6 ILJ (1977) 1; P. Davies and M. Freedland, *Labour Law Text and Materials*, 2nd edn. (Weidenfeld & Nicolson, 1984), pp. 306–18.

[32] Ibid., p. 11.

interest, the workforce threatens the viability of the firm. If it secures such an interest, it exposes the firm to the risk of insolvency.

Employers have adopted a unitarist perspective when arguing for the control of their schemes. They have argued that since the employer will have to meet all (or most) of the future cost of funding pension benefits, it should have control over matters which increase the cost of those benefits. Without such control, the future viability of the firm is threatened. It is not enough for the employer to control its pension costs by discontinuing its contributions. This would be too blunt an instrument of control, since employers would only be able to do this at the risk of considerably damaging their industrial relations. In a competitive environment, management needs to control the cost of pensions without resorting to such draconian methods. Thus is must be able to control funding, benefit levels, and investment either through its own powers, or through its appointment of the trustees.[33] These arguments were accepted by the Vice-Chancellor in *Imperial Group Pension Trust Ltd.* v. *Imperial Tobacco Limited*,[34] who felt that the power to discontinue contributions provided the employer with insufficient control of its costs, and proceeded to hold that the trustees had no independent power to increase benefits. Discontinuance was too 'fundamental' a step.

The unitarist perspective has been attacked, within industrial relations, by more pluralistic approaches. The latter are premised upon the relative inefficiency of market forces. If the market is inefficient, then the survival of the firm will not depend upon production being organized in such a manner as to maximize profits. This allows the workforce to assert its own competing interests.[35] It can question the management's need to control the pension scheme even where this results in greater costs to the enterprise.

But one does not need to abandon the unitarist perspective, as it has been described here, in order to question the management's right to control pension schemes. One can question the legitimacy of interpreting pension schemes solely by reference to employers' interests without challenging the primacy of market forces. This is because pension funds are created in order to *insulate* employees from market forces. Pension schemes are funded in order to protect the employees' welfare in retirement from the effects of an employer's insolvency. They are premised upon the need for the employees'

---

[33] Employers have undoubtedly tried to present pension schemes as an area of industrial relations in which there is no conflict of interest. Schuller notes that employers resisted their inclusion within collective bargaining: 'The most common strategy is to foster the feeling that pensions are an integrative rather than a distributive issue; in other words, that employers and employees have a common interest in improving pensions and there is therefore no place for bargaining with its inherent implication of an opposition of interest' (n. 22 above).

[34] (Ch. D) [1991] 2 All ER 597; [1991] 1 WLR 589.

[35] Or alternatively, on the inevitability of conflict and the claim that such conflict is more efficiently dealt with through compromise than by simply asserting the management's right of control. See A. Fox, *Beyond Contract: Work, Power and Trust Relations* (Faber, 1974).

pension rights to survive the demise of the firm. Management's interest in continued profitability and survival is therefore expected, *in some circumstances*, to conflict with the members' interest in adequate pensions. Pension benefits represent rewards for past service which accrue over periods of up to forty years. Action taken to ensure the firm's survival may offer the prospect of job security, increased wages, and even increased pensions, but it cannot *always* justify placing pension rights at risk. The unitarist approach is especially suspect when applied to long-serving employees, who have large pensions to lose, little opportunity to gain through increased wages, and a low priority on winding up if the employer's strategy should fail to save the firm.

Another problem with the unitarist perspective is that it does not address the legitimacy of long-term agreements. The logic of the unitarist perspective is that management should not reduce its ability to react flexibly to market forces. But what if it decides to enter into long-term agreements, whether these be three-year legally enforceable collective-bargaining agreements, five-year contracts of employment, or pension schemes lasting half a century? Whilst the unitarist perspective may indicate that such arrangements are unwise, a court must be expected to give them legal effect.

Before leaving the unitarist framework, as described by Batstone, one should note that this is but one version of unitarism. The claim that there is no conflict between the interests of the workforce and management is not always based upon arguments of market efficiency. As Alan Fox has shown, the unitarist perspective has its historical origins in the ideology of master–servant relations, with the status of master carrying a responsibility for the general welfare of the servant.[36] The paradigm which underlies the master–servant relationship is not the efficiency of the market, but the idea of family, with the employer in the position of *paterfamilias*.[37] Pension provision can be seen as part of the employer's desire to create a:

style of personal relations cultivated by management, characterised by respect, consideration, and fair dealing, on the basis of which 'the good employer can establish a feeling of sympathy and co-operation between himself and his people akin to the old family feeling that existed between the master and his apprentices in the days before machinery and industrial centres'.[38]

There is some evidence that the courts will accept a unitarist perspective based upon the 'good' employer who is concerned with the welfare of its workforce, but seek to restrain 'bad' employers who are concerned only with profit maximization. The best example of this has been the court's antipathy to those employers who seek to exploit their power over the pension scheme of a company which they have recently acquired through a take-over. Millett J's judgment in *Re Courage Group's Pension Schemes, Ryan v. Imperial*

---

[36] Ibid. pp. 185, 248–9.   [37] Ibid., p. 184.
[38] Ibid., p. 196.

Brewing and Leisure Ltd.[39] captures this contrast between employers who can be trusted and those who cannot:[40]

In the present case, the members of these schemes object to being compulsorily transferred to a new scheme of which they know nothing except that it has a relatively small surplus. While they have no legal right to participate in the surpluses in the existing schemes, they are entitled to have them dealt with by consultation and negotiation between their *employers with a continuing responsibility towards them* and the [trustees] with a discretion to exercise on their behalf, and not to be irrevocably parted from these surpluses by the unilateral decision of a *take-over raider with only a transitory interest in the share capital of the companies which employ them.*[41]

Balance of Cost Arguments   As an alternative to the unitarist approach, employers argue not for total control of all pension fund assets, but for control of those assets which are not required to secure the scheme's existing fixed benefits (what is often called a 'surplus'—see Chapter 7). This represents a compromise between the employer's interest in the control of funding and the employees' interest in security of benefits. Employers argue that their contribution is made for a particular purpose: to achieve a balance of costs and liabilities on a basis calculated by the actuary. If it should turn out that the scheme has more than sufficient funds to meet its accrued liabilities, the balance represents a kind of overpayment, akin to a mistaken overpayment into a bank account. This excess should therefore be used for their benefit rather than that of the employees. Employers are entitled to control the scheme in order to ensure that this occurs. Such control is in the employees' interest as well as the employers'. If there is no fear of losing control of contributions which turn out to be more than were strictly necessary, the employer is encouraged to continue to fund on a generous basis, and thereby increase future security of the members' benefits.[42]

A variation of this argument starts from the observation that if the employer has only to meet the balance of cost, excess funding will lower the employer's future contribution rate. Since excess funding benefits the employer in the future, through a lower contribution rate, what is wrong with accelerating that benefit by allowing the employer to benefit from the surplus immediately?

---

[39] *Re Courage Group's Pension Schemes; Ryan* et al. v. *Imperial Brewing and Leisure Ltd.* et al. [1987] 1 All ER 528, [1987] 1 WLR 495.

[40] See also Browne-Wilkinson VC's judgment in *Imperial Group Pension Trust Ltd.* v. *Imperial Tobacco Limited* Ch. D) [1991] 2 All ER 597; [1991] 1 WLR 589, discussed at greater length in Chapter 4.

[41] Note 39 above at 545; 515 (emphasis added). This statement is actually a mixture of unitarism (based on the responsible employer), and pluralism (in that the trustees are expected to negotiate with the employer). The concern that take-overs may lead to a change from a paternalistic management style to a more profit-orientated approach is also evidenced in the OPB's 1989 report (n. 11 above) which devotes three chapters to the problems which may follow take-overs.

[42] See 100 Group Pensions Working Party Report, March 1992, p. 28.

The third form of this argument tries to draw an equation between the right to surpluses and the employer's practice when facing deficits. Since the employer has undertaken to make up any deficit between liabilities and assets which is identified by the actuary, it is only fair that it should have the right to enjoy any surplus over liabilities and assets which is similarly identified.

If one accepts these arguments, a pension trust should operate something like a mortgage. The assets of the scheme are there to secure the benefits of the employees, who are akin to mortgagees. Any excess thereafter should be held for the employer, who is like a mortgagor.[43]

The arguments which seek to give the employer a right to control and benefit from surpluses, whilst conceding the employees' interest in the assets which secure their fixed benefits, can all be countered.

The first balance of cost argument is an attempt to impose, retrospectively, a condition upon the employer's contribution. The truth is that employers have paid exactly what they agreed under the scheme rules: such contributions as the actuary required. The fact that such contributions might lead to a large excess of assets over liabilities had not been fully appreciated by employers or employees. If it had, the pension scheme rules would have been drafted to take account of it. An awareness that large surpluses could arise on winding up might have led to the drafting of rules regarding their distribution, akin to the detailed rules specifying how deficits were to be treated. Similarly, if it had been apparent that annual payments could, within an ongoing scheme, lead to actuarial valuations showing large surpluses, the rules might have been expected to give some direction as to their treatment. Since the schemes do not specifically address the treatment of surpluses, why should one imply conditions in favour of the employer?[44]

Employees can make exactly the same kinds of arguments. They have provided services in exchange for an employer's contribution to their pension scheme, without being fully aware of the possibility that such contributions

[43] The power of investment should be interpreted on the basis that the assets which secure the members' fixed benefits are invested for the benefit of the members, whilst those in excess of this amount are invested for the employer. Where a fund needs to be divided following a take-over or merger, the trustees should not object to the transfer of any assets in excess of those necessary to secure the members' fixed benefits. When receiving members into a scheme, the trustees need not have regard to the interests of the members until the influx of new members has removed a surplus from the existing scheme. The court should accept that the employer should control the power to increase benefits and use that power as it sees fit. With respect to the power of amendment, the trustees should only act to protect the security of members' benefits up to the point where there is a surplus. Having different duties towards such part of the fund as the scheme actuary considers to represent a 'surplus' means that the protection which the members receive from the trustees will depend on the actuary's opinion. As Chapter 6 shows, actuaries opinions are open to manipulation.

[44] The argument that the employer's contribution was made for the sole purpose of funding the scheme's fixed benefits is particularly difficult to apply to those schemes were there has been a practice of making discretionary increases. Such increases are often pre-funded, with the actuary setting a contribution rate which anticipates that they will be paid. Since the employer has funded for discretionary increases for the members, what could be wrong with ensuring that they receive them?

might lead to a large surplus of assets over liabilities. If they had realized that the employer had overestimated the cost of providing the promised benefits, they might have asked for higher benefits (or higher take-home pay), or they might have agreed to retain the agreed level of benefits, provided that any resulting surplus would be used for their benefit. But it seems unlikely that, had they been aware of the possibility that the employer's estimate of costs could be too high, employees would have agreed that any eventual surplus should be returned to the employer. And as to the claim that allowing employers to benefit from surpluses is for the members' future benefit, by encouraging a high rate of funding in future, there is simply no guarantee that allowing employers to reduce the amount of assets which currently secure the members' benefits will result in a higher contribution rate at some future date.

The second balance of cost argument (that surpluses ordinarily result in a reduced future employer's contribution rate, and so the surplus should be treated as the employer's property) suffers from reliance on a *non sequitur*. Why should the right to one form of benefit justify the receipt of others? One can just as easily argue the reverse. The ability of employers to claw back value from their past contributions by reducing future contributions is, from the employees' perspective, something to be deplored. There is absolutely no reason to worsen the employees' position by allowing employers immediate access to the funds.

The third argument (that employers have met deficits in the past, and should now benefit from surpluses) tends to oversimplify the situation somewhat. Employers have met deficits in the past, (particularly in the early 1970s, when stock-market yields were very low, which depressed the value of pension funds), but on their own terms. Employers were not legally liable for these deficits if the schemes were would up.[45] They only had to meet deficits if they continued with a scheme, and they would only do this where it suited their industrial relations policy. Their actuaries were free to choose methods and assumptions which allowed the deficits to be made good over long periods.[46] During the period in which these schemes were in deficit, it was the employees who were at risk. If the scheme had to wind up, their benefits would have been reduced. In these circumstances, the argument for a quid pro quo can be restated in favour of employees as follows: since the employees have born the risk of deficits in the past, should they not benefit now that their schemes are in surplus?

In future, employers will bear a greater portion of the risk, since they are now liable to make up any deficit arising on winding up.[47] But they still do not bear all the risk. One needs to remember that the event which is most likely to trigger a pension scheme wind-up is the insolvency of the employing

---

[45] The employer is now liable to make up deficits on winding up under the Social Security Act 1990, Schedule 4, para. 2.   [46] See Chapter 6.   [47] Note 45 above.

company, in which circumstance the employer's liability to make up a deficit may well be worthless.

In assessing balance of cost arguments, one should remember that, within an ongoing scheme, a surplus is not a physical fact, but simply an actuary's opinion. If economic conditions prove to be more harsh than the actuary has assumed when making his calculations, a scheme which is supposed to have a surplus may turn out to have insufficient assets to meet the fixed benefits.[48] Since the actuary's choice of methods and assumptions can be influenced by the employer (see Chapter 6), there is a danger that, by accepting balance of cost arguments, courts will allow the level of protection to be manipulated by employers.

The Courts' View of Balance of Cost Arguments   Whilst balance of cost considerations seem to have influenced the outcome of some cases, there is no judicial consensus as to what follows from such considerations, even when dealing with identical cases. In *Icarus (Hertford) Limited* v. *Driscoll*,[49] the court had to decide whether the winding-up clause gave the trustees a power or a duty to increase pensions. The relevant clause said that the trustee:

shall subject to Revenue Limitations at their discretion apply the whole or any part of such balance as they may determine to augment entitlements of Members or any of them.[50]

Aldous J had to decide which words had overriding effect: 'shall', or 'at their discretion'. He decided upon 'at their discretion'. The only reason which he gave in support of his preference was the basis of funding:

That surplus [£200,000] has to a large extent arisen due to the success of the policy, and if the scheme had not terminated, would have meant that the plaintiff could have reduced its contributions whilst still ensuring that funds would be available to meet the members' pensions. In that sense, the surplus is due to overfunding by the plaintiff during the period prior to the date of termination.[51]

By contrast, in *Mettoy Pension Trustees Limited* v. *Evans*,[52] another case dealing with the winding up of a pension scheme following the employer's insolvency, Warner J denied the relevance of the balance of cost funding to the construction of the rights of pension scheme members:

One cannot in my opinion, in construing a provision in the rules of a 'balance of cost' pension scheme relating to surplus, start from the assumption that any surplus belongs morally to the employer.[53]

---

[48] A point made by Lord Browne-Wilkinson in a speech given at an Australian conference on superannuation in 1992: 'Equity and its Relevance to Superannuation Today'.
[49] 4 December 1989. [1990] 1 PLR 1.   [50] Ibid., p. 5.   [51] Ibid.
[52] [1991] 2 All ER 513; [1990] 1 WLR 1587.
[53] [1991] 2 All ER 513 at 551; [1990] 1 WLR 1587 at 1619. Whilst Warner's judgment has been cited with approval in cases where an employer has sought to benefit from an ongoing pension scheme, there is some evidence that judges accept that employers should benefit from

In conclusion, one cannot interpret pension schemes solely by reference to management's right to manage, since the rationale for having funded schemes is to protect the members' pension rights from the consequence of the firm's insolvency, which would not be possible if management could control the scheme in whatever manner it saw fit. There has to be some compromise between management's right to manage and the members' right to protection for their pension benefits. The claim that management should have unrestricted control of those assets which are not required to secure the scheme's fixed benefits offers one such compromise. But the courts have not universally accepted the employer's right to control and benefit from surpluses. In denying the employer an uncontrolled right to manage pension trusts, or even to benefit from surpluses within such trusts, the courts have been influenced by another perspective: the view that pensions represent the members' deferred pay. And it is to this perspective that we now turn.

B. PENSIONS AS DEFERRED PAY

In its strongest form, the claim that pensions are pay refers both to the benefits that employees have been promised and the contributions which the employer makes to fund those benefits. From this perspective, the employer's contribution represents money that would otherwise be available to pay current wages. The promise to the workforce is in these terms:

We promise to pay you final salary benefits. This is not a free lunch. The money necessary to pay those benefits will represent a part of the payroll that will be diverted into the trust fund for the purposes of funding your pensions.

This is a double promise. The workforce expects to receive the promised benefits and its members expect all the money that is deducted from the payroll to be used in their interests. There is no question of the employer enjoying any benefit from the money diverted into the pension scheme. It, like the promised benefits as and when they become payable, represents the members' pay.[54]

---

surpluses on a final winding up. See *Davis* v. *Richards & Wallington Industries* [1991] 2 All ER 563; and Lord Browne-Wilkinson LJ's speech (n. 48 above), p. 19: 'The employer, being required to pay only the balance of cost, contracted to pay the amounts required from time to time by the actuary on the implied term that if the payments are excessive he is to recover the amounts overpaid.' (This is his preferred approach—he admits it may not represent the current legal position, which he finds it impossible to state.)

[54] This may seem like a strong claim, but it is not so very different from the position enjoyed by employers before the Social Security Act 1990, Schedule 4, para. 2 came into force. This provision makes employers liable for any deficit arising when a scheme is wound up. But employers previously offered their members a promise in the following terms: 'The employer will fund a pension scheme. If it has insufficient assets to pay the promised pensions these pensions will be reduced. If the scheme has more than enough to pay the promised pensions the balance will return to the employer.'

If one accepts this version of the claim that pensions are pay, much of what employers do, or seek to do, with their pension schemes appears as a form of exploitation. There are parallels with the type of abuses which led to the passing of the Truck Acts 1831–1940[55] (which required employers to pay their manual workers in coins of the realm and prohibited them from making deductions from their wages). One is reminded of the practice of paying some nineteenth-century employees in vouchers which could be redeemed only at the company shop, with that shop charging high prices for shoddy goods. The opportunities for exploitation are simply that much greater with a pension scheme. The value of a nineteenth-century labourer's wage was reduced very shortly after she had earned it. With pension schemes, the full value of the benefits earned through a single year's labour is not known until that member, and any member of her family who inherits a pension from her, has died. Pensions are pay that may be devalued by the employer failing to fund the benefits, by its winding up the scheme before retirement, by an investment policy which compromises the security of the scheme's assets, or by amending the terms of the scheme. The contribution level may be set at a level which is intended to provide discretionary increases in pensions, and the trust have sufficient assets to meet such discretionary increases, and those increases may still be denied.

The weakest version of the claim that pensions are deferred pay involves accepting that the benefits payable are pay, but denying that this term could be applied to any other part of the pension arrangement. It represents an assertion that members should expect no more than a minimum of legal entitlements. As a method of interpretation it is analogous to *caveat emptor*. The employees should have been aware that the funding of schemes, their administration, winding up, and amendment were in the control of the employer. They should have expected no more than the minimum level of benefits that were promised under the rules, and only those if the assets of the trust (and, since 1992, the assets of the employer),[56] prove sufficient.

It is very difficult to deny that pension benefits are in any sense pay, since the alternative is to view them as *ex gratia* benefits. It is also difficult to accept the minimum position. Employees are not just interested in a promise to pay pensions; they want to see that promise met. Even if the promise only related to the fixed benefits, this would give the employees an interest in the rules which governed the administration of the scheme. For a start, the investment policy could undermine the security of the fixed benefits. Once you accept that the employees can view the rules of the scheme regarding investments as part of the promise of pay, where do you stop? And if all the rules of the scheme form part of the promise of pay, how are those rules to be interpreted?

---

[55] Repealed by the Wages Act 1986.

[56] Social Security Act 1990, Schedule 4, para. 2. Social Security Act 1990 (Commencement Order No. 5) Order 1992 SI 1992/1532.

Logically, accepting that pensions are deferred pay leads one to regard all of the rules of the scheme as part of the pay arrangement, and to interpret those rules as the means to implement some kind of promise. Looking for such a promise, and interpreting the pension scheme and trust law in such a way as to ensure that the promise is being kept, rather than frustrated, is likely to result in the members of a pension scheme being treated differently, and probably more favourably, than beneficiaries of a family settlement. But the argument of deferred pay does not dictate what that difference will be, or how favourably members should be treated. The strongest version of the deferred pay argument is an assertion that everything should be done to see that current members receive the fixed benefits and enjoy the benefit of any money available to fund additional benefits. Even those who accept this assertion still have to decide what is feasible, and what the likely repercussions would be.

1. The Courts and Deferred Pay

The courts have recognized that pensions are pay in a number of contexts. In *Barber* v. *Guardian Royal Exchange Group*[57] the European Court held that pension benefits constituted a form of pay within the meaning of Article 119 of the Treaty of Rome which requires equal pay for men and women, not withstanding that pensions are paid after the termination of an employment relationship and through a trust instead of directly from the employer. The English courts have made similar admissions. Unpaid employer's contributions were allowed to be recovered as 'wages' in *Re The Halcyon Skies*[58] and in *Parry* v. *Cleaver*,[59] a House of Lords decision, Lord Reid held that an employer's contributions to a pension scheme were no different from payments made by a worker towards the worker's own insurance policy:

Take a simple case where a man and his employer agree that he shall have a wage of £20 per week to take home . . . and that between them they will put aside £4 per week. It cannot matter whether the man's nominal wage is £21 per week so that, of the £4, £1 comes from his 'wage' and £3 comes from the employer, or the man's nominal wage is £23 per week so that, of the £4, £3 comes from his 'wage' and £1 comes from the employer . . . His employer is willing to pay £24 per week to obtain his services, and it seems to me that he ought to be regarded as having earned that sum per week. The products of the sums paid into the pension fund are in fact delayed remuneration for his current work. That is why pensions are regarded as earned income.[60]

One can point to admissions such as this and claim that English law recognizes that occupational pensions are deferred pay. However, the crucial question is not whether the courts or other institutions do, on occasions, recognize pensions as pay, but whether they recognize that admission has implications for the manner in which schemes rules are interpreted. Is the

---

[57] [1990] IRLR 240.   [58] [1977] 1 QB 14.   [59] [1970] AC 1.
[60] Ibid., p. 16.

claim that pensions are a form of deferred pay something which can alter the law which the courts will apply to them at the moment, or is it a basis for criticizing that law and lobbying for legislative reform?

To date, the courts have shown some willingness to alter their interpretation of pension schemes, and trust law, to give effect to the idea that pension schemes represent the members' pay, and that therefore, the members deserve better treatment than trust beneficiaries who are mere volunteers. Thus Megarry VC in *Cowan* v. *Scargill*[61] stated that members of contributory schemes might deserve better protection than beneficiaries of a family trust, because the members had paid for their benefits whereas family trust beneficiaries were usually the object of bounty.[62] Warner J in *Mettoy Pension Trustees Limited* v. *Evans*[63] took the same view, but extended it to the members of non-contributory schemes on the basis that the employer's contribution is earned by the members through their service to the company:

If the discretion were in a will or in a private settlement in favour of beneficiaries who were volunteers, the conclusion that the person on whom it was conferred owed no duty to the objects of it would not be startling. However, in deciding [whether] the employer owed a duty to the objects of the power, one must in my view have regard to the fact that the beneficiaries under a pension scheme are not volunteers . . . their rights are derived from the contracts of employment of the members as well as from the trust instrument. Those rights have been earned by the service of the members under those contracts as well as by their contributions . . . [I]n construing the trust instrument, one must bear in mind as an important part of the background, the origin of the beneficiaries' rights under it.[64]

However, even if judges accept that beneficiaries who have earned their benefits should receive better treatment than those who have not, the question which remains is, how much better? The recognition that pension benefits have been earned does not, for example, necessarily commit the judges to accepting a strong version of the claim that pensions are deferred pay. A judge may accept that pension benefits are earned, and that the members therefore deserve better protection than beneficiaries of family trusts, without concluding that all of the employer's influence over the fund should be removed, or that the employer should have no right to participate in any surplus. Thus, for example, Browne-Wilkinson VC accepted, in *Imperial Group Pension Trust Ltd.* v. *Imperial Tobacco Limited*,[65] that pension benefits were part of the consideration which an employee receives in return for the rendering of services, but nevertheless denied that the trustees could be expected to have an independent power to increase benefits. Instead, he accepted that balance of cost funding gave the employer a right to expect to control benefit levels.

[61] [1985] 1 Ch. 270.   [62] Ibid. 290.
[63] [1991] 2 All ER 513; [1990] 1 WLR 1587.
[64] [1991] 2 All ER 513 at 549; [1990] 1 WLR 1587 at 1618.
[65] (Ch. D) [1991] 2 All ER 597; [1991] 1 WLR 589.

2. *How Can Trust Law Protect the Members' Deferred Pay?*

If judges wish to protect the members' pay, they have a wide range of legal doctrines which they can use. Discretionary powers must be used in accordance with their purpose. This is known as the doctrine of a fraud on a power. Where a power is used in a manner which appears unreasonable, it can be held to be *ultra vires*. Judges can also, if they wish, take an aggressive attitude to the duty to act in the members' best interests, and insist that trustees do not take decisions where they have an acute conflict of interest. Through these doctrines, discussed at length in Chapter 3, the courts can make the pension scheme operate more closely to the central idea of the trust as a fiduciary relationship described in the previous chapter. These trust doctrines can be supplemented by other devices from the law of contract, such as the introduction of implied terms, and the doctrine of *contra proferentum* (construing a document strictly against the party who drafts it).

C. PENSIONS AS CONTRACTUAL ENTITLEMENTS

Deferred pay and balance of cost considerations provide substantive reasons for approaching interpretation in the interests of employers or employees. By contrast, contract does not have the same substantive content. Instead, it provides a mechanism through which to give effect to conclusions already reached on the basis of a judge's view of the appropriate balance between management's right to manage, and the members' right to protection for their pay.

Until recently,[66] the contract of employment and the pension scheme were considered to give rise to separate legal relationships: the pension scheme member, *qua* member, had no contractual rights against the employer. The only term of the contract of employment which was generally acknowledged to refer to the pension scheme was the employee's right to become a member of the scheme in its current form.[67] Thus the value of the contractual promise depended on the terms of the trust, i.e., what benefits were promised and to what extent they were funded.[68] But in three recent decisions the courts have

---

[66] As late as 1982, the scheme rules were seen as something separate from the contract of employment. See *Duke* v. *Reliance Systems Ltd.* [1982] ICR 449; though Ellison calls this case 'exceptional', claiming that a willingness to see scheme rules as part of the contract of employment is evidenced much earlier. See R. Ellison *Pensions, Law and Practice* (Longman, 1992), 19.023.

[67] Whilst the contract of employment commonly required the employee to belong to the pension scheme (a term now void under the Social Security Act 1986, s. 15) 'many pension fund rules contain a clause, the effectiveness of which may be questioned, to the effect that nothing contained in the rules or granting benefit shall have any contractual effect . . .'. Ellison (n. 66), 19.002, 19.023.

[68] See e.g. *Beach* v. *Reed Corrugated Cases Ltd.* [1956] 1 WLR 807; [1956] 2 All ER 652; where damages for loss of wrongful dismissal arising from the loss of future membership were held to be zero, since the scheme rules gave the employer power to discontinue the scheme and to eject any particular member.

asserted that the contractual basis of an employee's right to belong to a pension scheme might give rise to rights in addition to those created under the law of trusts.[69]

The first of these decisions, *Mihlenstedt* v. *Barclays Bank Ltd.*,[70] involved the construction of an ill-health provision within the bank's pension scheme. The plaintiff, an employee of the bank, was entitled to retire early and receive an immediate pension:

> only when after consulting its medical adviser, the Bank is of the opinion that the Member . . . is unable by reason of physical or mental incapacity . . . to undertake any duties . . . and is likely permanently to remain so unable or suffering such loss.[71]

Peter Gibson J, in the High Court, held that the decision of the bank was not fiduciary and so the bank could not be required to come to any particular decision, whatever the evidence. The Court of Appeal took a more robust view. It felt the plaintiff had a contractual right to force the bank to consult its medical expert and to form an opinion that was honest and not erroneous. Nourse LJ put it thus:

> If the matter had rested on the trust deed and rules alone, I would have held that the Bank was under no obligation in regard to the plaintiff's application for an ill-health pension. But it was a term of her contract of employment with the Bank that she should be entitled to the membership of the pension scheme and to the benefits thereunder. From that it must follow, as a matter of necessary implication, that the Bank became contractually bound, so far as it lay within its power, to procure for the plaintiff the benefits to which she was entitled under the scheme.[72]

This seems, on its face, to be a far-reaching statement. What other implicit terms might the courts construe into pension schemes if the employer is bound 'to procure for the [member] the benefits to which she is entitled under the scheme'? Would there be, for example, an implied term that the benefits would be properly funded?

One should not get carried away. The statement is, for a start, circular. The employer must not act to frustrate the member receiving the benefits to which she is *entitled*. One still has to construe the *pension scheme* to see what is, or is not, being denied. The decision simply uses the law of contract to remedy limitations in the law of trusts. The court accepted that the decision of the employer was a precondition to the grant of an ill-health benefit, but decided that the bank could not, under the law of trusts, be forced to carry out its function because it was not a trustee or fiduciary. Instead it fell back on the law of contract, and held the bank to have contracted to act in good faith.

---

[69] For an example of the contract giving rise to less rights than are set out in the pension scheme rules, see *Duke* v. *Reliance Systems Ltd.* [1982] ICR 449 (pension scheme's stated normal retirement age for both sexes of 65 did not overturn the implied term of the contract of employment, based on previous practice, that women could be fired at 60).

[70] [1989] IRLR 522.   [71] Ibid., at 526.   [72] Ibid., at 525.

This approach may remedy other, similar, limitations in the law of trusts. (Thus, for example, where benefits are conditional upon the opinion of the scheme actuary, and this person has to be appointed by the employer, the employer may be compelled to appoint an actuary.) While this is commendable, its limitations must be recognized. The court had construed the clause as one which was intended to create a *right* to the ill-health pension, once certain conditions were satisfied. Having decided that the plaintiff had a right, they were not going to see it frustrated by the limitations of the law of trusts. Contract would fill the gap. The entitlement was construed out of *the trust deed*. There was no suggestion that the contractual relationship represented a separate source of entitlements. It simply provided a separate means for giving effect to scheme entitlements.[73]

The second case in which a pension scheme gave rise to additional contractual entitlements was *Scally* v. *Southern Health and Social Services Board*.[74] In this case the plaintiffs were entitled to make additional voluntary contributions to their pension scheme and thereby receive additional benefits. The plaintiffs were unaware of this right, and failed to exercise it in time. They sued for damages for breach of an implied term in their contract of employment which required the employer to inform them of this valuable option. The approach of the House of Lords was similar to the Court of Appeal in *Mihlenstedt*. Having decided that the regulations (this was a statutory scheme and not a trust) were intended to confer an entitlement on the employees, Lord Bridge was not prepared to see this entitlement lost through matters which were beyond the employees' control:

since the employee's entitlement to enhance his pension rights by the purchase of added years is of no effect unless he is aware of it, and since he cannot be expected to become aware of it unless it is drawn to his attention, it is necessary to imply an obligation on the employer to bring it to his attention to render efficacious the very benefit which the contractual right to purchase additional years was intended to confer.[75]

The approach here is again circular: having found an entitlement in the scheme rules, the court used contractual rights to make that entitlement effective.

The third case in which a court was prepared to imply contractual terms into the pension scheme was *Imperial Group Pension Trust Ltd.* v. *Imperial Tobacco Limited*.[76] The first point in this case (the meaning of a power to increase pensions by 'at least 5 per cent') was looked at in the previous chapter. The second point concerned the right of the employer to refuse to

---

[73] Following *Mihlenstedt*, a trust deed which gives powers to the employer can be construed in three ways: as a power that may be exercised in the employer's self-interest to grant or deny an entitlement as the employer sees fit; as a fiduciary power; or as a non-fiduciary power which gives rise to contractual entitlements.   [74] [1991] 4 All ER 563 (HL).
[75] Ibid., p. 571.   [76] (Ch. D) [1991] 2 All ER 597; [1991] 1 WLR 589.

consent to benefit increases. Imperial Tobacco argued that the requirement for consent was the same sort of power as might be given to an individual or retained by the settlor under a family settlement. The courts have refused to interfere with the exercise of such powers on the basis that they are intended to be exercised in whatever manner the holder of the power sees fit. In the VC's opinion, such uncontrolled powers were acceptable in a family settlement because the beneficiaries were the objects of the settlor's bounty. But the members of a pension scheme provide consideration for their benefits, not only through any contributions which they may make to the scheme, but because the benefits are part of the remuneration which they receive in return for the rendering of services. The presence of consideration arising out of the employment relationship entitled the VC to read aspects of the employment relationship into the provisions of the trust deed. In particular, the employer's powers under the trust were subject to the same duty of trust and confidence as applied to his powers under the contract of employment. Employers were not 'without reasonable cause, [to] conduct themselves in a manner calculated to destroy or seriously damage the relationship of confidence and trust between the employer and employee.'[77] In the case of a pension scheme, this duty extends to ex-employees and their dependants.

In its employment context, this duty refers to actions by the employer which are wholly unreasonable, or 'intolerable'.[78] The standard has its origins in cases in which the employee is claiming unfair dismissal on the basis that the employer's conduct amounted to a repudiation of the contract.[79] This may indicate that courts should ask themselves whether the employer's action under the pension scheme was such that the members were entitled (or would have been entitled if they were still employees), to commence an action for unfair dismissal. But whether the standard is one of reasonableness, or the prevention of what is wholly unreasonable, or the prevention of conduct which gives rise to a right of unfair dismissal, deciding what constitutes such action requires the court to consider what entitlements the members can legitimately expect from their pension scheme. And this requires the court to consider standards or perspectives which lie outside the law of contract. Thus it is not that contractual entitlements provide a different perspective for interpretation. Rather, the existence of a contractual relationship is used to legitimize the interpretation of pension schemes in accordance with ideas that they are pay. And it is ideas associated with

---

[77] (Ch. D) [1991] 2 All ER 597 at 606; [1991] 1 WLR 589 at 597.

[78] '[I]t must ordinarily be an implied term of the contract of employment that the employers do not behave in a way which is intolerable or in a way which employees cannot be expected to put up with any longer.' *British Aircraft Corp.* v. *Austin* [1978] IRLR 332 at 334.

[79] 'The obligation of the employer not to destroy or seriously damage the mutual trust and confidence between employer and employee has its origins in the common law including the law of wrongful dismissal.' S. Anderman, *The Law of Unfair Dismissal*, 2nd edn. (Butterworths, 1985), p. 82.

deferred pay, and not independent contractual entitlements, which establish whether an employer has breached the duty of trust and confidence.

Imperial Tobacco is really very similar to *Mihlenstedt* and *Scally*. Having formed a view that employees had entitlements that ought to be protected, the Vice-Chancellor then looked for ways to do this. The law of trusts did not seem to provide a remedy, since the employer was not a fiduciary. The Vice-Chancellor therefore looked to the law of contract to fill the gap. In *Imperial* and *Mihlenstedt*, a less restricted view of the law of trusts could have served as well.[80] The Vice-Chancellor could have simply said that the power held by the employer was intended to be exercised in accordance with a purpose, and was therefore bound by the principle that a power must be exercised in accordance with its purpose.[81] Instead, the VC introduced a contractual duty and used it to justify limiting the purposes for which the employer's power could be used. That said, *Imperial* is a more radical decision than the other two. In *Mihlenstedt* and *Scally* the courts had regard to *particular* contingent rights set out in the trust deed and rules, decided that it would be unjust for these rights to be defeated through circumstances which were within the employer's control, and introduced an implied term which prevented that. In *Imperial*, Browne-Wilkinson did not seek to supplement particular scheme rules. Instead, he had regard to the whole contractual relationship, and introduced a general contractual term not to exercise *any* right under the pension scheme in a manner that was wholly unreasonable.

1. Scheme Booklets

Employers usually provide employees with a booklet setting out the scheme's benefits at length, including employees' options on leaving the scheme. It may also contain a brief summary of the basis upon which the scheme is administered. Such booklets serve a number of purposes. First, it is considered good industrial relations to publicize the scheme amongst the employees, so that they appreciate that their remuneration includes pension benefits as well as current pay. Second, it allows the employer to comply with the Inland Revenue's requirement, as a condition of discretionary approval, that every member and every employee who has a right to be a member be given written particulars of all essential features of the scheme which concern him.[82] Third, it provides a means for complying with the Occupational Pensions Board's disclosure regulations.[83] These require new members to be

---

[80] Because *Scally* involved a statutory scheme rather than a trust, the doctrine of fraud on a power was inapplicable. The plaintiffs argued for damages for breach of statutory duty, relying on Northern Ireland's equivalent of s. 1 of the Employment Protection (Consolidation) Act 1978, but lost.

[81] Also known as the doctrine of a fraud on a power. See R. Nobles, 'Restrictions on the Use of an Employer's Powers under a Pension Scheme', 20 ILJ (1991) 130.

[82] Income and Corporation Taxes Act 1988, s. 590(2)(b) and Inland Revenue Practice Notes, IR 12 1991, para. 3.2.

[83] Occupational Pension Scheme (Disclosure of Information) Regulations 1986, SI 1986 No.

supplied with details of the conditions for becoming and remaining scheme members, on the method of calculation of employers' and, if applicable, members' contributions, and on the provisions regarding preservation and transfer of deferred pensions, and indexation of pensions in payment.

Where a scheme booklet or formal announcement offers some entitlement which is not present in the trust deed and rules, this may be recognized as a contractual right. The scheme booklet may be found to be incorporated into the contract of employment, or to constitute a collateral agreement.[84] However, the wording of scheme booklets is often designed to prevent this from occurring. They are likely to include a disclaimer, for example:

Although this booklet gives basic information about the Fund, the detailed provisions are set out in the Trust Deed and Rules and nothing in this booklet can override these documents, which may be inspected on application to the Pensions Department.[85]

In the face of such disclaimers, it is difficult for the courts to hold that the scheme booklet gives rise to rights, whether in contract, trust, or estoppel, which are different from those set out in the trust deed and rules. This is not to say that such disclaimers will always have this effect. If the parties have clearly acted upon the provisions set out in the booklet, rather than those set out in the trust deed and rules, they may be estopped from relying on such a disclaimer on the basis of estoppel by convention, discussed below.

The ability of booklets to create contractual rights which supplement those found in the trust deed and rules should not be exaggerated. First, booklets concentrate upon settling out the benefits, and contain only the most cursory description of the scheme's administrative provisions and methods of funding. Second, there is no guarantee that being able to enforce the provisions of the booklet will assist the members, since these may offer the members less rights than the trust deed and rules.[86]

2. The General Law of Contract

If pension rights are seen as contractual in nature, then the courts may look not only to the law of employment, but to the general law of contract. This contains a wide selection of rules of construction. From the employees' point of view, the most favourable of these rules of construction is *contra proferentum*. The rule requires contractual terms to be construed against the interests of the party which drafted it, and in favour of the party which did not. As the rules of the pension scheme are usually drafted entirely in accordance with the wishes of the employer, with little or no input from the

1046, as amended by SI No. 1717, SI 1987 No. 1105, SI 1988 No. 476, SI 1989/1641, SI 1991/167, SI 1991/2684 and SI 1992/1531.

[84] See B. Napier, 'The Contract of Employment', in R. Lewis, *Labour Law in Britain* (Blackwell, 1986), p. 246.

[85] Phillips Pension Fund Booklet, April 1981, p. 3.

[86] This was demonstrated in the context of estoppel by *Icarus (Hertford) Limited* v. *Driscoll*, 4 December 1989. [1990] 1 PLR 1. See pp. See pp. 61–2, below.

employees, this approach to construction would require that ambiguities in the scheme rules be construed in the employees' favour.

The application of this doctrine will depend on the court's acceptance of deferred-pay arguments. *Contra proferentum* is not applied automatically whenever a contract is drafted by one party and simply accepted by the other. It requires the court to identify some entitlement to which the plaintiff is reasonably entitled which the defendant, through specific terms, is seeking to avoid. This is the reason why it is generally discussed in the context of exclusion clauses.[87] The doctrine reduces the drafter's ability to obtain an inequitable advantage. But, before it can be used, the judge must first have accepted the view that the interpretation sought is in some way unreasonable. The need for this element of unreasonableness is illustrated in Evershed MR's application of the doctrine in *John Lee & Son (Grantham) Ltd.* v. *Railway Executive*:[88]

We are presented with two alternative readings of this document and the reading which should be adopted is to be determined, among other things by a consideration of the fact that the defendants put forward the document. They have put forward a clause which is by no means free from obscurity and *have contended . . . that it has a remarkably, if not extravagantly, wide scope*, and I think that the rule contra proferentem should be applied.[89]

Before *contra proferentum* is applied to pension schemes, the court must form a similar conclusion that the employer is asking for an interpretation which has a 'remarkably, if not extravagantly, wide scope'. In other words, the court must have already formed a view on the unreasonableness of what the employer is seeking, before using the doctrine.

Perhaps the greatest danger for the employees, from recognizing pensions as contractual rights, is the concentration of contract law on the need for parties to have agreed.[90] It is no use arguing that something is just, or a legitimate expectation of one of the parties, if there is no evidence that it was agreed to by the other. Nourse LJ seems to recognize this need for agreement in *Mihlenstedt* when he states that:

references to *'legitimate expectations'* in the field of contract are both unnecessary and undesirable. If an employer agrees with an employee to consult . . . [and] . . . form an opinion . . . I can see no reason why the law of contract should not be copious enough

---

[87] *Chitty on Contracts*, 24th edn. (Sweet & Maxwell, 1977), para. 726, cites it as a general rule of construction with exemption clauses as an important modern application of the doctrine.

[88] [1949] 2 All ER 581. [89] Ibid., p. 583.

[90] For an extreme example of this, see *Armour* v. *Liverpool Corporation* [1939] Ch. 422 where, in the absence of identifiable offer and acceptance, the court were not prepared to accept that the pension scheme formed part of the contract of employment, despite the employer's role in sponsoring and administering the pension scheme. Simonds J was only prepared to recognize as contractual terms matters of which *all* of the workforce were aware, and as only some of them knew of the representations made by company officials, these could not form part of a common contract.

. . . to enforce by injunction the obligation to consult or to declare that the employer's opinion has been formed dishonestly or on an erroneous basis . . .

In the context of pension schemes, looking for things which have been agreed to by both parties is unlikely to take you further than the deed and rules, and perhaps the scheme booklet. The employer is unlikely to have made any other formal statement of his intentions, and the employees are unlikely even to know the formula used to calculate their benefits, let alone the terms of the pension deed and rules.

3. *Contract vs. Estoppel*

Where employers and members have common expectations that differ from the terms of the pension scheme, this can give rise to additional rights in both contract and estopel. Estoppel can arise when two or more parties act upon a common understanding that their rights were different from those set out in the trust deed and rules. Thus, it does not require the additional element of agreement.

In practice, contract and estoppel become indistinguishable. This can be seen from *Icarus (Hertford) Limited* v. *Driscoll.*[91] In *Icarus,* the rules of the pension scheme provided that members should accrue at the rate of 1/80th of final salary, 1/60th for special members. In 1979, following the admission of manual employees to the scheme, the employer announced that benefits were to be reduced to 1/270th of final salary. Scheme booklets henceforth described the scheme benefits as 1/270th, but the scheme rules were not altered to take account of the employer's new policy. The scheme had been wound up with a surplus over liabilities of £200,000, if the benefits were 1/270th, or £40,000, if they were calculated in accordance with the scheme's rules. Aldous J held that the members were estopped from asserting that their benefits were based on the 1/60th and 1/80th formulas contained in the rules of the pension scheme. Instead, they could only claim pension at the rate of 1/270th of final salary, since this was the fraction used in the booklets produced for the employees. He relied on the principle, set out by Lord Denning in *Amalgamated Property Co.* v. *Texas*[92] that:

When the parties to a transaction proceed on the basis of an underlying assumption . . . on which they have conducted the dealings between them—neither of them will be allowed to go back on that assumption when it would be unfair or unjust to allow them to do so. If one of them does seek to go back on it, the court will give such remedy as the equity of the court demands.

Since all the parties to the scheme had proceeded on the basis that the rate of accrual was 1/270th, they could not now claim otherwise. It would be unjust or unfair to hold otherwise.

This decision represents a fairly liberal application of the doctrine of

[91] 4 December 1989. [1990] 1 PLR 1.   [92] [1982] 1 QB 84.

estoppel by convention, which applies when two parties act upon a common mistake of fact, or where one party makes such a mistake, and the other acquiesces in that mistake.[93] The employer seems to have been allowed to rely upon its own misunderstanding of the effect of the announcements and the members' failure to draw their employer's mistake to its attention. There was no evidence that each of the employees was aware of the basis on which they were to receive benefits, whether under the rules or the announcements, and so they could not all be said to have 'acquiesced' in the employer's mistake.[94]

If the approach to estoppel is to be that used in *Icarus*, then estoppel will operate very much in the same way as contract. There is not much difference between deciding a dispute on the basis of terms that you assert all parties have acquiesced to, and deciding by reference terms which you assert they have agreed to. On the other hand, if you assert that the beliefs or expectations in question were understood by only one party, be that party the employer or the employees, it is hard to justify giving effect to that expectation in either contract or estoppel. You will not have the agreement required for contract or the acquiescence required for estoppel.

Whilst contract and estoppel require similar assertions in order to operate, contract offers the court a more flexible basis upon which to interfere. Estoppel is generally regarded as being capable only of restricting pre-existing rights.[95] Thus it will not give the members or the trustees additional rights to those set out in the trust deed and rules. At best, estoppel may operate to prevent an employer from exercising some of the rights which it has reserved to itself under a scheme's rules. At worst, as *Icarus* illustrates, it will operate to reduce the members' rights.

With contract, there is no doubt that the court is not limited to restricting rights set out in the trust deed and rules. It can supplement and amend the trust by introducing new terms: implied terms.

4. Implied Terms

The law of contract provides for terms to be implied into an agreement, even when there is no evidence that the parties agreed to their inclusion. But the preconditions for implying terms into contract are more restrictive than those available under the law of trusts. According to the House of Lords in *Liverpool City Council* v. *Irwin*,[96] a term may not ordinarily be implied into a contract unless it is necessary to give business efficacy to the agreement. In

---

[93] See G. H. Treitel, *The Law of Contract*, 7th edn. (1987), p. 94.

[94] It would have been even more difficult to have applied promissory or proprietary estoppel, which require representations by one party which are relied upon by the other. If the ignorance and inactivity of these members and their dependants is hard to describe as acquiescence, it is even harder to describe it as a representation or reliance.

[95] Whilst Lord Denning was sure that it could do more than this, the other Court of Appeal judges in *Amalgamated Investments* did not share his view.

[96] [1977] AC 239.

other words, the agreement must be seen as unworkable, or wholly unreasonable, without the term in question.[97] This strict approach applies to the introduction of specific terms into a particular contract. The courts are more willing to imply general terms into particular classes of contractual relationship. Thus, when dealing with contracts of employment, the courts are willing to imply a term, 'based upon wider considerations . . . as a necessary incident of a definable category of contractual relationship.'[98] *Scally* and *Imperial Tobacco* provide examples of such terms.

With respect to challenges to the use of powers, the law of trusts already offers a doctrine that is, in some ways, more flexible that contract. The doctrine of a fraud on a power provides that a power should not be exercised other than in accordance with its purpose. This doctrine allows a court to introduce a term restricting the use of a power in any manner that it thinks appropriate to the general purposes of the instrument and the surrounding circumstances. The doctrine is not limited to what is necessary to give the whole relationship effect, nor must it be applied to trusts of a particular kind. If the purpose of a trust is unique, the doctrine can lead to a one-off restriction on the particular power in question.

D. CONCLUSION

Contract law is unlikely to provide a new source for members' substantive rights. Rather, it will legitimize the interpretation of schemes in accordance with ideas of deferred pay, and provide remedies where courts are reluctant to rely on the flexibility of trust law. This does not mean that rights introduced under the law of contract will not, in future, prove valuable to members. If the courts accept a radical view of the claim that pensions are members' pay, then the law of contract could provide useful additional protections for members. On the other hand, if they accept the legitimacy of employer control, it will not.

Whilst the contract provides a means to supplement trust law, one should not underestimate the flexibility of trust law itself. As shown in the discussion of pensions as management policy and as deferred pay, the trust form is capable of being drafted and interpreted in quite different ways. Judicial views on the appropriate balance of power, on the compromise between the management's claim for control and the employees' demand for independence, crucially affect the interpretation of scheme rules and the relationship between those rules and general trust duties. The next chapter explores further this flexibility contained within the law of trusts, taking as its subject a matter that is crucial to the balance of power within pension schemes: the duties of trustees.

---

[97] This approach has been adopted by one court in a pensions case, in order to justify not introducing a term. See *Aitken* v. *Christy Hunt PLC* [1991] PLR 1, discussed in Chapter 8.
[98] *Scally* v. *Southern Health and Social Services Board* [1991] 4 All ER 563 (HL) at 571.

[3]

The Exercise of Trustees' Discretions under a Pension Scheme

I. INTRODUCTION

When trustees exercise discretionary powers ('discretions'), they are required to exercise them on a fiduciary basis. But what, in the context of a pension scheme, does this mean? In particular, are pension scheme trustees there to represent the members' interests? Or are they there to decide between the interests of the employer and the members? In the latter case, what, if any, are the limits of their freedom to favour the interests of one party or the other?

In its 1989 report on the protection afforded to the rights and expectations of members of occupational pension schemes,[1] the Occupational Pensions Board (OPB) decided that trust law provided a suitable legal basis for pension schemes. In reaching this conclusion, the OPB took the view that trust law required trustees to act in the best interests of the beneficiaries, and impartially between all the categories of beneficiaries. The employer was not a beneficiary for these purposes, and the 'trustees have only limited obligations towards the employer unless such an obligation is specifically created in the trust deed and rules'.[2] In an appendix to the report it is said that a trustee 'must exercise powers reasonably and in good faith, and use them for the purposes for which the trust was created'.[3] The relationship between this statement of duties and the stronger statement contained in the main report is never discussed.

There are, in fact, many standards which can be applied to the exercise of discretions. Legal advisers and the courts have to choose which standard is appropriate to the discretion in question. There is no guarantee that pension scheme members will, in the event, be protected by duties as strong as those described by the OPB in its main report. Similar criticisms apply to the OPB's description of the status of the employer. It is unclear what status the

---

[1] Protecting Pensions: Safeguarding Benefits in a Changing Environment. A Report by the Occupational Pensions Board in accordance with s. 66 of the Social Security Act 1973. CM 573.
[2] Ibid., para. 4.4. [3] Appendix 2, para. 11.

employer has with regard to the trustees' discretions. Deciding that status will involve the courts in a complicated process of interpretation, the outcome of which is uncertain.

This chapter analyses the manner in which the courts approach the exercise of trustees' discretions in the general law of trusts, and then considers how the duties of pension scheme trustees fit into this general framework. The first section looks at the range of standards which can be applied to trustees' discretions. As well as looking at the alternatives to the standards of 'best interest' and 'impartiality', it also analyses the varying extent to which trustees are subject to the rule which prohibits them from having interests which might conflict with their duties towards the beneficiaries.

The second part of the chapter looks at how these various standards apply to pension schemes. It first discusses whether the employer is a beneficiary for the purpose of the exercise of discretions. It then examines application of the standard of 'best interests' to the exercise of the trustees' discretion on winding up. This provides a concrete example of an important discretion which cannot be combined with a duty to act in the members' best interests. The section then looks at the application to pension schemes of the rules against conflicting interests.

II. STANDARDS FOR THE SUPERVISION OF TRUSTEES' DISCRETIONS UNDER THE GENERAL LAW OF TRUSTS

A. THE GENERAL DUTY OF TRUSTEES

Attempts to state the general duty of trustees are hindered by the fact that there is no single standard. Instead, there are a range of standards which the courts can bring to bear, which depend on the rules of the trust and the circumstances in which those rules are interpreted. These standards range from duties to act in the beneficiaries' best interests down to a duty to act in good faith. In between there are duties not to exercise a power contrary to its purpose, to exercise discretions impartially as between different groups of beneficiaries, and not to act capriciously or wholly unreasonably.

1. The Duty to Act in the Beneficiaries' Best Interests

The highest standard is that trustees must act in the beneficiaries' best interests.[4] It is not enough for a trustee to have acted in good faith, and with the intention of benefiting the beneficiaries, if it is clear to the court that the actions taken were not in the beneficiaries' best interests. The most emphatic exponent of this standard was Lindley LJ in *Hampden* v. *Earl of*

---

[4] *Cowan* v. *Scargill* [1984] 3 WLR 501 at 513.

Buckinghamshire:[5] even where a trustee's actions are taken in good faith and with every good intention

> . . . still an honest trustee may fail to see that he is acting unjustly towards those whose interests he is bound to consider and to protect; and if he is so acting, and the Court can see it although he cannot, it is in my opinion the duty of the Court to interfere.[6]

2. The Duty to Exercise a Power in Accordance with its Purpose

Another standard applied to the exercise of discretions is that they must be exercised 'according to their purpose'.[7] According to P. Finn,[8] 'best interests' and 'purposes' are cumulative, not alternative, standards. The trustees have a general duty to act in the best interests of the beneficiaries, and this requires particular powers to be used for a specified purpose:

> [First, as donee of the power, the question is whether] the power has been exercised for a purpose or with an intention beyond the scope of, or not justified by, the instrument creating the power? Secondly and in addition, the fiduciary can be seen . . . as one who in the exercise of his powers is bound to act in, what he believes to be his beneficiaries' interests . . . These 'interests' . . . ordain both the ultimate purposes for which he must exercise his powers, and the overriding considerations which he must take into account in their exercise.[9]

However, purposes are not, as this statement suggests, simply spelled out from the duty to act in the beneficiaries' best interests; they are also constructed out of the rules of the particular instrument. On this basis, a power must not be used other than for the purpose which is expressly, or implicitly, authorized under the trust deed or rules. This allows a court to decide that powers were included to enable trustees to exercise discretions other than for the best interests of the beneficiaries. For example, in *Joseph Hayim* v. *Citibank*[10] the testator provided that his trustee was to have 'no responsibility or duty with respect to' a house occupied by his ageing brother and sister, neither of whom were beneficiaries of the trust. The house was held by the trustee on trust for sale, with the brother and sister paying no rent. The beneficiaries argued that the trustees were bound by a duty to act in their best interests and, in the circumstances, should sell the house. The trustee, acting in the interests of the brother and sister, insisted on postponing the sale. The Privy Council decided that this provision left the trustee free to allow the brother and sister to remain in the house, and that in making this decision, the trustee need have no regard to the interests of the beneficiaries.

---

    5 [1893] 2 Ch. 531.   6 Ibid., at 544.
    7 *Re Paulings Settlement Trusts* [1964] Ch. 303; *Re Hays Settlement Trusts* [1981] 3 All ER 786 at 792.
    8 P. D. Finn, *Fiduciary Obligations* (The Law Book Co., 1977).
    9 Ibid., p. 39.
    10 [1987] 3 WLR 83 at 90 (PC).

3. The Duty to Exercise Powers in an Impartial Manner

A purpose restriction may also work in conjunction with the general duty to exercise discretions in an impartial manner when choosing between the interests of different groups of beneficiaries.[11] This allows the courts to give specific directions as to what, in a particular context, is to constitute impartiality. Again, because purpose restrictions can also be spelled out of the trust deed and rules, they enable a court to decide that a power was included in order to enable trustees to act in a very partial manner as between different groups of beneficiaries.

4. The Duty of Good Faith

The above standards are not, however, always applied to the exercise of discretions. The courts have sometimes allowed settlors to place their trustees under quite minimal restrictions. Thus in *Gisborne* v. *Gisborne*[12] trustees were authorized

in their discretion, and of their uncontrollable authority, pay and apply the whole or such portion only, of the annual income . . . to or for the maintenance of my dear wife.[13]

The Lord Chancellor took the view that these words, in this settlement, meant that the trustees were to be outside the check or control of the courts, provided that the trustees acted in good faith. Good faith in this context was a low standard. It would presumably have covered such things as the taking of bribes, but it did not prevent the trustees acting in their own self-interest. The trustees in *Gisborne* were also the residuary beneficiaries of the trust: every £1 which they omitted to spend on the wife, was an extra £1 for themselves. In this case, a duty to act in good faith meant no more than a duty to avoid dishonesty.

Where a discretion is as wide as that in *Gisborne*, the function of the trustees is not to act in the best interests of the beneficiaries, nor to act in accordance with purposes, but to determine the purposes to be furthered, and the interests to be protected. When advising a trustee with such a discretion, one cannot say: 'here is what you must attempt to achieve, exercise your judgement.' Instead, the trustee must be told: 'you are the trustee, you have to decide what is appropriate.'

Gisborne reveals that a minimal control of trustees is possible; it does not tell one how to achieve that position. Obviously, the more one uses terms like 'uncontrollable', 'absolute', etc., the more sure the courts will be that the trustees are not subject to overriding considerations of purpose or interest. But there is no formula which is guaranteed to achieve this result.[14] One

---

[11] *Howe* v. *Dartmouth* (1802) Ves. 137; *Cowan* v. *Scargill* (n. 4 above), at 513.
[12] (1877) 2 App. Cas. 300.   [13] Ibid., at 302.
[14] See D. Parry, 'Control of Trustees' Discretions' [1989] Conv. 244 at 248.

cannot confidently assert that the phrase 'at their absolute discretion' has the effect of drastically reducing the court's supervision, whilst words such as 'in their discretion', or 'in their sole discretion' do not. The omission or addition of the word 'absolute' is largely a matter of drafting formality,[15] a fact which is known to the court, and allows it to put its own interpretation upon the freedom intended by the words used. There is also the example of *Bartlett* v. *Barclays Bank Trust Co. Ltd. (No. 1)*:[16] clauses which appear to exclude the supervision of the courts can be narrowly construed where the court is convinced that a trustee has acted without sufficient regard to the interests of the beneficiaries.[17]

5. Standards between 'Best Interests' and 'Good Faith'

As Moffat and Chesterman observe,[18] *Gisborne* represents the 'high water mark of judicial non-interventionism'. There are standards which lie in between the extremes of acting in the beneficiaries' best interests and acting in an honest manner. Some of these standards overlap with (or could be restated in the language of) the principle that powers must be used in accordance with their purpose. Trustees must not exercise their powers 'capriciously', meaning 'irrational perverse or contrary to any sensible expectation of the settlor'.[19] This standard allows the court to intervene when it feels that the trustees have acted in a manner that is wholly unreasonable. What counts as unreasonable in this context depends on what the court feels is the likely intention of the settlor, which leads in turn to a consideration of the purpose of the instrument as a whole, as well as the purpose of a particular discretion. In *Tempest* v. *Lord Camoys*[20] the court asserted that it would intervene if a discretion was exercised 'improperly' or 'in any way that is wrong or unreasonable'.[21] Some commentators[22] have equated these different standards with the general approach used in administrative law, the so-called *Wednesbury principles*:

[15] See M. Cullity, 'Judicial Control of Trustees Discretions' (1975), 25 University of Toronto Law Journal 99 at 113.

[16] [1980] 1. Ch. 515. The trustees were empowered to 'act . . . in such a way as it shall think best calculated to benefit the trust premises and as if it was the absolute owner of such . . . property'. This was interpreted to empower the trustees to undertake investments that would otherwise have been outside their authority, but to leave their duty of care unchanged (duty to act as a prudent man of business). Ibid., at 536–7. The court's willingness to read the power in this way may have been influenced by the fact that the case involved a professional trustee.

[17] P. Matthews, 'Trustee Exemption Clauses in English Law' [1989] Conv. 42 states that it is an 'established rule' that clauses which attempt to narrow the trustees' duties will be construed strictly against the trustee. As *Gisborne* shows, this statement may oversimplify matters. Once the court has decided which standard of care is appropriate to a particular power, it is reluctant to allow the trustees to excuse themselves from that standard. But it first has to decide, in light of the terms of the power, what standard is appropriate.

[18] Moffat and Chesterman, *Trust Law, Text and Materials* (Weidenfeld & Nicolson, 1988), p. 428.   [19] *Re Manisty* [1974] Ch. 17 at 26.

[20] (1882) 21 Ch. D 571 (CA).   [21] Ibid., at 578 per Jessel MR.

[22] See A. Grubb [1982] Conv. 432 at 438; Moffat and Chesterman (n. 18 above), at 439; and Parry, (n. 14 above), at 249.

The court is entitled to investigate . . . whether they have taken into account matters which they ought not to have taken into account, or conversely, have refused to take into account or neglected to take into account matters which they ought to have taken into account [or have] . . . come to a conclusion so unreasonable that no reasonable [person] could have come to it[23]

The task of identifying what standards are used by judges when deciding whether to interfere with trustees' decisions is made complicated by the use, or abuse, of language. Judges can appear to agree with the approach used in *Gisborne* by intervening solely in order to ensure that the trustees act in good faith, but interpret good faith to include not only dishonesty, but failing to take into account considerations that the court felt were relevant, or taking into account considerations that the court felt were improper. One of the most transparent and extreme examples of such abuse of language is in *Klug* v. *Klug*.[24] The trustee in that case declined to exercise a power of advancement in favour of her daughter (the life tenant) on the basis that her daughter had married without her consent. Neville J was 'loath to say that, where trustees have honestly exercised their discretion, the Court will interfere in the absence of special circumstances'.[25] He overcame this loathing by describing the trustee's decision to refuse the advance as a failure to exercise her discretion, and then ordered that the advance be made.

6. *The Relevance of Construction*

In choosing which of these standards to apply, a court is inevitably involved in a process of construction. Every discretionary power must be interpreted in the context of the instrument in which it is contained and in the light of any relevant and admissible evidence.[26] This process is well stated by M. Cullity:

[G]eneral statements to the effect that, in the exercise of his discretions, a trustee must act [in the best interests of the beneficiaries] and must maintain an even hand between the beneficiaries are misleading unless they are understood to apply only to the extent that the instrument which confers the discretion does not reveal an intention that those standards should be weakened or excluded. Conversely, the proposition that, in the absence of *mala fides* a Court will not interfere . . . requires qualification . . . Either the concept of *mala fides* must be regarded as sufficiently broad to comprehend a failure to observe the standards normally applied to discretions to the extent that such standards have not been excluded by the words of the instrument, or the proposition must be confined to cases where all such standards are inapplicable or intended to be excluded.[27]

---

[23] *Associated Provincial Picture Houses Ltd.* v. *Wednesbury Corporation* [1948] 1 KB 223 at 234 per Lord Greene MR.   [24] [1918] 2 Ch. 67.   [25] Ibid., at 71.
[26] M. Cullity (n. 15 above), p. 103.
[27] Ibid., p. 106. Cullity's text refers to the standard of the reasonable and prudent man of business instead of the duty to act in the best interests of the beneficiaries.

The process described by M. Cullity leaves plenty of room for judicial discretion. Is the power to be read as a possible exception to a duty of 'best interests', or a possible extension of 'good faith'?

B. CONTROLLING CONFLICTS OF INTEREST

Just as there are a range of standards regarding the manner in which trustees must exercise their discretions, so there is a range of standards regarding the effects upon trustees of conflicts of interests.

1. The Mere Possibility of Conflict

At one extreme, we have the standard set out by Lord Cranworth in *Aberdeen Railway Co.* v. *Balkie*, where he said:

And it is a rule of universal application, that no one, having [fiduciary] duties to discharge, shall be allowed to enter into engagements in which he has, or can have, a personal interest conflicting, or which possibly may conflict, with the interests of those whom he is bound to protect.[28]

This standard seems to be designed not simply to stop decisions which actually involve conflict of interest, but to stop persons from acting as trustees where their other interests might just possibly give rise to such a conflict.[29]

2. A Real Possibility of Conflict

Lord Upjohn, in his dissent in *Boardman* v. *Phipps*, took a less strict view of the scope of disqualification:

The phrase 'possibly may conflict' requires consideration. In my view it means that the reasonable man looking at the relevant facts and circumstances of the particular case would think that there was a real sensible possibility of conflict; not that you could imagine some situation arising which might, in some conceivable possibility in events not contemplated as real sensible possibilities by any reasonable person, result in conflict.[30]

Lord Upjohn was reiterating views originally expressed in *Boulting* v. *ACTAT*.[31] Insisting upon a 'real' conflict allows the court to relax the rule where it feels that the trustees are able to combine their interests and duty in a satisfactory manner. In *Boulting*, the court had no evidence that the

---

[28] 1 Marcq. 461, 471. This rule was approved by the majority of the House of Lords in *Boardman* v. *Phipps* [1967] 2 AC 46 at 124 (HL). See also *Bray* v. *Ford* [1986] AC 44 at 51 per Lord Herschell.

[29] 'No doubt it was but a remote possibility that Mr Boardman would ever be asked by the court to advise on the desirability of an application to court in order that the trustees might avail themselves of the information obtained. Nevertheless, even if the possibility of conflict is present between personal interest and the fiduciary position the rule of equity must be applied.' *Boardman*, ibid., at 111 per Lord Hodson.   [30] Ibid., at 124.

[31] [1963] 2 QB 606 at 638 (CA).

fiduciary duties of the plaintiffs as company directors could not be combined with their interests as trade union members. And the court was not prepared to assume, by the mere fact that the plaintiffs were both directors and union members, that such a conflict arose.

Similar approaches to that of Lord Upjohn were taken in *Holder* v. *Holder*;[32] and *Farrars* v. *Farrars Ltd.*.[33] In *Holder* the defendant was an executor only because he had signed a few cheques in connection with the administration of an estate and was deemed to be an executor under the doctrine which makes intermeddlers in estates into executors ('executor de son tort'). The court was not prepared to set aside a subsequent sale to him as he had never acted as trustee in connection with the sale, or with the general business of the estate. Since he had never acted to protect the beneficiaries' interests, and the beneficiaries never expected him to protect their interests, there was no conflict in the fact of his buying the trust property.

In *Farrars*, property was sold by three mortgagees to a company for which one of the mortgagees was the solicitor, and in which he also had a small shareholding. Lindley LJ was not prepared to assume that there was a conflict of interest on these facts alone:

It is necessary to see what his duties to the mortgagors were, and what he really did.[34]

3. *The Relation between Rules against Conflicting Interest, and Evidence of Conflicting Interests*

The courts not only have different rules as to what constitutes a conflict, they also apply different standards of evidence in connection with those rules. At one extreme, represented by *Aberdeen Railway*, the beneficiaries need only show a hypothetical possibility of conflicting interests. Once this is shown, the trustees are not allowed to adduce evidence that their actions were actually in the beneficiaries' best interests. *Aberdeen Railway* assumes that it is often impossible to prove that a trustee has acted unfairly, and responds with a standard intended to deter trustees from having conflicts of interest: the trustees' actions will be treated as breaches of trust *whatever the evidence*. This standard can be relaxed by allowing the trustees to provide evidence that their actions were, in fact, the best that the beneficiaries could expect. This was the approach adopted by the court in *Farrars*. It required the trustees to show that their actions were in the beneficiaries' best interests.[35]

The relationship between evidence and an insistence that conflicts be 'real' is quite flexible. At one extreme a court might find conflicts as soon as the possibility is more than theoretical, and then refuse to allow the trustees to produce evidence that they had acted in the beneficiaries' best interests. At

---

[32] [1968] Ch. 353.   [33] (1888) 40 Ch. D 395.   [34] Ibid., at 410.

[35] For an example of how hard it can be to discharge this burden, see the list of things which the Privy Council expected of a mortgagee who sold the mortgaged property to a company which he controlled. *Tse Kwong Lam* v. *Wong Chit Sen* [1983] 3 All ER 54.

the other extreme, a court might refuse to find a 'real' conflict so long as the trustees could show that their actions had not deprived the beneficiaries of any benefits.[36]

As with general standards of care, the conflict rule has to be interpreted against the trust deed and rules and the background matrix of fact. Exceptions to the rule may be express and implied. Examples of both kinds of exception are provided by *Sargeant* v. *National Westminster Bank PLC*.[37] In this case the settlor had leased his land to a partnership of which his three children were, at the date of his death, the partners. Under the terms of the partnership, when a partner died, the two remaining partners could purchase his share of the partnership. Under the terms of the settlor's will, the three children were trustees and beneficiaries of the freeholds. The will provided that the trustees could purchase trust property. When one of the children died, the remaining trustees acquired his interest in the partnership, and the lease. They then tried to purchase the freehold.

The Court of Appeal were not prepared to apply the rule against conflicts of interest, even though they accepted that there was an acute conflict of interest between the trustees' interest in the partnership and their duty to the beneficiaries. They felt that the trustees' interests under the partnership, including the tenancy and the right of pre-emption, were known to the settlor at the time the trust came into effect. As such, the holding of such positions, and the possible conflict of interest which could arise, must be taken to have been authorized by the settlor. Furthermore, the trustees could sell the freeholds to themselves under the express authority in the trust and, in the absence of any evidence that they were not acting in the beneficiaries' best interests, the court was not prepared to appoint an independent trustee for the purpose of this sale.

C. THE RELATIONSHIP BETWEEN DUTIES OF CARE AND THE RULE AGAINST CONFLICTING INTERESTS

Finally, it is worth noting the relationship between duties of care and conflicts of interest, using *Sargeant* as an example. The authority to self-deal in *Sargeant* meant that the conflict rule did not apply, and the beneficiaries had to prove that the trustees were preferring their own interests. But the authority to self-deal did not allow the trustees to carry out any transactions at the expense of the beneficiaries' interests. If such a sacrifice was to occur, it would have to be separately, and clearly, authorized.

---

[36] In *Boardman*, the dispute was over whether Boardman, the trust's solicitor, should disgorge profits made from the purchase of shares in a company in which the trust held a major shareholding. Lord Upjohn and Viscount Dilthorne stressed that the trust never expected to purchase the shares acquired by Boardman. As the trust had therefore lost no benefit, there was no conflict of interests. See *Boardman* v. *Phipps* (n. 28 above), pp. 92, 120, 125, 129, 130.

[37] 4 May 1990 (CA). Times Law Reports, 10 May 1990; Independent Law Reports, 14 May 1990. 61 P & CR 518 (1990).

D. SUMMARY

Section II of this chapter has shown that the general law of trusts provides a wide range of standards with which to regulate the exercise of trustees' discretions. When choosing amongst those standards, the court will have regard to the language used in the trust in question, and the surrounding circumstances, to see what level of control is appropriate. This is an indeterminate and flexible process. One should not assert that trustees must avoid all conflicts of interest and that they must act in the best interests of the beneficiaries, and then treat all lesser standards as if they were exceptions to a general rule. Such assertions ignore the creative role which courts have in interpreting the general law of trusts and deciding how it relates to the language of a particular trust, and to the surrounding circumstances. Every discretion is a potential exception to these strict standards.

The courts do not operate in a different manner when seeking to control the exercise of discretions by pension scheme trustees. They still have to decide which standards are appropriate, and that still requires them to select standards from the general law of trusts by reference to the language of the trust and the general circumstances. Millett J was correct to say in *Re Courage Group's Pension Schemes* that 'there were no special rules of construction applicable to a pension scheme' but only a requirement that 'its provisions should wherever possible be construed to give reasonable and practical effect to the scheme'.[38] But there are a number of factors which complicate this task. First, courts will have to interpret the general law of trusts, and the rules of particular schemes, to see whether the employer is a beneficiary. Second, in making this interpretation, and in choosing what standards of control to apply, the courts will have to decide whether the general circumstances of pension schemes should alter their willingness to hold trustees to strict standards. In particular, should the fact that the beneficiaries have paid for their beneficial interests, either through contributions, or through their service to the firm, make a difference to the process of determining what standards are appropriate?

III. APPLYING TRUST PRINCIPLES TO OCCUPATIONAL PENSION SCHEMES

A. WHO IS COVERED BY THE TRUSTEES' DUTY TO ACT IN THE BENEFICIARIES' BEST INTERESTS?

If pension scheme trustees are to be governed by the standard of 'best interests', then one must know who, for these purposes, is a beneficiary. In

[38] [1987] 1 All ER 528 at 537.

particular, is the employer a beneficiary? If so, then the trustees must act for the members and for the employer, and their independence from the sponsoring company is established, if at all, only by their personal views or their duty to act 'impartially' as between different categories of beneficiaries.

1. The Duty of Trustees in pre-1971 Schemes

The type of scheme which could most easily give rise to a duty to act solely in the interests of the members, their survivors, and dependants, are those pre-1971 schemes which make no provision for the employer to benefit under the trust deed and rules, and may even contain a provision stating that the employer is not to benefit under any circumstances.[39] As the employer is not a beneficiary under the terms of the trust deed, it is usually thought that the employer is not one of the parties whose interests must be considered when the trustees decide how to exercise their discretions under the trust deed and rules. But is the position really this clear?

The Trustee's Duty under a Resulting Trust   The employer's rights as a beneficiary under this type of scheme arise under the doctrine of resulting trust: property held by trustees which is not completely used up under the terms of the trust is automatically held on resulting trust for the settlor.[40] This doctrine can lead to a surplus on winding up being held by the trustees for the benefit of the employer as the main, or only contributor to the pension scheme. But what is the connection between the presence of this right and the trustees' general discretions under the terms of the original trust?

At one extreme, the beneficiary of a resulting trust deserves no more consideration from the trustees than the other claimant for undisposed surpluses arising within trusts: the Treasury (which takes all unowned property, under the doctrine known as *bona vacantia*). From this perspective, the employer's only right is to receive whatever surplus should arise after the trustees have carried out all their duties under a trust. At the other extreme, the settlor simply steps into the shoes of any beneficiary whose interest is invalid and, as the party who has contributed the trust funds, is entitled to be treated at least as well as the other beneficiaries. From this perspective, the employer, by reason of a resulting trust, becomes a residuary beneficiary for the purposes of the trustees' exercise of discretions under the pension scheme.

This is an example of the indeterminacy of trust law, and the difficulty of

---

[39] Before the Finance Act 1970, some Schedule D inspectors made it a condition of their allowing tax reliefs on contributions to occupational pension schemes that the scheme rules prohibit both a return of monies to the employer on winding up, and any refund that could result in such a refund. See D. Bates, 'Payments to the Employer', in *Pensions World*, February 1984, p. 88.

[40] For a clear statement of the automatic resulting trust, and how it may be distinguished from the presumed resulting trust, see *Re Vandervell's Trusts (No. 2)* [1974] Ch. 269 at 294–5.

being sure that rules, developed in one context, will be applied in another. Cases on the automatic resulting trust have centred on the question of who should, or could, benefit from a surplus when a trust comes to an end.[41] The courts have not been called upon to decide whether, or how, trustees should treat a party who has an interest under a resulting trust when exercising their powers under the original trust. General principles do not assist a great deal. On the one hand, one can argue that since the resulting trust arises by operation of law, it takes effect outside the terms of the original trust, and therefore the beneficiary of the resulting trust is not someone whose interests the trustees must consider when exercising their powers under the terms of the original trust.

On the other hand, resulting trusts arise in situations in which this kind of division would be unworkable. The doctrine is not limited to interests arising on the termination of a trust, but covers all undisposed interests arising under trust. Where the income of a trust fund was held for the settlor under a resulting trust, would the trustees really have to exercise their powers of appointment and investment solely in the interests of the remaining beneficiaries, i.e., those entitled to the capital?

The Courts' Attitude towards the Employer   The cases in this area of law show an increasing willingness to treat employers favourably under schemes which purport to exclude the employer from benefit. At one time it was thought that the type of scheme which made no provision for an eventual surplus would be unlikely to give rise to a resulting trust, so that the employer could have no type of beneficial interest under such a scheme. In *Re ABC Television, Goodblatte* v. *John*,[42] Foster J had to interpret a scheme which made no provision for a residual surplus, and contained a restriction on the power of amendment which provided that no money contributed by the employer 'shall in any circumstances by repayable to the Principal company'. He decided that such a provision negated the possibility of implying a resulting trust. In *Palmer* v. *Abney Park Cemetery Co. Ltd.*[43] Blackett-Ord J provided another reason why employers should not expect to benefit from a resulting trust. A number of authorities had held that resulting trusts could not arise when the contributions to the original trust were made under contract. These cases concerned unincorporated associations, but in *Palmer* v. *Abney Park Cemetery Co. Ltd.*, Blackett-Ord J applied the same reasoning to a pension scheme:

Under the deed and the rules the company was entitled to no return or benefit other than that of goodwill with its employees, and the members were entitled only to what

---

[41] See e.g. *Re Gillingham Bus Disaster Fund* [1958] Ch. 300; *Re Printers and Transferers Society* [1899] 2 Ch. 184; *Re Customs & Excise Officers Fund* [1917] 2 Ch. 18.
[42] *Re ABC Television, Goodblatte* et al. v. *John* et al., 22 May 1973, reported in R. Ellison, *Private Occupational Pension Schemes* (1979), p. 347.   [43] 4 July 1985, unreported.

they had contracted for. That they have obtained. And on that ground it seems to me that the balance of the fund can only pass to the Crown as *bona vacantia*.[44]

In two recent cases involving pension schemes the courts have, however, taken a different view. In *Jones* v. *Williams*,[45] Knox J held that a resulting trust was to be excluded 'only where it was absolutely clear that in no circumstances was a resulting trust to arise',[46] and in *Davis* v. *Richards & Wallington Industries*,[47] Scott J felt that the presence of a contract was insufficient evidence of intention to exclude a resulting trust. *Davis* is a particularly favourable case for employers, for not only was the employer entitled to a resulting trust, but it was the only party entitled to a resulting trust despite the fact that employees had made contributions as well. When excluding the employees from the benefit of any resulting trust, Scott J relied on the fact that employers pay the balance of cost. He likened the presence of a surplus to a mistaken overpayment into an account:

The actuarial calculations were, I am sure, impeccable. But the [winding-up] having invalidated some of the assumptions underlying the calculations, the case is, in my opinion, strongly analogous to that of an account drawn up under a mistake. In my opinion, equity should treat the employers as entitled to claim the surplus, or so much of it as is derived from overpayment.[48]

One must be wary of seeing an inevitable upgrading of the employer's position under these pre-1971 schemes to that of an employer under a post-1971 scheme. If the opinion of the former Vice-Chancellor is anything to go by, judges currently assume that the trustees of pre-1971 schemes do not have to take the employer's interest into account when exercising their discretions. This was one of the reasons why, in *Imperial Group Pension Trust Limited* v. *Imperial Tobacco Ltd.*,[49] Browne-Wilkinson VC would not treat the employer's power to veto amendments to the scheme as a fiduciary power:

if this were a fiduciary power the company would have to decide whether or not to consent by reference *only to the interests of the members, disregarding its own interest*.[50]

However, this one line of authority is hardly reassurance for scheme members.[51]

---

[44] Quoted by Scott J in *Davis* v. *Richards & Wallington Industries* [1991] 2 All ER 563 at 590.
[45] [1989] 1 PLR 21.   [46] Ibid., at 33.   [47] Note 44 above.
[48] Ibid., at 594.   [49] [1991] 1 WLR 589, [1991] 2 All ER 597.
[50] [1991] 1 WLR 589 at 596, [1991] 2 All ER 597 at 604.
[51] As *Haig* v. *Lord Advocate* [1976] SLT 16 demonstrates, the rules of a scheme may not, by themselves, prevent the employer from receiving consideration by reason of a resulting trust. There, Lord Kinscraig argued that the fact that an employer was not entitled to be given an interest in the pension fund under the scheme rules did not mean that it could not have an interest in the fund under a resulting trust. The same logic allows a court to say that the fact that an employer is not to be given an interest under the rules does not mean that it cannot be the object of the trustees' discretions by reason of an interest under a resulting trust.

2. The General Duty of Trustees in New Code Schemes

Following the Finance Act 1970, Revenue approval for new schemes required that the winding-up clause stipulate for an eventual surplus to be returned to the employer.[52] There is no evidence as to the Revenue's motives in introducing this requirement. The most likely reason is that in its absence, trustees might have been persuaded to augment benefits on winding up to levels which exceed Revenue maximum. It is even possible that the Revenue were trying to remove the possibility that property could go to the Treasury under the doctrine of *bona vacantia* (a valuable but unsolicited and perhaps embarrassing benefit). There is no evidence that the Revenue were trying to ensure that the trustees exercised their discretions in the interests of employers as well as members. That said, the employer is clearly a beneficiary of the trust and, in the circumstances of a family settlement, would be one of the parties whose interests the trustees should consider when deciding how to exercise their discretions. Unless the rules of the scheme indicate otherwise, the employer, as a beneficiary, is entitled to the same consideration as other beneficiaries. But, as we shall see, there are some indications that the employer should be treated less favourably than this.

The 'Sole Purpose' Rule   The rules of a scheme usually provide that it has been established for the sole purpose of providing pensions.[53] If all the trustees' powers can only be exercised for this purpose, it would mean that the trustees would be able to take account only of the interests of those parties who receive pensions: the members, their dependants and survivors.[54]

The Winding-up Clause   Another provision which may reduce the status of the employer is the wording of the winding-up clause. In some schemes it is provided that on commencement of winding up, the 'trusts shall cease' and the terms of the winding-up clause take effect in their place. The effect of such a clause may have the effect of creating two trusts, with the employer being beneficiary of the trust arising on winding up, but not under the trust which governs the operation of the scheme on an ongoing basis. In this context it does not matter if the trust arising on winding up supplements the original trust, or replaces it, so long as it does not come into effect before the commencement of winding up.

---

[52] See Occupational Pension Schemes: *Notes on Approval under the Finance Act 1970*, IR 12 (Oct. 1970), p. 39. The condition was retained when the Revenue issued new versions of 'IR 12' in 1979 and 1991.

[53] Tax relief is, and has always been, subject to a 'sole purpose' restriction. See Finance Act 1921, s. 32(3)(b) (now Income and Corporations Act 1988, s. 590(2)(a)).

[54] And would not be able to secure them benefits in other capacities such as that of employees, or as absolute owners of property. On trusts to benefit individuals in a particular manner, see J. Hackney, *Understanding Equity and Trusts* (Fontana, 1987) pp. 71–4.

Re Courage Group's Pension Schemes—Trustees are Not to Advance the Employer's Interests   In *Re Courage Group's Pension Schemes*[55] Millett J expressed a firm opinion that the trustees are not there to protect the interests of the employer, even when the employer has an interest under the trust under the terms of the winding-up clause. This case arose out of a take-over. The Courage Group of companies had been purchased by Hanson Trust PLC ('Hansons'), who had subsequently sold them to Elders IXL Ltd. ('Elders'). The pension schemes of these companies were substantially in surplus. Hansons wished to retain these surpluses (totalling £80 million) for their own benefit. In the sale-agreement with Hansons, Elders undertook to set up new schemes for the employees of the Courage Group, and to procure the execution of deeds which would have the effect of substituting Hansons as the principal employer under the rules of the Courage pension schemes. The schemes were currently closed to new members,[56] but if they could be reopened with Hansons as the principal employer, the surpluses could be used to fund the pensions of Hansons' employees. Courage employees were to have the choice of transferring into the new schemes set up by Elders, or having deferred pensions under the Courage pension schemes.

The trustees of the Courage schemes refused to execute the proposed amendments. They were concerned that the amendments would leave the pensioners and deferred pensioners in schemes where future discretionary pension increases would be determined by Hansons, a company with which the pensioners enjoyed only the most tenuous of relationships. The trustees' other concern was that the employees of the Courage Group were to be separated from their fund and transferred to a scheme which had only a small surplus (£10 million)

In Millett J's opinion:

A pension scheme is established not for the benefit of a particular company, but for the benefit of those *employed* in a commercial undertaking . . .[57]

This premiss formed the basis of his interpretation of the way in which powers could be used within a pension scheme. The power to substitute a new principal company could be used to benefit these employees by preventing the scheme from being wound up when the company which happened to be the principal company was the subject of an amalgamation or reconstruction, but it could not be used to stop the schemes from continuing to operate for these employees' benefit. Such a use of the power of substitution was *ultra vires*. As such, it could not be agreed to by the trustees and, by implication, could not have been carried out by the employer even had the power of amendment not required the trustees' consent.

---

[55] Note 38 above.
[56] The pension schemes had been closed to new members shortly before the take-over by Hansons, in order to ensure that the surpluses were retained for the benefit of the existing members.   [57] Note 38 above, at 541.

B. THE DUTY OF PENSION SCHEME TRUSTEES WHEN WINDING UP
AN OCCUPATIONAL PENSION SCHEME

Section II of this chapter stressed the relationship between general standards and the express terms of the trust. Pension trusts provide a very good example of this interaction in the form of the rule which allows trustees to augment benefits on winding up and the duty to act in the members' best interests. Such a duty cannot assist the members in the exercise of this particular discretion. It is, as the subsequent discussion will show, a situation in which the wording of the discretion cannot readily be combined with the application of such a general duty.

1. The Relationship between a Duty to Act in the Beneficiaries' Best Interests and a Discretion to Increase Benefits

The discretion to augment benefits on winding up would seem to be the classic case for deciding whether trustees are subject to an overriding duty to act in the best interests of the members. For a start, the implications of finding that such a duty exists are so clear: the trustees should use their power to augment rather than see the money returned to the employer. But ironically, this situation is also one in which it is almost impossible to give such a duty an independent effect. There is almost no room for such a duty, once you have decided what type of discretion the trustees have. If the trustees are under a duty to use the surplus to augment benefits, but can use discretion to decide which of the benefits to augment, then the trustees will have to augment, and the duty to act in the members' best interests adds nothing.[58] If instead the trustees can decide not only how to augment, but whether to augment in the first place, then one has to accept that they cannot be required to act in the members' best interests. (At most, they can be required to consider their best interests.)[59] The major question therefore becomes, is this the kind of power which *must* be exercised, leaving the trustees only to decide *how* to exercise the power ('a trust power'), or is it the kind of power where the trustees are not only free to decide how to exercise it, but *whether* to exercise it (a 'mere power')?

In a pre-1971 scheme, where the employer has no residuary entitlement to surplus under the scheme, it is possible to interpret a discretion to augment benefits on winding up as a trust power rather than a mere power. But under a post-1971 scheme, this is more difficult. The presence of an express employer's entitlement to surplus indicates that there will be circumstances in which the trustees will not exhaust the surplus through an increase of benefits. Where the trustees' power to increase benefits is expressly limited to Inland Revenue maximum (or where the court implies this restriction) one

[58] Though the duty to act impartially between beneficiaries will be relevant to the allocation of increases between the members.

[59] See *Mettoy Pension Trustees Limited* v. *Evans* [1991] 2 All ER 513; [1990] 1 WLR 1587.

can interpret the employer's residuary entitlement as a device for dealing with any surplus that cannot be absorbed within these limits. This still allows the discretion to be treated as a trust power. But where the trustees' power to augment is not limited in this way, it is extremely difficult to treat the power to augment as a trust power. How can the employer ever receive a refund of surplus, if the trustees have a duty to increase benefits which places no limit on the amount of such increases? The same logic which makes it difficult to construe a power to augment benefits as a trust power, also prevents one from interpreting such discretions as being subject to a general overriding duty to act in the members' best interests. If the members' best interests so obviously require an increase of benefits, how can a duty to act in their interests be reconciled with a clause giving surpluses to the employer?

One can make an attempt to reconcile the employer's right to a surplus with the trustees having an overriding duty to act in the members' interests. The employer can enjoy a surplus, without this being directly and obviously in conflict with the interests of the members, when the winding up is for the purposes of introducing a replacement scheme.[60] Where winding up is part of a reorganization of the company's pension arrangements, a replacement scheme might be in the interests of the members, even where a surplus is to be returned to the employer. On this basis, the trustees can have a mere power and still be subject to an overriding duty to act in the members' best interests. This interpretation of the winding-up clause is, however, very strained. One has to assume that the employer's right to receive a surplus has only been put into the winding-up clause to allow the employer to obtain a refund as part of a reorganization.

Icarus (Hertford) Ltd. v. Driscoll   The way in which the wording of a discretion can remove the possibility of trust power (or a duty to act in the members' best interests) can be illustrated by *Icarus (Hertford) Ltd.* v. *Driscoll.*[61] In this case, the trustee of the scheme was the employer. The employer was in liquidation and the scheme was being wound up. The trustee had a discretion to decide whether to augment the members' benefits. Any surplus which remained after securing members' benefits was to be returned to the employer. The discretion was worded as follows:

The employer shall subject to Revenue Limitations at their discretion apply the whole or part of such [surplus] as they may determine to augment entitlements of Members . . .[62]

In Chapter 2, we looked at Aldous J's decision that the word 'shall' was not mandatory, but permissive. Once one accepts that the discretion is permissive, i.e., that it need not be exercised, one has accepted that the

---

[60] See the letter by Raymond Ainscoe in 30 *Pension Lawyer* (January 1990), p. 3.
[61] 4 December 1989. [1990] 1 PLR 1.   [62] Ibid., at 5.

trustees have the right to allow part or all of the surplus to return to the employer. Such freedom cannot be reconciled with an overriding duty to act in the members' best interests.

2. No Duty to Augment in post-1970 Schemes

The provision in post-1970 schemes for the return of a surplus to the employer on winding up is incompatible with a duty to augment. Such clauses clearly envisage that the trustees may, in some circumstances, fail to augment, or at least fail to augment sufficiently to wipe out the surplus. If the trustees were under an overriding duty to exercise the power of augmentation in the members' best interests, there would be no surplus, since they would have to augment without limit. It therefore follows that, with respect to their discretion to augment on winding up, the trustees are not under such a duty.

C. CONFLICTS OF INTEREST

1. A Strict Standard? Brooke Bond & Co. Ltd.'s Trust Deed

On the authority of *Brooke Bond & Co. Ltd.'s Trust Deed*,[63] pension schemes are subject to the strict standard for conflicts of interest set out in *Aberdeen Railway*.[64] In *Brooke*, a pension scheme was administered by trustees, but employed an insurance company as a custodial trustee. The insurance company had no duties other than to provide safe custody for the scheme's assets. When the other trustees wished to take out a policy with the insurance company, they asked the court whether the fact that the company was already a trustee, albeit in this limited capacity, prevented them from entering into the contract. Cross J held that the rule set out in *Aberdeen Railway* was an inflexible one, and because there was still some risk of a conflict of interest and duty, albeit a much lower one than with managing trustees, the insurance company could not enter into the contract.

2. Reasons for Doubting That Aberdeen Railway will be Applied

Despite the authority of *Brooke Bond*, the consequences of the strict application of *Aberdeen Railway* to occupational pension schemes causes one to doubt whether the strict standard will be applied. If no possible conflict of interest were allowed, then hardly any of the current trustees could continue to act, or should have accepted their trusteeship in the first place. Trustees are commonly directors of the employer, and might therefore be expected to have a conflict of duties. Those trustees who are not directors of the employer are still likely to be employees. As employees, they are also likely to be beneficiaries of the pension scheme and therefore affected, directly or indirectly, by the exercise of their own discretions.

If the *Aberdeen Railway* approach were to be applied to the administration

---

[63] [1962] Ch. 357.   [64] Note 28 above.

of pension schemes, it would cause chaos. All decisions taken by trustees who were directors, employees, or beneficiaries, would be open to challenge by the beneficiaries. Although, according to the Court of Appeal in *Boulting* v. *ACTAT*,[65] such decisions are only voidable, and not void, this would not prevent past decisions on benefit increases, scheme amendments, and investments being open to challenge long after they had been made. The court might protect such decisions by a liberal application of the doctrine of estoppel, but this is not a sensible manner for the occupational pensions industry to be administered. It would also require that, as soon as possible, trustees who suffer conflicts of interest and duty would have to be replaced, or their schemes altered (by independent trustees) to authorize trustees with conflicts to act.[66]

3. *Implied Exceptions to* Aberdeen Railways

Despite *Brooke Bond & Co. Ltd.'s Trust Deed*, pension trustees can expect to rely on a liberal application of the approach taken in *Sargeant* v. *National Westminster Bank PLC*,[67] and an approach to conflict of interest based on that applied in *Boulting*, i.e. that they are impliedly authorized to be trustees, despite their conflicts of interest or duty because, in the context of general practice in the pensions industry, it was always envisaged that such persons would be trustees and because, in the general administration of a pension scheme, there is no 'real' conflict.

The approaches set out in *Sargeant* and *Boulting* provide the courts with a flexible basis on which to intervene, whenever they feel that there is a significant possibility that the interests of the members will be sacrificed. They do not have to wait for evidence that such a sacrifice has, in fact, occurred. They can intervene by preventing the trustees from acting, or undoing transactions that have occurred, or they can put the onus on the trustees to prove that the interests of the members were, or will be, protected.

4. *Intervening Where the Conflict of Interest is Serious*—Mettoy Pension Trustees Limited *v*. Evans

In *Mettoy Pension Trustees Limited* v. *Evans*,[68] the court did not profess to intervene just because there was some possibility of conflicting interests, but because there was a certain and extreme conflict of interest. *Mettoy* involved the winding up of an insolvent company's pension scheme. The winding-up clause gave the employer power to increase benefits. The liquidator asked the

---

[65] Note 31 above.

[66] In some schemes, particular persons may be named as the original trustees. This is common where the scheme is to be administered by a corporate trustee. Such parties may be deemed to be excluded from the rule in *Aberdeen*, by reason of their express or implied authority, in the same manner as the trustees in *Sargeant*.   [67] Note 37 above.

[68] Note 59 above.

court to decide whether this power was fiduciary and, if so, whether it could be exercised by the liquidator. Warner J decided that the power was fiduciary and that it could not, in these circumstances, be exercised by the directors of the company, or a liquidator, or receiver. Instead, it must be surrendered to the court.

Warner J felt that the discretion to increase benefits on winding up could not be exercised by the directors of the company (had there still been any) because, in the context of a cessation of business, the directors would not be allowed to consider the interests of the past employees and their dependants.[69] The receiver and the liquidator could not exercise it because, in view of their duties to the creditors and the shareholders, it was inevitable that they would choose not to exercise the power so as to allow the largest possible surplus to be returned to the employer.[70] To ensure that the members' interests were properly considered, the power should be surrendered to the court.

5. Identifying a Serious Risk of Conflict

The decision in *Mettoy* was narrowly drawn. The judge was inclined to believe that the liquidator's prior duty to the creditors made sacrifice of the members' interests inevitable.[71] But this does not mean that the rule against conflicts will always be drawn so narrowly, i.e. that everything short of an inevitable conflict of duty is either not, in the terms of *Boulting* a 'real' conflict or, applying *Sargeant*, is impliedly authorized.

If the approach of the courts to rules against conflict is, as has been suggested, a flexible means to prevent abuse, then the central question for predicting future intervention is what types of behaviour are likely to be considered to give rise to an acute risk that the members' interests will be sacrificed. Certain transactions are easily identified. Self-investment by the trustees provides an obvious risk that the interests of the members will be sacrificed. Such investment is only allowed where there is an express authority in the trust deed and rules, and even then, according to Brighton J

---

[69] Because of the rule in *Parke* v. *Daily News Ltd.* [1962] Ch. 927 as modified by Companies Act 1985, s. 309.

[70] The receiver was also prevented from exercising an employer's fiduciary powers on the basis that these are not part of the assets of the company and therefore are not caught by the charge.

[71] The Social Security Act 1990 puts this right to be considered on to a statutory basis. When an insolvency practitioner (a receiver, administrator, or liquidator) is appointed to a company the powers of the trustees must be exercised by an independent trustee. Where there is no such trustee, one must be appointed. The independent trustee becomes the only person who can exercise the trustees' discretions. Where the employer is also the sole trustee, the independent trustee replaces the employer as trustee of the scheme. To take account of situations like that in *Mettoy*, the independent trustee will also exercise any power held by the employer which is fiduciary in nature, even when the employer is not a trustee. The act defines independent trustee to exclude the liquidator, receiver, administrator, employer (and all their associates and persons connected with them), and the beneficiaries of the scheme. It thus goes beyond *Mettoy* by removing the trustees' discretion from persons who suffer from conflicts of interest as well as those who suffer a conflict of duties.

in *Evans* v. *London Co-Operative Society*,[72] the trustees must be satisifed that such investment is in the interests of the members. Pension scheme trustees would be ill-advised to assume that the court will accept their word that such transactions involved no sacrifice of members' interests. They should be prepared to demonstrate that the members' interests were fully protected.

At the other extreme, certain potential conflicts of interest are easily excused. The trustees are often entitled to decide questions of individual entitlement to discretionary benefits. Consider, for example, a discretionary entitlement to a generous early leaver's pension where retirement is on grounds of ill health. There is some conflict here. Such generosity reduces the security of the benefits of the other members, and increases the cost of the scheme to the employer. But one can expect the court to understand the commercial realities of the situation. It, like the OPB,[73] is likely to accept that the benefits of having trustees who are familiar with the applicants outweighs the possibility of conflicting interest. The amounts involved in these individual decisions are relatively small when compared with the value of the fund, and one should not expect the trustees to be under pressure to exercise their discretion other than in a bona fide manner.[74]

6. *Dealing with Pension Fund Surpluses—a Serious Risk of Conflicting Interests?*

A type of decision which lies between these extremes is the amendment of a pensions scheme which has a large surplus. Many trustees are in the process of negotiating with the scheme's employer over changes in the scheme's rules. Millett J stated the need for such negotiations in *Courage*:

Repayment [of a surplus] will, however, still normally require amendment to the scheme and thus co-operation between the employer and the trustees or committee of management. Where the employer seeks repayment, the trustees or committee can be expected to press for generous treatment of the employees and pensioners, and the employer to be influenced by a desire to maintain good industrial relations with its workforce.[75]

Such negotiation does not involve the acute conflict of interest identified in *Mettoy*, whereby every £1 not used to increase benefits was £1 extra for the

---

[72] 5 July 1976. Reported in Ellison, *Private Occupational Pension Schemes*, (Oyez, 1979) p. 356.

[73] See Protecting Pensions: Safeguarding Pensions in a Changing Environment. A Report by the Occupational Pensions Board in accordance with s. 66 of the Social Security Act 1973. CM 573, para. 4.10.

[74] Although situations can arise in which access to ill-health pensions becomes costly, and controversial. Consider e.g., the treatment of nine journalists suffering from repetitive strain injury at the *Financial Times*, a company in which one-third of the workforce have been estimated to suffer from the same condition. See 'Inside Story: Keyboard Revolution—National Newspapers changed as computers redefined everything—especially the jobs. The FT launched into an uncertain future, then came RSI', The *Guardian*, 5 February 1992, p. 5.

[75] Note 38 above, at 545.

liquidator. The trustees will seek to improve the members' benefits. In return for such improvements (which increase the employer's future funding burden), the employer seeks an immediate advantage, such as a refund. These negotiations vary in the means which are used to effect the change, and the trade-off which takes place. Thus the trustees may be asked to amend their scheme, or to transfer the scheme assets into a scheme which has different rules. The advantage sought by the employer may be that a scheme which is closed to new members becomes open, or that early retirement benefits are introduced which reduce the cost of a redundancy programme, or that a scheme which prohibits refunds will be changed into one that allows them, or that a scheme which allows refunds on winding up will henceforth allow them on an ongoing basis.

With respect to these negotiations, it is far from clear that the benefits of having trustees who know the membership and the company outweigh the danger that the members' interests will be sacrificed to those of the company. Handing back part of the trust assets in exchange for benefit increases seems no less of a conflict of interest situation than self-investment. In fact, the dangers may be more acute in this situation, since it is far harder to assess whether the decision reached was, in reality, in the best interests of the members. At least with self-investment, evidence of market rates of return can be used to form a judgment on the extent to which the employer was advantaged, and the members' interests sacrificed. But in negotiations over surpluses there is no such benchmark.[76] Given the difficulties of proving that their interests were sacrificed, the conflict of interest rule should be applied in one of its forms: either the trustees should be disqualified from acting where their interests are linked with the employer, or they should have the onus of proving that the deal was the best that could be reached in the circumstances.

IV. CONCLUSION

Although the OPB's statement of the duties of trustees was, as this chapter has shown, misleadingly simplistic, that does not mean that trust law cannot provide a suitable legal framework for the control of trustees' discretion. There is a case for regulating pension schemes by reference to a body of indeterminate principles and rules, with the strictness of supervision being tailored to the circumstances in which a particular discretion is exercised, and the wording of the discretion in question. Such a system offers a flexible basis for the review of the reasonableness of trustees' actions.[77]

---

[76] Whilst the members may show that other trustees have achieved better results in their negotiations, such evidence will not have the objectivity of a market price.

[77] The same 1989 OPB report which so confidently stated that trustees were under a duty to act solely in the interests of the members, also claimed that one of the major benefits of trust law was its inherent flexibility. N. 73 above, para. 8.11.

But there are powerful counter-arguments. First, if one believes that the duties of pension trustees should be as strong, or stronger, than the OPB's description, then it is inappropriate to rely on a body of law which is capable of delivering a much lower standard. Second, and this is the subject of Chapter 5, if one prefers to have a flexible basis of review, should that system for review be as expensive, and as difficult, as that offered by the law of trusts and the High Court?[78]

In assessing these arguments, one needs to remember that the suitability of trust duties cannot be isolated from the question of who the trustees are. A residual and flexible system of review may be quite satisfactory where all trustees are chosen by the scheme members and pensioners. Gross abuses can be restrained, and the employer, because of its economic interest in the scheme, is likely to fund any application to court. By contrast, if the employer is the trustee, or appoints the trustees, a system of flexible review may be quite unacceptable. The duties may be too weak to curb the employer's influence, and the members may in any case be unable to afford to bring the matter to court.

Trustees are not the only parties who have legal duties under a pension scheme. Another party who may have legal duties is the employer, and these are explored in the next chapter.

---

[78] Although the OPB recommended the introduction of a pensions tribunal (n. 73 above, paras. 13.10–13.17), they undermined much of the case for its introduction by overstating the protection offered by the law of trusts. The government has instead introduced a pensions ombudsman. This person is not expected to review the exercise of trustees' discretions: 'My view is that we should concentrate the new service on the types of problem that individuals, rather than schemes, can face. Disputes involving trustess, concerning large sums of money, are likely to end up in the courts in any case. That is not really our concern here'. Tony Newton, in a speech given to the Society of Pension Consultants on 7 November 1989. SPC News, No. 6, quoted in J. Mesher's annotations to the Social Security Act 1990, Schedule 3, in *Current Law Statutes Annotated* [1990] vol. 2 Ch. 27.55.

[4]

The Duties of the Employer under a Pension Scheme

1. INTRODUCTION

Until recently, the duties of employers under their pension schemes were basically limited to certain duties arising under the regulations requiring men and women to be given equal access to schemes, and the contracting-out procedure.[1] Unless the employer undertook to be a trustee, its liability was otherwise limited to the covenant to contribute, which could be discontinued on giving notice. The employees were to enjoy no contractual right other than the right to join the pension scheme on its current terms. All other employee pension rights were intended to exist in trust rather than contract, and to be enforceable against the trustees rather than the employer.[2]

If an employer was a trustee, its duties as trustee were clearly fiduciary,[3] and therefore had to be exercised on behalf of the scheme's beneficiaries (although, as Chapter 3 showed, exactly what this means is unclear). But where employees reserved scheme powers and were not trustees, or where they were trustees but reserved particular powers for the exercise of 'the employer' instead of 'the trustees', it had been thought, until recently, that they could exercise such powers in whatever manner they saw fit.[4] The one exception to this was the power to appoint trustees, which was generally accepted to be a fiduciary power,[5] and therefore required to be exercised in the beneficiaries' interests.

Three recent decisions indicate that the employer's duties under their

---

[1] See Ellison, *Private Occupational Pension Schemes* (Oyez, 1979), pp. 50–1.

[2] Ibid., p. 29: 'In the majority of cases the contract of employment will refer merely to the employee's right to become a member of the employer's pension scheme . . . In such cases the rights against the employer will be limited to the enforcing of the right to membership of the scheme, unless evidence can be shown of an oral variation of the written contract (for example by a personnel officer promising specific benefits).'

[3] See e.g. *Icarus (Hertford) Limited* v. *Driscoll* 4 December 1989, [1990] 1 PLR 1 and Nobles, 'Don't Trust the Trustee', 53 MLR (1990) 377 at 379.

[4] Subject only to the constraints of company law such as, e.g., the doctrine of *ultra vires*. See Ellison (n. 1 above), ch. 3.

[5] See N. Inglis-Jones, *The Law of Occupational Pension Schemes* (Sweet & Maxwell, 1989), pp. 40–2. P. Docking, 'Acting in Good Faith', *Pension World*, March 1990, p. 40. But see D. Pollard, 'Appointment and Removal of Trustees—a Fiduciary Power?', British Pension Lawyer, March 1991, p. 1.

scheme may be greater than this. *Mettoy Pension Trustees Limited* v. *Evans*[6] raises the possibility that employers' discretions can be interpreted as fiduciary powers, and therefore subject to the general duty of trustees. In *Mihlenstedt* v. *Barclays Bank PLC*[7] and *Imperial Group Pension Trust Ltd* v. *Imperial Tobacco Ltd.*[8] the employers' rights under the scheme were found to be subject to an implied contractual duty of good faith. This chapter analyses the scope of these duties, beginning with *Mettoy,* and the circumstances in which the employer may be subject to fiduciary duties.

II. INTERPRETING AN EMPLOYER'S POWER AS A FIDUCIARY POWER

In *Mettoy,* the court was called upon to interpret a power to increase benefits on winding up which, following an amendment of the scheme, had been taken from the trustees and given to the employer. The employer was in receivership and the receivers sought guidance on whether they could exercise the employer's scheme powers, and the basis upon which those powers should be exercised. Warner J did not accept that an employer was free to exercise this power in its own interests:

If that discretion is not such a fiduciary power it is, from the point of view of beneficiaries under the scheme, illusory. As I have pointed out, the words conferring the power mean no more, on that construction of them, than that the employer is free to make gifts to those beneficiaries out of property of which it is the absolute beneficial owner, so that at best those words amount to . . . a true but pointless assertion.

Accordingly, he held that the employer held this power as trustee. As was seen in Chapter 3, fiduciary duties range from a duty to act in the beneficiaries' best interests down to a duty to act in good faith. What gave this duty substance was Warner J's conclusion that it was a type of duty which could not be exercised by a liquidator or receiver because of their conflicting interests. By contrast, in *Icarus (Hertford) Limited* v. *Driscoll*[9] a case of almost identical facts, Aldous J saw nothing wrong with fiduciary powers being exercised by the employer's receiver, provided the receiver acted in 'good faith'. Good faith was no more than a procedural requirement, since the receiver had already announced her inclination not to increase benefits, so that the scheme's surplus could go to the employer's creditors.

The *Mettoy* decision, if followed elsewhere, could change the balance of power in schemes. Those drafting schemes might have supposed that giving a power to the employer gave it greater powers than sharing the power between trustees and the employer (by giving the employer a veto over its exercise) or

[6] [1991] 2 All ER 513; [1990] 1 WLR 1587.   [7] [1989] IRLR 522.
[8] (Ch.d) [1991] 2 All ER 597; [1990] 1 WLR 589.
[9] 4 December 1989, [1990] 1 PLR 1.

giving the power to the trustees alone. The interpretation in *Mettoy* collapses the difference between trustee and employee powers, and leaves the employer with greater control when it shares power with the trustees than when it seeks to exercise that power alone. But one should not interpret *Mettoy* as an indication that all employer powers will now be interpreted as fiduciary in nature. The reasoning which underlay the decision was Warner J's view that the members' rights to benefit from discretionary powers should not be 'illusory'. His interpretation was designed to ensure that these rights had some substance. He was not saying that all of the employer's powers are fiduciary, only that this power needed to be fiduciary in order to protect these particular rights. As we shall see, this reasoning is common to all three decisions on employers' duties: the court finds an entitlement which cannot be given effect without placing the employer under a duty.

III. THE DUTY OF GOOD FAITH

A. *MIHLENSTEDT* V. *BARCLAYS BANK PLC*

In *Mihlenstedt*, the Court of Appeal looked at a clause which 'permitted' the payment of an ill-health, early retirement pension and decided that this pension was not something which the employer could withhold at will, but was available to the employee of right once the necessary precondition had been met. The condition was the employer's opinion that she could no longer work. The employer argued that as it was not a trustee, it could form this opinion on any basis it saw fit. Had this been accepted, the right to an ill-health pension would have been, in effect, something which the employer could withhold at will. Instead, the Court of Appeal held that the employer, when forming its judgment, had a contractual duty to act in good faith. This was part of a wider principle that the employer 'was contractually bound, so far as it lay within its own power, to procure for the plaintiff the benefits to which she was entitled under the scheme'. The decision itself seemed to be limited to powers which required the holder to form an opinion on the existence of some sort of facts—powers which one commentator has described as 'quasi-judicial'.[10] But the wider principle suggested that the duty of good faith might be extended to other kinds of discretions. The meaning of good faith in this case seems to approach an administrative law standard. Nourse LJ felt that a decision by the employer could be set aside if it was formed dishonestly, 'or on an erroneous basis'.[11] The bank had to ask itself the right questions, and there had to be evidence before it which could justify its conclusion. Nicholls LJ accepted that it was not enough for the bank to act in good faith, if it had never 'properly considered' her case.[12] And

[10] See 'Attacking and Protecting Trustees', a talk given by E. Nugee QC on 6 June 1990, reported in the British Pension Lawyer, June 1990, p. 1.
[11] [1989] IRLR 522 at 525.   [12] Ibid., at 531.

Sir John May would have overturned the bank's decision, on the basis that there was material before it which 'ought to have been considered, but was not'.[13]

B. *IMPERIAL GROUP PENSION TRUST LTD* V. *IMPERIAL TOBACCO LTD*

Both *Mihlenstedt* and *Mettoy* involved powers which were held by the employer alone. With respect to powers that were divided between trustees and the employer, at least where the power involved a pure discretion rather than a quasi-judicial decision, it might have been expected that the employer could act in its own interests, and leave the trustees to act on behalf of the members. But in *Imperial Tobacco*, the Vice-Chancellor decided that *all* the powers of an employer under a pension scheme were subject to an implied duty of good faith, even, as was the case in *Imperial Tobacco*, when those powers were assigned to the trustees with the employer reserving only a right of veto. This right existed both in contract, and in trust.

The Vice-Chancellor articulated this duty of good faith in a number of ways. Employers must not, 'without reasonable and proper cause, conduct themselves in a manner calculated or likely to destroy or seriously damage the relationship of confidence and trust between employer and employee'.[14] An employer must not exercise a veto 'capriciously'.[15] The company must exercise its rights 'for the efficient running of the scheme . . . and not for the purpose of forcing the members to give up their accrued rights in the existing Fund'.[16] The Vice-Chancellor expressly denied that the duty to act in good faith was a duty to act reasonably. In deciding whether or not to give its consent, the company was free to look after its own interests, financial or otherwise, in the future operations of the scheme.[17]

These verbal formulas make it quite clear that the employer is not required to exercise its powers in the best interests of the members, but the boundaries thereafter are unclear. Is it, like the duty in *Mihlenstedt*, akin to judicial review, or does it go further? To find the substance of this duty, as understood by the Vice-Chancellor, we need to find what, if anything, he thought was wrong with the employer's conduct, and to do this we have to understand the context in which the employer had exercised its veto.

1. The Facts of Imperial Tobacco

The Imperial Tobacco pension scheme had been closed to new members when the Imperial Group was taken over by Hanson Trust PLC. Imperial Tobacco was able to enjoy a contribution holiday with respect to this scheme as it had a surplus, at minimum, of £130 million. But new employees could not join a closed scheme. They had to have a new scheme set up to provide

---

[13] [1989] IRLR 522 at 532.
[14] (Ch.D) [1991] 2 All ER 597 at 606; [1990] 1 WLR 589 at 597.
[15] Ibid.   [16] Ibid., at 608; 598.   [17] Ibid., at 607; 598.

their pensions and, with respect to this scheme, Imperial Tobacco was having to make contributions. The new management of Imperial Tobacco tried to get the Imperial scheme reopened, so that all their employees could belong to the one scheme. If this occurred, they would not have to make any contributions. The trustees asked for benefit increases as a condition of reopening and, when Imperial Tobacco refused, negotiations broke down. The Imperial management then tried to persuade the members to transfer their entitlements into a new scheme. The new scheme offered increased benefits and, for the members who were also employees, the additional advantage that it was a non-contributory scheme. If all the members transferred, then all of the fund, including the surplus, would go with them.

Aside from the difference in fixed benefits, there was only one major difference between the schemes. The new scheme was open to new members, whilst the old one was not. Both schemes required members to have their benefits augmented to Inland Revenue limits on winding up. An excess over this amount would, under the old scheme, either go to the Crown under the doctrine of *bona vacantia*, or to the employer under the doctrine of resulting trust.[18] The new scheme met current Revenue requirements, including an express provision for residual surplus on winding up to be refunded to the employer.[19] The trustees understood that the only basis upon which members of the Imperial scheme were going to enjoy benefit increases was if they transferred into the new scheme. On this basis they were prepared to recommend that the members transfer, and to alter the Imperial scheme in such a way as to allow a share of the surplus to be transferred with them. If the members had a right to benefit increases within the Imperial scheme, then they had no need to transfer to the new scheme. The Vice-Chancellor was therefore asked to decide on what basis, if any, the employer could refuse its consent to benefit increases within the Imperial scheme.

2. The Holding

The Vice-Chancellor felt that the employer could not announce a blanket policy of refusing to consider benefit increases. This seems to follow logically from his statement that the employer's rights are held by it in order to promote the 'efficient running of the scheme'. What is efficient for the scheme will alter as circumstances change. In order to meet this part of the duty, employers can be expected to state their decisions in terms which make it clear that, whilst they are firm in their resolve, they will review their decision should circumstances change.[20] This will inconvenience employers

---

[18] Depending on whether the law in this area is represented by *Davis* v. *Richards & Wallington Industries* [1991] 2 All ER 563, or *Re ABC Television, Goodblatte* et al. v. *John* et al. 22 May 1973, reported in Ellison, (n. 1 above), p. 347.

[19] Occupational Pension Schemes, *Notes on Approval under the Finance Act 1970 as Amended by the Finance Act 1971*, IR 12, para. 15.4.

[20] Employers must not say that benefit increases will 'never' be granted in the existing scheme, or that they will 'never be granted unless' or even that 'they will only be granted if'. All of these

who wish to persuade their employees to change schemes, since the employees will be more willing to do this if they can be sure that there can be no improvements to their benefits in their current scheme. But the underlying message 'don't expect improvements', should still get through, even if the employer has to add a formal rider with respect to changing circumstances.

Whilst the procedural content of this duty ('never say never') is fairly clear, identifying what else will amount to a breach of the duty of good faith is not. The Vice-Chancellor was clear that powers could not be used to favour membership of one trade union over another. They could also not be used 'if the sole purpose of refusing to consent to an amendment increasing benefits is the collateral purpose of putting pressure on members to abandon their existing rights'.[21] If this statement refers to rights held by trustees on behalf of members, as well as to rights held by the members themselves, then it has potentially far-reaching implications for the relationship between trustees, members, and the employer. If employers cannot use any of their powers to pressure members to give up rights, or to persuade trustees not to exercise discretions on behalf of members, then the balance of power within schemes has been altered significantly in the members' favour. The Vice-Chancellor was quite clear that the duty covered all the employer's powers. Thus the employer could not use the power to wind up, the power to make transfers, the power to make or veto amendments, or the power to discontinue contributions, in a manner which 'forced' the sacrifice of existing rights. This undermines the ability of the employer to influence trustees in the exercise of their discretions, or members in the exercise of their options. The power to wind up, especially where the rules provide for surplus assets to return to the employer, has been viewed as a means by which the employer could ensure that trustees, no matter how 'independent', would always have regard to their interests. Similar considerations apply to the power to discontinue contributions.[22]

On a more mundane level, how are employers to negotiate with trustees for changes in scheme rules,[23] if they cannot 'force' the trustees or the members to give up existing rights? Such negotiations are premised upon the assumption that the employer will agree to benefit increases if, but only if, the trustees agree to give the employer rights which it does not currently

---

forms of expression suggest that the employer has reached a blanket policy on the basis of which the power to increase benefits will be exercised. A well-advised employer will phrase the decision to deny benefits in a way that shows the employer is prepared to consider exercising the power in future: 'at present we do not intend to allow benefit increases . . .'.

[21] (Ch. D) [1991] 2 All ER 597 at 608; [1990] 1 WLR 589 at 599.

[22] See R. Nobles, 'Conflicts of Interest in the Trustee's Management of Pension Funds: An Analysis of the Legal Framework', 14 ILJ (1985) 1.

[23] Along the lines suggested by Millett J in *Re Courage Group's Pension Schemes, Ryan v. Imperial Brewing and Leisure Ltd.* [1987] 1 All ER 528 at 545; [1987] 1 WLR 495 at 515.

enjoy, such as a right to a refund. What distinguishes those negotiations where an employer 'persuades' trustees or the members to give up rights by the offer of benefit increases, and those where it 'forces' trustees or members to give up rights by refusing otherwise to make benefit increases?[24]

Another problem with *Imperial Tobacco* is that the Vice-Chancellor never identified exactly what rights the members were being 'forced' to give up. He seemed to think that the employees were being forced to give up their rights on winding up, by transferring from a scheme in which the company could not benefit from a winding up into one where it could enjoy any residual surplus:

> IMPACT [an association of pensioners from the scheme] suspects that the only reason why the benefits are not being provided in the Fund (as opposed to the [new scheme]) is the Company's wish to transfer the surplus of the Fund (to which the members of the scheme are currently entitled) to the [new scheme] where the surplus will belong to the Company . . . If so, in my judgment the Company would be acting unlawfully.

But the surplus was not something to which the members were 'entitled' now, or on the determination of the scheme. The surplus was currently allowing the employer to cease contributing to the scheme (a contribution holiday). In the event of winding up, a residuary surplus would not go to the members, but to the Crown or, if *Davis* v. *Richards & Wallington Industries*[25] applied, to the employer.[26]

The only way in which one can say that the surplus belonged to the members in these cases is that it currently secured their benefits and, after the proposed changes, those benefits would be less secure. The members were moving from a closed scheme into one in which the surplus would secure not only their benefits, but those of new employees. But the Vice-Chancellor raised no objection to the employer securing the opening of the

---

[24] Consider *Vauxhall Motor Pension Fund; Bullard* v. *Randall* [1989] 1 PLR 49. The Vauxhall pension fund had a surplus of £200 million. The trust deed did not allow refunds to the company, and the power of amendment prohibited alterations which would have this effect. In order to obtain a refund the company proposed a scheme: 'whereby the . . . trustees, with the consent of the members or such members as agree, pay over to trustees of new pension funds under which assenting members will receive substantially greater benefits than they get under the existing scheme but (and this is the big 'but') the surplus assets are under the terms of the new scheme returnable to the subscribing companies.'

[25] Note 18 above.

[26] But whilst the employees were not losing anything by transferring from the old scheme, they were not *all* gaining either. The employees would be getting a major benefit: non-contributory scheme membership. The current pensioners were getting a good indexation arrangement. They had to forgo some of their current pension in exchange for increased indexation, but the terms of this exchange seemed reasonable. The most disadvantaged group was the deferred pensioners. The amount of pension which they would have to sacrifice in order to gain increased indexation was not even worked out at the time of the court case. They were being asked to transfer merely in the hope that the indexation arrangement would prove to be a good deal, a situation which the Vice-Chancellor called 'a pig in a poke' during the hearing.

Imperial scheme in exchange for benefit increases (and implicitly refusing those benefit increases unless the Imperial scheme were opened). His concern seems to be that the employer wanted something *more* than this:

> The [trustees have] no objection to reopening the Fund to new members, provided that those benefits are made available to all members of the reopened Fund. Why then is the Company seeking to induce Members of the Fund to give up their rights in the Fund and transfer to the [new] scheme?'[27]

3. The Scope of the Duty in Imperial Tobacco

What the above analysis seems to show, is that the duty of good faith, as announced in *Imperial Tobacco*, is a duty without specific content. The Vice-Chancellor was clear that some entitlement was being undermined by the employer's use of powers, and that a general duty of good faith would prevent this, but never identified exactly what that entitlement was. As such, the case itself provides little guide as to how this duty will operate in future. There are plenty of ways in which transactions similar to that in *Imperial Tobacco* can be distinguished. The giving up of existing rights was 'forced' and the withholding of consent was for the 'sole purpose' of obtaining rights currently enjoyed by the members. A future court may, on careful examination of similar transactions, find that no 'rights' are being sacrificed. It could also find that the level of coercion does not warrant the judgment that the exchange is 'forced' rather than voluntary. Lastly, employers will be careful to justify transactions such as this on the basis of at least some gains in terms of 'efficient running of the scheme', even if these amount only to the lower administrative costs involved in having all one's members in one scheme.

Whilst *Imperial Tobacco* can be narrowed and distinguished, it could also provide a basis for a general right to review employers' actions to prevent whatever a court finds objectionable. The statement that the purpose of the power was the 'efficient running of the scheme' opens up the possibility of a challenge based on the sort of principles which are commony associated with administrative law:

> The court is entitled to investigate . . . whether they have taken into account matters which they ought not to have taken into account, or conversely, have refused to take into account or neglected to take into account matters which they ought to have taken into account [or have] . . . come to a conclusion so unreasonable that no reasonable [employer] could have come to it.[28]

---

[27] The Vice-Chancellor was actually wrong to think that the trustees were prepared to open the Imperial scheme in exchange for the same benefit increases as were being offered in the new scheme. The trustees had wanted a continuation of the level of indexation offered by Imperial Tobacco before the take-over. The new management were not prepared to offer this. When negotiations broke down, the company tried to persuade members to transfer to the new scheme.

[28] *Associated Provincial Picture Houses Ltd.* v. *Wednesbury Corporation* [1948] 1 KB 223 at 234 per Lord Greene MR (slightly amended).

There are also elements of administrative law reasoning in the Vice-Chancellor's conclusion that the employer's powers could not be exercised on a once-and-for-all basis, but had to be periodically considered. This has echoes of the rule that persons entrusted with discretions should not adopt blanket policies.[29]

The duty of good faith will allow the courts to articulate further restrictions of purpose, or to adopt a more ad hoc process, and simply intervene whenever the actions of an employer are considered so outrageous that they breach the duty of trust and confidence. The ad hoc approach typifies the way in which this duty has operated in its employment context. For example, in *British Aircraft Corp.* v. *Austin*[30] the duty was expressed thus 'it must ordinarily be an implied term of the contract that the employers do not behave in a way which is intolerable or in a way which employees cannot be expected to put up with any longer.'[31] With this approach, whilst employers cannot be required to behave reasonably, they cannot act wholly unreasonably. But if good faith covers only what is 'wholly unreasonable', only transactions which are clearly seen as abuses are going to be caught. Doubts have to resolved in the employer's favour. As H. Collins has said of this approach in the context of unfair dismissal:

The [court] . . . simply endorses the practices of management in all but the most unreasonable and irrational abuse of managerial . . . power.[32]

The duty of good faith leaves enormous scope for interpretation. What is 'wholly unreasonable'? What is 'capricious'? What rights can employees be expected to give up, and on what terms? When have employers failed to properly consider the exercise of their powers under the scheme? And the answer to these questions is not found in verbal formulas but in judicial views of what constitutes the proper function of a pension scheme or, to put this another way, judges' opinion as to when the administration of a pension scheme becomes exploitation of the scheme members. In order to identify this dividing line, judges will have to consider the perspectives outlined in Chapter 2, and in particular, the claim that pensions are deferred pay.

In the context of unfair dismissal, where individual claims are pursued in

---

[29] What Galligan calls the 'no-fettering doctrine'. See D. J. Galligan, *Discretionary Powers: A Legal Study of Official Discretion* (Oxford University Press, 1986), pp. 281–4.

[30] [1978] IRLR 332.

[31] Ibid., at 334.

[32] H. Collins, *Justice in Dismissal* (Clarendon Press, Oxford, 1992), p. 39. Collins likens the shift from a test of what is reasonable to one of what is wholly unreasonable, to the assessment of the sharpness of a knife. Requiring a sharp knife means that all knives that are not sharp must be rejected. (This is like a test of reasonableness—all unreasonable behaviour is an abuse.) Saying that the knife must not be blunt means that any knife with some cutting edge must be accepted. (Any action which is not clearly an abuse has to be accepted.)

the *relatively* informal, low-cost, and speedy tribunal system, such indeterminancy over what constitutes an unreasonable exercise of managerial prerogative may be acceptable. But as the next chapter will show, the barriers to bringing a review of trustees' or employers' actions in the chancery courts may make residual duties such as that of 'good faith' difficult, if not impossible, to enforce.

[5]
Enforcing Trust Law

This chapter looks at the two major factors which inhibit members' access to the courts: legal costs, and lack of information. The chapter begins by looking at the kinds of rights which need to be enforced. It then examines the way in which legal costs, and lack of information, prevent members from enforcing their rights. It ends by considering the likely effectiveness of the new legal forum in pension matters: the Pensions Ombudsman.

I. WHAT NEEDS TO BE ENFORCED?

A 1989 OPB report intended, amongst other things, to consider 'measures to safeguard the rights of members',[1] found 'near-unanimity' amongst witnesses that:

(i) It is very unusual indeed for scheme beneficiaries not to obtain their rights (although their expectations may be disappointed).[2]

Such evidence assumes a narrow view of what constitutes a legal right. Whilst there may be little difficulty in enforcing a member's right to the fixed benefits promised under scheme rules, these do not comprise all of the members' rights. The members' interest in funding, surpluses, and investment are not mere expectations. The duties placed upon trustees, actuaries, and employers in connection with these issues give rise to correlative rights enjoyed by the members.[3] To describe all such rights as 'expectations' is to adopt an extreme version of the balance of cost argument: that the only thing definitely promised is an unsecured fixed benefit.

When assessing the need for access to the courts, it should not be forgotten

---

[1] Protecting Pensions: Safeguarding Benefits in a Changing Environment. CM 573, para. 1.1.

[2] Ibid., para. 7.11

[3] Whilst not every duty gives rise to a correlative right, these duties would seem to give rise to such rights. Non-correlative duties arise under the criminal law, and when there are statutory duties which give rise to no private cause of action. Where duties can be enforced by individuals who assert that their private interests have been adversely affected, one has the classic case of a correlative right. See R. W. M. Dias, *Jurisprudence*, 5th edn. (1985) pp. 25–7. Cf. W. Hohfeld, in W. Cook (ed.) *Fundamental Legal Conceptions* (Yale University Press, 1966), p. 38: 'even those who use the word and conception "right" in the broadest possible way are accustomed to thinking of duty as the invariable correlative.'

that courts are not simply means to enforce rights which are clear, but a forum in which to establish what rights the parties should enjoy. This is particularly the case with respect to discretions, where the standards used to assess the legality of a particular decision are, in the context of trust law at least, quite general, and also subject to variation depending on one's interpretation of the rules of the scheme and the purpose of the scheme as a whole. Access to the court establishes both what standards are applicable, and whether those standards have been breached. Without access to the courts, or an equivalent forum, the interpretation of standards and the enforcement of entitlements will be decided purely on the basis of the relative strength of the parties. In the context of pension schemes, this would depend on such factors as the employer's ability to control the trustees and the scheme actuary versus the members' ability to bring industrial relations and media pressure to bear on the employer. Individual members are in a very weak position to adopt any kind of self-help. The OPB's 1989 report does not reveal whether the perceived inadequacies of the courts arose out of their role as enforcers of existing rights, or as bodies who decide what rights the parties have. Pensioners had complained about surpluses being used too much to the employer's advantage, changes of policies on discretionary increases following take-overs, lack of communication, and inefficiency of administration.[4] Whilst these complaints could relate to breaches of the rights of members and their dependants, they could also be the result of uncertainty as to the duties of the trustees and the employer, or they could represent appeals for amending legislation in order to give more substantive rights to the members and their dependants. The OPB also noted a 'not insignificant' number of respondents criticizing the following practices:

(i) trustees appearing to act in the interests of the employer rather than the members;
(ii) trustees appearing to give inadequate weight to the interests of the pensioners and ex-pensioners;
(iii) trustees being put under pressure by the parent company to vote shares or dispose of assets in particular ways.[5]

These criticisms could be interpreted as evidence that the courts are failing to prevent trustees from breaching their duties towards the beneficiaries; or as evidence of the need to require trustees to disclose the reasons for their decisions; or as calls to make trustees' duties towards members and past members more stringent. The only other evidence noted by the OPB came from the Occupational Pensions Advisory Service (OPAS), which claimed that its advisers encountered a hard core of cases in which there was maladministration or misinterpretation of scheme rules which was not accepted by the scheme authorities. The OPB understood that scheme

---

[4] Note 1 above, para 7.5.   [5] Ibid., para. 7.12.

authorities were intransigent in about 10 per cent of those cases in which OPAS advisers had identified a need for redress.[6]

II. LEGAL COSTS

One factor which makes pension litigation expensive[7] is the number of parties who must be represented before the court. Because pension fund litigation may result in an order affecting many hundreds or thousands of members and pensioners, the court needs to be satisfied that expediency has not been allowed to override the interests of any one class of member which may be numerically, or physically weak—for example the pensioners—so as to unduly advantage another class such as the active members.[8] Deferred pensioners and members' dependants may also need separate representation and, where the current scheme has replaced an earlier scheme, there may have to be separate representatives for each class of beneficiary with respect to each scheme. Given the enormous sums which may be involved, and the uncertainties over what arguments may be made at trial, solicitors will prefer to err on the side of caution and insist that a large number of parties be separately represented.[9] If they attempt, for reasons of cost, to restrict the number of parties, they may find that the Master (who deals with High Court pre-trial matters) is unwilling to declare the action ready for trial until further parties are added. The late addition of parties will create even greater delay and expense.[10]

The risks of incurring legal costs depend on whether litigation is seen as hostile or not. If the litigation is not hostile, the court will usually order that all legal costs be born by the fund itself. By contrast, with hostile litigation all parties, other than the trustees, are at a substantial disadvantage. If they lose the action, they will have to pay their own legal costs in full, and those of the other parties on a party and party basis.[11] The trustees, because of their indemnity clause, are in a special position. They will be indemnified for their own costs, and for any costs which they have to pay to another party unless

---

[6] Ibid., para. 13.10. Don Hall of OPAS felt that the OPB's figure was too high. About 40% of cases referred to them required redress, the rest being the result of poor communication between the person seeking advice and the scheme authorities. Of this 40% who had a genuine grievance, only about 4% could not be solved by OPAS. Telephone conversation, Wednesday, 19 June 1991.

[7] The litigation in *Stannard* v. *Fisons Pension Trust Limited* [1990] PLR 179 (HC) cost £1.5 million. R. Ellison, *Pensions: Law and Practice* (Longman, 1992), para. 8.024. It was then appealed!

[8] See J. Stephens, *Pension Fund Litigation* (Nicholson, Graham & Jones), p. 9.

[9] Ibid.   [10] Ibid.

[11] Costs between parties are awarded on the standard basis. Order 62, r. 3, *The Supreme Court Practice* (Sweet & Maxwell 1991). This entitles the receiving party to all costs reasonably incurred, but requires doubts on the reasonableness of any costs to be resolved against the receiving party. By contrast, where costs are awarded on an indemnity basis, doubts are resolved in favour of the receiving party. Order 62, r. 12(1) and (2).

they are found to have acted in wilful default.[12] Members may not be able to afford even to win hostile litigation, since they may not recover all of their legal costs. The crucial importance to members of whether their litigation is seen as hostile or not is well captured in the following account taken from *Pension Fund Litigation* by John Stephens:

> In a case a number of years ago (which never came to trial), some members of a scheme commenced proceedings by Originating Summons, with the idea that an Order should be obtained at an early stage [and] that their costs should be met from the fund at any event. The reality of the complaint, however, was that an attack was being mounted on the Trustees' exercise of their discretions over the past years, with the result that the Plaintiffs were ordered to continue the action on a hostile basis, that is though they had begun it (correctly) by Writ. Being thereafter at risk for their own, and the Trustees' legal costs, the Plaintiffs discontinued.[13]

The definition of hostile litigation is not precise. To accuse trustees or another party of breaching the trust is usually viewed as hostile litigation. This is clearest where the accusation is one of dishonesty or fraud. But where it relates to an incorrect exercise of discretions, the boundary is hard to draw. Members are entitled to have the fund administered in accordance with its terms, and to have the trustees,[14] the actuary,[15] and the employer[16] act in accordance with their duties. But what those terms require, and what duties are applicable is, as has been seen, often open to argument and interpretation. Obtaining directions on the meaning of the trust deed or rules is typically thought of as non-hostile litigation. But how does one categorize an attempt to challenge the basis upon which trustees have, or propose, to exercise discretion? Are the members entitled to use an originating summons to determine how the discretion ought to be exercised, and then commence a hostile action where the interpretation given on the originating summons indicates that the parties' actions, or proposed actions, are wrongful? Or do the members have to start with a hostile action accusing a party of acting wrongfully and find out, in the course of that action, what standard is applicable?

The division between actions which can be paid for out of the fund and those which cannot is determined not only by the degree of hostility between the parties but also by the amount and nature of the evidence that will be involved in the action. Actions for interpretation are begun by originating summons and supported by affidavit evidence. The assumption is that a dispute of interpretation can be undertaken without the need for cross-examination, as there will be no arguments over the facts. If the evidence of

---

[12] In *Re Vickery* [1931] 1 Ch. 572, Maugham J held that these words meant a consciousness of committing a wrong or at any rate a recklessness as to whether or not a wrong was being committed. For a discussion of the likely effectiveness of trust deeds which attempt to lower the standard even more, see P. Matthews, 'The Efficacy of Trustee Exemption Clauses in English Law' [1989] Conv. 42.   [13] Note 8 above, p. 30.   [14] See Chapter 3.
[15] See Chapter 6.   [16] See Chapter 4.

the relevant parties is to be challenged, the action is likely to be deemed hostile, and required to be begun by way of writ, with full liability for costs.[17]

The need to avoid liability for costs severely restricts the ability of members to obtain review of the actions of trustees, actuaries, or their employer. They must avoid any accusation that implies moral turpitude, and they cannot challenge the evidence of the trustees, actuary, or employer. Arguments as to the members' need for protection have to be cast in hypothetical form, since the members cannot question the good faith of these parties.

Even where actions commence, and are fought out, as non-hostile ones, there is still some risk of liability for costs. In *Aitken* v. *Christy Hunt PLC*[18] the trustees, faced with a request from the employer's parent company to amalgamate the pension schemes of the employer and the parent company, sought to amend the scheme to enable them to use their scheme's surplus to fund benefit increases for the current and past members of the scheme, and to prevent the parent company's employees from enjoying any benefit from the scheme. These amendments were challenged by the employer, with the result that the trustees applied to court for directions. A summons for directions is ordinarily viewed as non-hostile litigation, with the result that all parties have their legal costs indemnified out of the trust fund. But Ferris J took a different view. Because the parent company had disputed the validity of the trustees' proposed course of action, and thereby caused the trustees to take the matter to court, it was hostile litigation, and the company would have to bear its own costs, even though the case only involved questions of construction. Whilst such a last-minute decision to treat a construction summons as hostile litigation will be a shock to an employer, its implications for members are more drastic, since they are far less likely to be able to afford their own legal costs.

On the other hand, as the discussion of costs in *Aitken* illustrates, the courts are less likely to view the plaintiffs and defendants to a completed construction summons as hostile parties where they take part in a representative capacity. It is presumably felt to be unfair retrospectively to penalize a minority of members, or even a minority of employers, where they have argued for an interpretation of the trust deed which will benefit others as well as themselves. Whilst employers will rarely join an action in a representative capacity, members will invariably represent particular classes of beneficiaries.

---

[17] 'A useful rule of thumb as to whether proceedings are genuinely hostile is whether there is some dispute as to the facts: if so the proceedings will have to be begun by Writ, with proper Pleadings, Interrogatories, Discovery and so forth and the loser will have to pay the costs.' Stephens (n. 8 above), p. 16. See also *Re Buckton* [1907] 2 Ch. 406. There are, however, procedures for dealing with disputed facts in actions commenced by originating summons. See n. 11 above, Order 38, 2(3) and generally, Order 5, 4(2).   [18] [1991] PLR 3.

A. BYPASSING A COURT HEARING BY OBTAINING THE OPINION OF QUEEN'S COUNSEL

There is a relatively low-cost way in which trustees can establish their legal duties. Under section 48 of the Administration of Justice Act 1985, trustees can obtain immunity from breach of trust if their intended action is lawful in the opinion of a barrister with ten years' standing, and that opinion is subsequently approved by a judge. The judge can give approval without a formal hearing, or representation by the members.

There is considerable scope for barristers to give favourable opinions in such an indeterminate area of the law. However, one hopes for the members' sakes that recent litigation will have alerted judges to the fact that deciding upon members' entitlements involves complex questions, which should not be resolved without the members being separately represented and which, ideally, should not be settled without a formal hearing.

III. INFORMATION

Members have various statutory rights to information, but these give them limited insight into the administration of the trust fund. The Employment Protection Consolidation Act 1978, s. 1, requires that they be given written details of the terms of their contract of employment within thirteen weeks of taking up employment.[19] But this is unlikely to refer to the pension scheme except to mention the right to join it and, perhaps, to refer the employee to the scheme's booklet. The Inland Revenue, as a condition of discretionary approval, require that every member and every employee who has a right to be a member must be given written particulars of all essential features of the scheme which concern her.[20] This requirement has led to the practice of issuing scheme members with booklets setting out the benefits and options available to the member.[21]

The Disclosure Regulations are more substantial.[22] They require new members to be supplied with details of the conditions for becoming and remaining scheme members, on the method of calculation of employers' and,

---

[19] Under the Trade Union Reform and Employment Bill, clause 23, Schedule 4, this is to be reduced to two months in order to comply with the Directive on 'An Employer's Obligation to Inform Employees of the Conditions Applicable to the Contract or Employment Relationship', Directive 91/533/EC; OJ No. L 288/32, 18.10.91; on which, see generally, H. Clark and M. Hall, 'The Cinderella Directive? Employee Rights to Information about Conditions Applicable to their Contract or Employment Relationship', 21 ILJ (1992) 106.

[20] Inland Revenue Practice Notes, IR 12 (1991), para. 3.2; Income and Corporation Taxes Act 1988, s. 590 (2)(b).

[21] K. Muir, T. Round, and M. Fairclough, *Hoskings Pension Schemes and Retirement Benefits*, 5th edn. (Sweet & Maxwell, 1985), p. 187.

[22] Occupational Pension Scheme (Disclosure of Information) Regulations 1986, SI 1986 No. 1046, as amended by SI No. 1717, SI 1987 No. 1105, SI 1988 No. 476, SI 1989/1641, SI 1991/167, SI 1991/2684, SI 1992/1531.

if applicable, members' contributions, and the provisions regarding preservation, and transfer of deferred pension, and indexation of pensions in
payment. (Any change in this basic information must be notified to all
members.) Members who retire or otherwise leave the scheme are entitled to
statements showing their benefit entitlement and, in the case of early leavers,
setting out the alternatives to taking a deferred pension. Current members
are entitled, on request, to an annual statement setting out their accrued
benefits, calculated on the basis of existing or projected future salaries.
Members are also entitled, on request, to copies of the annual audited
accounts, and the latest actuarial report (which must be produced every three
and a half years). They can also request copies of any ad hoc actuarial
valuation prepared for the trustees (though not those prepared for the
employer). The accounts will reveal how that year's transactions have
affected the scheme's balance of liabilities and assets, and confirm whether
the contributions due have been received. The actuarial report should reveal
the basis of funding and the ability to secure benefits on winding up.
Members are also entitled, on request, to copies of the trust deed, and any
other document constituting or amending the scheme (which covers booklets
and scheme announcements where these supplement or amend the trust
deed).

These information rights enable members to monitor the value and
security of their benefits, and to learn the rules of their scheme. But they do
not provide information about the administration of the scheme, except with
regard to scheme security, and then only in the broadest terms.[23] If members
wish to find out such information as why trustees have taken particular
decisions, or what instructions were given to the scheme's actuaries prior to
the recommendation of a rate of contribution, they have to rely on the general
law of trusts regarding the right of beneficiaries to information, or the High
Court rules of procedure governing discovery and interrogatories.

A. TRUST LAW AND THE RIGHT TO INFORMATION FROM THE TRUSTEES

According to the Court of Appeal in *Re Londonderry's Settlement Trusts*,[24]
trustees do not have to provide beneficiaries with reasons for their decisions.
Harman LJ felt that this was a 'long-standing principle'[25] which was superior
to the beneficiaries' right to see trust documents, with the result that the
trustees in question did not have to disclose such of their minutes and agenda
of meetings, or correspondence, as would reveal the reasons why their power
of appointment had been exercised in a particular manner.

---

[23] With some specific exceptions; for example, Occupational Pension Scheme (Disclosure of
Information) Regulations 1986, SI 1986 No. 1046, Schedule 3, para. 6 as amended by
Occupational and Personal Pension (Miscellaneous Amendment) Regulations 1992, reg. 5,
requires self-investment in excess of 5% to be disclosed.   [24] [1964] 3 All ER 855.
[25] Ibid., at 857.

If this 'principle' represents a general rule,[26] then pension fund members cannot demand to learn the reasons for a trustees' decisions, whether that decision concerns investment (including self-investment), scheme amendments, benefit increases, contribution rates, or whatever.[27] Beneficiaries who wish to learn the reasons for their trustees' decisions will have to commence hostile litigation, alleging that the trustees have committed some impropriety, in the hope that the trustees' reasons will be revealed through the pre-trial processes. Megarry VC felt that it would be 'simple' to avoid the effects of *Re Londonderry* by this expedient, since the general rights of litigants to see documents before trial are so wide.[28] On discovery, an applicant may see any document 'which may fairly lead him to a train of inquiry [that may] either directly or indirectly enable the party requiring the [document] either to advance his own case or to damage the case of his adversary'.[29] However, hostile litigation involves liability for costs which, even at the pre-trial stage, will often deter members from commencing actions. Moreover, if the courts are really committed to protecting trustees from disclosing their reasons, they are not likely to allow pre-trial processes to nullify *Re Londonderry* so easily. The rights to discovery, and to serve interrogatories, can themselves be nullified through a successful application to strike out proceedings on the basis that they reveal no cause of action. If members have no evidence of impropriety, then their action may not survive such an application.[30]

B. THE RELATIONSHIP BETWEEN INFORMATION AND DUTIES OF CARE

If members cannot obtain trustees' reasons, then standards of care (discussed in Chapter 3) are less effective than they might appear. A duty to act in the best interests of the beneficiaries becomes, in practice, a duty not to act in a manner which is self-evidently contrary to the best interests of the beneficiaries. A duty to act in accordance with the purpose of a power, or a duty to act in good faith, is similarly restricted by the need for a breach to be self-evident.

---

[26] Textbooks seem to accept that trustees can always refuse to give reasons for their decisions, and only discuss the conflict between this rule and the beneficiaries' proprietary right to see trust documents. See G. Moffat and M. Chesterman, *Trust Law: Text and Materials* (Weidenfeld & Nicolson, 1988) p. 433; Parker and A. Mellows, *The Modern Law and Trusts*, 4th edn. (Sweet and Maxwell, 1979), p. 282.

[27] The courts have expressed greater willingness for beneficiaries to be provided with the information necessary to supervise the trustees' investment powers: 'It is the duty of trustees to afford to their [beneficiaries] accurate information of the disposition of the trust fund; all the information of which they are, or ought to be, in possesson: a trustee may involve himself in serious difficulty by want of the information which it was his duty to obtain.' *Walker* v. *Symonds* (1818) 3 Swan 1 at 57 per Lord Eldon LC.

[28] R. E. Megarry (1965) 81 LQR 196.

[29] *Compagnie Financière et Commerciale du Pacifique* v. *Peruvian Guano Co.* (1882) 11 QBD 55 at 63 per Brett LJ. Although the material must be necessary, and not merely relevant. See *Science Research Council* v. *Nassé* (1978) 3WLR 762.

[30] See Alec Samuels, 'Disclosure of Trust Documents', 28 MLR (1965) 220 at 222.

1. *Reassessing* Londonderry

If the courts wish pension trustees to be under strict duties to act in the best interests of their members, then there is a case to be made for requiring trustees to give reasons for their decisions, and to allow beneficiaries access to documents in which those reasons are recorded. If the courts wished to narrow the application of *Re Londonderry* in the context of pension schemes, they would have little difficulty. Much of the case consists of questionable assertions about the likely consequences of requiring trustees to reveal their reasons. Harman LJ asserted that no one would agree to be a trustee if he were liable to have his motives or reasons called into question by the court.[31] This assertion seems to ignore the fact that many trustees are paid for their trouble, and protected from innocent liability for damages by indemnity clauses. In the case of pension schemes, and particularly with regard to trustees who are senior managers or directors, it is simply an incredible assertion. Trusteeship of the pension scheme is, for such persons, not a voluntary act of kindness but (whatever the precise relationship to their contracts of employment) something undertaken as part of their general employment duties.

Dankwerts LJ accepted that requiring reasons would cause quarrels and embitter the relationship between the beneficiaries, or between the trustees and the beneficiaries.[32] However, he was talking about the importance of family harmony in the context of a trust in which beneficiaries are the objects of the bounty of the head of that family. Pension trusts exist within the context of industrial relations, where some degree of conflict is to be expected. Members are not the objects of bounty, and can therefore expect greater protection from the courts even, on occasion, at the cost of some disharmony. Even within family trusts, it is implausible to argue that all kind of discretions will, if reasons had to be given, create intolerable risks of disharmony. Having to explain investment strategy carries less risk of disharmony than justifying individual appointments of capital and income.

Dankwerts LJ also asserted that trustees should not be compelled to reveal their reasons where their discretion is 'confidential', on the basis that such a discretion cannot be properly carried out where 'at any moment there is likely to be an investigation for the purpose of seeing whether they have exercised their discretion in the best possible manner'.[33] Whilst there may be decisions, even in the context of a commercial trust,[34] in which it is necessary

---

[31] '. . . nobody could be called on to accept a trusteeship involving the exercise of discretion unless, in the absence of bad faith, he were not liable to have his motives or his reasons called in question either by the beneficiaries or by the court.' N. 24 above, p. 857.

[32] Ibid., at 861.   [33] Ibid.

[34] The facts of *In Re Gresham Life Assurance Society Ex Parte Penny* (1872) 8 Ch. App. 446, a case relied upon by Harmon LJ, show how confidentiality may be necessary to protect the beneficiaries. The directors of an insurance company were unable to state why they could not accept a transfer of shares without running the risk of libel actions, since the most likely reason

for the trustees to keep their reasons secret, this will not always be the case.

Salmon LJ added a further reason. He said the trustees had only to act in good faith and as such, their reasons for acting were immaterial.[35] But, as Chapter 3 showed, there are higher standards of care than the duty to act in good faith. And, even if the standard were this low, the reasons might disclose that the trustees have been acting in bad faith and would therefore be very material.[36]

In light of the reasons given by their Lordships, *Re Londonderry* should not be interpreted as a general statement of the right of all trustees, on all occasions, to refuse to give reasons. Instead, it should be read as a statement that trustees who have to exercise discretions which involve judgments on the worthiness of particular individuals, and other, similar, 'delicate' decisions, should not be required to give their reasons.[37]

IV. THE PENSIONS OMBUDSMAN

A. CHOOSING AN OMBUDSMAN INSTEAD OF A TRIBUNAL

Although the OPB discussed alternatives to the courts under the heading of 'Help for the Individual',[38] they clearly expected their proposals to result in an alternative forum for all sorts of disputes, including disputes involving many individuals and disputes between different sets of trustees. They felt that the sums of money at stake could be very large, that the scale of operations of pension schemes was vast, and that the problems which required to be tackled were extraordinarily diverse, and included legal, actuarial, and accounting issues amongst others.[39] They also expected the new body to be able to provide guidance to trustees and managers on the propriety of proposed actions.[40] The OPB felt that a tribunal, rather than an ombudsman, was the appropriate body to tackle issues of such scale and complexity.

In the event, the government declined to introduce a tribunal, preferring to have an ombudsman. In choosing to appoint an ombudsman, the government decided to concentrate upon cases where an individual was prejudiced by unjust administration or a breach of the scheme rules which intransigent scheme managers had refused to correct (the type of cases identified by OPAS) and to leave the courts to deal with disputes between the whole membership, or sections of it, and the employer or the trustees. Tony Newton, then Secretary of State for Social Security, in a speech given to the

was the transferee's insolvency. If the directors had to give reasons, they might sacrifice the security of the company to avoid this liability.

[35] Note 24 above, at 862.   [36] See Samuels (n. 30 above), at 221.

[37] *Re Londonderry* may not have completely settled the question of what documents may be disclosed. For problems over the definition of trust documents and the right to see accounts and supporting documents, see *Tiger* v. *Barclays Bank Ltd.* [1952] 1 All ER 85.

[38] The title of chapter 10 of Protecting Pensions (see n. 1 above).

[39] These were their reasons for rejecting the proposal for a pensions ombudsman. Ibid., para. 13.12.   [40] Ibid., para. 13.6.

Society of Pension Consultants on 7 November 1989, made no secret of the government's limited ambitions:

My view is that we should concentrate the new service on the types of problem that individuals, rather than schemes, can face. Disputes involving trustees, concerning large sums of money, are likely to end up in the courts in any case. That is not really our concern here.[41]

B. THE POWERS OF THE PENSIONS OMBUDSMAN

The Pensions Ombudsman is empowered to investigate and determine any dispute of fact or law which arises between a complainant (a member, past member or their widow or surviving dependant)[42] and the managers or trustees of an occupational or personal pension scheme or the employer.[43] In addition, the Pensions Ombudsman may investigate whether a complainant has suffered an injustice by reason of 'maladministration' by the trustees or managers of a scheme or by the scheme's employer. Maladministration covers behaviour which may not be in breach of the law of trusts or any statutory duty. The term is not defined in the Social Security Act 1990 or the subsequent regulations. The complaint to the Pensions Ombudsman must be made within three years of the event complained about. The Pensions Ombudsman cannot investigate disputes in connection with any public-service scheme except the NHS scheme in England and Wales, unless the complaint relates to maladministration.

The Pensions Ombudsman will expect the complainant to have first attempted to sort out the matter with the scheme managers/trustees/employer. The complainant is then expected to contact OPAS to see if they can sort it out.[44] (This is a charitable body, staffed mostly by volunteers, who provide advice and conciliation service to members of occupational pension schemes.)[45] Only thereafter will the Pensions Ombudsman normally be prepared to start an investigation. In practice, most referrals to the Pensions Ombudsman will come from OPAS, and be the consequence of a failure to provide a response which OPAS (or the complainant) regards as satisfactory.

The courts and the Pensions Ombudsman are alternative means for

[41] SPC News, No. 6. quoted in J. Mesher's annotations to the Social Security Act 1990, Schedule 3, in *Current Law Statutes Annotated* [1990], vol. 2, ch. 27.55.

[42] Where someone of this description cannot act for themselves, another person may complain on their behalf.

[43] Social Security and Pensions Act 1975, s. 59C(1). The ability to consider disputes with the employer was added by the Personal and Occupational Pension Schemes (Pensions Ombudsman) Regulations 1991, para. 2(1), SI 1991 No. 588.

[44] Annual Report of the Pensions Ombudsman 1991–2, para. 14.

[45] Most of OPAS' volunteers are persons employed, or previously employed but now retired, within company pensions departments, or with insurance companies. Few are, or ever were, trade unionists, although the present director of OPAS, in a speech given to the Second Northern Independent Pensions Research Group Conference, July 1991, stated that he was keen to recruit more advisers from amongst employees and trade unions.

obtaining redress. Members cannot apply to the Pensions Ombudsman where a matter is already the subject of a court action. Conversely, where there is an application to court in respect of a matter in which the Pensions Ombudsman is already involved, the court may (not must) stay proceedings unless it concludes that the matter ought not to be investigated by the Pensions Ombudsman. At the end of the investigation, the Pensions Ombudsman will make a determination and, where remedial action is justified, can order the trustees, managers, or the employer to take, or abstain from taking, such actions as he thinks appropriate. This determination and order is final and binding on all the parties, unless there is an appeal to the High Court on a point of law.

The Pensions Ombudsman's responsibility for maladministration gives him power to establish and enforce standards of administration above those currently required by the courts, which cannot intervene unless poor administration also amounts to a breach of trust or statutory duty. What the Pensions Ombudsman considers to amount ot maladministration should gradually become apparent from his annual reports. However, the kinds of problems identified by the parliamentary Ombudsman as falling within this description[46] are:

(a)   mistakes, errors, and oversights;
(b)   failing to provide information or providing inadequate explanations;
(c)   giving inaccurate information or misleading advice;
(d)   misapplication of rules;
(e)   peremptory or inconsiderate behaviour on the part of officials;
(f)   unjustifiable delay;
(g)   not treating, so far as possible, like cases alike;
and,
(h)   with regard to the exercise of discretions, failing to take account of all the circumstances, and taking into account irrelevant circumstances.[47]

There is an important restriction to the Pensions Ombudsman's powers of investigation. He cannot ask for any documents or evidence which could not be demanded before a court. This may prevent him from forcing trustees to disclose the reasons for their decisions, or obtaining copies of documents which reveal those reasons,[48] unless he has at least prima-facie evidence of breach of trust. He relies on the members to provide evidence of

---

[46] R. Gregory and P. Hutchesson, *The Parliamentary Ombudsman* (Allen and Unwin, 1975), p. 281. See Mesher (n. 41 above), at p. 57.

[47] Gregory, *The Parliamentary Ombudsman*, p. 309.

[48] Social Security and Pensions Act 1975, s. 59G(3): 'No person shall be compelled for the purposes of any such investigation to give any evidence or produce an document which he could not be compelled to give in civil proceedings before the court.' The limited right to see trust documents is discussed on pp. 103–7.

maladministration or breach of trust[49] and, as we have seen, the members' right to such information is limited.

The Pensions Ombudsman's power to settle disputes of fact allows him to determine whether a complainant is eligible for a particular benefit. For example, where an ill-health pension is dependent upon a claimant suffering from a medical condition which makes it unlikely that he will work in future, the Pensions Ombudsman can decide what medical condition the claimant has, and how that condition is likely to affect his ability to work. However, scheme rules will often severely restrict the ability of members to challenge findings of fact. To use the same example, the rules may make the payment of an ill-health pension conditional upon the trustees 'forming the opinion' that the claimant is unable to continue in employment. With such a rule, the fact that the Pensions Ombudsman takes a different view of the claimant's medical condition from that of the trustees does not entitle him to intervene. He can only do this if the trustees' conclusions are wholly unreasonable, or erroneously reached.[50]

The Pensions Ombudsman's power to determine questions of law allows him to determine the duties of trustees and employers. Thus he is empowered to decide what constitutes a breach of the employer's duty of good faith;[51] when a trustee's conflict of interest disqualifies him from acting; what amendments can be made under a scheme's power of amendment; and whether transfer payments have been correctly calculated.[52] The full range of legal questions that could arise is vast, particularly when one remembers that the interpretation of the rules of a pension scheme is itself a legal question. However, the Pensions Ombudsman has decided he will not investigate the exercise of trustees' discretions unless that exercise is in breach of a scheme's rules or 'had been so arbitrary and irrational that no reasonable person would, on the facts of the case, have exercised it in that way'.[53] Where the dispute involves the use of a scheme surplus, he will only intervene where there has been a breach of scheme rules or of a statute.[54]

Even if the Pensions Ombudsman were prepared to decide cases which involved large sums of money (such as the disposal of surpluses),[55] there are

---

[49] 'I am generally not able to undertake an investigation where a group of members *suspects* that all is not well but does not yet have any evidence of maladministration.' N. 44 above, para. 52.   [50] See *Mihlenstedt* v. *Barclays Bank PLC* [1989] IRLR 522.

[51] See *Imperial Group Pension Trust Ltd.* v. *Imperial Tobacco Ltd.* [1990] 2 All ER 597; [1991] 1 WLR 589. (Ch. d), discussed in Chapter 4.

[52] See *Stannard* v. *Fisons Pension Trust Limited* [1992] IRLR 27 (CA), discussed in Chapter 6.

[53] Note 44 above, para. 30.

[54] Ibid., para. 46. The Pensions Ombudsman has power to refer cases which raise points of law to the High Court. But so far he seems to prefer to refuse jurisdiction and leave the members to decide whether or not to instigate court proceedings. This may be motivated by a desire to avoid the liability for costs which could follow from such a referral.

[55] The Ombudsman declared that a dispute over the legality of a £130 million refund from the Lucas pension fund was outside his jurisdiction. See 'Lucas Pensioners Seek Return of £150 million Funds', *Daily Telegraph*, 31 August 1992.

tactical reasons why it may be unwise to bring such a case to the Pensions Ombudsman. Firstly, the Pensions Ombudsman has no power to grant an injunction. Thus, if the complainant is trying to prevent a decision from being taken, it may be better to start, or to threaten, a High Court action. Secondly, the ability of the Pensions Ombudsman to dispose of such cases is undermined by the right of appeal. Where the Pensions Ombudsman finds against the complainant, the costs of an appeal are likely to deter the complainant from taking the matter further. By contrast, where cases involving significant sums are decided against the trustees or the employer, there is still likely to be an appeal to the High Court.

The Pensions Ombudsman will probably provide a useful service where the facts, or the law, are reasonably clear, and the problem is one of intransigence or sloth on the part of scheme administrators or trustees. But where the dispute is complex, or the law unclear, a matter which begins with the Pensions Ombudsman may still end up in court by way of a referral from the Pensions Ombudsman, or an appeal against the Ombudsman's decision on a point of law. In these circumstances, the Pensions Ombudsman's inquiry may simply represent an extra stage in the process of obtaining a ruling from the court.

V. CONCLUSION

The costs of legal action, coupled with lack of access to the sort of information necessary to mount a legal challenge, considerably undermine the members' ability to enforce the duties placed upon employers, trustees, and actuaries in connection with their administration of the pension scheme. Legal action becomes a threat of last resort, used to frighten trustees into seeking directions from the court (with every party's legal costs met from the fund), and otherwise only likely to be proceeded with when the action complained of is self-evidently, and indisputably, a breach of the trust.[56] As we saw in Chapter 3, the standards applied to trustees can amount to no more than a duty of good faith. To be sure of winning an action, a challenged action will have to be a self-evident breach of subjective good faith. If the enforceable standard of trust law is this low, the protections offered by trust law are, to say the least, somewhat illusory.

One should not overestimate the ability of alternative forums, such as tribunals, to reduce the costs of pension disputes. There is no reason to believe that a pensions tribunal which applied the law of trusts, and offered legal representation to all affected parties, would be less formal or costly than the High Court. There would be a need for legal representation in any

---

[56] Or, in the case of the employer, in breach also of the duty of good faith, which exists in both contract and trust.

disputes involving arguments over the interpretation to be given to trust documents, or the relevant standards to apply. The combination of complex arguments and legal representation is likely to make tribunals act in a court-like fashion.[57]

[57] As happened with industrial tribunals. See L. Dickens and D. Cockburn, 'Dispute Settlement Institutions and the Courts', in R. Lewis (ed.), *Labour Law in Britain* (Blackwell, 1986), p. 563.

[6]

Funding, and the Role of the Actuary

I. INTRODUCTION

UK pension schemes are, as we have seen, funded schemes, with the assets of the scheme being held by trustees. Funded pension schemes offer two major advantages over unfunded ones: discipline and security. Discipline comes from the employer bearing the cost of pensions in advance instead of paying them, as they become due, out of current profits. This deters employers from promising to pay pensions in excess of what, in the future, the enterprise will be able to afford. Funding also increases security, since it increases the likelihood that those pensions will be paid. Security is further enhanced when the funding takes place through a trust. The assets held by the pension scheme's trustees are not part of the company's property. They must be used to pay the members' benefits and should only be returned to the employer (if at all), once these have been satisfied. Thus they are not available to pay the employer's creditors until the members' rights have been secured in full.

The level of funding is in practice determined by the scheme actuary. The actuary decides the employer's contribution rate: the percentage of the payroll which will be paid into the pension scheme. The employees' contribution rate requires no particular expertise. Employees either make no contribution (non-contributory schemes), or they pay a fixed percentage of their salary (contributory pension schemes). The scheme rules require the employer to contribute 'such amounts as the actuary shall recommend'.[1]

The peculiar expertise of the actuary is the ability, using assumptions and methods, to make decisions about the future; in the context of pension schemes, to determine what level of assets will be required to pay for a given level of pensions.[2] But the question which remains is whether actuarial judgments are made according to strict criteria, so that the involvement of

---

[1] K. McKelvey, T. Round, and Michael Fairclough, *Hoskings Pensions Schemes and Retirement Benefits*, 5th edn. (Sweet & Maxwell, 1985) p. 49. Or 'such amounts as the trustees, having taken the advice of the scheme actuary, decide.' Bryn Davies, of Union Pension Services, questions McKelvey *et al.*'s claim that the clause quoted in the text is the most usual one.

[2] This skill is relevant for unfunded schemes as well as funded ones: a prudent employer would wish to know what pensions were likely to cost in the future, even if it did not intend to make provision in advance.

this profession enhances the protection offered by trust law. Or are actuarial judgments so flexible that the involvement of the actuary may operate so as to disguise what is, in effect, managerial control of pension scheme funding? To answer this question we need to look at the professional standards and methods of actuaries, as well as the law which regulates them.

II. PROFESSIONAL STANDARDS

Although many actuaries may share the same opinion on what is an acceptable minimum level of funding, there is no minimum standard laid down by their professional bodies. The profession seems reluctant to adopt the role of policeman in connection with funding. Their concern is not to ensure a minimum level of funding, but to see that actuaries use methods that meet the needs of their clients.

The lack of mandatory professional standards can be understood once you appreciate that the skill of an actuary is the ability to determine what contributions, at any particular time, are necessary to fund any given benefit formula over any period. The actuary can calculate the lump sum which, if paid on the day of the scheme's introduction, would fund all its benefits. Alternatively, she can calculate the sum that would fund the benefits of each member if it were to be paid on the day of that member's retirement. Both these extremes put a heavy burden on the firm at one time, and may have adverse tax consequences.[3] In response to these practical difficulties, actuaries have devised methods which allow the pension benefits to be funded through a system of annual payments. Actuaries have had to develop methods of funding which meet the needs of the employer for liquidity, the employer's accountants' need to calculate the true annual cost of employing scheme members,[4] and the employees' needs for security.[5]

Some actuaries stress the need for funding to provide security. The authors of *Hoskings Pension Schemes and Retirement Benefits*, 5th edn., all actuaries, consider that:

A reasonable minimum funding objective . . . would be to ensure the availability at any given time in the life of the pension fund of sufficient assets to provide, were the

---

[3] The Income and Corporation Taxes Act 1988, s. 592 (4)–(6), limits relief on the employer's *ordinary* annual contributions. Extraordinary contributions can receive relief only on a discretionary basis. See *Notes on Approval under the Finance Act 1970 as Amended by the Finance Act 1971*, issued by the Inland Revenue Superannuation Funds Office, IR 12 (1991), para. 5.6.

[4] See C. Napier, *Accounting for the Cost of Pensions* (Institute of Chartered Accountants in England and Wales 1983); and M. Davies, R. Paterson, and A. Wilson, *Ernst & Young: Generally Accepted Accounting Practice in the United Kingdom* (Macmillan, 1992), Ch. 17.

[5] 'The choice of funding method will depend on a consideration of the employees' requirement for security for their benefits, and the employer's requirement for a stable contribution rate. The employer's cash flow position may also have a bearing.' 'Report of a working party of the Pensions Standards Committee on terminology of pension funding methods' (published jointly by the Institute of Actuaries and Faculty of Actuaries, 1984), p. 3.

fund to be terminated, the pensions for the rest of their lives of all members already retired, together with deferred pensions for life, to start at the normal retirement age, for all active members on the termination date, based upon their pensionable service up to and salary at that date.[6]

This 'reasonable minimum' represents the legal liabilities of the scheme under its winding-up clause. But it is not an absolute minimum. It is 'subject like all such rules to exception'.[7]

Whilst the actuary's decision is vital to the interests of the scheme members, the members are not the actuary's clients. Employers directly or indirectly choose their schemes' actuaries,[8] and pay their fees.[9] Until 1984, the Institute of Actuaries required an actuary to act solely in the interests of the person who employed her. The actuary's only responsibility to other parties was to make it clear that she was not there to serve their interests.[10] Since 1984, in a guidance note, the Institute has required its members to have regard not only to the interests of whichever party pays them, but also to those persons who could reasonably be expected to rely on the actuaries' advice, namely, the members.[11] But this guidance note will, at best, only lead actuaries to point out the risks involved in adopting low funding standards. It does not require the actuary to act in the members' interests when setting the contribution rate.

The actuary's lack of independence raises two problems for scheme members. First, their benefits may be underfunded from the start, leading to the illusion that their scheme will be in a position to pay the fixed benefits, and to maintain their value after retirement, when it has, or will have, insufficient funds. Second, a new management, or a change in management attitudes, may lead the actuary to recommend a reduction in the targeted funding level. Such a reduction can be both large and sudden. By a change of method and assumption, an actuary can justify a complete suspension of the employer's contributions, thereby allowing the security of members' benefits

---

[6] Note 1 above, p. 103.

[7] Ibid. A common reason for falling below the minimum is where a new scheme gives generous benefits in respect of service before the scheme began ('back service benefits'). The cost of these can be spread over future years, with the result that the scheme will, in its early years, be funded below its winding-up liabilities. See OPB, 'Greater Security for the Rights and Expectations of Members of Occupational Pension Schemes', Report by Occupational Pensions Board, Cmnd. 8649 (1982), para. 6.11. Interestingly, the 6th edn. of *Hoskings* makes no reference to minimum funding levels, stressing instead the requirement to disclose funding below this level in the actuary's report.

[8] Either by choosing the actuary themselves, or by having one chosen by the trustees which they have appointed.

[9] This is partly a consequence of tax law. Pension funds are not registered for VAT. In order to reclaim VAT, employers ensure that they, and not the funds, are the advisers' client.

[10] 'Matters . . . [must] be so ordered that all concerned are clear as to who is the [actuary's] principal and in what capacity the [actuary] is serving his principal.' Institute of Actuaries Year Book 1983–4, p. 31.

[11] GN9. 'Retirement Benefit Schemes: Actuarial Reports'. Since the disclosure regulations now require copies of the actuaries' report to be given to the members, it is quite clear that members can be expected to rely on the actuary's advice. Indeed, this was the OPB's intention.

to be run down over a far shorter period than it was built up. When a pension scheme is divided (a consequence of members leaving the scheme due to, for example, the sale of subsidiaries), the loss of security can be even more alarming. The actuary has to decide what assets are necessary to secure the benefits of the transferring members. She can calculate the transfer payment using methods and assumptions which drastically reduce the security of members' benefits at the moment of transfer. Similar problems arise when pension schemes are combined. The actuary has to advise whether the amount of assets being transferred into a scheme will adequately secure the benefits of the incoming members. An insufficient payment into a scheme will dilute the security of the existing members' benefits.

III. FUNDING: TWO IMPORTANT CONCERNS

Funding a final salary pension scheme requires one to pursue a moving target: the benefits of current members are fixed by reference to salaries, which ordinarily increase over time due to inflation. When calculating the ability of assets to secure such liabilities, the actuary is crucially concerned with the return on investment, relative to earnings inflation. This is referred to as the 'real rate of return'.

A second important consideration is the fact that the cost of securing an employee's pension rises steadily during that employee's service with the company. This is because contributions made early in an employee's life can be invested for more years than those made later. Thus, the cost of funding the pensions of the current workforce will rise steadily over their working lifetime. Whether this will actually necessitate a rising contribution rate depends on whether new, young members join the scheme. The contributions paid by, or on behalf of such members are usually more than enough to fund the benefits which they accrue in the early years of their scheme membership. But prudent funding dictates that the solvency of the scheme should, ideally, be dependent neither on the introduction of new members, nor on a steadily rising employer's contribution rate.

IV. CHOOSING THE LEVEL OF FUNDING[12]

When funding a pension scheme, the actuary has to make a number of choices, each of which has an effect on the scheme's solvency and the contribution rate. The first choice is that of method. The second concerns the assumptions to be used with that method, the most important of these

---

[12] The following description relies heavily on 'Report of a working party of the Pensions Standards Committee on terminology of pension funding methods' (n. 5 above). For a general description of funding methods which is more accessible than this report, see B. Escolme, D. Hudson, and P. Greenwood, *Hoskings Pension Schemes and Retirement Benefits*, 6th edn. (Sweet & Maxwell, 1991), 5.46.

assumptions, in the typical defined benefit scheme, being the rate of interest which he expects the scheme to earn on its assets, and the rate at which the members' salaries will increase in future. The third choice relates to the speed at which surpluses, or deficits, must be eliminated. It requires more drastic measures to eliminate a surplus over five years than forty. For convenience we shall look at these choices in a slightly different order, starting with the assumptions, which can be dealt with quite simply, and then moving on to the methods, which are more difficult to understand.

ASSUMPTIONS

Actuaries will make a large number of assumptions, including such matters as expected average life of the workforce, the turnover of staff, the rate of return on investments, and the rate of earnings inflation. The most important of these assumptions are investment return and earnings inflation, or rather, the gap between the two: real investment return. The real rate of return on investments determines the extent to which the scheme's investments will be able to reduce the burden of funding. A high real rate of return means that the assets can be expected to make a large contribution, and vice versa. Actuarial assumptions on the real rate of return vary widely. In a recent survey they were found commonly to vary from 1 per cent to 2½ per cent.[13]

B. VALUING THE SCHEME'S ASSETS

The investments of the fund are not usually valued according to their stock market quotation.[14] Instead, the actuary values them according to the income which they can be expected to produce.[15] So again, this involves the use of assumptions. The actuary has to look at current income yields, form some view of the income that can be expected in future, and then calculate the present value of that future income. Because the actuary is concerned with expected future income, and not current market values, the valuation process is shielded from the effect of day-to-day fluctuations in the stock market. On the other hand, large movements in the market find their way into the valuation. If, for example, the yields on investments are well above those used in a previous valuation, actuaries may be prepared to adjust upwards their estimate of future income, which will increase their valuation of the present assets. In the same way, lower income yields than expected may

---

[13] See Paul Greenwood, 'Choosing Actuarial Assumptions—Best Estimates for SSAP 24 or Funding', paper presented at the 1991 Actuarial Convention at Harrogate'. An earlier survey found a distribution of between ½% and 2½%; see D. Renn and M. Stewart, 'Actuarial Reports on Pension Fund Valuations', 109 Journal of the Institute of Actuaries (1982), 113.

[14] Even if market values are used, they are usually averaged over some period to iron out day-to-day fluctuations. See Escolme, (n. 12 above), at 5.49.

[15] This is the most common method of valuation. Ibid., at 5.49.

result in the actuary reducing the assumed future yield, and lowering the valuation of the scheme's assets.

Thus, it was not the rise in the *Financial Times* index of quoted share prices which caused the higher valuation of scheme assets at the beginning of the 1980s, but the relatively high dividends on which those share prices were, in part, based. Those high dividends caused actuaries to increase the value which they put on the existing scheme assets.[16]

This form of valuation insulates funding from the effects of day-to-day changes in market valuation and short-term changes in investment returns.[17] However, a scheme which was solvent on the basis of such asset valuation would not necessarily be able to meet its obligations on winding up if this required scheme assets to be sold.

V. METHODS OF FUNDING PENSION SCHEMES

There are five basic methods for funding pension schemes in the UK. Before setting out the methods, it is necessary to outline how they are used. The first method, the aggregate method, is a method of directly setting a contribution rate. It makes no assessment of how solvent a scheme is, but only calculates the contribution rate necessary to ensure that, in the long term at least, it becomes solvent. The remaining four methods perform a somewhat different function. They are methods of assessing the relative solvency of a scheme at a particular date. They do not, by themselves, fix a contribution rate. Once these methods are used, the actuary can state whether a scheme is in surplus, or in deficit. The imbalance can be stated in percentage or money terms. Having established the solvency of the fund, the actuary will consider the possible ways of bringing the fund into balance. The manner in which the fund can be balanced will be discussed after the description of the methods.

A. THE AGGREGATE METHOD

Until the start of the 1980s, the most widely used method was the aggregate funding method.[18] This method aims to equate a scheme's liabilities with its assets in order to ensure that, as each member retires or leaves, there are sufficient assets to fund his or her pension. The method treats the expected benefits of the current membership as liabilities, and the expected

---

[16] This does not mean that movements in share price have no effect on valuation. Where income is reinvested, the market price determines what the scheme receives. If market prices rise, the scheme can purchase less assets than expected from its reinvested income. Where market prices fall, the reverse applies.

[17] It also allows the scheme's assets and liabilities to be compared, which is the main point of the exercise. The scheme's liabilities will increase with earnings inflation. The market price of assets does not indicate whether they will secure such liabilities. What the actuary needs to identify is the likely rate of return on investments after allowing for earnings inflation.

[18] Colbran, 'Valuation of Final Salary Pension Schemes', 109 Journal of the Institute of Actuaries (1982), 359 at 361.

contributions, investments, and income therefrom as assets, and sets a contribution rate whereby the present value of the assets equals that of the liabilities. If investments achieve a better yield than expected, then, at the next valuation, this will reduce the contribution rate necessary to balance assets and liabilities. Similarly, if the actuary's assumptions have turned out to be too optimistic, an increase in the contribution rate will be required. The aggregate method thus spreads deficits or surpluses arising from unexpected economic trends over the remaining careers of the scheme members by adjusting the contribution rate.

The aim of the aggregate method is to achieve solvency on the basis that the fund is ongoing, and it does not guarantee that the fund would be able to meet its liabilities if it were wound up. The method reflects a desire to keep the employer's contribution rate stable rather than a desire to ensure security of benefits. However, the aggregate method, as applied in the UK, has been based on cautious assumptions which increase the security offered. Actuaries have assumed that there will be no new scheme members. New members are likely to be younger than the existing members, and calculating the contribution rate without taking their benefits or the contributions made on their behalf[19] into account is likely to increase the solvency of the fund. This is because the contributions paid on their behalf are usually more than enough to fund the benefits which they accrue.[20]

B. THE OTHER METHODS

As was stated above, the other basic methods are means to assess the current solvency of the scheme, rather than a method of directly fixing the contribution rate. These methods require the assets of the fund to be valued, and to be compared with a notional or target fund.[21] As in the aggregate method, the future contributions of the scheme are valued, and treated as an asset, which, when subtracted from the current value of the scheme's liabilities, gives the target fund. One then compares the actual fund with the target fund to see how solvent the scheme is.[22]

---

[19] The contribution rate will be levied on the entire payroll, so even if it is fixed without reference to new members, their wages will still increase the amount paid into the pension fund.

[20] The contributions of younger members can be invested for longer before their retirement and are therefore worth more. The cost of their benefits is also reduced by the fact that more of them will leave the scheme before their retirement than would be expected amongst the membership as a whole (there will be a higher percentage of early leavers, whose benefits are cheaper because they are eroded by inflation). The value of the benefits of younger employees is further reduced by the fact that, when they become early leavers, their benefits have longer to be eroded by inflation than is the case amongst leavers from the existing workforce.

[21] In the working party report, (n. 12 above), the target fund is called 'the standard fund'.

[22] A caveat: this description of what the methods entail is based on the authoritative definition of methods set out in the working party report (n. 12 above). In practice, actuaries will often make their calculations in a somewhat different fashion. For example, where a method requires future contributions to equal future liabilities, the actuary may short-circuit the calculation by simply comparing past service liabilities with the actual fund.

1. The Entry-age Method

The entry-age method is a complicated manner of assessing whether the fund has acquired a prudent level of assets. The strength of this method is that it assumes that the employer will have difficulty in meeting a high contribution rate in the future. The method requires the actuary to ask herself the question: 'How solvent is this fund if I assume that the contribution rate will, in future, be sufficient only to fund the (relatively cheap) benefits of new entrants?' The scheme is only solvent if, even with this relatively low contribution rate, the past and future benefits of the current members will be secure. The rate of contribution is then adjusted according to the deficit or surplus revealed by the valuation. A deficit requires an increase, a surplus a decrease.

To go through the mechanics of the method: the target fund is calculated as the difference between the current value of all the benefits likely to be earned by the current membership, less the current value of the contribution required for a new entrant to earn all her expected future benefits over her expected working lifetime. The actuary then assesses how much would be received by the fund if this rate were paid on behalf of all the existing membership for the rest of their working lives. The present value of this sum is then subtracted from the current value of the members' past and future benefits. This subtraction gives you the value of the target fund, which must be compared with the actual fund held by the trustees.

To return to more simple language. As the benefits for new members' benefits are relatively cheap, a contribution rate sufficient only to fund their benefits will not fund the future benefits of the existing members. Thus a scheme which had only sufficient assets to fund the existing members' accrued benefits would show a deficit under this method. To be in balance, the actual fund must be greater than this. It must hold sufficient assets to secure all of the existing members' past benefits, and some part of their future benefits.

2. The Attained Age Method

The attained age method is like the entry-age method but without the benefit of the conservative assumption about what future contribution rates will be. Instead of assuming that the contribution rate will only be sufficient to fund the benefits of new members, the actuary assumes a contribution rate that will be sufficient to fund the future benefits of all the existing members. This rate, unless there is a surplus or deficit, will be the contribution rate set by the actuary. To assess the adequacy of the assets held by the trustees, the actual fund is compared with the present value of the accrued benefits, taking account of the effect on those liabilities of future salary increases.

This method, like the two which follow, has abandoned the entry-age method's conservative assumption that the future contributions will be inadequate. It has also become almost indistinguishable from the projected unit credit method, although its manner of setting the contribution rate remains slightly more prudent. Whilst the projected unit credit method attempts only to fund each year's liabilities as they accrue, the attained age method fixes a contribution rate sufficient to fund the average future annual cost of current membership's future benefits. Since the cost of funding a membership's benefits increases as that membership ages, a method that looks at the average cost of future benefits is more conservative than one that only funds the cost of this year's benefits.

But the benefits of setting such a contribution rate are lost by the manner in which the target fund is calculated. Everything over the cost of the accrued liabilities is treated as a surplus, ignoring the fact that some of this 'surplus' is an attempt to anticipate the rising cost of funding the current members' benefits. The only advantage of the method over the two which follow is that, *between valuations*, a reserve is allowed to build up over accrued liabilities.[23]

The attained age method, and the two which follow, will, if there are no new members, result in a steadily increased contribution rate in order to cover the increasing annual cost of the current membership's benefits. This represents a major deterioration in prudence. One is either assuming that the employer is content to pay such an increased rate, or one is anticipating that the scheme will have new members and, due to cross-subsidies from those new members, no such increases will be required.

3. The Projected Unit Method

The projected unit method (the 'PU method'),[24] like the attained age method, requires the actuary to calculate the scheme's accrued liabilities by reference to projected future salaries and compare this figure with the value of the scheme's assets. The method differs only in the manner by which the contribution rate for future service is calculated. Instead of calculating the contribution rate necessary to fund the average annual cost of future entitlements, the actuary only looks to see what rate will fund the next year's entitlements. It is this figure which is then adjusted to take account of any surplus or deficit on the valuation of current entitlements.

4. The Current Unit Credit Method .

The current unit credit method[25] is basically the same as the projected unit method, only the actuary will make no allowance for future salary increases except for those likely to take place in the next year. In effect, the method

---

[23] A prudent variant of the attained age method would find the target fund by calculating the value of all the benefits likely to be earned by the existing members, and subtract the value of a contribution rate sufficient to fund the cost of their future service benefits.

[24] See Colbran (n. 18 above), p. 363 (described there under the title of 'Projected Unit Credit Method'); and the working party report (n. 5 above), p. 15.

[25] Working party report, ibid., p. 15.

values benefits on the same basis as if the fund were to wind up within the next twelve months.[26] The method offers less security than the projected unit method. In the circumstances of most UK pension schemes, the method also requires the employer to increase his contribution rate in the future.[27]

C. FIXING THE CONTRIBUTION RATE

The aggregate method is the only method which directly fixes a contribution rate for a given level of benefits. The others merely indicate the current solvency of the scheme, and leave the actuary to decide how to eliminate any consequent surplus or deficiency. As was stated before, a major area of choice is the period over which to eliminate any surplus or deficiency. If the time-frame taken for elimination is the maximum working lifetime of membership (forty years), then very large surpluses or deficits will lead to relatively small alterations to the contribution rate. In contrast, if the time-scale chosen is very short, drastic changes will be indicated. Prudence indicates that surpluses should be eliminated over the long term, and deficits in a much shorter period. As we shall see, practice has been exactly the reverse. The deficits of the 1970s were dealt with under the aggregate method, and funded over forty years, whilst the surpluses of the 1980s and 1990s have been dealt with under the other methods, and absorbed over much shorter periods.

D. HYBRID METHODS

The above methods are, to a certain extent, ideal types. In practice, actuaries use variations of each of them. By varying these methods, actuaries considerably reduce the differences between them. Using an attained age method but looking at the total liabilities and contributions accrued by the end of only one year is the same as using the projected unit method. If you calculate the total benefits likely to be accrued over half the expected working lives of the existing members, which of these two methods are you using? Similar problems arise with the aggregate and projected unit methods. If you use the aggregate method but consider only liabilities and assets accruing within the next five years, you reduce the difference between it and the projected unit method. Similarly, if you use the projected unit method but

---

[26] The method is sometimes called the discontinuance method of funding. For a discussion of the merits of discontinuance funding, see D. McLeish and C. Stewart, 'Objectives and Methods of Funding Defined Benefit Pension Schemes', paper presented to the Institute of Actuaries, 26 January 1987. The method is criticized by Colbran (n. 18 above), p. 364.

[27] The number of years of past service which have to be funded to take account of increases in salaries grows with each year the scheme is in operation. It begins as a small burden and grows with each year until the scheme is mature (when the average past service is constant). By contrast, the projected unit method anticipates the burden of having to fund the past service to take account of salary increases up to retirement.

have regard to the next fifteen years of liabilities and assets, your method begins to resemble the aggregate method.

E. ASSESSING THE METHODS

One cannot say that one method is inherently good, whilst another is bad. Methods have to be looked at in conjunction with the assumptions used, and the period over which surpluses or deficits are to be eliminated. Using the current unit method with a low assumed real rate of return could produce a higher level of solvency than using the projected unit method with a higher rate of return.

F. ADAPTING THE METHODS FOR TRANSFER PAYMENTS

Each of the above funding methods can be used not only to calculate the employer's contribution rate but, in the somewhat different context of a take-over, to calculate the payment that must be made in order to secure the benefits of transferring employees. And it is in this context, rather than the fixing of contribution rates, that funding methods have been challenged in the courts. It is therefore necessary to end this section with a brief introduction to the use of funding methods in the calculation of transfer payments.

When making transfer payments on behalf of large numbers of scheme members transfering from one scheme into another ('bulk transfers'), actuaries have to choose the basis upon which such transfers will be made. In so doing, they have to assess the accrued liabilities of the transferring members and calculate an appropriate sum to secure those benefits. The methods generally used are as follows.

1. The Total Service Reserve Method

This is a variant of the aggregate method. The actuary divides the scheme's assets with a view to producing acceptable contribution rates in each of the schemes. So the actuary might divide the scheme's assets in such a way as to ensure that the employer's contribution rate in the two schemes will, after the transfer payment, be equal. To do this, you have to transfer an amount so that, when you do an aggregate funding method calculation of the two schemes after the transfer, you come out with the same future funding rate. A variation of the method is to divide the fund so as to produce different contribution rates, e.g. with one employer paying 12 per cent and the other 15 per cent. But as we shall see, trustees who endorse such deliberate discrimination may have to justify their decision.

2. Value of Accrued Rights by Reference to Accrued Salaries—the 'Early Leaver' or 'Cash Equivalent' Method

This method comes close to the current unit credit method, only there is no need to calculate the benefits likely to accrue during the year, or the contributions necessary to fund them. The actuary need only have regard to benefits accruing through service up to the date of transfer, and to calculate those benefits by reference to the salaries being paid at the date of transfer, taking account of the statutory obligation to index deferred pensions.[28] This method, like the current unit credit method, will ordinarily lead to a higher funding burden in future. The basis on which the transferring employees will receive their eventual pensions will not be the salary paid at the date of transfer, but that paid at the date of their retirement.[29] The receiving employer will therefore have to fund not only the employees' future service benefits, but the increase in the value of their accrued benefits which results from any increase in pay between transfer and retirement.[30]

3. Past Service Reserve with Allowance for Future Salary and Pension Increases—'Past Service Reserve' Method

This method again values benefits accrued up to the date of transfer but, instead of using current salaries as the basis of valuation, has regard to the salaries on which those accrued rights will actually be based, i.e. those paid at retirement.[31] As such, the method is the same as the projected unit credit method, except that it does not have regard to benefits earned, or contributions paid, in the coming year.

4. Share of the Fund

This is not a method as such. It can be used in conjunction with the past service reserve or early leaver methods. If there is still a surplus after calculating the accrued liabilities on the basis of either of these two methods, it could be retained by the transferring scheme, or transferred to the new scheme, or shared between them. If shared, the actuary would have to calculate an appropriate basis. This might be in proportion to the liabilities as calculated using either the past service reserve or the accrued service/early leaver methods. Another basis of sharing might be based on the relative numbers in each group, or the amount of each member's contributions. If the scheme was found to be in deficit when the accrued liabilities were calculated (using the past service or early leaver methods) then the transfer payment might be reduced, with the receiving scheme suffering a 'share' of the deficit.

[28] The payment will approximate to the sum of transfer values payable if the relevant members opted to leave their employer's occupational pension scheme and asked for the individual transfer payments to which they would be statutorily entitled. Discussed below at pp. 135–6.

[29] Some of the transferring members will not in fact continue in this employment through to their retirement, due to death, redundancy, job changes, etc.

[30] An early leaver basis for the transfer payment will fund increases in deferred pensions resulting from price indexation up to 5% p.a. It is likely increase in salaries above this level which the new employer will have to fund.

[31] There will be some allowance for the likelihood that not all members will stay in the scheme until their retirement.

VI. THE COMMON-SENSE POSITION

One can cut through the terminological and mathematical barriers to understanding the work of actuaries, and reach a few common-sense conclusions.

First, the more prudent the assumptions that a valuation involves, the more secure the pension scheme will become. For example, reducing the assumed real rates of return, which in turn reduces the current value of the scheme's assets, will result in the actuary stating that the scheme is less solvent. If such a valuation results in an increase in the contribution rate, then the scheme's benefits will become more secure. Similarly, if a conservative method or assumption results in a greater transfer payment following a take-over, then the benefits of those transferring workers will be more secure (though the security of the benefits of those remaining will be correspondingly reduced).

Secondly, the faster you take remedial action over a deficit, and the slower you react to a surplus, the more secure pensions will be. So, eliminating surpluses quickly reduces solvency, with the reverse being true of deficits.

Thirdly, with equal assumptions and time-scales for corrective action, the methods can be ranked to a certain extent. The entry-age method produces more security than the attained age method, which is slightly better than the projected unit method, which is superior to the current unit method.

To summarize the common-sense position: the combined method and assumptions which results in the largest accumulated fund by the earliest possible date, gives the most security; and any combined method and assumptions which results, or will result, in a lower fund by the same date gives less security. Thus you can rank the security of methods and assumptions by the amount of funds which they require the employer to maintain in the trust fund. The method and assumptions which require the largest trust fund give the greatest security. The larger the contribution rate in any period following a valuation, the more that security increases. As we shall see in the next section, this crucial common-sense understanding seems to have been lost in *Re Imperial Foods Pension Scheme*,[32] one of the first attempts to define the actuary's responsibilities, but reasserted itself in the Court of Appeal's decision in *Stannard* v. *Fisons Pension Trust Ltd*.[33]

VII. THE LEGAL DUTIES OF THE ACTUARY

A. JUDICIAL VIEWS ON THE ACTUARY'S DUTY

The funding of a pension scheme is just one example of a problem which is common to many areas of the law: what attitude should the courts adopt when adjudication involves the court in passing judgment on the methods

---

[32] [1986] 1 WLR 717.   [33] [1992] IRLR 27.

adopted by another discipline or profession? Where an expert has done something which an authoritative member of her profession will denounce as a technical mistake, the courts have little problem agreeing with this verdict. But the situation becomes more problematic where the dispute is over the method chosen, rather than a mistaken application of method. Here the court has a number of choices. It can defer to any expert who uses methods which another expert would find acceptable, or it can seek to define what the expert should be seeking to achieve. The court may even go so far as to judge upon the suitability of particular approaches.[34] And, quite crucially, it can decide whether the expert is entitled to take the decision in question, or is merely to assist another party to take that decision.

There has been no reported decision in which a judge has interpreted the rule which provides for the setting of the employer's rate of contribution. But solvency levels have been litigated in connection with the interpretation of another set of rules: those dealing with the division of a fund following the sale of one of the companies which participates in a pension scheme. The two leading decisions on actuarial methods in connection with such divisions are *Re Imperial Foods Pension Scheme*[35] and *Stannard v. Fisons Pension Trust Ltd.*[36] Much of the Court of Appeal's judgment in *Stannard* criticizes the approach taken by Walton J in *Re Imperial Foods Pension Scheme*. In order to understand the content and validity of the Court of Appeal's criticisms, it is useful to begin with a thorough analysis of the decision in *Re Imperial Foods Pension Scheme*.

1. Re Imperial Foods Pension Scheme

This case arose out of the sale of two subsidiaries of the Imperial Foods group. The purchaser established a new scheme to receive the employees of the subsidiaries. The rules of the Imperial scheme required the scheme actuary to calculate an 'appropriate' amount to secure the pensions of the transferring members. This sum was to be transferred from the Imperial Food scheme to the new scheme. The new scheme's actuary objected to the method used by Imperial scheme's actuary to calculate the transfer payment.

The judgment contains contradictory approaches and conflicting statements and can be cited as authority for at least four propositions: that the method of calculation is entirely a matter for the actuary, provided she uses a method acknowledged by her profession; that the method used must be fair; that the method used makes no difference to the welfare of the scheme members; and that the past service reserve method deals adequately with the entitlements and expectations of members.

---

[34] For an analysis of this problem in the field of tax law, see J. Freedman, 'Profits and Prophets', 1987 BTR 61 and 104. This article shows how the courts have never completely conceded that profit for the purposes of taxation should be calculated by reference to methods which the accountancy profession has developed for quite different purposes.

[35] Note 32 above.

[36] Note 33 above.

The Choice of Method is a Matter for the Actuary   Walton J says at one point:

[U]pon [the actuary for the transferring trustees] indicating the method that he proposed to adopt, [the purchaser's actuary] did not at once say words to the effect 'You can't be serious'. And I am not sure that that is not really a complete end to the challenge . . .[37]

What this quotation seems to indicate is that the actuary may use any method which is recognized by her profession. The trustees' actuary describes six methods used to calculate transfer payments. One of these methods, 'value of accrued rights calculated by reference to current salaries', involves treating the transferring members as early leavers.[38] At the other extreme, the share of the fund method requires that the transferring members participate in the scheme's current surplus.[39]

The Method Must be Fair   At another point in his judgment, Walton J acknowledges that the duty of the actuary is not, as the above quotation would suggest, to choose any method of valuation recognized by the profession, but to choose a *fair* basis for dividing the fund. Endorsing the decision of Buckley J in *Re George Newnes Group Pension Scheme*,[40] he states that:

the function of an actuary in any situation which is not governed precisely by the provisions of the Trust deed is to achieve the greatest possible degree of fairness between the various persons interested under the scheme.[41]

The Method is Irrelevant   At yet another point in his judgment, Walton J seems to assert that the method chosen by the actuary is irrelevant to the welfare of the members. Referring to what he calls the 'economic point of view',[42] Walton J asserts that the presence of a surplus, or even a deficit, makes no difference to the calculation of a transfer payment provided that the employing company is sound and there is no question of discontinuance of the fund.

Past Service Reserve (Projected Unit Method of Calculation) is OK   Walton J's fourth proposition was that the past service method (a sum sufficient to

---

[37] Note 32 above, at 723. He also felt that an admission by the purchaser's actuary that the method used amounted to 'a view that can be held by a competent actuary' was really the end of the purchaser's case. Ibid., at 727.

[38] Essentially, this is the application of the current unit method to the calculation of transfer payments.

[39] The actuary would still have to choose a basis for sharing the surplus. It could be the relative values of early leavers' entitlements; or of past service entitlements adjusted to take account of future pay increases (past service reserve); or of numbers of members; or of the relative value of member contributions; or such division as would enable two continuing funds to have the same contribution rate (total service reserve method).

[40] (1969) 98 J. Inst. of Actuaries 251.   [41] Note 32 above, at 729.

[42] Ibid., at 728.

secure accrued liabilities up to the date of transfer, with those liabilities calculated by reference to the future salaries on which they would be based):

adequately [met] the entitlements and the expectations of the separating members and [did not alter] the strict entitlements and realistic expectations [of the continuing members] in any manner whatsoever.[43]

Walton J even went so far as to state that, in his opinion, it would be unfair to use the more generous 'share of the fund' basis.[44] This part of his judgment seems to accept that solvency is a benefit to members, but simply places a ceiling on the amount of solvency that they can reasonably expect, as measured by this particular method.

Assessing Fairness   The starting-point for making sense of the law in this area is to accept that the role of the actuary is to be fair. There is little reason to believe that a judge is going to accept that a transfer value that he regards as wholly unreasonable or unfair is beyond judicial remedy simply because it has been reached in a manner which other actuaries would regard as competent.[45] This is especially so when that judge has authority, including parts of *Re Imperial Foods Pension Scheme* and *Stannard* v. *Fisons Pension Trust Ltd.*, which allows him to interfere. Having said this, the burden of proof on those who seek to challenge an actuary's choice of methods is heavy, if only because of the difficulty of explaining actuarial methods to judges. If one accepts that the duty of the actuary is to adopt a fair basis for calculation, and that the method adopted is subject to review in the courts, the next question is, what methods, under what circumstances, can produce unfair results?

The fairness of a transfer payment, from the point of view of pension scheme members, is about sharing the advantages of funding. There is no guarantee that funded schemes will, in the event, pay out larger pensions than unfunded ones, or that well-funded ones will pay out larger pensions than poorly funded ones. It all depends on what happens in the future. Provided that an employer remains in business, it can make up for low (or no) funding by greater funding in the future. Similarly, where a scheme is well funded at the moment, the solvency level may be reduced by contribution holidays, or the admission of new members.

---

[43]   Ibid., at 729.

[44]   This part of Walton J's judgment initially gained some acceptance. In *Stannard* v. *Fisons Pension Trust Ltd.* [1990] 1 PLR 179 at 210 (HCt), Steinfield QC said that his client 'would not be claiming more [than past service reserve] because that would fly in the face of what Mr Justice Walton had said in the *Imperial Foods case*'.

[45]   In tort law, the courts have been quite robust in their rejection of actuarial evidence on occasions: 'as a method of providing a reliable guide to individual behaviour patterns, or future economic and political events, the predictions of an actuary can be only a little more likely to be accurate (and will almost certainly be less entertaining than those of astrologer.' *Auty* v. *National Coal Board* [1985] 1 All ER 930 at 939 per Oliver LJ.

But the fact that solvency levels can be restored or eroded in the future does not prevent high levels of solvency from being an advantage to the members. High solvency produces an immediate benefit in that it increases the security of benefits. It also offers two contingent benefits: an increasing likelihood that the scheme will be continued in the future, and a greater probability that the members will receive discretionary increases to their benefits. The actuary in *Re Imperial Foods Pension Scheme* was asked to divide these benefits fairly.

Walton J's judgment loses sight of what is being divided. Instead of recognizing that solvency is a current benefit that can be shared equally between transferring and remaining members, he looks for legal rights, for ownership. He looks to see who can require that the assets of the scheme be used in their sole interests. Because the members have no such legal rights, he concludes that they have no right to any particular level of transfer payment:

the fallacy . . . is . . . in assuming that the fund existing at the moment of separation belongs exclusively to the two classes of members, namely the transferring and the continuing members together, and to nobody else . . . the most cursory consideration will establish that this is not the case.[46]

Because the members cannot force the employer to maintain the high level of solvency, or to use it solely in their own interests, they cannot be said to have any legal right to the increased security which it represents.

This part of Walton J's judgment undermines the idea of fairness when dividing a fund. If it were generally followed, it would allow worse treatment of transferring members than most actuaries would ever contemplate. For a start, consistency of approach when calculating the funds necessary to secure the benefits of two different groups of members would seem to be a basic requirement of fairness. On this basis, an actuary should normally be expected to calculate a transfer payment using the same assumptions regarding discretionary increases as are being used by the transferring scheme. This is in fact what happened in *Re Imperial Foods Pension Scheme*, since the transfer was made on the basis of past service reserve, taking account of the same future salary increases and discretionary benefits as were being funded for within the transferring scheme. But Walton J, concentrating on the members' legal entitlements, describes the actuary's consistent approach as:

a generous one, in that it certainly preserves for the transferring members not only their strict contractual rights, but a considerable surround of likely increases and additional discretionary benefits.[47]

Walton J's approach invites discrimination between different groups of members. Transferring members from a scheme with high levels of solvency

---

[46] Note 32 above, at 728.   [47] Ibid., at 725.

could be provided with transfer payments that covered only their accrued rights calculated by reference to current salaries (early leavers' benefits). Such a basis of transfer would put a heavy funding burden on the receiving scheme's employer. This increased burden would lower the probability that the members would receive any discretionary increases in pensions, and would increase the possibility that the employer would, at some future date, find the scheme too expensive to continue to fund.[48]

To summarize, Walton J's approach to the question of fairness invites actuaries to manipulate transfer payments through the use of inconsistent methods. He does not require that they assume that the same discretionary payments will be made when calculating the transfer payment as are made when calculating how to fund the transferring scheme. He does not even require that the same *method* be used to calculate the transfer payment as is used to fund the transferring scheme. He fails to explore the relationship between funding levels and the welfare of the members. Unless surpluses can be guaranteed to lead to increased benefits, he seems to think that they should be ignored. He expresses a preference for the past service reserve method, but fails to show why this method is to be preferred.

2. Stannard v. Fisons Pensions Trust Ltd.[49]

The approach adopted in *Re Imperial Foods Pension Scheme* was criticized by the Court of Appeal in *Stannard* v. *Fisons Pension Trust Ltd*. The case concerned the division of the Fison pension scheme following a sale of one of its businesses.[50] The dispute arose because the fund increased in value between the date of sale, when the basis of division was agreed between Fisons and the purchasing company, and the date of the transfer payment. The plaintiff, sponsored by the purchaser, argued that the transfer payment was insufficient. The Court of Appeal's approach differed from that of Walton J in a number of important respects.

---

[48] In an ordinary transfer, the benefit of solvency levels might not be maintained within a receiving scheme even at the moment of transfer, since the transfer payment would be used to secure the benefits of that scheme's other members. This should be considered by an actuary. But in the Imperial transfer this complication is removed, since the transfer was expressly stated to be for the sole benefit of the transferring members in respect of their current entitlement.

[49] Note 33 above.

[50] The sale here was of a business rather than a company, and the transfer was to be made to a new pension scheme specially set up by the receiving company to provide pensions to the transferring employees. The equities of the situation differ only slightly from *Re Imperial Foods*. In the latter case, all of the transferred money was required to be used solely for the benefit of the transferred employees. In *Stannard*, it could also be used to fund the pensions of new employees. As such, there was *less* chance of the transferred monies being used for the sole benefit of the transferred workers in *Stannard* than in *Imperial Foods*. There was therefore even less reason to recognize that the transferred employees had rights with respect to the calculation of the transfer payment. Despite this, the Court of Appeal was willing to recognize that the transferring members had greater entitlements with respect to the calculation of the transfer payment.

Reducing the Authority of the Actuary   As part of the dispute, the plaintiff argued that the rule which should have been used to make the transfer payment would have meant that the actuary's decision on the method to be used should have been final. The rule in question was similar to that discussed in *Re Imperial Foods*: the trustees were to transfer an amount 'advised by the actuary'. Dillon LJ stressed that this wording still left the trustees with ultimate authority to refuse to make a payment which was not fair to both the transferring and remaining members. He drew no distinction between a rule which expressly required the trustees to assess the fairness of the payment, and one that did not.[51] In effect, and in line with the flexible nature of construction described in Chapter 3, he introduced an implied term into the pension scheme, which would not be excluded in the absence of express words to the contrary:

[This] rule . . . merely gives the trustees power to make a transfer to an associated scheme and does not oblige them to act blindly on whatever advice the actuary may give. If they decide to make a transfer they have to consider whether they are acting fairly as between those who will become members of the [new] scheme and those who will remain members of the Fisons pension scheme . . . [Whilst they] will necessarily be guided by the views of the actuaries . . . they will still . . . need to feel satisfied that the amount to be transferred is fair each way.[52]

Dillon LJ's judgment fails to discuss what form of words will suffice to exclude the trustees' duty to decide upon the fairness of a transfer. Staughton LJ expressly refused to hold that *Imperial Foods* was wrongly decided on this point, leaving open the possibility that the precise form of words found in the Imperial Foods pension scheme (the transfer payment 'shall be determined by the Actuary') will require the trustees to give effect to the actuary's decision.[53]

Factors Which Needed to be Considered for a Transfer Payment to be Fair   The Court of Appeal set out some guidelines as how to assess the fairness of a transfer payment. First, it did not think that trustees should attempt to favour their employer's (in this case Fison's) interests over those of the receiving employer, or vice versa.[54] Secondly, the trustees were required to

[51] The Fison scheme contained both types of rules. Dillon LJ did not think that the absence of an express requirement for the trustees to consider the fairness of the payment in one of these rules was significant.   [52] Note 33 above, p. 29.

[53] Though, on the basis of the varying treatment given to the term 'absolute authority', one should not expect the courts always to apply identical words in the same way, especially when they have accepted the unfairness of the result produced by such words. See Chapter 3, pp. 67–8.

[54] Note 33 above, p. 33 (para. 62). This appears to have been directed at remarks made by Walton J regarding the right of a parent company to benefit from a surplus arising in a group pension scheme. Walton J had expressed the view that, as between parent and subsidiary companies, the parent company had the greatest claim to benefit from a surplus, since the parent company bore the ultimate cost of funding. These remarks suggest that the parent company has a special right to a surplus. However, Walton J stated quite firmly that such considerations could not be taken into account when considering the fairness of transfer payment.

calculate the fairness of a transfer payment on a properly informed basis. In this case, the trustees were ill informed because, although they had been told that the fund had increased in value between the date of sale and that for transfer, they were not told how this fact might affect the fairness of continuing to use the total service method.[55] In particular, they should have been told that the past reserve method, which the trustees had originally been inclined to use, but which had been abandoned because it was thought the fund could not secure both the transferring and remaining members on this basis, could now be afforded. In addition, they should have been told the implications of continuing with the method already adopted (the total service reserve method) once the fund's investments had risen in value. The transfer had been calculated on the assumption that both schemes would need a future employer's contribution of 16 per cent. But the increase in the value of the scheme's assets meant that such assets as would, with an employer's contribution rate of 16 per cent, secure all of the present and future benefits of the *transferring* employees, would leave enough investments in the Fison's scheme for their present and future benefits to be secured with a contribution rate of only 12½ per cent. This would mean that the present and future benefits of the transferring employees would depend on a higher contribution rate from their employer, than would those of the employees remaining with Fisons. Whilst the Court of Appeal did not say that such an outcome was necessarily unfair, it felt that the trustees should have considered the implications of the greater funding burden on the transferring employer when deciding if the transfer payment was fair.

Fairness Requires the Trustees to Have Regard to More Than Legal Rights   In deciding what was relevant to the fairness of a transfer payment, the Court of Appeal showed a much better understanding of the value of funding than did Walton J. Instead of concentrating on the members' legal rights to fund assets, the Court of Appeal considered how solvency might be expected to benefit members. Dillon LJ was aware that the members had only the possibility of benefiting from an actuarial surplus. Walton J had felt that the lack of a legal right to benefit from a surplus meant that the members should not expect to receive any part of that surplus, which should be considered to be the property of the funding company. Staughton LJ took a quite different view:

The surplus might . . . disappear if Fisons decreased its rate of contribution, as it was free to do so. But it is very arguable that one should attempt to assess the likelihood of Fisons taking that course. Would it cause discontent and industrial unrest? Is Fisons a hard-hearted employer who would not be deterred by that, or likely to fall on hard times to such an extent that a reduction of contributions would be essential? . . . there

---

[55] This seems to be an example of the administrative law approach to trustees' duties discussed in Chapter 3, p. 67–9.

was some degree of likelihood that the existing employees and pensioners would receive some benefit from that surplus in future, in the form of increased pensions or other benefits. When the trustees came to consider what was just and equitable upon a division of the fund . . . they ought to have borne those points in mind and made some evaluation of them.[56]

Thus, whilst Walton J had felt that mere possibilities could be ignored, the Court of Appeal felt that the trustees could, indeed must, take such matters into account.[57] To do so, the trustees must have regard not only to the members' legal rights, but to the company's industrial relations policy.

A Substantive Basis for Fair Treatment?   Whilst most of the Court of Appeal judgments relate to the procedural requirements for a fair division of the fund, Staughton LJ's judgment contains indications as to how, at least prima facie, trustees should divide their trust fund between different groups of members. He concentrated on the relationship between asset levels and the likelihood of benefit increases. This possibility should be equal as between the two groups. The complications on sharing out surpluses, deciding the basis of a pro-rata share in the surplus, did not concern him.[58] But he was sure that some part of the surplus should ordinarily go to each of the members. He stressed that the effect of the method in this case was:

to award any likelihood of increased benefits in the future, arising from the actuarial state of the fund, wholly to employees who remained with Fisons, and not at all to those who [transferred].[59]

Whilst he did not hold that excluding one group of members from a share of the surplus was always unfair, his approach seems to suggest that the trustees must have a good reason for taking such an approach. In the case before him, Staughton LJ thought that the transferring members could have been excluded from the surplus on the basis that none of them were retired, presumably because the trustees could reasonably take the view that the first call on the surplus should be to increase the benefits of existing pensioners. Other reasons might relate to the trustees' assessment of the industrial relations record of one or other employers: there is no point transferring surplus assets to a scheme which is shortly to be wound up by its employer in order to extract a surplus for itself. But the basis of division, in the absence of

[56] Note 33 above, p. 32.

[57] Dillon LJ felt that the possibility that members might not, in the end, benefit from surplus assets, represented: 'possibilities which . . . are merely questions of practicality for a practical question, and not binding rules of law'. Ibid., at 31.

[58] A decision to share the surplus between the two groups still leaves open the question of the basis of those shares. They could be in some relationship to the numbers in each group, to their respective winding-up benefits, to the accumulated contributions paid by each member, to their past service benefits calculated with allowance for future salary, or to the total benefits which each member can expect to receive under the scheme if they continue in service through to retirement.   [59] Note 33 above, p. 33.

valid reasons to the contrary, should be equal distribution between different groups of members.

Staughton LJ also anticipated the kind of extreme discrimination which Walton J's judgment would have allowed, whereby one group of members receives no more than is necessary to secure their legal entitlements on winding up, so-called early leaver benefits. Whilst acknowledging that such a division could be approved by the trustees in the case before him, since it was expressly authorized under one of the scheme's rules, he questioned its appropriateness in ordinary circumstances.[60]

Past Service Reserve Method   The Court of Appeal neither endorsed, nor criticized, the method of calculating transfer payments which had found such favour with Walton J: the past service reserve method. But the implication of their remarks on the treatment of surpluses suggests that this method must be used in a different way from that applied in *Re Imperial Foods Pension Scheme*. It can be used to calculate members' initial share of the fund's assets and, where this still leaves a surplus, it can presumably be used to calculate the pro-rata allocation of that surplus. But the trustees cannot simply allocate one group a sum based upon their past service reserve, and then leave the other with an amount greater or less than this method would produce, unless they have good reasons for discriminating.

What Protections are Offered by Stannard *v.* Fisons Pension Trust Ltd.*?*   To summarize the Court of Appeal's judgment, the trustees must not blindly adopt the opinion of the actuary, but must form their own opinion on the fairness of the treatment afforded to different groups of members. This judgment must be made on a properly informed basis and, where one group is treated differently from another, the trustees must be prepared to justify the fairness of that discrimination. The judgment also recognizes the industrial relations expertise which trustees need to exercise in their dealings with the fund. When assessing whether a particular group of members is likely to receive discretionary benefit increases, the trustees have to consider the employer's likely industrial relations strategy. They must then decide whether the relevant employer will be willing or able to use all, part, or none of the actuarial surplus for its own benefit.

One should not exaggerate the protection afforded by *Stannard* in comparison with *Imperial*. For a start, any challenge like that in *Stannard* depends crucially on obtaining access to information regarding the basis upon which the trustees and the actuary reached their decision. In *Stannard*, the plaintiff appears to have become aware of the discrimination only accidentally, when a report to the members who remained with the original scheme came

---

[60] 'If an employee leaves voluntarily, or is dismissed for redundancy or misconduct, he may have to suffer those disadvantages. But is it appropriate when he is, more or less compulsorily, transferred to another employer?' Ibid., at p. 32.

to his attention. The report made reference to the actuarial position of the remainder of the fund having been favourably affected by the terms of the transfer out. Only through this chance remark, and the fact that the new employer was willing to finance a legal action, was the plaintiff able to obtain full discovery of the basis upon which the trustees had acted.[61]

Stannard encourages independently minded trustees to stand up to the scheme actuary and the employer, and refuse to do what they are told. It also gives more legitimacy to trade union trustees, who are well placed to form an assessment of the likelihood that the employer can be persuaded to use a surplus to increase benefits rather than to reduce contributions. But it will not radically alter the behaviour of more passive trustees. Trustees who are inclined to do whatever the employer or the scheme trustee advises may simply have to be provided with more information in order to make their decision unimpeachable. With such trustees, *Stannard* simply increases the formality of the trustees' meeting, with trustees being provided with lists of relevant factors, and statements justifying each of the possible methods of division, whilst they continue to adopt the actuary or employer's decision.

B. STATUTORY RESTRICTIONS ON EMPLOYERS' CONTROL OF FUNDING

1. The Need for Consent before Transferring Members into Less Secure Schemes

Whilst some scheme rules provide that bulk transfers may take place without the consent of the transferred members, this does not mean that a member will, in the event, be forced into a receiving scheme with lower security. Before there can be a compulsory transfer, the actuary to the transferring scheme must certify that the rights and expectations to be provided in the new scheme to the transferring members in respect of their past service are equivalent, on an overall basis, to their rights and expectations in respect of pensionable service in their original scheme.[62] The difficulty in ensuring overall compatibility in benefit promises, let alone solvency levels or administrative provisions, means that, in all but 'mirror' replacement schemes, actuaries will be reluctant to give these certificates. The result is that members are usually given the choice to whether to transfer their accrued rights to the new scheme or take a deferred pension in the old one.

The need for consent reduces the employer's ability, through transfer payments, to reduce the security of the members' benefits. However, a current member may face the choice between less secure benefits in a new scheme, or secure, but less benefits in the employer's existing scheme. Where the option to transfer follows the sale of a subsidiary or business, employees of that subsidiary or business will be unable to continue to be members of the

---

[61] See, generally, Chapter 5.
[62] Occupational Pension Schemes (Preservation of Benefit) Regulations 1991 (SI 1991 No. 167).

vendor's scheme except for a limited transitional period. After this period, the member's rights are limited to the receipt of a deferred pension calculated on an early leaver basis. In addition, by refusing to transfer, the member will forgo any additional benefits being offered by the new scheme. For young employees, for whom the right to accrue benefits in future may be far more important than the security of accrued rights, there is little point in refusing to transfer. For older employees, whose accrued rights are relatively more valuable, refusing to transfer may maintain the security of their benefits, but as those benefits will now be calculated on an early leaver basis, the cost of maintaining security may be simply too great.

The right to refuse to transfer is really only a realistic protection in two cases. First, older workers coming up to retirement, where the value of accrued rights is great, the loss of further accrual is slight, and there is relatively little time for the deferred pension to be eroded by inflation prior to retirement. Second, existing pensioners, who will receive no further accruals of benefit, and have already had their pension calculated by reference to their retirement salary.[63] But even these two groups may be 'persuaded' to take a transfer to a less secure scheme, due to their reliance on discretionary pension increases. Without discretionary increases, which are usually within the power of the employer, pensioners cannot maintain the real value of pensions in payment. If the old employer makes it clear that such discretionary increases will not be forthcoming in the old scheme, then a pensioner may be persuaded to transfer to the new one, even if the level of security is somewhat lower. The only restriction against forcing members to transfer from one scheme to another in this way is the employer's duty of good faith.[64]

2. The Statutory Right to Individual Transfer Payments

Current members who are unhappy with any aspect of their scheme's administration, including the level of security, may exercise their statutory right to leave the scheme[65] and take a transfer payment, equivalent in value to their deferred pension, and have this paid into a personal pension.[66] Pension schemes have to offer transfer values to members with more than two years' worth of benefits. The amount must be calculated by an actuary and be at least the cash equivalent of the member's deferred pension, allowing for the indexation of that pension required under the Social Security Acts or, where this is more generous, the scheme rules.

The major drawback for anyone exercising this right is that the benefits paid to such early leavers are less than will be paid if they remain in the scheme through to retirement, for all the reasons discussed in the previous section. When calculating the cash equivalent, actuaries are required to give

---

[63] Or where those pensioners were themselves early leavers, on their salary at the date of leaving the scheme.

[64] See *Imperial Tobacco Pension Trust Ltd.* v. *Imperial Tobacco* [1991] 2 All ER 597; [1990] 1 WLR 58; discussed in Chapter 4.   [65] Social Security Act 1986, s. 15.

[66] Social Security and Pensions Act 1975, s. 52B, Schedule 1A, part II.

credit for any discretionary increases which are paid under established custom, but the inclusion of a sum representing such increases can be waived by the trustees.[67]

A member can be sure to receive the cash equivalent of her deferred pension without allowance for discretionary increases. But calculating this cash equivalent is, as with bulk transfer payments, largely a matter for the actuary's discretion. The regulations require the actuary to use the same methods and assumptions for transfer payments out of the scheme as are used when granting benefits to members transferring in. This restriction is irrelevant to those schemes which do not accept transfers in. And even where transfers in are allowed, this regulation may not overly restrict the actuary. The actuary clearly has to calculate transfers in and out which occur at *precisely the same time* on the same basis. But the actuary does not have to give this year's transfers out on the same basis as last year's transfers in. Without a stipulated time-frame during which these two types of transaction must remain consistent, there is an obvious risk of manipulation. The terms applied to last week's transfers in may, once the actuary has looked again at the scheme's security, provide an unsuitable basis for this week's transfers out. Similarly, next week's transfers in may, after a similar review, not need to take place on the same basis as this week's transfers out. In the end, any restriction on the actuary's discretion will not be based on the regulations themselves, but on some underlying notion of good faith. Or, to express the same idea in a different manner, on the courts' willingness to prevent gross manipulation and exploitation of members' rights.

3. Restrictions on Overfunding: Maximum Funding Levels

The Inland Revenue are concerned to prevent occupational schemes being used as a mechanism to avoid tax. As such, they have always been concerned with overfunding. Before 1986, their remedy was somewhat draconian: schemes which would not reduce their level of funding when asked would be threatened with the withdrawal of exempt-approved status.[68] This would expose the scheme to tax on future employee and employer contributions, future investment income and, most serious of all, capital gains tax on all future disposals of investments.[69]

The Finance Act 1986 introduced a more formal but less draconian regime for overfunding.[70] At least every three and a half years[71] the actuary must

[67] The Faculty and Institute of Actuaries have expressed their concern at reports that in an increasing number of cases, trustees are directing that discretionary increases should be ignored in total or in part. See Bryn Davies, *What's Wrong With Transfer Values?* (PIRC/Union Pension Services, 1990), p. 7.

[68] IR 12, n. 3 above, para. 24.2.

[69] For a full discussion of the consequences of losing exempt approved status, see N. Inglis-Jones, *The Law of Occupational Pension Schemes* (Sweet & Maxwell, 1989), p. 29.

[70] The relevant provisions are now found in Income and Corporation Taxes Act 1988, Schedule 22, and the Pension Scheme Surpluses (Valuation) Regulations 1987 (SI 1987 No. 412). See generally Escolme (n. 12 above), paras. 5.101–5.108.

[71] Pension Scheme Surpluses (Valuation) Regulations 1987, SI 1987/412, reg. 2.

value the scheme by a specified method (effectively the projected unit method) and standard assumptions.[72] If this valuation reveals that the scheme has assets worth more than 105 per cent of liabilities, and the trustees do not submit proposals, which are acceptable to the Revenue, for the elimination of the excess, the scheme will suffer a partial loss of approval. A percentage of capital gains and income investment (equal to the percentage of the total fund which is in excess of the Revenue limits) becomes subject to taxation. Actuaries will not wish to recommend contributions which cause or increase partial loss of approval.

Partial loss of approval can be avoided by increasing the fund's liabilities through benefit increases, or by reducing its solvency through contribution reductions or holidays, or refunds, or a combination of these methods. The proposals must provide for the excess over 105 per cent to be eliminated. Allowance can be made for the effect of taking a contribution holiday for up to five years.[73]

Lowering or suspending the employer's contributions is usually within the employer's control,[74] but this alone will often not suffice to avoid partial loss of approval since an excess may remain even with no contributions for five years. In such a situation, avoiding partial loss of approval requires benefit increases or a refund of assets.

Trustees who act in their members' best interests can be expected to resist refunds, and press instead for benefit increases. Employers may prefer refunds, though this is not a costless option for them. The fiscal treatment of refunds makes them relatively unattractive. Refunds are subject to a free-standing tax of 40 per cent. Future contributions will enjoy only 33 per cent relief[75] (assuming no change in tax rates). This means that a refund will result in the loss of 7 per cent of the sum refunded, assuming that the refund is eventually returned to the scheme in the form of contributions, or a loss of 40 per cent, if it is never paid back in. Refunds are also caught by the Social Security Act 1990, s. 11 (3). This provision makes a refund conditional upon the scheme providing indexation to pensions in payment up to a maximum of 5 per cent p.a. Where the scheme rules do not already provide for this, the benefits must be altered to offer this level of indexation as a precondition to any refund.[76]

---

[72] Ibid., regs. 4–9.

[73] Fifteen years in the case of new schemes. With schemes of less than thirty members, the surplus can be eliminated over the entire expected working lifetime of the youngest scheme member.

[74] Though some schemes require substantial minimum employer contributions, for example, requiring the employer to pay some multiple or fraction of the employees' contributions.

[75] 25% on small companies.

[76] Section 11 (3) reads as follows: 'In the case of an occupational pension scheme—(a) such as is mentioned in subsection (1) of s. 58A of the Pensions Act . . . no payment shall be made out of the resources of the scheme to or for a person who is or has been the employer of persons in the description of category of employment to which the scheme relates until such time as provision has been made by the scheme for every pension which commences or has commenced under it to be increased as mentioned in paragraph (b) of that subsection.'

Where an employer will not agree to benefit increases, it may be in the interests of both members and the employer to accept a stalemate, rather than to propose a refund. The statute provides that failure to submit proposals acceptable to the Revenue will result in partial loss of approval. As such, there is no duty to submit acceptable proposals, but simply a price to be paid in terms of partial loss of reliefs if no acceptable proposals are forthcoming.[77] Loss of capital gains can be mitigated by reducing or suspending the trading of assets. To calculate the cost to the employer of a partial loss of relief, one needs to compare a 7 per cent loss of the sum refunded, with a 33 per cent tax on the capital gains and income accruing to that same sum over the expected period of partial loss of approval. If the refund works out more expensive, and yet is still desired by the employer, this probably indicates that the employer is suffering from some kind of liquidity problem. This should make the trustees even more reluctant to agree to a refund. There is nothing in the statute which allows trustees to grant a refund where this is forbidden under the scheme's rules. Unless the scheme rules can be changed by amendment to allow for refunds to the employer, a refund may necessitate the present scheme being wound up, and a replacement scheme being introduced.[78]

From the members' point of view, a refund represents an immediate loss to the scheme of 100 per cent of the amount refunded, with only the hope that it will be returned to the scheme in the form of future employer contributions. As such, it must be justified by significant immediate benefit increases.[79]

4. Disclosure Requirements

Whilst an actuary is relatively free to choose her methods and assumptions, the timing and presentation of valuations is regulated by statute.

Where a scheme is contracted out, the actuary must prepare a certificate[80] at least every three and a half years which specifically states whether the contracted-out part of a member's pension, the Guaranteed Minimum Pension (GMP), is adequately funded,[81] and whether, in event of a scheme

---

[77] One commentator has argued that this provision places a duty upon administrators to eliminate surpluses, and gives them a power to make a refund which overrides any scheme rule to the contrary; see J. Quarrell, 'More Sap than Solution?', *Pensions*, October 1986, p. 51, and J. Quarrell's replies to letters published in *Pensions*, March 1987, p. 51. However, this mandatory language is belied by para. 9 (2), which envisages that administrators may be unable to carry out their proposals, and stipulates the consequences for the scheme if this occurs.

[78] Where the scheme assets are below the maximum set out in ITCA 1988, Schedule 22, the Revenue will not allow an employer to take a refund from a continuing scheme, or to wind up that scheme and replace it by a less well funded one. IR 12 (1991), n. 3 above, paras. 13.20, 13.28.

[79] See *Re Courage Group's Pension Schemes* [1987] 1 All ER 528 at 545.

[80] This certificate does not require a separate valuation. It can be based upon the last valuation, provided that the actuary has been provided with full details of any relevant changes in circumstances (large-scale redundancies, changes in the scheme's investments, etc.).

[81] Social Security and Pensions Act 1975, s. 41, as amended by Social Security Act 1980, s. 3 (6) and the contracted-out Employment (Miscellaneous Provisions) Regulations 1983, SI 1983 No. 338.

winding up, its financial resources are likely in the normal course of events to be sufficient to meet GMPs in full or buy the members back into the state scheme. This certificate must reveal any self-investment or concentration of investment in excess of 10 per cent[82] of the fund. A further certificate is required if self-invested assets have to be taken into account by the actuary before he can be satisfied that the GMPs and other priority liabilities are covered. The OPB lacks the resources to check the accuracy of these certificates.[83]

Following two reports by the OPB,[84] the system of disclosure previously confined to GMPs was extended to all defined benefit schemes with respect to all of their benefits. Trustees are now required to obtain, at intervals not greater than three and a half years, an actuarial valuation[85] which is prepared in accordance with the guidelines published by the Institute of Actuaries and Faculty of Actuaries.[86] These guidelines state that the valuation report must contain 'sufficient information to enable the expected future course of a scheme's contribution rate and funding level to be appreciated.'[87] They require the actuary to set out the methods, assumptions, and funding objectives adopted and to draw attention to those assumptions which have a large effect on the contribution rate, and to changes in the funding of discretionary benefits, and to comment on any significant difference between the assumptions used to prepare the last report, and the actual experience of the scheme since then. The actuary must also state the ability of the scheme to meet its accrued liabilities if it were wound up at the date of valuation, and indicate, by reference to the winding-up clause, which benefits might have to be abated.

Members who are to be transferred without their consent must be given 'full information' about the proposed transfer, including the value of all accrued rights to be transferred.[88] This is, on the surface, a quite open-ended obligation. But it will probably simply lead to scheme members receiving a statement of the rights available in the respective schemes, together with a copy of the actuary's valuation of those respective rights. The member will

[82] This requirement has been rendered superfluous by the prohibition on self-investment in excess of 5% of the fund contained in the Occupational Pension Schemes (Investment of Scheme's Resources) Regulations 1992, SI 1992/246.

[83] The OPB have approximately one hundred and thirty eight staff, forty-three of whom work in the new pensions registry, and five carry out general administration. The remainder are divided equally between rule examinations and financial supervision. (Information supplied by the general inquiry section of the OPB, 31 March 1993).

[84] 'Solvency, Disclosure of Information and Member Participation in Occupational Pension Schemes', Cmnd. 5904 1975; 'Greater Security for the Rights and Expectations of Members of Occupational Pension Schemes', Cmnd. 8649 (1982).

[85] Occupational Pension Schemes (Disclosure of Information) Regulations 1986, SI 1986/1046 reg. 8 (4).   [86] Retirement Benefit Schemes—Actuarial Reports (GN9).

[87] Appreciated by whom? Another actuary? Lay trustees? Scheme members?

[88] Occupational Pension Schemes (Disclosure of Information) Regulations 1986, SI 1986/1046, Schedule 2, para. 13, as amended by Occupational and Personal Pension Schemes (Miscellaneous Amendments) Regulations 1992, SI 1992/1531 reg. 14 (e).

have to form her own judgment on whether to accept the transfer, or leave the employer's scheme and ask for an individual transfer payment.

Disclosure was recommended by the OPB as an alternative to mandatory minimum funding standards.[89] The OPB were unconvinced of the need for funding controls, in view of the small number of scheme failures. Instead, they preferred to see established a practice whereby:

warning signals on scheme solvency can be picked up in good time by all concerned—scheme members, trustees, employers and their advisers—in the hope that they will be able to take their own preventative measures.[90]

Where the problem arose through deliberate underfunding by the employer, members were expected to bring pressure to bear on their employers through their trade unions, and collective bargaining.[91] With respect to large, unionized companies, this approach will afford some protection against underfunding, particularly where some of the trustees are appointed from the workforce and supported by their unions. Trustees who are supported by their trade unions can monitor funding, and seek independent actuarial advice which can spell out the amount and likely effects of underfunding. With respect to small, non-unionized firms, the expectation that employees will be able to monitor and counter underfunding may be no more than a pious hope.

Individual members are even less likely to understand what constitutes good or bad funding, and will be both less able and less likely to seek independent advice. For such individuals, the best that may be hoped for is that disclosure will alert them to the need to exercise their right to leave their employer's scheme and take a transfer payment into a personal pension plan. Such a strategy is, for the reasons set out in the earlier section on individual transfer payments, a strategy of last resort.

VIII. CONCLUSION

Since employers are under no obligation to introduce pension schemes in the first place, it can be argued that a pension scheme, however funded, is better than no scheme at all. However, there is a danger that employees will rely on promised levels of retirement income which, not being properly funded, fail to live up to their expectations. Given the limited ability of at least some employees to monitor the solvency of their schemes, there is a strong case for a minimum statutory level of funding. However, such a system will not solve all the problems of funding, not least because any level chosen is likely to be relatively low, as there would be pressure to set a minimum which would be within the capacity of all but a small number of the employers who currently

---

[89] See n. 84 above: OPB 1975, para. 53; OPB 1982, para. 6.21.
[90] OPB 1982, para. 6.21.
[91] Ibid., para. 6.33; OPB 1975, (n. 84 above), para. 58.

offer pension schemes. These standards would not prove satisfactory to members whose employers could afford greater contributions, and these employees would continue to rely on trust law and actuarial practice to ensure that their benefits were secured to a higher level. In the light of the *Stannard* decision, which approves Walton J's treatment of the actuary's decision, but reaffirms the role of trustees, employees must put most of their faith in trust law.

The *Stannard* case goes some way to ensuring that employees who currently enjoy high funding levels do not see those levels substantially reduced through the employer's ability to split up a pension scheme and control the level of transfer payments made into each of the replacement schemes. However, the protection afforded by a requirement for trustees to justify discriminating against different groups of employees may not prove substantial in practice. Aside from the fact that discrimination motivated by a desire to advantage the employer can sometimes be dressed up in reasons associated with the characteristics of the respective groups of employees, there are also the major obstacles discussed in Chapter 5: how do members get access to the reasons for trustees' decisions, and how do they finance an application to the court to submit those reasons to judicial review?

Statutory minimum funding, or indeed any accepted minimum level of funding, will continue to give rise to a dispute which currently receives great attention: who is entitled to benefit from assets in excess of that minimum, that is, who is entitled to the pension fund surplus? And it is to this issue that we now turn.

[7]

Surpluses and the Right to Augmented Benefits

I. INTRODUCTION

'Who owns the pension scheme surplus?' If the assets in the pension fund exceed the amount required to secure the promised benefits, who is entitled to benefit from the excess: the employer, the employer's creditors, the employees, or the members and their dependants? Recent cases on this question have involved millions of pounds, and the total at stake may run into hundreds or thousands of millions.[1] The members may wish to see surpluses used to increase their benefits. Contributing members may prefer to see their contributions reduced, suspended, or eliminated altogether. The employer may want a refund of assets, or the reduction or suspension of its contributions. This may lead the employer to seek to change some of the scheme provisions: to insert a provision for refunds where they are prohibited; to provide for refunds from an ongoing scheme where the present rules allow them only on winding up; or to open the scheme to new employees where it is presently operating for the benefit of a closed class of members. Thus the general question, 'Who owns the pension fund surplus?' is a question about the ability of the parties to enforce these conflicting claims under a scheme's existing rules, or to secure changes in the rules which will enable them so to do.

Sections II and III of the chapter provide a description of what surpluses are, how they have arisen, and what claims are made upon them. Section IV sets out the rights of the various parties to benefit from such surpluses. It begins by considering the rights arising when a surplus occurs within an ongoing scheme, and then proceeds to consider the position on a scheme's final winding up. Section V examines the scope for judicial discretion in disputes involving surpluses. It will demonstrate why any description of the law relating to surpluses, including the one which has just preceded it, is an extremely speculative exercise.

---

[1] In their report on surpluses, the Labour Research Department claimed that, in the two years to the end of 1989, over 2,000 pension schemes had reported a surplus in their funds. Report on Surpluses, LRD, 1 September 1990, p. 1.

II. SURPLUSES WITHIN CONTINUING SCHEMES

A. HOW THEY ARISE: ACTUARIAL JUDGMENTS

When a scheme is continuing, the judgment that it is in surplus is entirely an actuarial one. Whether the actuary's report reveals a surplus depends on the methods and assumptions used, and this depends in turn on the questions which the actuary is instructed to address. If the employer wishes to fund the scheme over a long period with an extremely stable contribution rate, then the actuary will choose a method suitable for this purpose. She might, for example, use the aggregate funding method and set a contribution rate which will, over the forty-year period, balance the liabilities against the value of the scheme's existing assets and its future contributions. When this process is repeated at the next valuation, there are three possible outcomes. If the assets have risen in value relative to the liabilities, the contribution rate required to balance them will fall. If the assets have fallen in value relative to the liabilities, the contribution rate will have to rise. If the relative value of assets and liabilities is exactly the same, the contribution rate will remain unchanged. Because the actuary is asked to set a contribution rate which will bring the assets and liabilities into balance over forty years, the change in the contribution rate is unlikely to be large. For example, an unexpectedly large increase in the value of the scheme's assets can be absorbed by a small reduction in the contribution rate.

This approach to funding, which was fairly typical in the UK until recently, does not usually produce a figure that can be instantly recognized as a 'surplus'. If the assets of the scheme are greater than expected, or the liabilities less, the two can be brought into balance by a change in the contribution rate. If this method were followed slavishly, a suspension of contributions, ('a contribution holiday') would not be recommended unless the scheme needed no contributions for the next forty years. Only if even a forty-year holiday would not balance assets and liabilities, would benefit increases or a refund be required. In practice, the aggregate funding method has not been used in quite this way. Where assumptions have resulted in an increase in scheme solvency, the employer has often preferred to increase benefits rather than to reduce the contribution rate by a small amount.

Large actuarial surpluses are the combined result of changes in the general approach to funding, and economic events. We shall look at each of these in turn.

B. CHANGING APPROACHES TO FUNDING

Finance directors are no longer so concerned with maintaining an even contribution rate, and in consequence, have adopted a more short-term approach to pension scheme funding. It is not good enough for assets and liabilities to balance *only* at the end of forty years; they must be made to balance throughout the life of the scheme. It is not practical to balance the value of accrued liabilities and existing assets on a daily, on weekly basis. But it is possible to balance the value of assets and liabilities over periods shorter than forty years. A compromise position is to insist that the scheme's assets and liabilities balance by the date of the next actuarial valuation, typically within three to five years.

Changing the basis of funding[2] has increased the demands which employers, and employees, can make. If the assets and liabilities of the scheme have to balance over five years instead of forty, then the company may be able to justify not only a reduction in contributions but a complete suspension of contributions. It may even demand a refund. By the same token, the benefit increases that are required to absorb an improvement in solvency over five years are far greater than those needed to achieve this over forty years.

This change in funding has long-term implications. Benefit increases which absorb a surplus over five years may considerably increase the burden of funding the scheme after that date. For example, an increase in the accrual rate (the fraction of final salary earned by each member for each year's pensionable service) from 1/80th to 1/60th may be sufficient, over five years, to bring the assets and the liabilities into balance. But what of the years after? Benefits will continue to accrue at this increased rate, but without a surplus to fund them. Will the employer meet the cost of these improved benefits when contributions recommence? Similar questions arise with contribution holidays or refunds. If a company suspends contributions or takes a refund, in order to balance the liabilities and assets that are expected to have accrued within five years, will it be able to recommence contributing at the old rate, or perhaps an even higher rate, once the five years have expired?

C. ECONOMIC EVENTS

Changes in funding have coincided with economic events which have significantly improved the solvency of pension schemes. There has been a wide swing in investment returns over two decades. In the 1970s, a period of low real rates of return,[3] actuaries valued scheme investments on a conservative basis.[4] Low valuations led to increased contribution rates, and a

---

[2] The move to a more short-term approach to funding has usually been accompanied by a change from the aggregate to the projected unit method of funding. This is largely a question of terminology. The major difference between the aggregate and projected unit methods is the period by which assets and liabilities must balance. Shorten the period used in the aggregate method, or lengthen that used with the projected unit method, and the methods become practically indistinguishable.

[3] B. Escolme, D. Hudson, and P. Greenwood, *Hoskings Pension Schemes and Retirement Benefits*, 6th edn. (Sweet & Maxwell, 1991), p. 114, fig. 4.

[4] They reduced the assumed real rate of return. Ibid., p. 113, paras. 5–43.

consequent high rate of investment acquisition.[5] In the 1980s, a period of relatively high rates of return,[6] actuaries have used more optimistic assumptions for the long-term rate of return. A period of high investment acquisition has therefore been followed by a sharp increase in the value placed upon scheme investments. The result, in actuarial valuations, is a sharp increase in scheme solvency.

Another economic event which has relevance for scheme solvency is the recession in manufacturing which occurred in the late 1970s and early 1980s.[7] This resulted in unexpectedly high numbers of redundancies and early retirements in some schemes. The benefits of early leavers who take deferred pensions are cheap relative to those who remain in a scheme through to retirement. These unexpected savings can create, or increase, scheme surpluses.

D. CLAIMS TO SURPLUS

Employers claim that surpluses represent overfunding and should be used to reduce contributions or even to provide a refund. The surplus is the result of assumptions and methods adopted during a period when the Stock Exchange was performing badly. If they were prepared to increase their contributions in response to poor investment returns, should they not now benefit from good investment returns? Members view contribution holidays as a devaluation of their deferred pay. If the surplus has been created by assets purchased from part of their pay, it should be used to increase their benefits.[8] Had they known that their employer's contribution would provide a surplus at a future date, and that this surplus would be claimed by the employer, they might not have been prepared to accept that such a high percentage of their payroll should have gone into the pension fund. Pensioners, both existing and deferred, will feel that they have a very strong claim. Unless their pensions are indexed to earnings, they will have financed part of the surplus through a loss in the real value of their pensions. With existing pensioners, this occurs

[5] Some actuaries went so far as to persuade their companies, and the Inland Revenue, of the need for special, large contributions to bring schemes up to acceptable levels of solvency. See, for example, 'BP Gives its Pension Fund £38 Million "Topping up" to Counter Inflation', *The Times*, 4 December 1974—although some of these payments were probably motivated by the desire to defer corporation tax.

[6] The average annual return on pension fund investment during the period 1980–9 was 19.6%, whereas the average annual increase in earnings for this period was 9.4%. See Income Data Services, *Focus 58*, March 1991, p. 13.

[7] Between 1975 and 1985 unemployment rose from 4.8% of the workforce to 13.1% (from 1.29 million to 3.25 million). *Economic Trends*, Dec. 1985, table 39.

[8] 'Pensions are the deferred pay of our members and . . . when a surplus arises that surplus should be used to bring about improvements to the scheme rather than being appropriated for the sole benefit of the employer. Such improvements should be the subject of negotiation between the employer and the trade unions representing the employees.' Motion passed at the 1990 Trades Union Congress, quoted in the Labour Research Department's report on Surpluses (n. 1 above), p. 4.

from the date of their retirement.[9] With deferred pensioners, this occurs from the date of leaving service.[10]

III. SURPLUSES ARISING ON FINAL WINDING UP

A. SURPLUS: FACT, OR ACTUARIAL JUDGMENT?

When a scheme winds up, the trustees must secure the fixed benefits. This may be done by purchasing annuities from insurance companies, by the trustees retaining sufficient assets to pay pensions as they fall due, or by transferring assets to a scheme that undertakes to provide the members' benefits.[11] Where the trustees buy annuities, the amount of surplus can be calculated exactly. Where they secure the benefits by retaining scheme assets or transferring them to another scheme, the existence of a surplus is still a matter of actuarial judgment. Only experience will show whether the retained assets will turn out to be insufficient, more than sufficient, or by some miracle, exactly the right amount, to pay the last pension instalment of the last surviving pensioner.

B. WHY THERE SHOULD BE A SURPLUS ON WINDING UP

Surpluses are likely to occur on final winding up even within a scheme that showed no surplus when valued on an ongoing basis. This is because the benefits which must be secured are usually lower on winding up than they are within a continuing scheme. Within an ongoing scheme, the actuary will value the current entitlements of the membership on the assumption that these entitlements will increase in value as the salaries of the members increase. (The benefits in a defined benefit scheme are fixed by reference to the salary earned by the member. As this salary increases, the accrued entitlement of the member increases in value.) If the scheme is wound up, the members no longer receive benefits increased by reference to their salaries at the date of retirement, but current salaries. Instead of that entitlement being increased every time that the member's salary increases, it will only increase under the indexation requirements of the Social Security Act 1990 (price inflation up to a maximum of 5 per cent p.a.). This is a lesser liability, and a

---

[9] Except for the 5–6% of pensioners who are in private-sector schemes which promise full cost-of-living increases. Occupational Pension Schemes 1987: Eighth Survey by the Government Actuary HMSO (1991), p. 47, table 9.5.

[10] Except in those few schemes which are fully indexed. Ibid., para. 11.4.

[11] Note that a scheme which is contracted out cannot secure GMPs within a scheme that is contracted in. The alternative to keeping the GMPs is to pay the state to undertake these liabilities. The amount which must be paid is known as a transfer rights premium. Social Security and pensions Act 1975, s. 44 (A), Occupational Pension Schemes (Contracting-out) Regulations 1984, SI 1984/380, regs, 18–20.

scheme which had no surplus when valued on an ongoing basis can therefore still show a surplus in final winding up.[12]

C. CLAIMING AGAINST A SURPLUS ON WINDING UP

Since there will be no future contributions, there can be no contribution holiday for the employer or the employees. The choice is whether to augment benefits for the members, refund money to the employer for the benefit of the creditors and shareholders, or treat it as unowned property (*bona vacantia*), and give it to the Treasury.

IV. LEGAL QUESTIONS ARISING IN CONNECTION WITH A SURPLUS

One cannot simply state who 'owns' the surplus, whether that surplus arises on final winding up or within an ongoing scheme. For a start, within an ongoing scheme, a surplus does not represent any particular assets. It is simply an actuarial opinion that the scheme is better funded than a particular method requires. There is nothing to own. In this context one should not speak of owning the surplus, but ask who can expect to benefit from it. On final winding up, where the benefits are secured by the purchase of annuities, one has an identifiable share of assets which the different parties can claim. But even here, it is difficult to speak of the surplus being owned by a particular party, since entitlements will usually depend upon the trustees exercising, or failing to exercise, their power to augment benefits.

The overall question of entitlement to surplus has been broken down into questions as to who, in what situation, can expect to benefit from a surplus, starting with surpluses arising within ongoing schemes, and then looking at those arising on final winding up.

A. SURPLUSES ARISING WITHIN ONGOING SCHEMES

1. Do Employees Have a Right to Benefit from a Surplus through Reduced Contributions?

Where employees contribute to their pension scheme, their contributions take the form of a fixed percentage of their salary. This means that they

[12] This does not always follow. Some actuaries only fund the benefits which will be paid on final winding up: the scheme's minimum legal liabilities. (The current projected unit or discontinuance method—see Chapter 6.) Also, where the winding up involves the realization of scheme assets, and the purchase of annuities for the members, the valuation of the scheme's assets is based on a different basis from that used for an ongoing valuation. The winding-up valuation must be based on market values. The ongoing valuation will have been based on the income and capital gains that the assets were expected to produce. Where the market price is below the actuaries' estimated value, the difference in these figures can be larger than the savings which result from only having to provide benefits fixed by reference to current salaries (indexed up to 5%).

cannot be required to make greater contributions when their scheme is in deficit, and they must continue to contribute even when their scheme is in surplus (regardless of whether their employer is currently making contributions to the scheme). This led Millett J to observe, in *Re Courage Group's Pension Schemes*,[13] that:

Employees have no right to complain if while the fund is in surplus, the employer should require them to continue their contributions while itself contributing nothing. If the employer chooses to reduce or suspend their contributions, it does so ex gratia and in the interests of maintaining good industrial relations.[14]

So far there has not even been a suggestion that employees have the right to be 'considered' for a contribution reduction where a scheme is in surplus, either by the trustees, or by the employer under its duty of good faith.[15] However, one group who do have a right to be 'considered', when an employer decides to reduce employee contributions, are the deferred and existing pensioners. Suspending or reducing employee contributions benefits current members, but does nothing for these other two groups. Unless there are some benefit improvements for pensioners, trustees who agree to an amendment which lowers or terminates the employees' duty to contribute can be accused of unfairly favouring the interests of one group of beneficiaries. For the same reasons, although with less chance of success (since the employer can adduce industrial relations reasons to justify concentrating benefits upon his current workforce), the employer could be accused of a breach of good faith.[16]

2. Do Employees Enjoy a Right to a Refund of Their Contributions?

Employees who leave a contributory fund with less than two years' pensionable service are not required to be given a deferred pension,[17] so their scheme may provide for them to receive a return of their contributions plus interest. Outside of this situation, Revenue rules prohibit the payment of any monies to the employees other than in the form of benefits.[18]

3. Can Employers Benefit from a Surplus through Reduced Contributions?

Because of the balance of cost basis upon which the employer's contribution is calculated, it is very difficult to prevent employers from benefiting from

---

[13] [1987] 1 All ER 528.   [14] Ibid., at 545.

[15] Although many employers have reduced or eliminated employee contributions in order to make their own contribution holiday or refund more acceptable. In 1988, 25% of private schemes reduced or suspended members' contributions. See National Association of Pension Funds Annual Survey 1988, p. 4, para. 2.3.1.   [16] See, generally, Chapter 4.

[17] Social Security Act 1973, section 63, Schedule 16, para. 6(1)(b).

[18] The preservation requirements, ibid., para. 6(5), prohibit the payment of lump sums to short-service employees before normal pension age. The return of a member's contributions, disqualifies that member from the payment of benefits with respect to that period. Practice Notes on Approval of Occupational Pension Schemes, IR 12 (1991), para. 10.45.

surpluses, within ongoing schemes, through reduced contributions.[19] While some schemes' rules require a minimum employer contribution,[20] and thus prevent a complete suspension of employer contributions, this still leaves the employer able, in the long term, to absorb a surplus by making less contributions. Schemes which provide for no minimum employer contribution can absorb surpluses somewhat quicker. Here the actuary can recommend that the employer make no annual contributions, i.e. that it takes a contribution holiday. While there may be some circumstances in which a contribution holiday would amount to a breach of the employer's duty of good faith,[21] this is only likely to occur if the employer announces its unwillingness even to consider using the surplus to fund increased benefits.[22]

4. What Other Rights Does the Employer Have in Consequence of his Right to Take a Contribution Holiday?

Whilst the employer's right to absorb surpluses, in the long term, through contribution reductions or even holidays has been accepted,[23] there has been a lack of consensus as to what other rights might follow from this. In particular, is the employer to be given a similar right to benefit from surpluses in the short term, through refunds fron an ongoing scheme, by splitting up schemes and controlling transfer payments, or by seeking a refund when a scheme is finally wound up?[24]

5. The Employer's Right to a Refund from an Ongoing Scheme

The Need for Amendments Since 1986, the Revenue have allowed new schemes to contain a clause which allows for refunds to the employer provided these are approved by the Revenue.[25] Older schemes are unlikely to provide for refunds except on winding up, and pre-1971 schemes are likely to

---

[19] The Labour Research Department surveyed 77 schemes and found that 81% had reduced their contributions in 1990. See n. 1 above, p. 12. In 1989, the National Association of Pension Funds found that 45% of schemes had reduced contributions. See National Association of Pension Funds 1989, Annual Survey, p. 6, para. 2.3.1.

[20] For example, that the employer's contribution must at least equal the annual contributions of the members.

[21] Staughton LJ in *Stannard* v. *Fisons Pension Trust Ltd*. [1992] IRLR 27 at pp. 32 suggested that a reduction in the employer's contribution rate might, in some circumstances, be a breach of this duty.   [22] See, generally, Chapter 4.

[23] Though there have been cases in which the trustees have been found to hold a power to increase benefits without the employer's consent and thus frustrate the employer's ability to absorb a surplus through a contribution holiday. See *Aitken* v. *Christy Hunt PLC* [1991] PLR 1, discussed on p. 157.

[24] In one of the first decisions to consider this question, *Re Imperial Foods Pension Scheme* [1986] 1 WLR 717, the employer's right to benefit from surpluses in the long term was used to justify allowing it to benefit immediately. Had this approach been followed in subsequent cases, then pension schemes would have come to resemble mortgages, with the employer, like some kind of mortgagor, having an absolute right to claim any monies deemed by the actuary to be surplus to current liabilities.

[25] The Inland Revenue's Superannuation Office approved 44 refunds in 1987–8, 47 in 1988–9 and 55 in 1989–90. See Labour Research Department's report, (n. 1 above), p. 13.

prohibit refunds even then. The upshot of this is that procuring a refund to an employer from an ongoing scheme will ordinarily require amendment to the scheme.

The Power of Amendment   The ability to amend a scheme in order to provide for a refund was considered by Millett J in *Re Courage Group's Pension Schemes*.[26] In this decision, Millett J came to a number of important conclusions: that scheme trustees must act on behalf of the members to protect their interests; that the purpose of a pension scheme was to benefit the past and present employees of businesses covered by the pension scheme, and the powers contained within the scheme should not be exercised in such a manner as to defeat these purposes; and that members had a right to maintain a relationship with the employer who had employed them.

Courage arose out of a take-over. The Courage group of companies had been purchased by Hanson Trust PLC ('Hansons'), which had subsequently sold them to Elders IXL Ltd. ('Elders'). The Courage pension schemes were substantially in surplus, and Hansons wished to retain the surpluses (totalling £80 million) for their own benefit. The pension schemes had been closed to new members shortly before the take-over by Hansons, so as to retain the surpluses for the benefit of current members. In the sale agreement with Hansons, Elders undertook to procure the execution of deeds substituting Hansons as the principal employer under the rules of the Courage pension schemes. Hansons wished to reopen the Courage schemes and, as principal employer, to admit its own employees as members. It could then use the surpluses to fund the pensions of Hanson employees instead of Courage employees. Courage employees were to have the choice of transferring into new schemes set up by Elders, or remaining with the Courage pension schemes as deferred pensioners.

The trustees of the Courage schemes refused to execute the proposed amendments. The amendments would leave Courage pensioners (actual and deferred) in schemes which were operated by Hansons. Their right to discretionary benefit increases would then be determined by Hansons, a company with which the pensioners enjoyed little or no employment relationship. The trustees were also concerned that Courage employees were to be separated from their fund and transferred to a scheme which had only a small surplus (£10 million).

The arguments of the employer in *Courage* were based upon the reasoning adopted by Walton J in *Re Imperial Foods Ltd.'s Pension Scheme*.[27] *Imperial Foods* concerned the transfer payments made on behalf of employees of a subsidiary. Walton J decided that the transfer payment need have no regard to the scheme's surplus. Walton J based the members' rights to share in the surplus in a transfer on the amount which they had a right to demand, if the

---

[26] Note 13 above.   [27] Note 24 above.

scheme continued, in future. Since the members had no such future right, given the employer's ability to absorb all of the surplus through contribution holidays, he concluded that they had no present right to the surplus either.[28]

The reasoning used by Walton J in *Re Imperial Foods* would seem to indicate that the trustees had no reason to object to the proposed amendments in *Courage*. If the fairness of the pensioners' treatment were to be decided by asking what, in a continuing scheme, they had a legal right to receive, then the answer would be: only their current level of benefits secured to the weakest actuarial standard. At the time of the proposed amendment, the employees were to have their fixed benefits fully secured, and the pensioners were to have their benefits secured by an amount which included all but £10 million of the surplus.

The employer's arguments in *Courage* went beyond those advanced by Walton J in *Imperial*. It asked Millett J to assess the rights of the members not only by what an employer could do, over time, under the scheme's funding provisions, but to take account of what could be achieved by a determined employer using commercial powers which lay outside the scheme. It was open to an employer to separate the current membership from its pension scheme by transferring businesses between companies. The company which was currently named as the principal company could be reduced to a shell with a few employees. This shell and the surplus could then have been retained by Hansons whilst the group's business was sold to Elders. Since the purpose of Hansons' proposals could be achieved by this roundabout route, what if anything, was wrong with using the power of amendment to secure the same objective?

Millett J accepted that the members could not, in the long term, be sure to benefit from the surplus.[29] But he avoided the *non sequitur* that underlay Walton J's reasoning and the employer's arguments. Just because a party has rights which mean that, in all probability, it will be the only party which benefits from an asset, this does not mean that its rights over that asset should be increased. Conversely, the fact that a party is in a relatively weak legal position does not mean that its rights should be further reduced. Millett J was not prepared to interpret the members' current right to protection from a pension scheme on the basis of what could, in future, be perpetrated upon them by a determined employer. The fact that members could not be

---

[28] As the remaining members had no legal right to benefit from the surplus, he concluded that the transferring members should be similarly disadvantaged. On this basis he expressed disapproval of the share of the fund method of dividing the fund. Walton J also sought to justify his approach by pointing out that the surplus was the result of payments by the parent company, either directly, or through its subsidiaries, and therefore the parent company had the best claim on the surplus. However, he referred to these latter arguments as 'economic' ones, presumably to differentiate them from 'legal' ones.

[29] He went so far as to deny that any part of his judgment was based on the assumption that the proposal in question would 'deprive the employees of an accrued legal entitlement'. N. 13 above, p. 545.

guaranteed to enjoy the surplus in the long term did not mean that they could not enjoy rights which increased the *possibility* that they might benefit from it[30] and, conversely, just because a determined employer could gain full control of the surplus did not mean that the members should have no rights which might restrict or impede an employer's access to the surplus.[31]

The Purpose of a Power of Amendment   Millett J decided that the members had rights other than their entitlements to fixed benefits. In particular, they had a right to have the trustees act on their behalf to protect their interests, and they had a right to maintain a relationship with the employer who had employed them. More generally, the purpose of a pension scheme was to benefit the past and present employees of the business covered by the pension scheme, and the powers contained within the scheme should not be exercised in such a manner as to defeat these purposes.

The purpose of a power of amendment, with respect to the substitution of a new principal employer, was to allow a group of companies to be reorganized, and the original company wound up, without winding up the group's pension scheme. It could not be said that the scheme existed for the purpose of the parent company, since its purpose could survive that company. Nor could it be said that the scheme existed for the purposes of that company and its subsidiaries, since again, with the demise of the parent company, the rest of the group would no longer be its subsidiaries. Millett J had to look for a definition of the purposes of the scheme, which linked it with the group, but did not rely on the continued existence of the parent company.

Millett J defined the purposes of the scheme by reference to the group as a 'commercial undertaking'. By this he meant the business which the group undertakes, as defined by the employees who carry out that business. If the business of the group is transferred from one company to another, as part of a corporate reconstruction, it might be proper to alter the identity of the principal employer under the scheme rules, so as to allow the pension scheme to continue to operate for the benefit of the employees who carried out the group's business. But where, as here, the aim of the amendment is to separate the pension scheme surplus from the undertaking, it is *ultra vires*.[32]

This rule might seem to invalidate all attempts to introduce amendments

---

[30] Through benefit increases or as a consequence of increased security for their current benefits.

[31] This acceptance of the need to protect the *possibility* that members may benefit underlies the approach taken by the Court of Appeal in *Stannard* v. *Fisons Pension Trust Ltd* (n. 21 above).

[32] It is not clear how far one may extend the reasoning in *Courage*. Is it equally applicable, for example, to transfer payments? Where all of the employees and pensioners in one pension scheme are transferred into a new pension scheme, are the trustees bound to make a transfer payment of the whole of the fund? If the correct position is that powers should not be exercised so as to separate a scheme's membership from its fund, then such a situation dictates that the whole of the fund should be transferred.

allowing employers to take refunds. After all, what is a refund but the separation of members from all or some part of their scheme's surplus? But Millett J was not prepared to go this far. Whilst memberships should not be separated from a surplus by the manipulation of the identity of the principal employer, this did not mean that all amendments which allowed employers to extract a surplus were invalid. For Millett J, the distinction was between those extractions which were the result of unilateral actions by a hostile 'raider', and those which were the consequence of negotiation between the trustees and the employer.

The Duty to Negotiate Benefit Increases before Using a Power of Amendment
At the end of his judgment, Millett J looked at the rights of the members in the event that the employer should seek to introduce a provision allowing a refund of surplus. (One of the Courage schemes allowed no refunds, the other two allowed them only on final winding up.) Millett J felt that an amendment to allow refunds was an increase in the rights of the employer over the pension fund, which should not be agreed to by the trustees unless the members received something in return:

Repayment will, however, still normally require amendment to the scheme and thus co-operation between the employer and the trustees or committee of management. Where the employer seeks repayment, the trustees or committee can be expected to press for generous treatment of the employees and pensioners, and the employer to be influenced by a desire to maintain good industrial relations with its workforce.[33]

Millett J saw trustees as persons who might be expected to advance and protect the members' interests against demands made by the employer. This view of the trustees' role underlies the trustee's duty to negotiate benefit increases before agreeing to refunds, and it also influenced Millett J's interpretation of the precise words used in the power of amendment. The power stated that when the employer proposed amendments, the trustees 'shall concur'. The employer argued that this rule meant that the trustees were bound to concur in whatever amendments the employer desired. Millett J felt that this was an improbable interpretation. Unless the trustees had an independent discretion, the interests of the members could not be protected:

[T]he interests of the employed members, pensioners and deferred pensioners do not necessarily coincide with those of the company. They cannot be effectively protected at all if the all-important power to amend the trust deeds and rules is left to the company's sole discretion.[34]

The members were entitled to an interpretation of the scheme which enabled the trustees to protect their interests.

[33] Note 13 above, at 545.   [34] Ibid., at 536.

Millett's judgment clearly envisages that an amendment introducing a refund can come within the purposes of the power of amendment, so this judgment, although an improvement on *Re Imperial*, is actually a defeat for those persons who wish to see employers' contributions treated as the inalienable pay of the members. What the members are offered instead, is a refusal to interpret powers of amendment to give employers a unilateral right to introduce provisions which are contrary to the members' interests, and a right to expect trustees to negotiate before agreeing to any provision which increases an employer's access to the pension fund. As such, in the circumstances of many pension schemes, it does not offer substantial protections. Trustees who are themselves directors or senior managers of the employer are required to negotiate with themselves or at best, with their peers. As noted in Chapter 3, there has not yet been judicial recognition of the conflicts of interest inherent in this position.

The Ability to Separate the Workforce from its Scheme's Surplus Where companies have offered substantial benefit increases as a means of securing an amendment allowing refunds, this is more likely to be the result of industrial relations pressures than through the demands of scheme trustees. But this may not run contrary to what Millett J foresaw and intended. The *Courage* judgment is mostly an attempt to prevent employers from circumventing the industrial relations pressures which might force them to exercise pension scheme powers in a manner which is sympathetic to the interests of the members. This underlies Millett J's unwillingness to see the pensioners separated from an employer who might be made to feel responsible for them, or the employees separated from a fund upon which they might make demands:

While [the members] have no legal right to participate in the surpluses, they are entitled to have them dealt with by consultation and negotiation between their employers with a continuing responsibility towards them and the [trustees] with a discretion to exercise on their behalf, and not to be irrevocably parted from these surpluses by the unilateral decision of a take-over raider with only a transitory interest in the share capital of the companies which employ them.[35]

He felt that the relationship between the company as employer, and the members of the pension scheme as its past and present employees, was 'an essential feature of a pension scheme'.[36]

Where Scheme Rules Prohibit Refunds—The OPB's Power to Modify Schemes As mentioned before, pre-1971 schemes are likely to contain no provision for a refund to the employer, even on winding up, and to prohibit

---

[35] Note 13 above, at 546.　　　[36] Ibid., at 545.

amendments which would allow such refunds.[37] In these circumstances, the trustees will be unable to consent to the introduction of an amendment allowing refunds, even when they consider that it would be in their members' interests for such refunds to occur. In such circumstances, the trustees may consider securing an amendment through an application to the Occupational Pensions Board.

The OBP have power, under section 64A of the Social Security Act 1973[38] to make modification orders to introduce a power to make a refund where the power of amendment would not permit this, or where it would involve delay or difficulty. In view of the costs of obtaining rulings on the full scope of a power of amendment, the OPB will have jurisdiction in almost all cases. The procedure for obtaining a right to refunds is set out in the Occupational Pension Schemes (Modification) Regulations 1990.[39] The refund must only extend to assets that cause the scheme partial loss of approval under Schedule 22 of the Income and Taxes Act 1988. The OPB have to be satisfied that the modification order is reasonable, and the trustees of the scheme have to be satisfied that the amendment is in the interests of the beneficiaries of the scheme.[40]

The wording of the section and the relevant regulations envisage a process whereby the employer offers increased benefit to the members in exchange for the right to take a refund and, when the trustees are satisfied with the increases offered, an application is made to the OPB to introduce a right to refund which overrides the provisions of the scheme and the general law of trusts. It remains to be seen whether the OPB will exercise independent judgment in these matters and refuse orders where benefits to members are considered too low.[41] They have no power to bypass the trustees where the benefit increases demanded are too high.

What is the Maximum Refund an Employer May Receive from an Ongoing Scheme?   The OPB have no power to authorize a refund which brings the level of solvency below that which leads to a partial loss of approval, i.e. 105 per cent of liabilities. Where a scheme is being wound up and replaced, a

---

[37] Part of the *Courage* judgment indicates that such schemes could be amended by a two-stage process: one amendment removing the prohibition on the introduction of refund provisions, and another introducing the right to take refunds. Millett J suggests that the validity of any amendment needs to be considered only by reference to rules of the scheme at the time of amendment. However, removing the restriction with the intention of making an otherwise invalid future amendment is likely to be deemed a fraud on the power of amendment.

[38] As amended by the Social Security Act 1986, Schedule 10, para. 3.

[39] SI 1990/2021.   [40] Ibid., reg. 3.

[41] The ability of the OPB, or trustees, to make demands for benefit improvements is somewhat undermined by the decision in *Davis* v. *Richards & Wallington Industries* [1991] 2 All ER 563, in which Scott J held that any surplus arising on the winding up of a pension scheme which forbids refunds to an employer could nevertheless go to the employer via the doctrine of resulting trust. Against this background, any benefit improvement may seem preferable to winding up, since that may result in a much larger surplus going to the employer.

refund can be obtained by transferring less than the full value of the wound-up fund into the replacement scheme. Here the maximum refund is determined by the Inland Revenue. At present, they will not give approved status to the replacement scheme if the amount of the refund brings the replacement scheme's solvency below 105 per cent.[42] If the scheme's rules allow ongoing refunds, the Inland Revenue insist on the 105 per cent standard being maintained if the scheme is to continue to enjoy approved status.[43] Taking a refund increases a scheme's liabilities, which in turn increases the amount of assets required to secure them to 105 per cent. (The increase in benefits which results from a refund is dealt with in the next section.)

6. What Rights Have Members to Receive Benefit Increases When a Scheme Has a Surplus?

Mandatory Benefit Increases   At present, scheme members are guaranteed benefit increases only in one circumstance: where the employer takes a refund. Under the Social Security Act 1990, s. 11(3), schemes cannot make a refund to an employer unless their rules provide for the indexation of pensions in payment by up to 5 per cent. Where the rules make no such provision, the refund is conditional upon its introduction through amendment. The amount which may be refunded is reduced by the need to ensure that this indexing provision is adequately secured.[44]

Discretionary Benefit Increases   The members' rights to benefit increases over and above those contained in s. 11(3) depend on who has power, under the scheme, to increase benefits or to introduce amendments which have this effect. If the power to increase benefits is held by the employer alone, or is held by the trustees but subject to a power of veto by the employer, then that power or veto must be exercised in good faith. The courts are unlikely to treat an employer's desire to control its pension costs as a breach of that duty. They certainly will not require an employer to grant pension increases which will increase the employer's immediate funding burden. Nor are they likely to require increases which will increase the employer's funding burden in the future, by terminating a contribution holiday more quickly than might otherwise be the case.

---

[42] IR 12, n. 18 above, paras. 13.20, 13.28.   [43] Ibid.

[44] See e.g. *Thrells Ltd. (1974) Pension Scheme (In Liquidation)* v. *Peter Lomas* [1992] PLR. 1P. Similar rights to those contained in s. 11(3) are found in s. 11(1), Schedule 2, para. 3. This provision provides for the indexation of pensions in payment up to 5% p.a., whenever, and to the extent, that a scheme's valuation reveals a surplus which can be used to fund such levels of indexation. In effect, the provision gives increases of this type first call on any scheme surplus. The provision applies in all scheme valuations (not simply those occurring on winding up, and it is not limited to the periodic valuations required under the disclosure provisions). But the provision will not take effect until the appointed day, which, as at 7 December 1992, had yet to be announced.

The members' strongest case for a right to pension increases arises when their scheme is closed to new members and so well funded that the scheme's actuary concludes that future contributions from the employer will never be required. In these circumstances, the members can argue that refusal to increase benefits is the consequence not of a desire to control future funding burdens, but of one to obtain, either now or in the future, the benefit of a refund. Aside from the question of whether a desire to obtain a refund is, of itself, a breach of the duty of good faith, this argument only works if judges accept that contributions will never be required in future. Whilst judges may not understand the intricacies of actuarial judgments, they can be expected to understand that the same factors which have created surpluses can make them disappear: a gap between an actuary's reasonable estimate of what is likely to occur on the stock market and what actually occurs.[45] In the face of such awareness it is difficult to sustain the argument that benefit increases can *never* give rise to an increased future funding burden.

This is not to say that the power to increase benefits can never be independent from the employer, as is shown by *Aitken* v. *Christy Hunt PLC*.[46] Here an employer tried to convince the court that in a scheme where the employer paid the balance of cost, the trustees could not be given an independent discretion to increase benefits. In that case, the trustees had a power to amend the scheme which they could exercise 'in such manner as they shall in their absolute and uncontrolled discretion think fit . . .'. The scheme had a substantial surplus. The power to augment benefits was subject to the employer's consent. Following the take-over of the employing company, the trustees proposed to use the power of amendment to delete the need for the employer to consent to benefit increases. The employer argued that the consent required under the power to augment benefits was entrenched, and could not be deleted by the power of amendment.

The company says that if this is not so, then the consequence is the extraordinary one that . . . trustees who may have no connection with the company can unilaterally increase the burden of the pension scheme so far as the company is concerned, because the trustees can increase pensions . . . and, in effect the trustees have, if they are right, the benefit of something equivalent to a blank cheque in favour of the Fund.[47]

The employer asked Ferris J to imply a restriction on the power of amendment preventing the trustees from deleting the need for their consent. They argued that the requirement for their consent for benefit increases

---

[45] 'An actuarial surplus is *not* a real surplus. The same imponderables that falsified the original forecast as to the necessary funding which produced the present "surplus" are equally capable of falsifying the forecasts on the basis of which that "surplus" is calculated.' Browne-Wilkinson LJ, 'Equity and its Relevance to Superannuation Today', paper given at an Australian conference on Superannuation, 1992.

[46] Note 23 above. [47] Ibid., p. 5.

would be 'pointless' if this restriction were not read into the power of amendment.

Ferris J refused to read in the restriction requested. He did not think that it was necessary in order to give business efficacy to the pension scheme, nor did he think that, without it, the requirement for consent was pointless. As far as he was concerned, the company's argument was destroyed by the presence of a clause giving it the right to discontinue contributing to the pension scheme. This removed the blank cheque. He expected the trustees to act responsibly in making amendments, including one to remove the need for the employer to consent to benefit increases, since the employer could retaliate by ceasing to contribute. This gave some substance to the requirement for consent. The balance of power in the scheme, whereby amendments could lead to the termination of the employer's contributions, was a workable one. He was fortified in reaching this finding by the knowledge that the requirement for the employer to consent to benefit increases had only been introduced in 1981. Before that, the power to increase benefits, like the power to make amendments, had contained no requirement for the employer's consent.

If *Aitken* confirms that the courts will accept that trustees can have power over funding, then *Imperial Group Pension Trust Ltd.* v. *Imperial Tobacco Ltd.*[48] suggests that such powers will not be readily implied into a trust scheme. In *Imperial Tobacco*, the Vice-Chancellor Browne-Wilkinson was asked to decide whether the trustees had power to increase the scheme benefits without the employer's consent. The court was asked to construe a rule which provided that the pensioners should have their benefits increased annually by 'at least' the lesser of 5 per cent or price inflation. The members argued that this clause created a discretion for the Imperial scheme's trustees to award benefit increases greater than 5 per cent without the consent of the employer. The members argued that such a power would not represent an unduly heavy burden for the employer, even though the employer was under a duty to fund such increases. The trustees would exercise the power responsibly and, if the employer felt the burden of increased benefits was too great, it could exercise a power to reduce its contributions to 7 per cent or terminate them altogether. The provision to be interpreted was introduced just before Hansons made their take-over bid. It could therefore be interpreted as a poison pill: a device designed to make the pension scheme less attractive to the company seeking a take-over.

Browne-Wilkinson VC was not convinced. He found it extremely improbable that a management would wish to give trustees an independent power to increase benefits. As far as he was concerned, the protection which the employer enjoyed by reason of its power to cease contributing to the scheme was not sufficient:

[48] (Ch. D) [1991] 2 All ER 597; [1991] 1 WLR 589.

True it is that . . . the Company's liability to pay the balance of cost is limited to an amount not exceeding 7% of the pensionable pay of contributing members and the Company has power to terminate its liability to pay contributions. But the 7% limit is itself a large figure and the total termination of the scheme a fundamental step.[49]

Even in the context of a take-over, the Vice-Chancellor was not inclined to interpret the provision as an independent power. An independent power of this kind would have been far too drastic a deterrent. To use his own words, 'a poison pill can cause serious illness without being lethal.'

7. Summary

Whilst in *Imperial Foods* Walton J saw a surplus as essentially a matter for the funding company (and within a group scheme, a matter solely for the parent company), other judges have taken a less pro-employer view of the members' entitlements. Millett J was not prepared to see employers increasing their right to benefit from surpluses without some quid pro quo in the form of benefit increases. He wished to see the issue of surpluses dealt with by negotiations, and was not prepared to allow scheme powers to be exercised in such a way as to circumvent the possibility of effective negotiation. Browne-Wilkinson VC, in *Imperial Tobacco*, was not willing to give the trustees an independent power to increase benefits, and seemed to accept the legitimacy of the employer's right to protect itself against even the possibility that its pension costs might be increased. He totally accepted that employer's right to enjoy what might turn out to be a permanent contribution holiday.[50] Ferris J was less hostile to the idea of trustees having powers which reduced the employer's ability to enjoy a contribution holiday.

B. FINAL WINDING UP

1. The Employer's (or its Creditors') Right to a Refund on Final Winding Up

What is the Maximum That May be Refunded?   Refunds on final winding up are not affected by the Inland Revenue's requirement to maintain solvency at 105 per cent of liabilities. Instead, the winding-up clause determines the amount that may be refunded. This clause will usually require the purchase of annuities which duplicate the pensions, deferred and in payment, to which each of the members and their dependants are entitled. Before a refund can be paid, those benefits must be increased in accordance with the Social Security Act 1990, s. 11(3). Any amount in excess of this level will, if the trustees fail to increase benefits, be returned to the employer.

What Arguments Justify a Refund?   Employers (or their creditors) are likely to seek refunds from their pension schemes when they are wound up. From

---

[49] [1991] 2 All ER 597 at 604; [1991] 1 WLR 589 at 596.

[50] But, as we saw in Chapter 4, he would not regard an employer's attempt to increase its rights over the surplus with the same tolerance. Like Millett J, he would restrain the employer's ability to increase unilaterally its right to enjoy surplus assets.

the employees' point of view, refunds in this situation are even more threatening to their welfare in retirement than refunds from ongoing schemes. Where there is to be no replacement scheme, any refund represents a once-and-for-all loss to the fund, since there will be no future employer contributions, and little chance of future discretionary increases to their benefits. Where the winding up is due to the employer's insolvency, the position of the current members is particularly acute. They will have lost their jobs, and their benefits will now be based on their current salaries and can be expected to be eroded by inflation.

The employer's right to a refund is justified here, as with ongoing schemes, by reference to the balance of cost basis of funding. The employer will argue first that, had the scheme continued, it could have benefited from surplus assets through reduced contributions, and that it should not be deprived of this benefit just because the scheme has been wound up early. Another argument is that because the contributions were intended only to fund the members' benefits, and not to allow increases in those benefits, any surplus should be treated as a mistaken overpayment, and returned to the employer.

These arguments oversimplify the balance of cost basis of funding. The benefits funded by contributions often include expected discretionary increases, and it cannot therefore be considered a mistake when there are more funds than are required to secure fixed benefit. The benefits funded on an ongoing basis are usually based on projected future salaries, rather than the current salaries used on winding up, so again, if there is a surplus, this is not necessarily any indication of mistake.

Does the Employer Have a Right to a Refund Where the Scheme Rules Prohibit Refunds to the Employer on Winding Up?   Pre-1971 schemes are likely to prohibit refunds to the employer under any circumstances. As we saw in Chapter 3, such provisions had, prior to *Davis* v. *Richards & Wallington Industries*,[51] resulted in any funds not used to increase benefits being handed over to the Treasury under the doctrine of *bona vacantia* (unowned property). *Davis* indicated that ordinarily, the presence of an express prohibition on refunds to the employer in the scheme rules would not prevent the employer enjoying such a refund under the doctrine of resulting trust.

Davis not only reversed earlier decisions which indicated that resulting trusts should not apply in these situations, but applied a novel and, from the employer's point of view favourable, version of the resulting trust in these circumstances.

Where money is held by trustees, and the beneficial interests fail to exhaust that money, the balance is normally held for the settlor on resulting trust. Where more than one person has contributed to the trust, the balance is held for each contributor in proportion to their respective total contribution. In

---

[51] Note 41 above.

Davis the fund had come from three sources. There had been employer and employee contributions, and transfer payments from other pension schemes.[52] Scott J felt that the employer had a particularly strong claim to a resulting trust of the surplus, likening the employer's contribution to an accidental overpayment into an account.[53] By contrast, he felt that the employees and the transferring pension schemes had received exactly what they expected in exchange for their contributions: the members' fixed benefits. Thus, either they could not participate in the resulting trust or, at best, they should participate only once the employer had received a refund of all its past contributions. Only where the surplus would still have arisen without the employer's contributions, could there be a resulting trust for the employees. Thus, in a scheme where the employees do not make contributions from their pay packet, there is no possibility of a resulting trust in their favour.[54]

While *Davis* purports to decide what should happen in an inadvertent winding up, one should not conclude that a court will take the same approach in a case in which the winding up is part of a deliberate attempt to extract surplus assets from a scheme which prohibits refunds. As stressed in Chapter 3, the process of construction does not require a court to give an identical construction even to identical words, where the general circumstances are perceived to be different.

Do Employers Have a Right to a Refund on Winding Up Where the Trustees Have a Power to Increase Benefits?   The presence of a power to increase benefits on winding up indicates that the holders of that power have a discretion whether to increase benefits or not. As such, the presence of such a power is incompatible with a duty to augment, or a duty to act in the members' best interests,[55] or a duty to allow all of the surplus to return to the employer (whether by way of a resulting trust or an express provision for refunds). In place of such duties, the courts have accepted that such powers carry with them a duty to consider the interests of the members, and not to exercise the power when suffering from an acute conflict of interest. We shall look at these in turn.

---

[52] Transfer payments would have occurred when members gave up benefits in their old schemes in exchange for benefits in the Richards & Wallington fund.

[53] 'The actuarial calculations were, I am sure, impeccable. But the [winding up] having invalidated some of the assumptions underlying the calculations, the case is, in my opinion, strongly analogous to that of an account drawn up under a mistake. In my opinion, equity should treat the employer as entitled to claim the surplus, or so much of it as is derived from overpayment.' N. 41 at 594.

[54] Scott's analysis of the resulting trust is impossible to reconcile with the idea that pensions are a form of pay. If you accept that the *only* contribution which employees make towards the cost of their pension arrangements is their money contribution, you are treating the employer's contribution as a gratuity. See R. Nobles, case comment on *Davis* v. *Richards & Wallington*, 19 ILJ (1990) 204 at 206.   [55] See Chapter 3, p. 79.

2. The Power to Augment Benefits and the Trustees' Duty to Consider the Interests of the Members

The Scope of the Duty to Consider the Members' Interests   The duty to consider the interests of the members when exercising a power to augment benefits on winding up (or any other power in the scheme) does not represent a startling development in the law of trusts. Powers are put into trusts to be considered, not ignored, and the parties whose interests are to be considered when deciding to exercise them are usually the beneficiaries. Thus the announcement, in *Mettoy Pension Trustees Limited* v. *Evans*[56] and *Thrells Ltd. (1974) Pension Scheme (In Liquidation)* v. *Lomas*[57] that members can reasonably expect their interests to be taken into account when considering whether or how to exercise such a power does not necessarily offer members any greater right than they would receive under the general law of trusts as beneficiaries of a modern discretionary trust. Indeed, as *Icarus (Hertford) Limited* v. *Driscoll*[58] showed, a right to be considered can be reduced to a mere formality.

In *Threll*, the Vice-Chancellor Sir Donald Nicholls placed two restrictions on this duty to consider the members' interests. First, the fact that a surplus arising on winding up might be attributable to the overpayment by the employer was not, by itself, a sufficient reason to refuse to exercise the power and thereby to allow the surplus to return to the employer. Second, the power had to be exercised in a manner which was fair and equitable in all the circumstances. Underlying these restrictions is a judicial preference for balance between the perspectives set out in Chapter 2. Surpluses should not automatically go to the employer because it has paid on the basis of balance of cost, nor should they all go to the members as their deferred pay. But as the VC's own decision illustrates, this 'balance' may leave members with little more than their statutory rights, and represent a much closer approximation to the employer's claims for a full return of surplus than the employees' claim that pension funds should be used for their sole benefit.

Threll is the first reported case in which a court has exercised the power to increase pension benefits on final winding up. The scheme in question had a surplus of £505,000 after securing the scheme's fixed benefits on winding up, but this surplus fell to only £345,000 if the benefits were increased under s. 11(3) of the Social Security Act 1990, which makes indexation of pensions in payment up to 5 per cent p.a. a precondition of any refund to the employer. What was the members' entitlement to benefit increases in excess of this statutory precondition to a refund?

The Vice-Chancellor's understanding of what was 'fair' affected both his interpretation of the power to augment benefits, and his view of how that power should be exercised. The power came at the end of the list of benefits

---

[56] [1991] 2 All ER 513; [1990] 1 WLR 1587.   [57] Note 44 above.
[58] 4 December 1989. [1990] 1 PLR 1, discussed in Chapter 2, p. 41.

to be secured, immediately before the provision for the return of any residual surplus to the employer. Unfortunately for the current pensioners, the power was not separated from the clause dealing with the last class of benefits to be secured: deferred pensions.

Sixth in securing . . . pensions . . . for prospective pensioners . . . provided that the pension . . . may be increased if the value of the policies will permit and the trustees so decide.[59]

The Vice-Chancellor accepted that the words beginning with 'provided that' could, with the addition of a paragraph break and a capital letter 'p', be read as a general power to increase the benefits listed in all the preceding paragraphs, and not simply those described in this clause. He accepted that such omissions could be the result of typographical errors. But he could see 'no sufficient justification for ignoring [the] textual arrangement'. To put this another way, the consequences of restricting the power in this way were not so unreasonable as to convince him to treat it as a typographical error. Indeed, the Vice-Chancellor could find a quite reasonable explanation for the power being limited in this way. Its purpose was, he concluded, to:

enable the trustee . . . to increase prospective pensioners' pensions to compensate for the fact that early leavers' pensions are geared to the amount of salaries at the date which is earlier . . . than the date on which the pensions will actually be paid [and will thus be] subject to erosion by inflation.[60]

Having found a reasonable explanation for the presence of a power capable of benefiting only the deferred pensioners, the VC went on to consider how it should be exercised. As the scheme had wound up in 1984, its deferred pensioners were not protected by the protections given to early leavers in the Social Security Acts 1985 and 1991, or the Health and Social Security Act 1984. The 1985 and 1991 Acts had given early leavers the right to have deferred pensions increased up to the date of retirement by reference to price inflation up to a maximum of 5 per cent p.a.[61] The VC awarded the deferred pensioners this same level of protection through the exercise of the power to increase benefits.

The Health and Social Security Act 1984[62] outlaws 'franking'. This refers to a practice whereby contracted-out schemes sought to meet their liability to fully index GMPs up to retirement by reducing the amount paid to members in excess of the GMP. The scheme would increase the GMP, but leave the total amount of the deferred pension unchanged, so it was actually the member who met the cost of this requirement. The 1984 Act required that increases in the GMP should not result in a reduction in the balance of the

---

[59] Note 44 above at 4P. [60] Ibid., at 9P.

[61] Social Security Act 1985, s. 2, Schedule 1, para. 3; Social Security Act 1990, Schedule 4, para 4.

[62] Schedule 6, Social Security and Pensions Act 1975, s. 41 A–E. See also Contracted-out (Protection of Pensions) Regulations 1991 (SI 1991 No. 166).

pension. Thus, without franking, it was the scheme, and not the member, who had to meet the cost of increasing the GMP.

The cost of giving the deferred pensioners a right to indexed benefits up to 5 per cent of RPI was £154,000, but this fell to only £10,000 if the scheme was able to offset this liability against the duty to fully index GMPs ('franking'). Again, the VC decided to exercise the power to augment benefits in order to give the deferred pensioners the benefit of current levels of social security protection. Deferred pensions in excess of the GMP were to be indexed by the RPI up to a maximum of 5 per cent. The GMP itself was to be separately indexed. The cost of these protections was £154,000, leaving a balance of £200,000.

The VC had claimed that the purpose of this power was to compensate deferred pensioners for the devaluation of their pensions through pre-retirement inflation. One might therefore have expected him to use the balance of £200,000 to fully index deferred pensioners by earnings inflation, or at least as close to this level as the scheme could afford. Earnings inflation would, if the scheme had continued, have increased the value of the members' accrued benefits up to their retirement. By indexing deferred pensions to earnings inflation, the VC would simply be protecting members from the loss of expectations caused by the winding up.[63]

Instead, the VC held that the balance of £200,000 should go to the employer's unsecured creditors, who were owed some £2.4 million. In reaching this conclusion, the VC saw no need to take any evidence as to the financial situation of any particular pensioner or creditor.

Implicit in this judgment is the VC's view that current levels of social security protection provided an adequate standard for what the members could reasonably expect, and that any excess over this should, where a company has large debts, be returned to the creditors. However, this does not mean that all judges must adopt this same standard in future cases. What is just and equitable in this case need not be so in another, given 'all the circumstances'. In particular, one must remember that if this case involved a post-1991 winding up there would be no question of using the power to bring the members up to these levels of benefit: they would already enjoy these benefits under the Social Security Acts. Insisting that the members could only enjoy the benefits given in *Threll* would be tantamount to abandoning the power and giving the employer an automatic right to a maximum refund. On the other hand, the VC's sympathy for the employer's creditors, and his willingness to sacrifice the expectations of the deferred pensioners in order to relieve their assumed distress, indicates that members cannot be sure of receiving much more than their statutory rights if trustees sacrifice their discretion to the court.

---

[63] Those who expected salary increases above the level of inflation due to, for example, promotion, would still have suffered a loss in the expected value of their accrued benefits.

Who Must Consider the Members' Interests?   Where a final winding up has been brought about by the employer's insolvency, the Social Security Act 1990[64] provides that the trustees' discretions should be exercised by an independent trustee. Where there is no such trustee, the insolvency practitioner (a liquidator, receiver, or administrator) is required to appoint one. An independent trustee is defined negatively to exclude the liquidator, receiver, administrator, employer (and all their associates and persons connected with them) and the beneficiaries of the scheme. Where the employer is also the sole trustee, the independent trustee replaces the employer as trustee of the scheme. The independent trustee will also exercise any power held by the employer which is fiduciary in nature, even when the employer is not a trustee.[65]

The requirement for an independent trustee does not resolve who is entitled to benefit from a surplus arising on winding up; it simply attempts to allocate that decision to a person whose judgment is not biased by self-interest. Since the independent trustee is appointed by the insolvency practitioner, there must be some danger that the expected degree of independence will not be achieved, since insolvency practitioners are free to appoint persons who can be expected to take a pro-creditor approach, such as other insolvency practitioners.

Whilst the Act provides that the fiduciary powers of employers will be exercised by the independent trustee, it does not identify which powers will be considered fiduciary in nature. This is important because the scheme may provide that the employer, rather than the trustees, is to decide whether to increase benefits on final winding up. Alternatively, the scheme may provide that the trustees' power to increase benefits is subject to an employer veto. If this power, or veto, is not considered to be fiduciary in nature, then the insolvency practitioner will not have to surrender it to the independent trustee, and will be free to exercise it in the interest of the creditors, subject only to the duty of good faith. This is likely to result in no benefit increases and a maximum refund of surplus.

In *Mettoy*, Warner J argued that the members' right to be considered should be a right of substance and, where the power to increase benefits on winding up was held by the employer rather than the trustees, it should be treated as a fiduciary power:

If that discretion is not such a fiduciary power it is, from the point of view of the beneficiaries under the scheme, illusory . . . the words conferring the power mean no more, on that construction of them, than that the employer is free to make gifts to those beneficiaries out of property of which it is the absolute beneficial owner. . . .[66]

---

[64] Schedule 4, para. 1.
[65] For example, the power to appoint trustees.
[66] [1990] 1 WLR 1587 at 1618; [1991] 2 All ER 513 at 549.

Similar arguments can be made where the trustees have power to augment, but the employer reserves a right of veto. If the employer's power of veto is not fiduciary, and is therefore allowed to be exercised by the insolvency practitioner, then the trustees' power to consider increasing benefits will also be 'illusory', since it will represent no more than a power to *ask* the employer to make 'gifts' out of property of which it is the absolute beneficial owner.[67] Does this mean that such a veto is also fiduciary in nature? If trustees and the employer can both have fiduciary duties under the scheme, why can't they both have fiduciary duties with respected to the same provision?

One can argue that an employer who allows trustees to exercise a power, but reserves a veto, is more clearly intending that power to be non-fiduciary than an employer who generally gives powers to trustees throughout the scheme, but reserves a particular power to itself. But once one accepts that employers can reasonably intend to share fiduciary responsibility with the trustees, such distinctions appear somewhat arbitrary.

In a solvent winding up the trustees' powers are not affected by the Social Security Act 1990, and there is no need to appoint an independent trustee. A solvent winding up might be undertaken as part of the process of scheme reorganization, in which case the scheme will be replaced by a new scheme. It might also be actually final, prompted by the employer's desire to cease offering pensionable employment and/or to seek a refund from the scheme. In these circumstances there is no statutory protection other than the need to index benefits up to 5 per cent p.a. under the Social Security Act 1990, s. 11(3). The power to trigger a winding up, when coupled with a right to veto benefit increases, provides employers with a strong weapon in any dealings with the scheme's trustees. In light of these powers, there is a sense in which any share of a surplus in excess of the amount needed to fund early leaver benefits is a discretionary benefit.

3. Summary

The courts have denied the automatic right to members or employers to benefit from a surplus arising on winding up. They have also attempted to ensure that the identity of the trustee will not, in practice, give employers or their creditors automatic access to the maximum surplus. But in the only case so far in which the power to augment has been surrendered to the court, Sir David Nicholls saw nothing wrong with allowing the employer's creditors to share in the surplus.

V. THE SCOPE FOR JUDICIAL DISCRETION WHEN DEALING WITH A SURPLUS

Whilst the legal question of who 'owns' surpluses necessarily breaks down into a set of questions as to the rights of various parties to benefit from

---

[67] Subject only to the duty of good faith announced in *Imperial Tobacco*.

surpluses in different situations, this does not mean that the question is meaningless. The question really means which party should, in all of these situations, be treated as closely as possible as if they were the absolute owner of this part of the fund? As such, it is really an appeal to the two major perspectives which underlie questions of entitlement: deferred pay (the claim that all of the fund should be treated as if it were the property of the members); and balance of cost (the claim that any part of the fund not required to secure the scheme's fixed benefits should belong to the employer). Judicial commitment to these opposing perspectives may radically alter what rights may be found to exist in a particular dispute.

This section looks at four questions whose answers depend crucially upon the perspective adopted by the courts: what rules will be found to apply in any given dispute? How will those rules be interpreted? What standards govern the exercise of discretionary powers? And what constitutes a precedent in this area?

A. WHICH RULES TO INTERPRET

In any litigation, one of the first questions to address is, which set of rules governs the current dispute? This is the result of statements made in *Courage* and *Mettoy* regarding the validity of earlier scheme amendments.

Millett J's statement in *Courage* (that trustees should bargain before they agree to changes in a scheme's rules which increased the employer's access to a surplus) can be put into effect in the future, but what about past alterations? Will amendments be invalid where the trustees failed to ask for increases in exchange? Similar questions follow from Millett J's treatment of the particular amendment sought in *Courage*. He decided that the holding company could not be substituted for the principal employer unless the holding company had taken over the business of the former principal company. Yet there will be schemes in which the definition of the principal company was altered following a take-over, with the holding company having no more interest in the principal company than a majority shareholding at the time of the change. Will these substitutions be undone?

In *Mettoy*, the scheme had been changed following the Finance Act 1971.[68] The trustees received no legal advice of the effect of these amendments.[69] Warner J decided that the court could look at amendments made by trustees

---

[68] There were three important changes. First, the proviso to the power of amendment was altered. The old power of amendment contained a prohibition against making any amendment which would allow refunds to go to the employer. This bar on refunds was omitted from the new power of amendment. Second, the power to increase benefits on winding up was taken from the trustees and given to the employer. Third, the class of members who could receive increased benefits on winding up was widened.

[69] At least one trustee gave evidence that, had he been aware of the possible effect of the alterations, he would not have agreed to them or at least, would not have agreed to them without compensating benefit increases at the time.

and uphold those which the court felt would have been made even if the trustees had been told of their effect, and strike down those which would not; or even sever parts of amendments that were acceptable from those that were not.[70] But the implications of this approach are far-reaching. Where schemes have been regularly amended, the court may, depending on its view of what amendments trustees should have agreed to, find itself picking and choosing from the different sets of rules when deciding which provisions should govern the question at issue.[71]

Another doctrine which may affect the choice of rules is the doctrine of estoppel. In both *Icarus* and *Mettoy*, amendments that were prima facie contrary to the power of amendment were upheld on the basis that since all the parties had acted on the basis that the amendments were valid, they were now estopped from challenging them. But estoppel is a discretionary remedy, and therefore one which cannot be expected to be applied where the results which it produces are felt to be unjust. On the other hand, where no injustice results, it can be used to bypass restrictions on the power of amendment and, for example, allow the court to recognize the substitution of a principal employer who did not, at the time of substitution, employ the majority of the current scheme members.

B. HOW ARE RULES TO BE INTERPRETED?

Whilst any attempt to describe the law of trusts will discuss powers and duties in a general way, the reality of interpretation is always particular: one is looking for the appropriate interpretation to give to a particular power in a particular context. As such, there is considerable scope for different judges to take different views as to the powers and duties which arise in the dispute before them. The previous section gave some examples of the manner in which rules need to be categorized before duties can be applied to them. The employer's powers must be considered to see whether they are fiduciary or not. The power of amendment needs to be examined to see whether the amendment proposed lies outside its purpose. There is the question of whether a particular provision gives rise to a power at all, or whether it is required to be exercised and is therefore not a power but a duty.[72] There is also the need to decide whether powers can only be exercised for particular

---

[70] Relying on *Re Hastings-Bass* [1975] Ch. 25. In the event, he was satisfied that all of these amendments were valid, but only because the employer's power to agree to benefit increases (and thereby prevent refunds) was a fiduciary one.

[71] The *Mettoy* decision is likely to affect large numbers of schemes. Insurance companies have consistently updated and altered the trust deeds which they provide to companies. As insurance companies do not undertake to provide detailed legal advice to the trustees of these schemes, many of these amendments will have taken place without the trustees being aware of their legal effects.

[72] A power which is required to be exercised in a particular way is commonly called a trust power.

purposes, or in a particular manner. With respect to winding up, a common and important question is whether the power of amendment survives the commencement of the winding-up process, thereby allowing any surplus to be dealt with in a manner different from that set out in the current winding-up clause.[73]

Whilst the cases referred to above contain some indications as to how future judges may approach the construction of particular scheme rules, it is open to another judge to adopt a different construction, whether for reasons of syntax, the general arrangement or structure of the scheme in question, or simply through a lack of sympathy with the perspective which informed the first judge's interpretation of the rule in question. Thus, for example, if a future case arose on the facts of *Aitken*, would a judge still decide it in the same way if, like the Vice-Chancellor, she took the view that it was unreasonable for a company to face an increased funding burden? The doctrine of fraud on a power, which requires powers to be used in accordance with their intended purpose, allows a court to decide how a power was intended to be used and prevent its *ultra vires* exercise. If it is 'improbable' that an employer expected to lose control over benefit increases, then this doctrine would allow a court to restrain trustees who proposed to use the power of amendment for such a purpose. And one can apply a similar reasoning to the *Imperial* judgment. Judges who accept that the trustees can reasonably exercise independent powers which affect scheme funding have no reason to avoid implying such powers into the scheme where there are words which are capable of bearing that construction.

C. DISCRETIONARY STANDARDS

Except where a scheme rule, or the general law of trusts, sets out exactly what may or may not be done in particular circumstances, one is dealing with powers which are subject to discretionary standards: which range from 'best interests' to 'good faith'.[74] As well as deciding which standard applies to the exercise of a particular discretion, there is also the problem of identifying what that standard requires in the particular facts of the case. One judge's interpretation of 'good faith' may involve something which another judge would only require if the standard to be applied were 'best interests'.

D. WHAT CONSTITUTES A PRECEDENT IN THIS AREA?

This area of law brings into sharp focus the question (if not the answer to it) of what constitutes a precedent in the law of trusts, or in the common law generally. According to the formal rules of precedent, there are in fact

---

[73] Contrast *Threll*, n. 44 above (winding-up power did not survive commencement of winding up) and *Re Edwards Benevolent Fund* 8 March 1985 (unreported) (where it did).

[74] See Chapter 3.

virtually no precedents in this area, since almost all the decided cases are High Court decisions which are not binding in later High Court actions. But the need to have authoritative decisions in the absence of Court of Appeal or House of Lords decisions, as well as factors such as respect for other puisne judges, has led to the situation in which High Court decisions are said to have 'persuasive' authority in later High Court actions. This suggests a situation of one puisne judge considering the reasoning of another and probably deciding to follow it even if he is not required to do so.

But how does such a system of precedent operate when judges are giving substantively different reasons for adopting particular constructions of pension rules and general trust duties? *Imperial Tobacco* and *Aitken*, discussed above, provide examples of cases decided by reference to very different value-judgments. Others are *Davis* v. *Richards & Wallington Industries* and *Mettoy*.

In *Davis*, Scott J accepted the employer's claim that surpluses were caused by past overfunding by the employer, and that having overpaid, it should be entitled to benefit from its own mistake, even to the extent of receiving a refund. As a result, he ordered that monies not distributed under the pension scheme should, on final winding up, be returned to the employer under a resulting trust. In *Mettoy*, which involved the right of members to receive discretionary benefits in a winding up, similar arguments to those which were to be accepted in *Davis* were made by the employer's counsel and rejected by Warner J. In *Mettoy*, the employer's counsel argued that members were entitled only to their mandatory benefits and had no right to be considered for discretionary benefits. The money available to pay discretionary benefits was the result of the employer's contributions which, as they had been made on a balance of cost basis, were intended to fund only the mandatory benefits. As such, the surplus 'belongs in principle'[75] to the employer.

Warner J rejected counsel's arguments:

One cannot . . . when interpreting the rules of a 'balance of cost' pension scheme relating to surplus, start from an assumption that any surplus belongs morally to the employer.[76]

In his opinion, the excess could be attributed to the success of the scheme's investments, and to the relatively poor benefits paid to members who leave schemes before their retirement. The balance of cost basis gave the employer the right to reduce funding, a right which this employer had enjoyed during the period leading up to the insolvency, but this was no reason to interpret the scheme in such a manner as to increase its right to benefit from the surplus. Warner J was persuaded to interpret the scheme to make the employer's power to increase benefits on winding up a fiduciary one, which it

---

[75] A phrase used by the employer's counsel. [1990] 1 WLR 1587 at 1619; [1991] 2 All ER 513 at 550.   [76] [1990] WLR 1587 at 1619; [1991] 2 All ER 513 at 519.

could not therefore exercise solely in its own interests. As the employer was now in liquidation, he ordered the fiduciary power to be surrendered to the court.

If the perspective adopted in *Davis* had been applied in *Mettoy*, it seems unlikely that Warner J would have felt that it was so wrong for the liquidator to exercise the power to increase benefits on winding up, or for that power to have been fiduciary. There would have been nothing wrong with the money being returned to the party which had paid more than had been intended, and used to pay that party's creditors.[77] By contrast, if Scott J had accepted that the contributions of the employer had been earned by the employees through their past service, he might have been less inclined to exclude the employees from the benefit of a resulting trust. After all, the belief that the *Davis* scheme would continue through to the members' retirement was shared by the employer, the employees, and the trustees of the schemes which paid transfer payments. No one was contributing, or providing services, on the assumption that the members would receive no more than their early leavers' benefits.[78]

It seems difficult to envisage such contrary approaches building into a single, consistent body of precedent, particularly when each precedent has only 'persuasive' status. The desire for High Court judgments to provide guidance for potential litigants may result in these decisions, although based on contradictory reasoning, being applied in 'very similar' or 'identical' fact situations, and effectively operating as a binding rather than only a persuasive system of precedent. Whilst this may reduce, it will not overcome the problems created by inconsistent reasoning, since 'fact' here is a complex blend of scheme rules and surrounding circumstances, whose ability to be viewed as 'similar' or 'different' depends upon the judicial perspectives brought to bear.[79]

VI. CONCLUSION

The right of members, employees, and employers to benefit from surpluses depends upon a complex and indeterminate process of construction. Interpreting a scheme's rules, and relating those rules to the standards appropriate to the conduct of trustees and employers, is a far from straightforward process. As such, this chapter could not provide a simple answer to the question of who 'owns' a surplus. At best it has given some idea of the difficulties of answering that question in the present state of the law.

---

[77] See *Icarus (Hertford) Ltd.* v. *Driscoll*, n. 58 above.

[78] See on this *Thrells*, n. 44 above. For discussion of the way in which opposing perspectives affect the outcome of cases with similar facts, see R. Nobles, 'Don't Trust the Trustee', 53 MLR 377 (1990).

[79] As the Chapter 3 analysis of *Gisborne* showed, even identical words, interpreted by the House of Lords, can receive different interpretations once the assumption that persons using those words intend to achieve the exact same consequences no longer applies.

One must not presume that such indeterminancy is entirely unacceptable. Uncertainty in the law may facilitate negotiation.[80] Any division of surpluses can be presented as some kind of 'balance'. Members can be encouraged to accept their employer sharing in some part of a surplus on the basis that the law is unclear, and they might lose any litigation. Similarly, employers may be encouraged to share some part of a surplus with a workforce in order to head off a legal challenge which may have some possibility of success. However, one should not assume that such indeterminancy works in an even-handed way between employers and members. As in other areas of the law, indeterminancy may work in favour of whichever party has most resources and is least risk-averse. Between members and employer, this is most likely to be the employer.

[80] For example, the 1964–8 Labour government enacted a formula for fair rent which it knew to be meaningless. But the formula made it easier for landlords and tenants to agree to 'fair rents'. See P. Watchman and P. Robson, 'The Operation of the Rent Acts', unpublished paper, 1981 SSRC Economics and Low Seminar Group.

[8]

Investment

I. INTRODUCTION

The funding of a pension scheme affects the security of members' benefits. The treatment of surpluses also affects that security, and forces one to examine the nature of the employer's contribution to a pension scheme. Both these topics are easy to see as labour law issues, provided that one accepts that pension benefits, like other aspects of working conditions, are of direct concern to the workforce. But investment powers are less easy to understand as labour law issues. How do they relate to the employment relationship?

From the perspective of deferred pay, investment powers raise two issues. The first is related to the security and size of benefits. The claim that the employer's contribution is the members' pay indicates that the assets held in the fund should be invested for the benefit of the members and not for the employer. Thus, for example, the trustees should be extremely wary of requests to invest scheme assets back into the employing company; and they should not undertake high-risk investment strategies where the rewards of such strategies will only go to the employer in the form of reduced future contributions or refunds. The second connection between investment and the claim that pensions are deferred pay relates to the political implications of investment strategies. Should employees have 'their' money invested in industries or countries which pursue policies which are against the interests of the members of a particular pension scheme, or those of the industry which employs them, or those of UK employees in general? Should their money be invested in companies which support the Conservative party, or any other political party? Should pension funds invest in enterprises which the members, or their representatives, regard as unethical? The third way in which investment relates to labour law again involves security, but from the point of view of the safe custody of pension funds. Without this, pension schemes may be literally worthless.

II. TYPES OF SCHEME

In the vast majority of schemes, investment is largely a question of ensuring that the employer has paid premiums to an insurance company, and monitoring the performance of that insurance company relative to other insurance companies. These type of schemes, known as 'insured schemes', make up the bulk of occupational pension schemes. Of the 136,000 occupational schemes approved by the Inland Revenue, 100,000 were insured schemes.[1] This does not mean that such schemes could not, on surrender of those policies, produce a surplus, or that the trustees could not, in their dealings with those insurance companies, fail to meet the standard expected of trustees.[2] But it does significantly reduce the role played by trustees in the establishment and monitoring of scheme investments. The task of selecting investments that will enable the promised benefits to be paid when due has largely been transferred from trustees to the insurance company.

A further 30,000 schemes administer their own investments, but have only twelve members. Many of these schemes are not aimed at ordinary employees. They enable directors and senior employees to have a pension scheme whose investments are under their control. Such schemes do not raise the same problems as large, self-administered schemes, as the members are likely to be fully aware of the investments undertaken, and the risks involved.

This chapter is principally concerned with self-administered, final salary schemes where the members are not all directors or senior employees. There are some 6,000 to 7,000 such schemes.[3] Section III of the chapter looks at investment issues which affect these schemes. Section IV looks at the manner in which the courts have approached investment by trustees.

III. INVESTMENTS ISSUES

A. COST

Contributions to a pension scheme are but one source of the assets which secure the pensions promised to scheme members. The other source is return on investments. Contributions are used to purchase assets which are expected, in the course of time, to yield income or capital gains. The choice of investments is of central concern to the employer. The return on investments affects the contribution rate. The greater the return, the less that

---

[1] See 'Study of Self-Investment by Pension Funds: A Report to the Department of Social Security by Ernst & Young' (1991) HMSO, p. 4.

[2] Consider the scandal surrounding the loss of £6.7 million from the Averling Barford pension fund. A large part of this sum took the form of commissions, paid to parties who had persuaded the trustees to change their investment from policies with Equity and Law, to an unsuitable investment bond, marketed by a subsidiary of Royal Insurance. One of the trustees, who was also a director of the company, was sentenced to two years' imprisonment for his part in the affair. See 'Three Convicted of Pension Plot', *Financial Times*, 7 August 1992, p. 3.

[3] Ernst & Young's estimation of the total number of self-adminsitered final salary schemes with more than twelve members in 1991. Note 1 above, at p. 5.

the employer will have to pay to finance the 'balance of cost' of the pensions. Conversely, the lower the returns, the less that the employer will need to contribute. This leads to employers making similar claims to those made in respect of surpluses: that the balance of cost basis of funding means that the investment policy is mainly, if not wholly, their concern.

B. SECURITY

Employees can, however, advance claims with respect to investment policy. Investment policy affects the security of their pension benefits. If the scheme's assets are high-risk investments, which turn out to be worthless, their benefits are no longer secure. The fact that the employer is liable, under the Social Security Act 1990,[4] to fund any deficit arising on winding up, does not remove the members' interest in investment policy. An unsecured debt against the employer (who may well be insolvent) is a poor substitute for a fully secured pension.

The fact that employers and employees have different interests in the pension fund's investments should not lead one to the conclusion that their interests are always in conflict, with the employees favouring specific kinds of 'safe' investments such as government securities, and the employer preferring high-risk equities. Deciding on the appropriate portfolio of investments for a pension scheme is not a straightforward decision.

C. MATCHING AND DIVERSIFICATION

The security of pension benefits is achieved by two processes: matching, and diversification. Matching involves identifying types of liability and seeking to find investments whose value matches that of the liability in question. It is important for two reasons. First, if the assets and liabilities are not matched, the scheme may find that it cannot meet liabilities when they fall due, or can only meet liabilities by selling assets on unfavourable terms. Second, mismatch has implications for the contribution rate. If the assets increase in value substantially more than the liabilities, then, as we saw in Chapter 7, surpluses may arise. More worrying, if the assets are outstripped in value by the liabilities, a deficiency will arise. According to Martin and Grundy (both actuaries):

The primary objective of the trustees will be to invest the scheme monies in such a way as to ensure that the scheme will always have resources available to meet its liabilities to pay benefits as and when they fall due at all times in the future; and, in so doing, to take account of the risk factors inherent in any investment situation.[5]

---

[4] Schedule 4, para. 2.
[5] 'Principles and Practical Objectives of Pension Fund Investment', Ch. 1 in A. G. Shepherd (ed.), *Pension Fund Investment* (Woodhead-Faulkner, 1987), p. 3.

1. Matching Current Members' Benefits

In a pension scheme, the past service benefits of the current members are calculated by reference to their current salary. As such, they are increased by earnings inflation. One cannot safely secure such benefits by investing in the safest kind of security: fixed-interest government securities, or 'gilts'. Such securities are guaranteed to pay a definite sum of money each year, and, in the case of gilts which have a redemption date, can be certain to pay a fixed capital sum at some point in the future. But the benefits of current members are not fixed in money terms. They increase as the members' salaries increase. To secure them safely, one needs an investment whose value is closely related to earnings inflation. Index-linked government securities might seem to offer the safest way to secure such a benefit.[6] However, the possibility of adopting such a strategy is limited by two factors. First, there simply are not enough index gilts available.[7] Second, the yield on them has been low relative to other investments such as equities, making them an expensive means for securing pensions. Security achieved through the purchase of indexed gilts is achieved at a cost of greater employer contributions and forgone opportunities for benefit increases. It may simply be considered too expensive.

2. Matching Pensions in Payment

The benefits of pensioners differ from those of current members in two ways. First, they are actually in payment, so matching involves not just security but liquidity. Will there be sufficient cash to pay the pension each month? Second, there is no requirement to index such pensions. Since they are fixed in nominal terms, they can be secured by assets which are also fixed in nominal terms. The obvious asset to use for this is a fixed-interest government security with a given redemption date.

Any part of a GMP in payment attributable to service after 5 April 1988 must be price-indexed in payment up to 3 per cent p.a.[8] This requirement of limited indexation has made the use of gilts to secure pensions in payment less well matched. But as the indexation is limited to a maximum of 3 per cent fixed interest, securities can still be used with some certainty.[9]

[6] K. Ayers, 'Indexed Linked Gilts', ibid., pp. 82, 84.

[7] The total net assets of pension funds in 1990 were estimated to be worth £302,670 million. The amount of index-linked gilts outstanding at the end of 1990 was only £12,888 million. CSO Financial Statistics, No. 368, December 1992, p. 91, table 7.10.

[8] Social Security Act 1986, s. 9 (7); Social Security and Pensions Act 1975, s. 37A.

[9] The Social Security Act 1990, s. 11(1), Schedule 2, para. 3, will require all pensions accruing after the appointed day to be price-indexed up to 5% p.a. and, where a scheme's valuation shows a surplus, for service prior to the appointed day to be similarly indexed. The appointed day is yet to be announced.

3. Matching Deferred Pensions

Similar considerations apply to the GMPs of early leavers. These are required to be indexed to earnings from the date of leaving to the date of retirement. By payment of a premium,[10] the *scheme*'s requirement to index these benefits can be changed to price inflation with a ceiling of 5 per cent p.a. (The member's total state benefit remains unchanged, since the state then undertakes to meet the remaining cost of full earnings indexation.) Another alternative, which can be matched with even greater certainty, is for the GMP to be increased at a fixed rate.[11]

4. To Match, or Pursue Higher Returns?

So, should trustees of pension funds adopt the safest course, and choose an appropriate mix of indexed and fixed-interest government stock, avoiding equities, property, and overseas investments? This is not a perfect match for the liabilities, but it is probably the closest they can get. The lower rate of return which would probably result from such a narrow investment policy would lead to an increased funding burden in future. But is this any concern of the trustees? According to one view, it is:

In practice, however, the employer's resources are not open-ended and the control of pension funding costs is no less significant than the control of other business costs. In the usual private sector position, where pension increases are to a significant extent discretionary, overcautious investment is as likely to emerge as an impairment of the scheme's ability to increase pensions as in the form of increased employer contributions.[12]

The treatment of surpluses, as set out in the last chapter, should be kept in mind when considering the reasonableness of undertaking increased risk in the hope of securing higher returns. If the benefits of higher returns go entirely, or mostly, to the employer, through contribution holidays or refunds, one can see (with the benefit of hindsight), that the increased risks which the members faced (of inadequately secured pensions) have not been rewarded by higher returns.

5. Diversification

Trustees, for whatever reasons, have been persuaded to undertake investments in sectors other than government stocks.[13] In so doing, they have increased the risk that the assets of the scheme will fail to match the accrued liabilities.

---

[10] Known as a Limited Revaluation premium. See Social Security and Pensions Act 1975, s. 45.

[11] Currently 8.5% where contracted-out employment terminated before 6 April 1988, and 7.5% where it terminated on or after that date.

[12] Shepherd (n. 5 above), at p. 7.

[13] In 1990, pension funds held £148,350 million worth of UK company securities. See n. 7 above.

But having done this, the trustees can reduce the risk of such a mismatch by the process of diversification. Diversification is well summed up by the old adage: 'do not put all your eggs in one basket.' Trustees who invest in real assets such as equities or property, here or abroad, have to ensure that they are not exposed to a major loss if one of those assets performs less well than expected, or even collapses completely. Instead of having large investments in a single company, a fund will have a portfolio of investments. If a scheme owns a representative selection of all the shares in the UK Stock Exchange, the risk of that portfolio performing less well than expected is no greater than the risk that the entire UK market for equities will perform less well than expected. By investing overseas, the scheme can ensure that the fund does no worse than the average performance of a number of stock markets.[14]

D. THE NEED FOR LIQUIDITY

Different types of scheme have different abilities to take risk. A closed scheme made up entirely of pensioners has very little ability to invest outside of government gilts. Assets have to become liquid on a regular basis in order to meet pensions in payment, and there are no incoming contributions to cushion poor results. By contrast, ongoing schemes may not have to sell any assets for a long time to come. Pensions in payment can be met from contributions. This cushions the scheme from the effects of any temporary fall in the value of an investment.[15] But the assumption that a continuing pension scheme can take risks over the matching of its assets and long-term liabilities assumes that the scheme will not need to be wound up in the meantime. If it is wound up, and the winding-up clause requires the purchase of annuities to secure accrued benefits, then the ability to meet the scheme's liabilities will depend on the current market-value of the scheme's assets. Unfortunately, there are no obviously safe investments to deal with the risk of premature discontinuance. Gilts, which closely track long-term liabilities, suffer wide fluctuations in value in the short term. Their price depends on their relative attractiveness as an investment when compared with other investments. They are affected by the return currently received from all other kinds of investment.

---

[14] See, generally, J. Rutterford, *Introduction to Stock Exchange Investment* (Macmillan, 1983). Rutterford concludes (on p. 318) that 'unless expected returns are *much* lower on overseas securities (due to transaction costs, taxes, or political risk), investors should not limit themselves to domestic investment.'

[15] Assets which do swing in value over a short period, and pay higher returns to compensate for this, may still achieve a predictable long-term rate of return. If pension funds were only concerned with the long-term rate of return, then short-term swings in value would not affect the security of the liabilities. Any premium or bonus paid to compensate for short-term fluctuations in value would, from the point of view of a continuing pension fund, be a bonus.

E. SELF-INVESTMENT

Pension schemes engage, to different levels, in self-investment.[16] Self-investment can take a number of forms. The most obvious is where the scheme owns shares in the employing company or its subsidiaries. Other examples of this phenomenon are loans to the employer, guarantees of its indebtedness, or the ownership of property which is let to the employer.

The rationale for such investment differs between companies and schemes. With regard to very small companies, the ability to undertake such investments has been used to persuade the employer to sponsor a pension scheme. Self-investment is contrary to the employees' interest in security but, if the alternative is no pension scheme at all, or lower levels of benefits, it is not obvious that the practice should be discouraged. Some schemes have received shares in the employer on a gratuitous, or subsidized basis. Again, since such transfers benefit scheme members it is not self-evident that the practice should be discouraged.

With public companies' schemes, self-investment can be a side-effect of diversification. For example, a fund manager who wishes to hold a representative selection of quoted UK equities will need to include some of the employer's shares, or his portfolio will not be representative of the market as a whole.[17] It can also be justified as a defence against unwelcome hostile take-overs. By putting a significant number of the employer's shares into the pension scheme, the employer may ensure that the decision whether to accept such a bid is not taken entirely on the basis of the potential for short-term profits. Instead, the trustees may wish to take account of the general long-term interests of the members[18] (or at least the long-term interests of the incumbent management).

Self-investment becomes particularly controversial where it is the result of a down-turn in the fortunes of the employing company. Should the pension scheme provide finance at below market rates, or with less security than an outsider would require, where this enables the company to continue in

[16] The National Association of Pension Funds, in a survey carried out amongst their membership, found that 3.8% of funds had self-investment at the level of 5% or more. *Report of a Working Party Established by the National Association of Pension Funds to Look into Self-Investment by Pension Funds*, June 1988. This provides some indication of the levels of self-investment in the larger funds which make up the association's membership. Ernst & Young estimated that self-investment exceeded 5% in 8% of contracted-in schemes with more than twelve members, and 6–7% of contracted-out schemes of this size. See n. 1 above.

[17] For the argument that diversification should take account of the members' dependence on the profitability of the employing company and construct a portfolio which reduces *this* risk, see B. Shaw, M. Hagagi, and W. C. Atherton Jr., 'Investment Policy and Fiduciary Responsibility in Managing Defined Benefit Funds under E.R.I.S.A.' 27 Suffolk UL Rev. (1988), 83.

[18] See, for example, the trustees who preferred to accept a lower bid (albeit with the support of a stockbroker's advice), so as to end up as part of the Murdoch empire instead of the Maxwell one; 'Judge Rejects Pensioners' Now Shares Plea', *Financial Times*, 2 January 1969. See also 'Support of Bryant's Pension Fund Purchases', *Financial Times*, 21 January 1987. (Pension scheme trustees purchase shares in the employer to fight off hostile bid.)

business? Since the rationale of funding schemes is to ensure that the benefits will be paid even if the employer fails, self-investment in these circumstances should, perhaps, be discouraged. On the other hand, one cannot pretend that the welfare of the members and their dependants can be separated from the fate of the employer. Employees are rarely made better off by their employer going out of business. Even pensioners, who have no further interest in employment, may need the employer to continue to make contributions to the scheme if they are to receive *ex gratia* increases in their pensions in payment. And the dangers of self-investment cannot be assessed without looking at the overall level of funding in the scheme. A scheme which has a very high level of funding but 20 per cent self-investment may have more secure benefits than a scheme with no self-investment but a poor funding level. Where self-investment is an alternative to lower funding, it can be in the members' interests.[19] It might also be more acceptable if it were undertaken by trustees who are elected by, and responsible to, the members, instead of by trustees who are appointed by the employer.[20]

F. SOCIAL AND ETHICAL INVESTMENT[21]

Both these terms refer to the claim that investors have concentrated upon too narrow a range of criteria when deciding on their investment strategy.

1. Social Investment

Social investment describes investment which seeks to look at the wider financial consequences of an investment decision. For example, the TUC has claimed that increased investment abroad may result in an inadequate supply of capital for British industry.[22] It claims that pension funds, which are the largest institutional investors, must invest more in this country if the welfare of their members is to be safeguarded. There are more local variants of this argument: the pension funds of companies which are located in depressed areas should be prepared to invest in local industries.

The case for social investment is very similar to that for self-investment. The welfare of the members, in terms of jobs or higher pensions, cannot be separated from the prosperity of the funding industry. The future of a local employer cannot be separated from the future of a local economy. The future of a British employer cannot be separated from the future of the British

---

[19] For a fuller discussion of the arguments for and against self-investment, see the NAPF's 1988 report, n. 16 above.

[20] The Social Security Select Committee felt making schemes truly independent from the employer would remove most of the objections to self-investment. See 'The Operation of Pension Funds', 2nd Report of the Social Security Committee. 4 March 1992 HC Papers 61–11 1991/2 HMSO, para. 67.

[21] For a general introduction to this subject, see S. Ward, *Socially Responsible Investment* (Directory of Social Change, 1991).

[22] See the TUC's report: 'Pension Fund Investment and Trusteeship', July 1983.

economy. The principal difference between these levels of social investment is the extent to which they depend, for their success, on the co-operation of other investors. If a pension scheme invests in local industries, it may still fail to reverse the decline in the local economy and, in any case, much of the benefit of its investment will go to other firms. At the national level, the rewards to a particular fund are even more problematic. One scheme, however large, cannot reverse the fortunes of the British economy.[23] But these same objections do not apply to the wide-scale practice of social investment. If large-scale pension scheme investment can reverse the decline in a local economy, or even the national one, it may be for the greater good of all concerned.

2. Ethical Investment

Ethical investment refers to investment that takes political and moral criteria into account as well as financial ones. Again, examples help to make sense of the label. Investors may wish to avoid investing in companies manufacturing armaments, or products hazardous to health such as tobacco. They might avoid investing in companies which operate out of, or trade with, South Africa, because of their abhorrence of the apartheid system. Similar considerations apply to companies operating out of, or trading with, countries whose governments are guilty of human-rights abuses.

These labels are not mutually exclusive. A policy of avoiding investments in enterprises which cause environmental pollution could be called social investment, or ethical investment. A polluting company may be unprepared for future environmental protection legislation, and its negative impact upon a local economy may decrease the prosperity of one's own company. Similar overlaps arise with more parochial concerns. Is a refusal to invest in companies which discriminate against trade union membership an ethical objection, or an attempt to protect one's company from non-unionized competitors?

G. FRAUD

The relevance of fraud to the security of members' benefits has been demonstrated by the discovery that the late Robert Maxwell had used some £400 million from the pension funds of Mirror Group Newspapers, Maxwell Communications, and several other companies in order to maintain his control over the companies within his publishing group in the face of that group's mounting indebtedness.[24] The scandal has highlighted the ability of

---

[23] A point made by Megarry VC in *Cowan* v. *Scargill* [1985] Ch. 270 at 296.

[24] According to evidence given by auditors Cooper & Lybrand, Deloitte, some £235 million represented securities sold to Maxwell's private companies, which were never paid for. The remaining losses were due to the use of pension fund shares as security for loans to Maxwell's companies. The money seems to have been used to finance a share-buying operation, designed to

trust law to provide adequate security for pension benefits, and the dangers that security may be too easily sacrificed in pursuit of other aims, such as lower administrative costs or the need for fund managers to pursue profits without restrictions which reduce their ability to make quick investment decisions.[25]

Whilst fraud can never be eliminated entirely, the Maxwell scandal does concentrate attention on issues which are vital to the security of pension benefits, but may be omitted in discussions of investment: the custody and control of investments. There is a need to ensure that assets cannot be diverted from a pension fund for purposes which have nothing to do with the purposes of the scheme and which are in breach of the rules of the scheme, or the general law of trusts, or both.

IV. THE LEGAL FRAMEWORK FOR INVESTMENT DECISIONS

A. THE GENERAL LAW OF TRUSTS

Under the terms of pension trust deeds, investment is the responsibility of the scheme's trustees. Employers do not reserve the right to tell the trustees how to manage the scheme's assets. The trustees' power of investment is usually in very wide terms.[26] Typically, the power will authorize them to invest in any type of investment that would be open to persons who were investing their own money.[27] The trustees will also have wide powers to delegate investment to fund managers.[28]

---

keep up the value of other shares pledged as security to the banks, and thus prevent these secured loans from being called in. See the Report of the House of Commons Social Security Select Committee (n. 20 above).

[25] The Social Security Committee criticized the decision to place many separate trust funds into one common investment fund and the use of a Maxwell-controlled company, Bishopsgate Investment Management Limited, as fund manager. Whilst both of these developments probably reduced the administrative costs of running the Mirror Group's pension funds, they considerably increased the risk of fraud. Ibid., para. 139.

[26] Pension funds very rarely rely on the powers of investment set out in the Trustee Investment Act 1961. See J. Quarrell, *The Law of Pension Fund Investment* (Butterworths, 1990), p. 1.

[27] 'It is usual for the trust deed to specify that the trustees have the same unrestricted power of investment of the assets of the pension funds as if they were the absolute beneficial owners of those assets'. Ian Pittaway and P. Docking, 'Social Investment: Can It be Done?', Trust Law and Practice (1990), p. 26. For an example of such a clause, see W. Phillips, *Pension Scheme Precedents* (Sweet & Maxwell, 1957), para. 911.

[28] The powers of delegation contained in the Trustee Act 1925, s. 23, will allow trustees to delegate the execution of investment to agents, but this does not cover the making of investment decisions. Section 25 allows twelve months' delegation of all investment responsibility, but the trustees remain fully liable for the agent's acts as if they were their own. All but a few modern pension funds contain wider powers to delegate than the statutory ones set out in the Trustee Act 1925. See Quarrell (n. 26 above), p. 27. Note that delegations within the scope of such a power may still be imprudent, and therefore in breach of trust.

But in exercising such powers, the trustees are subject to a number of standards found in the general law of trusts. Trustees have a duty to act in the best interests of the beneficiaries:[29] to act impartially between classes of beneficiary;[30] to exercise such care as an ordinary, prudent man of business would take if he were minded to make an investment for the benefit of other persons for whom he felt morally bound to provide;[31] to have regard for the need for diversification;[32] and not to allow themselves to be placed in a position where their duty to the beneficiaries conflicts with their interests or with their duty towards a third party.[33]

These standards do not provide a simple legal 'answer' to the investment issues set out in Section III of this chapter. They provide a starting-point for the interpretation of the rules of a particular trust, and for the assessment of trustees' behaviour. With respect to many questions of investment, the meaning of these terms has yet to be worked out. The standards provide the courts with a basis for intervention. When deciding how and when to intervene, the courts have to determine what conduct they wish to allow or forbid, and the extent to which they will allow employers to devise a form of words which reduces, or eliminates, the court's supervision.

In the area of pensions, there has been some attempt to give substance to these standards, though the approaches of the courts have not been consistent. Investment issues were considered in *Evans* v. *The London Co-operative Society*;[34] *Cowan* v. *Scargill*;[35] *Martin* v. *City of Edinburgh District Council*;[36] and *Bartlett* v. *Barclays Bank Trust Company Ltd.*[37] The first three of these cases throw some light on the right of trustees to undertake self-investment and social investment, and on their freedom to take different decisions from those recommended by their schemes' financial advisers. The last of them deals with the trustees' duty to be diligent.

1. Evans *v.* The London Co-operative Society

The entire funds of the Society's pension fund were, from 1933 to 1962, lent to the Society at below market rates of interest. From then on, most of the annual contributions not used to pay pensions continued to be loaned to the Society. In 1970 the practice was challenged. Brightman J decided the case on the basis that the trustees had mistakenly believed that they had no discretion to refuse to lend to the Society. But he went on to consider the position if the trustees had known of their discretion and had decided that loans to the Society were in the beneficiaries' best interests:

[29] *Cowan* (n. 23 above), p. 513.
[30] *Howe* v. *Dartmouth* (1802) 7 Ves. 137; *Cowan*, ibid., p. 513.
[31] *Re Whiteley* (1886, 33 Ch. D p. 347 at 355 (CA); *Learoyd* v. *Whiteley* (1887) 12 App. Cas. 727 (HL).   [32] Trustee Investments Act 1961, s. 6(1).
[33] See *Bray* v. *Ford* [1896] AC 44; and the discussion of trustees' duties in Chapter 3.
[34] Reported in full in R. Ellison, *Private Occupational Pension Schemes* (Oyez, 1979), p. 356.
[35] Note 23 above.   [36] [1988] SLT 329 (Court of Session).
[37] [1980] 1 All ER 141.

Self-investment of a pension fund may be undesirable in ordinary commercial undertakings but it is to my mind consistent with the aims and principles of a co-operative undertaking . . . It should also be borne in mind that a co-operative society does not have the same facilities for raising working capital as are available to a joint stock company. [The shares of a Co-operative are withdrawable on demand, so all of its working capital is borrowed money or reserves] I also bear in mind that the members of the Pension Fund are all employees of the Society and therefore dependent for their employment on the financial health of the Society. *No doubt that is always so in the case of the pension fund of a trading concern* . . . [If the rules give the trustees power to lend to the parent concern] . . . it would in my view be wrong to suppose that the trustees are forbidden to give the parent concern financial accommodation on preferential terms if the trustees consider that the security of the employment of their members may otherwise be imperilled.[38]

Brightman J accepted that investment policies which favoured the employer could, in the right circumstances, be in the members' best interests. Once you accept that the members' interests are linked to the prosperity of the employer, the reasonableness of the trustees' actions becomes a matter of fact and judgment. Social investment may be harder to justify than self-investment, but only because the link between social investment and increased profitability is harder to demonstrate. Ethical investment is not directly authorized by this statement from *Evans* but, once you can take account of the members in their capacity not only as pensioners, but as employees, can you not look at the beneficiaries as real people with interests in morality, politics, etc.? There are authorities from other parts of trust law in which the interests of the beneficiaries have been held to include moral and social considerations at the expense of financial ones.[39] Lastly, the statement makes no mention of a need to seek expert advice. Brightman J accepts that if the employer tells the trustees that it needs preferential treatment, they can form a judgment on that statement without calling in accountants, industrial relations experts, or financial advisers. A wide reading of *Evans* would accept that other investment issues can be decided on a similar basis. For example, the trustees can form an opinion on ethical investment and the degree to which they will sacrifice security for high returns (or vice versa), without seeking the advice of investment advisers.

This widest possible reading of *Evans* puts trustees largely outside the control of the courts. The standard of 'best interests' of the beneficiaries is reduced, in effect, to what the trustees honestly and reasonably (or perhaps not wholly unreasonably) believe to be their best interests. Unless this standard is to be buttressed by the rule against conflicts of interests,

---

[38] Note 34 above, p. 365.
[39] *Ward* v. *Ward* (1843) 2 HL Cas. 777 (not in beneficiary's interest to have debt due to trust enforced, where this would make beneficiary's family bankrupt); *Re Clores Settlement* [1966] 1 WLR 955 (benefiting a beneficiary by giving his capital to charity); *In Re Pilkington's Will Trusts* [1964] AC 612 (benefiting a 5-year-old by giving her capital to other members of her family).

investment decisions will depend on the personalities and interests of the persons appointed to be trustees. In the case of most pension schemes, these will be persons chosen by the employer. But, as the facts of *Cowan* demonstrate, this will not always be the case.

2. Cowan v. Scargill

In *Cowan*, Megarry VC discussed the principles of pension scheme investment, and proceeded to give *Evans* a very narrow interpretation. In *Cowan*, the union-appointed trustees of the National Coal Board pension fund refused to approve the investment plan proposed by the scheme's investment advisers. The union trustees objected to the proposal that the scheme's overseas investments be increased. They proposed instead that the scheme divest itself of overseas investments at the most opportune time. They also wished to prohibit new investments in industries which competed with coal. This policy had been the subject of a motion which had been put to the NUM's conference and approved unanimously.

Megarry VC decided that *Evans* was an exception to the general law of trusts, and that self-investment was only possible where there was a specific rule authorizing it. Ordinarily, such investment could not be allowed because it was contrary to the trustees' duty to invest in a manner which was in the best interests of the beneficiaries:

In considering that duty, it must be remembered that very many of the beneficiaries will not in any way be directly affected by the prosperity of the mining industry or the Union. Miners who have retired, and the widows and children of deceased miners, will continue to receive their benefits from the fund even if the mining industry shrinks: for the scheme is fully funded, and the fund does not depend on further contributions to it being made. If the Board fell on hard times it might be unable to continue its voluntary payments to meet cost-of-living increases . . . [But] . . . the impact of that remote possibility falls far short of [an] imminent disaster . . . and I cannot regard any policy designed to ensure the general prosperity of coal mining as being a policy which is directed to obtaining the best possible result for the beneficiaries, most of whom are no longer engaged in the industry, and some of whom never were. The connection is far too remote and insubstantial.[40]

This argument disposed of the case for both social and self-investment without the need for evidence as to the likely success of such a policy. Even if likely to succeed, such policies were still indefensible, since they sacrifice the interests of the pensioners to those of the members.[41] Ethical investment was dealt with by interpreting the 'interests' of the members as their financial

---

[40] Note 23 above, at p. 292.
[41] Megarry VC is wrong on this point. The group whose interests are sacrificed by self- and social investment are the deferred pensioners. The current pensioners are protected by their ranking in the order of priority under the winding-up rule. See R. Nobles, 'Who is Entitled to the Pension Fund Surplus?', 16 Industrial Law Journal (1987) 164 at 174.

interests, and excluding ethical and moral considerations. Whilst conceding that there may be some trusts in which the interests of the beneficiaries include moral and social considerations (he gave the example of a trust for adults who all condemned alcohol, tobacco, and armaments), this trust was simply not one of this 'rare type'.

Megarry VC concluded that all trustees, including those of pension schemes, were required to put 'on one side' their political and social views when making an investment decision. If they failed to do this, they would be in breach of trust, and face personal liabilities which could be enormous. Megarry VC would require the trustees to guarantee the success of an ethical investment policy. If the ethical investment strategy proved less successful than a conventional strategy, the trustees might have to make up the difference.[42] Such a breach of trust could, if challenged, be treated as a wilful breach and therefore outside a trustees' normal indemnity clause. Thus trustees could, as did the NUM trustees, find themselves liable for enormous legal fees even where the fund had not suffered at all.[43]

Megarry VC also felt bound to restrict the general ability of trustees to refuse to follow the advice of their financial advisers:

the standard required of a trustee in exercising his powers of investment is that he must 'take such care as an ordinary prudent man would take if he were minded to make an investment for the benefit of other people for whom he felt morally bound to provide' . . . That duty includes the duty to seek advice on matters which the trustee does not understand, such as the making of investments, and on receiving that advice to act with the same degree of prudence. This requirement is not discharged merely by showing that the trustee has acted in good faith and with sincerity. Honesty and sincerity are not the same as prudence and reasonableness . . . Accordingly, although a trustee who takes advice on investments is not bound to accept and act upon that advice, he is not entitled to reject it merely because he sincerely disagrees with it, unless in addition to being sincere he is acting as an ordinary prudent man would act.[44]

---

[42] 'The assertion that trustees could not be criticised for failing to make a particular investment for social or political reasons is one that I would not accept in its full width. If the investment in fact made is equally beneficial to beneficiaries, then criticism would be difficult to sustain in practice, whatever the position in theory. But if the investment in fact made is less beneficial, then both in theory and in practice the trustees would normally be open to criticism.' Note 23 above, at 287. Where conventional investments are found to have performed better than ones chosen for moral or ethical reasons, trustees may have to make up the difference. This goes beyond the usual concept of loss, which looks at immediate loss suffered, rather than the loss of opportunity. Examples of such immediate losses are the sale of investments at below market rates, or at times when the market is depressed, or the acquisition of investments at inflated prices. But the liability envisaged by Megarry VC (liability for opportunity costs) is not entirely novel. In *Evans* the Society had to pay the fund the difference between the return on investment which had been earned, and the return which *would have been earned* if the investment had been properly made: 'The proper course is to compensate the fund for what it may be assumed to have lost'. Note 34 above, p. 367.

[43] In *Cowan* the NUM trustees were each liable for £50,000 in legal fees. Had they not been indemnified by their union, they would have had to find this sum from their personal savings, or be made bankrupt.   [44] Note 23 above, at p. 299.

Megarry VC is warning trustees not to challenge the advice of their financial experts. Investment is assumed to be something which trustees 'do not understand'. People do not 'prudently' refuse to follow advice on matters which they do not understand, without seeking the advice of other experts. Trustees should not therefore refuse to follow the advice of their financial advisers without first finding other financial experts who can support them.[45] This part of Megarry's judgment seems to be an attempt to prevent trustees from implementing ethical or social investment policies whilst insisting that their decisions are taken in the beneficiaries' best financial interests. Their own opinions of the financial best interests of their beneficiaries are not good enough, whether or not they are sincerely held. Only opinions supported by financial experts will do.

On the question of self-investment, Megarry VC ruled that there could be no special case for investments which could make the sponsoring industry or company more profitable. The interests of those beneficiaries who only stood to gain *ex gratia* increases in consequence were paramount, and *ex gratia* increases were of insufficient worth, and too speculative, to justify the sacrifice of security. They could only be undertaken where, as in *Evans*, the scheme contained a rule which authorized such investment. This does not necessarily rule out self-investment, even in the absence of a specific rule. What it rules out is giving any preference to the sponsoring company on the basis that this could help the majority of beneficiaries. It can still occur where it could be justified on financial grounds. Thus schemes may undertake investment on the ground that they hold no more shares of the sponsoring company than they hold of any other company with similar characteristics. This position leaves those who have no interest in the future profitability of the company facing no greater risk of loss. Self-investment may also be justified where it presents a financial bargain for the scheme—for example, the issue of shares at below market prices.

Where self-investment is authorized under a pension scheme's rules then, applying the approach taken in *Evans*, the trustees still need to demonstrate that the degree of self-investment undertaken was in the best interests of the beneficiaries. Here we encounter one of the paradoxes of trust law. If Megarry VC has ruled, in *Cowan*, that self-investment is not in the best interests of the beneficiaries, how can the trustees undertake such investment, even where there is an authorizing rule? In an essay written by Megarry VC on the *Cowan* decision,[46] we find another example of this paradox. Having ruled that a policy to restrict investments could not possibly be in the

---

[45] Even then, if they are known to hold strong ethical or political views, they may not be believed by the court. See, for example, the treatment of the NUM trustees in the interim hearing before Vinelott J in *Cowan* v. *Scargill*, 21 December 1983. Unreported.

[46] Sir Robert Megarry, 'Investing Pension Funds: The Mineworkers' Case', in T. Youdan (ed.), 'Equity, Fiduciaries and Trusts' (Carswell, 1989), p. 149.

interests of the beneficiaries, Megarry VC suggests in this essay that those trustees who wished to undertake social or ethical investment should exercise their powers of amendment (which they have to exercise in the best interests of the beneficiaries), to introduce permanent restrictions on investment.[47]

The Effects of Cowan   Megarry's statements on ethical and social investment are unlikely to be overruled by a future court. This is not just because Megarry VC was a more senior judge than Brightman J. A judgment like that in *Cowan* is necessary if trustees' investment is to remain open to control by the court. If ethical investment is allowed by trustees whenever they feel that it is in the interests of the beneficiaries, then judges face the spectre of either having no power to protect beneficiaries against the financial consequences of pursuing ethical investments, or having to adjudicate on which moral or ethical causes were acceptable: a political quagmire. Social investment provides less of a political dilemma but, at the end of the day, it is still a difficult subject for adjudication. If it is allowed in principle, then the question of the reasonableness of its pursuit in particular situations is an extremely complicated question, which is likely to involve the courts in the consideration of large amounts of economic evidence. In *Cowan*, Megarry VC felt able to dispose of the merits of the case for social investment by asserting that the assets of the Coal Board's fund were not 'large enough' to achieve a revival in the national economy by themselves. But if he had not also ruled out social investment in principle, future cases might have required the courts to decide what size or combination of funds could reasonably expect to revive the fortunes of a national, regional, or local economy.

At the other extreme, one may doubt whether judges really wish financial benefits to be pursued without any reference to ethical criteria. This is not just the problem identified by Megarry VC: that certain families or religious groups will hold strong ethical opinions. Requiring trustees to make investments solely on the basis of financial consequences is likely to place too great a burden on too many trustees. Trustees will not wish to be associated with funds that invest in concerns which outrage their moral opinions; for example, to be required to remain invested in a profitable film company which has been found to make (legal) pornographic films.[48]

Megarry VC's solution to these extremes was to rely on the financial advisers to exercise good sense. If they failed to recommend investments that were unethical, or if they, or other experts, could find financial reasons for making, or omitting to make, unethical investments, then all would be well. But if they did recommend an unethical investment, and other financial advisers could not find acceptable financial reasons against it, then the trustees would have to do what they were told.

---

[47] Ibid., p. 159.
[48] This actually occurred in the *Cowan* case.

3. Martin v. City of Edinburgh District Council[49]

In this Scottish case, Lord Murray gave *Cowan* his qualified approval. The authority was trustee of a number of funds and the Labour group on the authority wished to see those funds divested of their shareholdings in companies which had links with South Africa. Lord Murray would not allow the trustees to pursue a policy of ethical investment, but he disagreed with Megarry VC's suggestion that they were compelled to follow the advice of their financial advisers, or that they had to exclude all ethical considerations when deciding upon investment.[50] Where there was no policy being applied, Lord Murray was prepared to let the trustees give effect to their moral views so long as they were able to exercise a 'fair and impartial judgment on the merits of the issue before them'.

Lord Murray's approach restores the right of trustees to disagree with their investment advisers. From the point of view of the investment issues discussed in Section III of this chapter, this is an important admission. If investment is a matter on which trustees are considered to know nothing, then the trustees lose their right to determine the level of security in the scheme. They will be compelled to follow the advice of experts who may be chosen not by themselves but by the employer, and who may be more interested in pursuing high returns than in ensuring the security of members' benefits. If Megarry VC's view of the trustees were accepted, then they would have to play a very residual role: checking the honesty of their advisers, asking for explanations, and questioning any inconsistencies in what they were told.[51]

Lord Murray restores an ad hoc approach to questions of ethical investment. When finding such investments to be a breach of trust, the court will not have to declare that a particular moral or political belief is unreasonable, only that the particular trustee or trustees allowed their moral views to influence their decisions 'too much'. Megarry VC has himself suggested a similar approach. In the essay already referred to, he suggested that trustees could practice ethical or social investment provided that they did so in secret: announcing no policy and making no formal decision to that effect, and relying on financial reasons to justify the exclusion of unethical

---

[49] Note 36 above.

[50] 'Insofar as *Cowan* may be taken to imply that the duties of trustees in seeking to secure the best interests of the beneficiaries is merely to rubber-stamp the professional advice of financial advisers, I find myself unable to agree. I accept that the most profitable investment of funds is one of a number of matters which trustees have to consider. But I cannot conceive that trustees have an unqualified duty . . . simply to invest trust funds in the most profitable investment available. To accept that without qualification would, in my view, involve substituting the discretion of financial advisers for the discretion of trustees.' Ibid., at 334.

[51] The duty of diligence, discussed below.

investments—for example, stressing the political instability of countries where they did not wish to invest.[52]

The message from both judges on this issue is: do not make your moral and political views known. Trustees who are known to hold strong ethical or political views are unlikely to be believed if they claim that they are viewing each decision on its merits,[53] and are likely to have their decision impugned on the basis that it was the expression of a prior commitment.[54] They may even be disbelieved when they present expert evidence in support of the financial merits of their decision.[55] If they are considered to have applied ethical criteria to an unreasonable level, they face large personal liability.

Thus social and ethical investment may be safely pursued, to a limited extent, provided that the trustees can avoid leaving evidence that they have sacrificed the pursuit of maximum return or maximum diversification, and self-investment can be pursued provided that the trustees first introduce a rule allowing such investment.[56]

4. The Duty of Dilligence

The concern that trustees should not operate merely as the cyphers of their advisers is not simply the result of a desire to avoid a single-minded pursuit of profit in all circumstances and to the detriment of all other concerns. There is a danger that trustees who are cyphers will not be able to protect the security of the members' benefits. By making trustees do what their financial advisers tell them, the courts can avoid the risks inherent in an excessive ethical investment policy, but this may create even greater risks that trustees will make investments which offer financial rewards to their advisers (through

---

[52] Note 46 above, at p. 158. Hayton recommends a similar approach. 'Where confrontation is not sought (unlike the *Cowan* v. *Scargill* situation) there is still much scope for trustees quietly to take into account the moral, social and political views of beneficiaries and of themselves, since it will in practice be difficult to prove that at the time a particular investment was made it was not as equally financially meritorious as certain other possible investments.' D. Hayton, *Underhill and Hayton, Law Relating to Trusts and Trustees* (Butterworth, 14th edn., 1987), p. 530.

[53] Where trustees undertake ethical investment 'quietly' (without leaving evidence of their moral or social views), there will be no proof that the investments were undertaken for ethical reasons. Few investment decisions are explicable only on moral or political grounds. Conversely, where their views are known, it will be difficult to convince a court that such investments were not undertaken for ethical reasons.   [54] As happened in *Martin*.

[55] See e.g. the first hearing before Vinelott J in *Cowan* (n. 45 above). The union trustees were refusing to invest £60 million in a US property company, and submitted evidence from a chartered surveyor that such an investment should not be made unless the properties owned by the company were investigated in detail. Nevertheless, the union trustees were overruled and ordered to make the investment.

[56] But trustees should expect narrow construction of ethical investment clauses, at least where the policy to be pursued involves a risk of serious financial detriment. In *Bishop of Oxford* v. *The Church Commissioners* [1991] PLR 185, Nicholls VC examined the right of charities to pursue ethical investment policies, and decided that such policies are acceptable provided that there is no risk of serious financial detriment. Where such risks arise, the policy is *ultra vires* unless the clash between the charities objects and the unethical investments in question are obvious to all. For an alternative construction of the relationship between charitable objects and the power of investment, see R. Nobles, 'Charities and Ethical Investment' [1992] Conveyancer 115.

commissions or even fraud) at the beneficiaries' expense. Where the financial advisers are appointed by, or are a subsidiary of, the employer, the risk that benefit will be diverted from the members becomes even greater. And here we strike a paradox. Whilst the sophistication of pension fund investment makes a mockery of the principle that trustees should not delegate their discretions, but must make decisions personally and leave their agents with only the execution of those decisions,[57] the principle cannot be abandoned in its entirety.[58] Trustees must remain principals, required to seek advice from experts but not required to follow it; otherwise there may be great difficulties in trustees exercising their role as stewards of the pension fund, deciding what risks can be safely undertaken, and seeking to prevent speculation or fraud. Whilst the idea that trustees can understand financial risk may be ludicrous, allowing them to abrogate responsibility for concern over risk (whether of excessive investment risk or fraud) invites disaster.

Underlying the rhetoric of 'prudence' is concern that trustees, if they cannot be experts, must at least be diligent. They must do what they can to form a judgment on advice which they have received. This is, in the end, what one pension lawyer has called 'the ultimate responsibility'[59] of trustees, so that: 'however wide the provisions of an express investment clause may be, the trustees are not absolved from their duty to consider whether a proposed investment is such that in its nature it is prudent and right for them as trustees to make.'[60] However inadequate their efforts might appear in the face of the superior knowledge of financial experts, trustees must not cease their supervisory rule: asking for reasons, checking for consistency, seeking to understand.

Bartlett v. Barclays Bank Trust Company Ltd.   The need for trustees to maintain a supervision over their investments, and not to accept whatever experts might wish to do, is well illustrated by *Bartlett* v. *Barclays Bank Trust Company Ltd.*[61] In this case, the trustee company failed to involve itself adequately in the affairs of the company whose shares were the sole asset of the trust. The business of the company was that of property development. The directors were a solicitor, a surveyor, an accountant, and an estate agent.

---

[57] See *Speight* v. *Gaunt* (1883) 22 Ch. D 727 at 756 per Lindley LJ (CA); (1883) 9 App. Cas. 1 at 5 per Lord Selborne (HL).

[58] There is some suggestion in *Re Vickery* [1931] 1 Ch. 572 that, provided the trustee acts only in 'good faith', he may, under the Trustee Act 1925, s. 23, delegate even discretions: 'It is hardly too much to say that it revolutionises the position of a trustee . . . so far as regards the employment of agents. *He is no longer required to do any actual work himself*, but may employ a solicitor or other agent to do it, whether there is any real necessity for the employment or not.' But the standard of good faith is very flexible (see M. Cullity, 'Judicial Control of Trustees' Discretions' (1975) 25 University of Toronto Law Journal 99 at 106). A trustee who delegates all of his discretions without any necessity may find himself in breach of the duty of good faith. For a detailed statement of the reasons why *Re Vickery* should not be followed, see Gareth Jones, 'Delegation by Trustees', 22 MLR 381 (1959).   [59] Quarrell (n. 26 above), p. 4.

[60] Ibid., p. 2.   [61] Note 37 above.

The relevant employee of the trustee company regarded them as 'a team of well-equipped professionals and [he] was content to leave things to them.'[62] Brightman J took a different view of how a trustee might supervise investments:

> The prudent man of business will act in such a manner as is necessary to safeguard his investment. He will do this in two ways. If facts come to his knowledge which tell him that the company's affairs are not being conducted as they should be, or which put him on enquiry, he will take appropriate action. Appropriate action will no doubt consist in the first instance of enquiry and consultation . . . and in the last but most unlikely resort, . . . to replace one or more of the directors. What the prudent man of business will not do is to content himself with the receipt of such information on the affairs of the company as a shareholder ordinarily receives at annual general meetings. Since he has the power to do so, he will go further and see that he has sufficient information to enable him to make a responsible decision from time to time either to let matters proceed as they are proceeding, or to intervene if he is dissatisfied.[63]

Although Brighton J was examining the duty of a trustee to supervise a company in which it has a major investment, and is therefore referring to the trustee's duty to supervise directors through its powers as a shareholder, his remarks are equally applicable to a trustee's dealings with the trust advisers and fund managers. Trustees must be attentive to what the experts are doing and, if facts come to their attention which warrant further investigation, must ask questions. They cannot hand over responsibility to other people simply because those people possess the necessary expertise and the trustees do not. The danger of failing to ask questions, or to pick up on inconsistencies in the answers given, is again illustrated by *Bartlett*. The trustee was first told that the company needed to undertake property development in order to make itself more attractive for public flotation. But when the idea of flotation was abandoned, the trustee asked no further questions as to why property development was still being undertaken.[64] In view of this, Brighton J was right to consider that the bank had failed to do what might be considered prudent even for ordinary trustees,[65] let alone professional trustees, who might have been expected to meet a higher duty.[66]

---

[62] Ibid., at 145.   [63] Ibid., at 151.

[64] This was the first of many events in the history of the development when the trustee might have raised inquiries as to the soundness of continuing with the project which caused the loss.

[65] Brighton J's view that this investment was too speculative and therefore a breach of trust *per se*, is not relevant to most pension funds, which are not only authorized to undertake property development and other speculative investments under their scheme rules, but, given their size, may be allowed or even perhaps expected to include some speculative investments in their portfolio. See *Cowan* (n. 45 above) and *Trustees of the British Museum* v. *Att.-Gen.* [1984] 1 WLR 418, [1984] 1 All ER 337. His view also has to be considered in the light of Hoffman J's acceptance, in *Nestlés* v. *National Westminister Bank* 19 June 1988 (HCt.) (unreported) that modern trustees should be judged on the basis of current portfolio theory which concentrates on the risk level of the entire portfolio rather than the risk attached to each investment in isolation.

[66] The relevance of the higher duty in this case is unclear. Brighton J bases it on the 'special care and skill' which they profess to offer. But the skill offered by a bank's trust department is

In undertaking their supervisory role, trustees have to be careful not to intervene in the 'day-to-day' investment decisions. This is not simply a consequence of the need to take and ordinarily follow advice in order to be seen to be 'prudent', but to avoid contravening the Financial Services Act 1986,[67] which exempts trustees from the need to be licensed with a regulatory body, but only provided they do not undertake 'day-to-day' investment decisions.[68] For lay trustees, finding the right balance between unlawful intervention and imprudent abrogation of responsibility is not easy.[69] One needs some knowledge of investment theory and practice in order to know what can be safely left to experts.

B. THE IDENTITY OF THE TRUSTEES MAY BE MORE IMPORTANT THAN THEIR GENERAL DUTIES OF CARE

One must not exaggerate the protection offered by general standards of care, whether those standards are that of the members' best interests or a good-faith duty of diligence. The complexity of investment makes it difficult to know what is in the beneficiaries' best interests.[70] And even where breach can be shown, the remedy of compensatory damages will, at best, put the trust back in the position where it would have been if the breach had not been committed. In these circumstances, the identity of the trustees may be more important than their general duties of care. But there is simply no guarantee

the ability to put together and manage a balanced portfolio of assets. In a trust like that in *Bartlett*, where the only asset is the family's private company, this skill is largely irrelevant. A trustee who takes on a trust of this kind has not necessarily agreed to exhibit the same care that a private individual who owned 100% of the shares might show. Such an individual would ordinarily be the managing director.

[67] According to the Financial Services Act 1986, s. 3, no trustee can carry on investment business in the United Kingdom unless he is an authorized or an exempted person. See, generally, C. Francis, 'Trustees, Investment Managers and the Financial Services Act 1986', Trust Law and Practice (1989), 110.

[68] Occupational pension schemes' trustees not acting with a view to profit are exempt from the Financial Services Act 1986, s. 3, if they delegate all their day-to-day management decisions to a permitted third party; Financial Services Act 1986, s. 191. This has led to some trustees being advised not to exercise proper control over their financial advisers. See Social Security Committee's Report, n. 20 above, paras. 234, 238. Some trustees have been allowing the investment manager to place securities in its own name or that of a nominee, to retain custody of investment scrip, to place trust money with its own or that of other customers, and to make profits by selling its own securities to the trust or by purchasing securities from the trust. Ibid., p. 110.

[69] The trustees of the Mirror Group pension fund felt that the requirement to relinquish day-to-day control had reduced their power to protect the fund from Robert Maxwell. See 'IMRO Rules "Hampered Mirror Fund Trustees" ', *Independent*, 5 February 1992, p. 22.

[70] The complexities of trust law may also undermine the effectiveness of the criminal law, at least where the defendant is the employer. The law of theft will be complicated by the need to show the appropriation was dishonest and concerned appropriating the property of another. The defence may wish to open the whole question of who 'owns' pension fund surpluses. At the Aveling Barford trial, evidence was given that the defendants believed the company was entitled to the money. See n. 2 above.

that the persons who have responsibility for investments are genuinely committed to the members' best interests. The employer will usually be given the power to appoint the trustees, and may even be sole trustee or arrange for one of its subsidiaries to be sole trustee. The employer may also have the power to dismiss trustees. This may be direct, as in a formal power to remove trustees, or indirect, where the trustees cannot continue to serve unless they remain employees of the company. In the latter situation, by dismissing a trustee from employment, you terminate their trusteeship.[71]

Where there are member trustees, these may be removed from the supervision of investments by a rule which provides for investments to be undertaken by an investment committee on which only management-appointed trustees sit. In the face of such devices, any belief by the members that investment issues will be decided in accordance with their best interests, and that the scheme's investments are in safe custody, may be illusory.[72]

C. STATUTORY REGULATION OF PENSION SCHEME INVESTMENT

The government has recently limited self-investment to 5 per cent of the fund.[73] Prior to this, there was only a requirement of disclosure.[74] Ethical and social investment are neither restricted nor encouraged by statute, except for the duty under the Trustee Investments Act 1961, s. 6, to diversify investments, a duty which may not be excluded by the express terms of the trust.[75]

The lack of a statutory framework for the general regulation of occupational pension schemes is currently the subject of a review of pension law being undertaken by a committee chaired by Professor R. Goode.[76] The

---

[71] As was the case in *Imperial Group Pension Trust Ltd.* v. *Imperial Tobacco Limited*. (Ch. D) [1991] 2 All ER 597; [1991] 1 WLR 589.

[72] There is no statutory provision which affects the identity of the trustees so long as the employer remains solvent. Once the employer goes into receivership or liquidation, an independent trustee must take over the trustees' discretionary powers. Social Security and Pensions Act 1975, s. 57C, 57D; Occupational Pension Schemes (Independent Trustee) Regulations 1990, SI 1990/2075.

[73] Occupational Pension Schemes (Investment of Resources) Regulations 1992, SI 1992/246. Small schemes in which all the members are trustees, are exempt.

[74] The OPB required disclosure of self-investment by contracted-out schemes which exceeded 10 per cent of the fund. OPB, 'Contracted-out Salary Related Schemes Supervision of Resources', Memorandum No. 76, para. 81. This requirement has been overtaken by the Occupational Pension Schemes (Disclosure of Information) Regulations 1986, which require all deviations from the Accounting Standards Committee's Statement of Practice 1 to be mentioned in the audited accounts. As the Statement of Practice requires disclosure of more than 5% self-investment, the regulations turn that requirement into a statutory duty.

[75] Though it may be indirectly excluded, since it applies 'in so far as it is appropriate to the circumstances of the trust' (s. 6(1)(a)).

[76] Its terms of reference are to review the framework of law and regulations within which occupational pension schemes operate, taking into account the rights and interests of scheme members, pensioners, and employers, to consider in particular the status and ownership of occupational pension funds and the accountability and roles of trustees, fund managers,

committee has been set up in response to the Maxwell scandal and, whatever its general conclusions, is likely to suggest reforms which reduce the ability of employers to defraud pension schemes of their investments.

V. CONCLUSION

The failure of general trust law duties to indicate exactly how trustees should undertake investments does not provide proof that trust law should be abandoned in favour of some legal framework, such as that offered by company law.[77] Urging trustees to do their best for the members after taking account of all the circumstances may, once one has identified and excluded unacceptable investments, be an appropriate way to proceed. But again, it depends upon one's perspective. If one accepts the deferred pay arguments of employees, then one might support the control of pension scheme investment by a majority of trustees appointed by the members. And one would not allow the power of such trustees to be circumvented by the rules of the scheme by, for example, transferring responsibility for investments to a committee on which member trustees were not represented or were in the minority. If, on the other hand, one accepts the employer's claims that members are only entitled to their minimum benefits, then the current legal situation may, with a few amendments, be quite acceptable. If the employer accepts the major part of any risk of poor investment returns, then it is surely acceptable for the employer to appoint the persons who will decide the investment strategy and supervise the investments. And it is also appropriate to subject such trustees to a duty to pursue maximum financial returns, to pay close regard to the advice of advisers appointed by the employer, and to be diligent in supervising investment managers. Subject only to the need to prevent gross fraud like that of Robert Maxwell (which places even the basic benefits at risk), the current legal framework may be quite sufficient.

administrators, and pension scheme advisers, and to make recommendations. Pension Law Reform Committee, 'Consultation Document on the Law and Regulation of Occupational Pension Schemes', September 1992, para. 1.1.

[77] The author disagrees with the Social Security Select Committee, who favoured a company law approach. See n. 20 above, para. 74.

[9]

European Law and the Right to Equal 'Deferred Pay'

This chapter deals with a topic which is of central importance to the law of occupational pension schemes: the equalization of benefits for men and women. The topic does not fit into the same framework for analysis as the earlier chapters. The central issue in this chapter is not the interpretation of scheme rules and the general law of trusts, although these topics are still relevant, but the interpretation to be given to United Kingdom statutes and European Community law, particularly Article 119 of the Treaty of Rome ('Article 119'). Article 119 requires that men and women receive equal pay which, since pensions are deferred pay, requires occupational pension schemes to offer equal benefits, on the same conditions, to men and women.

The chapter will seek to identify the changes which occupational pension schemes must undergo in order to comply with Article 119. Section I identifies which rules and practices currently discriminate between men and women, and the reasons why these rules were introduced. Section II examines the sex discrimination law applicable to pensions, concentrating on Article 119. Since the European Court of Justice's (ECJ) decision in *Barber* v. *Guardian Royal Exchange*[1] (*'Barber'*), there can no longer be any doubt that pension scheme benefits are within the scope of Article 119. This section will therefore not deal at length with the arguments made, prior to *Barber*, that pension schemes were not pay but a form of social security or a working condition, and outside the scope of Article 119. Instead, it concentrates on four isssues: why the ECJ found pensions to be pay; why each benefit offered by a scheme must be provided to men and women on the same basis; why scheme rules which make no reference to the sex of a member may still be found to be contrary to Article 119 if they impact more adversely upon one sex; and on the need to equalize scheme benefits by increasing the benefits of the disadvantaged sex ('levelling up'). Section III is a detailed survey of the implications of Article 119 for particular scheme rules. Section IV analyses the ability of employers to reduce the costs of complying with Article 119 by altering the rules of the schemes or introducing replacement schemes.

---

[1] [1990] IRLR 240.

Section V analyses the ECJ's ruling on the retrospective effect of *Barber* in the light of the ECJ's ruling and the Maastricht Treaty, either of which may prevent men and women receiving equal deferred pay for another forty years.

I. EXAMPLES OF UNEQUAL DEFERRED PAY

Occupational pension schemes provide benefits to men and women on unequal terms.

i. Schemes provide for different pension ages. The most common difference is for women's normal pension age to be five years lower than that for men.

ii. Where they have early retirement provisions, these are linked to the normal pension age. Thus, where normal pension ages are lower for women than men, women can enjoy early retirement at an earlier age than men.

iii. The benefits paid to survivors can differ according to sex, with the survivors of male members receiving more generous benefits than those of female ones.

iv. Optional benefits are offered to men and women on different terms. Women have to pay higher additional voluntary contributions for equal extra pensions. They receive more when they commute their pensions into lump sums, or take a transfer value.

v. Women often have a lower maximum age at which they can join a pension scheme.

vi. Women are entitled to receive that part of their pension which represents their Guaranteed Minimum Pension (GMP) at 60, the state pension age, whilst men have to wait until 65.

vii. Men who retire between 60 and 65 may receive an additional payment (bridging pension) to compensate them for the fact that they will not receive the state retirement pension. Whilst this results in their receiving the same net income as women, who receive their state pension from age 60, the amount of benefit received from the scheme is unequal.

viii. Some schemes automatically reduce benefits to take account of a state pension (integrated schemes), and these also result in unequal provision of benefits to men and women aged between 60 and 65.

ix. Some older schemes even have different accrual rates for men and women.

All of the above practices afford different treatment to members on account of their sex. The remaining examples are practices which apply equally to individual men and women, but adversely affect more members of one sex than the other. Such practices will constitute indirect discrimination unless they can be justified.

x. The exclusion of part-time workers from scheme membership. Part-timers are excluded by making membership conditional upon employees working a minimum number of hours in the week, or achieving a defined level of salary. Because more women than men are part-timers, the rule disadvantages more women than men. Similar discrimination arises where pensions are restricted to particular trades, occupations, or grades of employee.

xi. Women may be disadvantaged by the definition of pensionable salary. Some schemes disregard earnings below the lower earnings limit for the payment of national insurance contributions. Because women usually earn lower wages than men, this means that a greater percentage of their salary fails to earn pension benefits.

A. WHY DO SCHEMES PROVIDE UNEQUAL PAY?

Pension schemes have been designed by reference to factors which inevitably result in the sexes being treated differently. The majority of them were created after unequal pension ages had been introduced into the state scheme (65 men/60 women), and have adopted the same ages, or the same five-year differential, on the assumption that members wish to retire at state pension age, or need to receive the state pension at the date when, or within the same period after, they retire. They have been designed on the assumption that women on average will live longer than men, and that women's pensions are therefore more expensive that men's. This difference in cost has been expressed in different contribution rates, different lump sums being offered in exchange for forgoing an equal amount of pension income, and even, in a few schemes, lower rates of accrual for women employees than for men. Married women are assumed to be dependent upon their husbands, and able to rely on their husbands to provide for them in retirement. Whilst this assumption is no longer as strong as it was at the beginning of this century, when married women were barred from work as well as schemes,[2] it still finds expression in the greater provision made for the survivors of male, as opposed to female, members. Lastly, the distribution and design of occupational pensions concentrate pension provision upon particular categories of employees. Whilst occupational pension scheme provision covers just under 50 per cent of the working population, only 35 per cent of pension scheme members are women.[3] Final salary schemes concentrate pension provision upon workers who remain in one employment for most of their working lives, and whose earnings peak at, or shortly before their retirement. Whilst only a minority of the working population come within this

[2] See J. Lewis, 'Dealing with Dependancy: State Practices and Social Realities, 1870–1945', p. 23, and D. Groves, 'Occupational Pension Provision and Women's Poverty in Old Age', in Jane Lewis (ed.), *Women's Welfare, Women's Rights* (Croom Helm, 1983).

[3] 49%. See Occupational Pensions Schemes 1987; Eighth Survey by the Government Actuary HMSO (1991), para. 1.2, table 2.1.

description, the ability ot women to do so is, by reason of their greater childcare responsibilities, significantly below that of men.[4]

II. SEX DISCRIMINATION LAW AND PENSIONS

A. UNITED KINGDOM LAW

Domestic legislation has largely failed to address unequal occupational pension provision. Pensions were excluded from the scope of the Equal Pay Act 1970 and the Sex Discrimination Act 1975 on the grounds that inequalities within pension schemes should be the subject of special and separate legislation.[5] The legislation which followed, s. 53 of the Social Security and Pensions Act 1975, failed to tackle the problems of unequal benefits within schemes. It required only that men and women be given *access* to pension schemes on the same terms with regard to length of service and age at the date of entry. It also did not address the problem of indirect discrimination: rules of entry which, when applied equally to both sexes, had the effect of excluding disproportionate numbers of one sex. Thus employers could continue to exclude women by setting age limits or minimum conditions of service whose effect was to exclude young women who left employment to have children. It was also lawful to make membership conditional upon minimum levels of salary or hours worked. These conditions disqualified part-time employees, most of whom are women.[6] Regulations made under the Act allowed the maximum entry-age for women to be up to five years lower than that for men.[7]

Subsequent domestic legislation has been closely related to developments in European law. The Sex Discrimination Act 1986, ss. 2 and 3, was introduced as a result of the ECJ's decision *Marshall* v. *South West Hampshire Area Health Authority (Teaching)*[8] that the 1976 Equal Treatment Directive[9] is contravened if men and women are required to retire at different ages. Section 2 amends the Sex Discrimination Act 1975 and the Equal Pay Act

---

[4] A survey carried out in 1984 recorded that only '4% of women with children we interviewed had been in the labour market continuously throughout their working lives'. See J. Martin and C. Roberts, *Women and Employment: A Lifetime Perspective* (HMSO, 1984), quoted in F. Davidson, 'Occupational Pensions and Equal Treatment' [1990] JSWL 310 at 311.

[5] See Equal Status for Men and Women in Occupational Pension Schemes: A Report of the Occupational Pensions Board in accordance with s. 66 of the Social Security Act 1973. (1976). Cmnd. 6599, para. 2.20–21.

[6] Of the 10.7 million males in employment, 1.1 million work part-time. Of the 10 million females in employment, 4.6 million work part-time. *Employment Gazette*, March 1993, table 1. Just over 10% of part time workers are members of occupational pension schemes, compared with 49% for the working population as a whole. Note 3 above, para. 1.2. See *R* v. *Secretary of State for Employment ex parte Equal Opportunities Commission* [1993] IRLR 10 (CA).

[7] The Occupational Pension Schemes (Equal Access to Membership) Regulations 1976, SI 1976/142, reg. 4.   [8] [1986] IRLR 140.

[9] The 1976 Directive on the implementation of the principle of equal treatment for men and women as regards access to employment, vocational training and promotion and working conditions. (76/207 EEC.)

1970 to make it unlawful to discriminate against a woman solely on grounds of her age. Section 3 equalizes the upper age-limit in unfair dismissal cases. The Social Security Act 1989, section 23 and Schedule 5, implements the 1986 Directive on equal treatment in Occupational Social Security Schemes.[10] The 1989 Act required 'that persons of one sex shall not, on the basis of sex, be treated any less favourably than persons of the other sex in any respect relating to an employment-related benefit scheme'.[11] These provisions were not due to come into effect until 1 January 1993. In passing this Act, the government had taken full advantage of all exceptions and opportunities for derogation allowed under the Occupational Social Security Directive.[12] The 1989 Act does not require pension ages, survivors' benefits, or optional benefits to be equalized; it permits the use of different actuarial tables when calculating the benefits of men and women; and does not require money purchase schemes to use unisex actuarial tables when calculating benefits.

B. EUROPEAN COMMUNITY LAW

Because of the failure of UK legislation to require equal occupational pension provision, those wishing to challenge discrimination within occupational schemes have sought to utilize European law and, in particular Article 119, which states boldly that:

Each member state shall . . . ensure and subsequently maintain the application of the principle that men and women should receive equal pay for equal work.

For the purpose of this Article, 'pay' means the ordinary basic or minimum wage or salary and any other consideration, whether in cash or in kind, which the worker receives, directly or indirectly, in respect of his employment from his employer.

There has been confusion over whether pension schemes were 'pay' within Article 119, rather than social security or working conditions, and therefore within Article 118 of the Treaty of Rome ('Article 118'). The importance of the distinction lies in the fact that Article 119 is capable of having direct effect between citizens of member states,[13] i.e. an individual can pursue a claim against another individual in the national courts based upon a breach of Article 119. By contrast, individuals only gain rights under Article 118 through the enactment of further secondary legislation, usually in the form of Directives. Directives are capable of limited direct effect: they can be relied upon in an action brought by an individual against a member state, but not in

[10] The 1986 Directive on the implementation of the principle of equal treatment for men and women in occupational social security schemes. (86/378/EEC.)

[11] Schedule 5, para. 2 (1).

[12] F. Davidson, n. 4 above. D. Curtin, 'Occupational Pension Schemes and Article 119: Beyond the Fringe?' [1987] CML Rev. 215 at 219.

[13] Case 43/75 *Defrenne* v. *Société Anonyme Belge de Navigation Aérienne Sabena* [1976] ECR 455 (Defrenne II). See generally Gráinne de Búrca, 'Giving Effect to European Community Directives', 55MLR (1992) 215.

an action brought by one individual against another. The relevant Directives here are the 1979 Social Security Directive,[14] the 1986 Occupational Social Security Directive,[15] and the 1976 Equal Treatment Directive.[16]

Directives may supplement Article 119, and indicate appropriate ways in which it can be implemented, but they may not be used to reduce its scope or effect.[17] But the European Community Commission, in the belief that pension provision was not pay within Article 119, but social security within Article 118, allowed the 1979 and 1986 Directives to contain important derogations and exceptions.[18] However, in *Bilka-Kaufhaus GmBh* v. *Weber Von Hartz*[19] ('*Bilka-Kaufhaus*') in 1986 and again in *Barber* in 1990, the ECJ affirmed that pension scheme benefits were pay within Article 119.

1. Pensions are Pay

Bilka-Kaufhaus   The plaintiff was a female part-time employee of a German department store who complained about her exclusion from the store's occupational pension scheme. The ECJ was asked to rule on whether a rule excluding part-time workers, the majority of whom were women, could constitute discrimination. The United Kingdom put forward the preliminary argument that pensions were not pay within Article 119, but social security and/or working conditions and within Article 118. The ECJ rejected the United Kingdom's arguments, ruling that, in the case before them, pension benefits were pay within Article 119.

In concluding that the benefits in question were pay, the ECJ had particular regard to their earlier judgment in *Defrenne* v. *Belgium*[20] ('*Defrenne I*'), where it decided that social security benefits did not come within Article 119, simply by reason of the fact that they were offered within an

---

[14] The 1979 Directive on the progressive implementation of the principle of equal treatment for men and women in matters of social security (79/7/EEC.)   [15] Note 10 above.
[16] Note 9 above.
[17] *Jenkins* v. *Kingsgate (Clothing Productions) Ltd.* [1981] IRLR 228, para. 22.
[18] The 1979 Directive on equal treatment of men and women in matters of social security excluded survivors' benefits, allowed member states to maintain unequal state pension ages, and did not cover occupational schemes. The 1986 Occupational Social Security Directive allowed each member state to delay implementation of equal pension ages in private schemes until they were equalized in their own state pension scheme or, if this was later, until equal state pension ages were required by a Directive; and to delay equalization of survivors' benefits until a Directive required this in the state scheme. The Directive did not cover the various optional benefits open to members such as additional voluntary contributions, commutation of pensions into lump sums, and early or late retirement options; and it did not require money purchase schemes to use unisex actuarial tables when calculating benefits. Member states had until 1993 to implement those parts of the Occupational Social Security Directive which were not subject to special rights of deferment.
The 1976 Equal Treatment Directive required member states to implement the principle of equal treatment with regard to working conditions. The Equal Treatment Directive is limited by the exclusions and deferments contained within the Social Security and Occupational Scheme Directives, although the ECJ has been inconsistent on the extent of the restriction. Contrast *Burton* v. *British Railways Board* [1982] IRLR 116 and *Marshall* (n. 8 above).
[19] [1986] IRLR 317.   [20] Case 80/70 (1971) ECR 445.

employment relationship. The ECJ had there held that Article 119 did not cover retirement benefits 'directly governed by legislation which do not involve any element of agreement within the undertaking or trade concerned and are compulsory for general categories of workers'.[21] The present case could be distinguished on the basis that the scheme was voluntary. Although it complied with statutory provisions, its introduction was not required by statute, and the scheme's benefits supplemented those available under the state social security scheme. Its benefits therefore had their origins in the contract of employment and were governed by Article 119.

The United Kingdom argued that conditions of entitlement to a pension were 'working conditions', which as the ECJ had ruled in *Defrenne* v. *Sabena*[22] ('*Defrenne III*'), included matters that did not come within the description of pay, even if those conditions had the consequence of making one contract more valuable than another. In *Defrenne III*, the ECJ had ruled that an earlier compulsory retirement age for women than for men was a working condition that did not come within the description of pay. In *Bilka-Kaufhaus*, the ECJ did not explore why certain working conditions constitute pay whilst others do not. They simply decided that pensions *were* pay.

The *Bilka-Kaufhaus* judgment was a clear warning that all of the United Kingdom's occupational pension schemes were governed by Article 119. But the warning was clearer with respect to contracted-in schemes than to contracted-out ones. In *Defrenne I* the ECJ had accepted that Article 119 did not apply to a 'statutory scheme to which workers, employers and in some cases the authorities contribute financially to an extent determined less by the employment relationship between the employer and the worker than by considerations of social policy'.[23] Contracted-out schemes' benefits were funded through a reduction in the national insurance contributions and were substitutes for state scheme benefits. Did this make them part of the state social security scheme? On the other hand, contracted-out schemes were not compulsory, and usually promised additional benefits to the GMP. Did this mean that their benefits were pay?

There were indications even prior to *Bilka-Kaufhaus* that contracted-out scheme benefits would be found to be pay. In *Worringham & Humphries* v. *Lloyds Bank Ltd.*,[24] the ECJ had decided that some aspects of a contracted-out pension scheme could fall within Article 119. In *Worringham*, to offset the extra contribution made by men towards their pension scheme, men received higher gross pay than women. Higher gross pay, even when immediately deducted to pay contributions to a contracted-out scheme, infringed Article 119, since it affected other salary-related benefits. Against this, those arguing for the exclusion of contracted-out scheme benefits from Article 119 relied upon *Newstead* v. *Department of Transport and Her Majesty's Treasurer*.[25] In this case, a bachelor objected to paying contributions to a fund for widows'

---

[21] Ibid., at 451.   [22] (1978) ECR 1365.   [23] Note 20 above, at p. 451.

[24] [1981] IRLR 178.   [25] [1988] IRLR 66.

benefits. Female members were not required to contribute, as widowers' benefits were not then required to be provided by contracted-out schemes. The ECJ upheld the employer's right to require contributions from only one sex:

> That scheme contains some provisions which are more favourable than the statutory scheme of general application, and is a substitute for the latter. [A contribution to such a scheme] must therefore, like a contribution to a statutory security scheme, be considered to fall within the scope of Article 118 of the Treaty, not Article 119.[26]

This has been accepted as a statement that contracted-out schemes fell outside Article 119.[27] But it really amounts to no more than a statement that where equal pay is received by each sex, a deduction to a substitute social security scheme which leads to unequal net remuneration does not infringe Article 119.[28] As such, it does not exclude the benefits of contracted-out schemes from Article 119.

The status of contracted-out scheme benefits was finally resolved in *Barber*.

Barber, a 52-year-old male employee, was made redundant. He was a member of the respondent's contracted out, non-contributory pension scheme which had normal pension ages for men and women of 62 years and 57 respectively. Persons made redundant within five years of their normal pension age were entitled to an immediate early retirement pension. Those made redundant more than five years from this date received an enhanced severance payment, and a deferred pension which became payable at their normal pension age. Barber complained that this provision discriminated against him by denying him the immediate early retirement pension which would be paid to a woman aged 52.

The ECJ upheld Barber's complaint on the basis that his inability to claim the immediate pension contravened Article 119. The Article covered remuneration received after employment, and it did not matter that the remuneration came from the scheme trustees rather than from the employer. Payment from the pension scheme was simply an 'indirect' payment from the employer. Article 119 applied because it was paid '*in respect of his employment*'.[29] The fact that the scheme provided benefits which were partly intended to substitute for state benefits did not prevent those benefits being

---

[26] Ibid., consideration 15.

[27] See D. Curtin, 'Scalping the Community Legislator: Occupational Pensions and "Barber"', 27 CMLR 475 at 480.

[28] See *Encyclopedia of Labour Law* (Sweet & Maxwell, 1992), para. 2611.

[29] Note 1 above, consideration 28. The ECJ did not address the Advocate-General's arguments, based upon *Burton* v. *British Railways Board* (n. 18 above), that there was a distinction between benefits and *access* to benefits, with the latter falling outside Article 119. If there was any doubt before, *Barber* seems to have overruled *Burton sotto voce*. See Curtin (n. 27 above), at 482.

pay. The schemes in question were voluntary, they did not cover all employees, and they gave additional benefits to those of the state scheme.

2. All *Benefits Offered by a Pension Scheme are Pay*

The specific conclusion reached by the ECJ in *Barber* was that:

> It is contrary to Article 119 to impose an age condition which differs according to sex in respect of pensions paid under a contracted-out scheme even if the difference between the pensionable age for men, and that for women is based on the one provided for by the national statutory scheme.[30]

This ruling means that UK pension schemes cannot continue to use different normal pension ages for men and women, even though their state pensions become payable at different ages. Nor can they offer different early retirement ages. But the basis on which the ECJ reached this conclusion has implications for *all* benefits offered within an occupational pension scheme. The ECJ declared that occupational pension scheme benefits were pay rather than social security, because of their voluntary nature. On this basis, it is difficult to see how any particular rule or practice can be excluded from the scope of Article 119. Provided scheme benefits are voluntary, rather than being required under the member state's social security scheme, it cannot matter whether they are paid to members or to their dependants, whether they take the form of a capital sum or income, and what conditions (such as age, death, or dependency) apply to them.[31] All voluntary payments are attributable to the contractual relationship between employer and employee rather than social policy, and come within Article 119.[32]

3. *Each Element of the Pension Scheme's Benefit Must be Provided on an Equal Basis*

In *Barber*, women received benefits that men did not, and vice versa. The ECJ was therefore asked to consider whether each element of the pay offered to men and women had to be the same, or whether it would be sufficient to offer men and women different benefits of equal value.

If the ECJ had accepted equal value was sufficient, the application of Article 119 to pension schemes would have become dependent upon actuarial evidence. You need an actuary to tell you whether a deferred pension plus an immediate redundancy payment is worth more than an immediate early

---

[30] Note 1 above, at p. 258.

[31] With redundancy benefits, the ECJ was prepared to treat even statutorily required payments as pay rather than social security. *Barber*, n. 1 above, consideration 16. This part of the ruling has been criticized as being incompatible with *Defrenne I* and the reasoning given on the pension issue in *Barber* itself. See V. Shrubsall, 'Sex Discrimination and Pension Benefits', 19 ILJ 244 at 249.

[32] The only exception to this suggested by the ECJ was a scheme which paid no more than state social security benefits and was financed solely through social security contributions. This exception would cover money purchase schemes which offer only 'protected rights' (benefits accruing from the investment of the national insurance rebate), and final salary schemes which offer only GMPs financed solely through the national insurance rebate.

retirement pension. And the values placed upon these different benefits by actuaries will depend crucially upon their assumptions about life expectancies, future rates of interest, and price inflation. Thus, if the ECJ had interpreted Article 119 to require only equal value, employees who wished to enforce Article 119 would have had to employ actuaries. And, unless member states passed legislation stipulating the actuarial basis for assessments of equal value, the national courts would often have had to assess conflicting actuarial evidence.[33]

In order to avoid these difficulties, and to ensure the effective implementation of Article 119, the ECJ held that it was not sufficient for each sex to receive total remuneration of equal value. Equal pay must be ensured with respect to each element of remuneration.[34]

Applying Article 119 to a pension scheme thus requires one to look at every provision separately, as if it were the only provision which might affect an otherwise equal remuneration. If a provision gives a benefit to only one sex, or gives a larger benefit to one sex, or gives it subject to a condition which applies to only one sex, then that provision contravenes Article 119. Equal pay does not mean total remuneration of equal capital value; it means giving equal payments (whether lump sums or income), to men and women who fulfil the same conditions.

4. Indirect Discrimination and the Meaning of Justification

Whilst there have been doubts about whether pensions are 'pay' within Article 119, there has been no doubt that Article 119 forbids the use of sex as a criterion for determining the pay of employees. By contrast, the ECJ has only recently developed a method for tackling forms of discrimination which do not refer to sex as the basis for discriminatory treatment, but which have discriminatory effect. In *Defrenne* v. *Société Anonyme Belge de Navigation Aérienne Sabena*[35] ('*Defrenne II*') it indicated that such provisions might not be subject to the direct effects of Article 119. The ECJ distinguished between':

direct and overt discrimination, which may be identified solely with the aid of the criteria based on equal work and equal pay referred to by the article . . . and . . . indirect and disguised discrimination which can only be identified by reference to more explicit implementing provisions of a Community or national character.[36]

But in *Jenkins* v. *Kingsgate (Clothing Productions) Ltd.*,[37] the ECJ confirmed that Article 119 covers practices which make no reference to sex,

---

[33] 'If the national courts were under an obligation to make an assessment and a comparison of all the various types of consideration granted . . . to men and women, judicial review would be difficult and the effectiveness of Article 119 would be diminished as a result.' Barber, n. 1 above, consideration 34.

[34] The ECJ relied upon *Handels-og Kontorfunktionaerernes Forbund i Danmark* v. *Dansk Aberjdsgiverforening (acting for Danfloss)* [1989] IRLR 532.   [35] Note 13 above.

[36] Ibid., at 473.   [37] Note 17 above.

but have a greater impact on one sex than the other. The decision seems to be restricted to practices which are intended to discriminate.[38] The ECJ was prepared to accept paying less to part-time workers, almost all of whom were women:

unless it is in reality merely an indirect way of reducing the level of pay of part-time workers *on the ground* that that group of workers is composed exclusively or predominantly of women.[39]

In *Bilka-Kaufhaus*, the ECJ reaffirmed that Article 119 could be infringed where 'a much lower proportion of women than men' were able to qualify for a particular element of pay, but went on to confirm that such infringements were not dependent upon showing that the discrimination was intentional. Article 119 covered practices which had an adverse impact on one sex which could not be objectively justified by economic factors. Provided that an employee can establish, by comparison with a relatively large number of employees,[40] that a rule or practice disadvantages a greater percentage of his or her sex, the rule or practice in question will constitute indirect discrimination unless it can be justified. To understand the scope of Article 119, one must therefore have regard to the case law on what constitutes justification.

Justification   Direct discrimination (offering different rates of pay to men and women) cannot be justified, whatever the employer's reasons.[41] It is simply forbidden by Article 119, and there are no excusing conditions. Even if the employer has a genuine economic reason for preferring male employees, this cannot excuse discriminatory pay. Thus, unequal pay cannot be justified on the basis that women, because of interrupted careers or child-rearing responsibilities, are willing to work for less than men. Nor can work which fits in with childcare responsibilities be offered to women on lower terms on the basis that this represents an additional value to them. Lastly, the employer may not take advantage of womens' own perceptions of their role in society. Thus, even if women employees regard the role of breadwinner as a male prerogative, this cannot justify lower pay and, in the context of pensions, the fact that some women may expect their husbands to provide retirement income for both of them is no excuse for giving women lower or no pensions.

By contrast, a provision which does not explicitly refer to a member's sex,

---

[38] This was certainly Browne-Wilkinson J's interpretation when the case returned to the EAT [1981] ICR 715 at 725.   [39] Note 17 above, at 234, emphasis added.

[40] A requirement made by the ECJ in *Handels-og Kontorfunktionaerernes Forbund i Danmark v.Dansk Arbejdsgiverfornening* (n. 34 above). See E. Szyszczak, 'European Court Rulings on Discrimination and Part-Time Work and the Burden of Proof in Equal Pay Claims', 19 ILJ (1990) 114.

[41] See *Worringham & Humphries* v. *Lloyds Bank Ltd.* (n. 24 above); *Dekker* v. *Strchting Vormingscentrum Voor Jonge Volwassenen (VHV-Centrum) Plus* [1991] IRLR 27.

but which impacts more adversely against one sex than another, does not amount to a breach of Article 119 if the employer can show that the discrimination in question is justified. According to the ECJ in *Bilka-Kaufhaus*, the employer must be:

able to show that its pay practice is unrelated to any discrimination on grounds of sex.[42]

The task of assessing whether a pay practice is justified by the reasons given is that of the national court, which must be satisfied that:

the measures chosen . . . correspond to a real need on the part of the undertaking, are appropriate with a view to achieving the objectives pursued and are necessary to that end.[43]

But the national court must have regard to the fact that:

Article 119 does not have the effect of requiring an employer to organise its occupational pension scheme in such a manner as to take into account the particular difficulties faced by persons with family responsibilities in meeting the conditions for entitlement to such a pension.[44]

While *Bilka-Kaufhaus* confirms that the standard to be applied is one of necessity and portionality,[45] rather than reasonableness, the basic problem remains the same: on what basis can an employer justify provisions which impact adversely on one sex? Whilst *de minimis* advantages will not justify adverse impact, the limits thereafter are a matter of opinion.

The impact of indirect discrimination law on pensions, as with all other aspects of the labour market, depends crucially on the extent to which the employer can produce market justifications for the practice in question.[46] The facts in *Bilka* illustrate this. The employer there offered the following justification for the exclusion of part-time workers: 'I do not need to offer pensions to recruit part-time labour, I cannot run my business entirely on part-time labour, and I can only recruit full-time labour by offering pensions.' It is very difficult for a tribunal to question such assertions. The first statement is self-evidently true, and the reason for the complaint. The second is plausible. The third is not only plausible, but forms part of the condition which disadvantages women in the first place: their child-rearing responsibiilties prevent them from exacting the higher rates of pay that are demanded by full-time workers. Once one accepts the truth of these assertions, a decision that the practice conflicts with Article 119 is simply a judgment that this employer should bear higher costs in order to avoid disadvantaging women. Such a judgment does not indicate what other

---

[42] Note 19 above, at 320.   [43] Ibid., at 320.   [44] Ibid., at 321.

[45] Though in a recent case, the ECJ failed to apply the principle of portionality: allowing a member state to justify a social security provision which adversely effected women even though there were less discriminatory means by which the state could achieve its objectives. See *Commission* v. *Belgium* [1991] IRLR 393.

[46] See S. Fredman, 'European Community Law: A Critique', 21 ILJ (1992) 119 at 131.

practices might be found to infringe Article 119, or whether a different tribunal might have accepted this practice, or even, within a more competitive industry, whether this tribunal would have reached the same decision with reference to this practice. In these circumstances, the requirement that the practice be 'necessary' as opposed to 'reasonable', seems little more than an exhortation that tribunals should require employers to undertake 'greater' expense than they might otherwise have done. And against the exhortation to show necessity, there is the counter-instruction that employers need not tailor their pension arrangements to take account of the disadvantages which women face through their childcare responsibilities.

There is another interpretation of 'necessity' which does not, by itself, require employers to sacrifice profit in order to reduce or eliminate the adverse impact. It can be seen as an instruction to the national courts that claims as to the 'necessity' of particular practices, however plausible, be subjected to a requirement of proof. The employer in *Bilka* claimed that it needed full-timers to cover particular days which were unpopular with part-timers. But the ECJ rejected this argument, as the employer had not tried to persuade part-timers to cover by offering them premium rates of pay or even pensions.[47]

While there have been other cases in which such questioning of established industrial relations practices has occurred,[48] one cannot be optimistic that courts and tribunals will always question widespread industrial relations practices, and require proof of their effectiveness and necessity in particular cases. It requires considerable knowledge of local labour markets, or at least great confidence, to tell employers that they could have organized their labour force in a less discriminatory fashion at no greater cost to themselves.

Lack of Uniformity as to What Constitutes Indirect Discrimination   The ECJ has not reconciled the employer's freedom to pursue profit with the need to stop employers from exploiting the disadvantaged position of women workers.[49] It has simply sent the problem back to the national courts. And the standards which it has announced will make it difficult for the superior courts in each member state to ensure uniformity in what constitutes

[47] See T. Hervey, 'Justification for Indirect Discrimination in Employment: European Community and United Kingdom Law Compared', 40 Int. Com. LQ (1991) 807 at 814. The employer could also have been asked how it could be sure that it could only attract full-timers by offering pensions? Had it recently tried to attract full-timers without this additional benefit?

[48] See *Home Office* v. *Holmes* [1984] IRLR 299, where the industrial tribunal and the EAT did not accept the Home Office's assertion that it could not offer the applicant part-time work. However, this applicant was assisted by two departmental reports which recommended the introduction of part-time employment.

[49] Advocate-General Damon's solution in *Bilka-Kaufhaus* was to restrict the application of Article 119 to circumstances where the employer intended to discriminate. The ECJ notably failed to incorporate this part of the Advocate-General's opinion, and preferred to identify exploitation by the test of whether the practice adopted what was a means to achieve a 'real need' which was 'appropriate' and 'necessary to that end'.

discrimination. There must be a great danger that the standard of what is justified, either in terms of requirements of proof that a particular practice is efficient, or the trade-off required between profit and a discriminatory rule or practice, will depend on the subjective viewpoint of the court, tribunal, or Pensions Ombudsman who decides the matter. The observations by Browne-Wilkinson in *Clarke* v. *Eley (IMI) Kynoch*,[50] although addressed to the interpretation of the Sex Discrimination Act 1975, are equally applicable to Article 119:

> On emotional matters such as racial or sex discrimination there is no generally accepted view as to the comparative importance of eliminating discriminatory practices on the one hand as against, for example, the profitability of a business on the other. In these circumstances, to leave the matter effectively within the unfettered decision of the many industrial tribunals throughout the country, each reflecting their own approach to the relative importance of these matters, seems likely to lead to widely differing decisions being reached.[51]

Bilka-Kaufhaus has clear implications for conditions of access, such as age bars or service qualification. Unless these can be justified, they contravene Article 119. However, even more fundamental aspects of pension scheme design may be challenged as examples of indirect discrimination. Final salary schemes adversely affect persons who suffer a career interruption and thereby become, in pension terminology, early leavers. Where it can be shown that, within a particular workforce, a higher proportion of women than men suffer from being early leavers, will the final salary formula contravene Article 119?

The economic justification for the final salary formula is that employers wish to retain long-serving employees, who might otherwise be tempted to take their expertise and experience to other employers. If this type of economic justification is not accepted, then the pension industry faces the prospect of wholesale reform. Employers would have to offer pension benefits which did not discriminate against earlier leavers. Employees would either have to be given the right to fully indexed early leaver benefits, or the scheme would have to be put on a money purchase basis. (But see below.)

In another context, the ECJ has indicated its acceptance of employers' need to encourage long-serving employees. When considering the practice of increasing pay with seniority, which has an adverse effect on female workers (since they often have less job tenure), the ECJ in *Handels-og Kontorfunktion-aerernes Forbund i Danmark* v. *Dansk Arbejdsgiverforening* (acting for Danfloss)[52] accepted that seniority nearly always had an effect upon the effectiveness with which an employee carried out his or her duties, and as such there was no need for an employer to justify the use of seniority pay systems. However, in *Nimz* v. *Frie Und Hansestadt*,[53] the ECJ retreated from a suggestion that seniority always justified higher pay, and reaffirmed the

---

[50] [1982] IRLR 482 (EAT).   [51] Ibid., at 487.   [52] Note 34 above.
[53] [1991] IRLR 222.

general principle that each discriminatory practice must be justified in the particular circumstances of the employment in question. Few employers can claim to have adopted the final salary formula because it fitted their particular circumstances.

Article 119 is also capable, theoretically, of challenging the alternative basic pensions formula: money purchase. Here the value of the eventual benefits varies with the amount contributed and the length of time that the contributions are invested. Women who leave service to raise children are likely to have poorer contribution records, with gaps concentrated in the earlier years of their working lives. The result, invariably, is that the value of a money purchase pension to women, expressed as an addition to their hourly rate of pay, is generally lower than that of men. One can require all schemes to make additional payments on behalf of individual women in order to equalize their benefits with those earned by men. But this runs the danger of being viewed as an addition to women's salary, which however well intentioned, is itself a breach of Article 119. The fact that such payments may result in men and women receiving an hourly pay rate of equal value will not excuse such discrimination, since *Barber* requires each element of remuneration to be equal.

An extreme solution to the problems of indirect discrimination would be for all schemes to adopt the final salary formula, with earnings-inflation indexation for early leavers' benefits. But industrial tribunals are unlikely, at least for the foreseeable future, to interpret Article 119 to require this kind of major reform.[54] And the ECJ, by its statement that employers need not design their pay structures to compensate for the disadvantages faced by women in the labour market due to their greater childcare responsibilities, also does not seem ready to demand such a radical measure.

5. *Remedying a Breach of Article 119—the Principle of Levelling Up*

The consequence of finding that a rule or practice discriminates against one sex should, according to the ECJ in *Defrenne II*,[55] result in the disadvantaged sex enjoying the same treatment as the favoured one ('levelling up'). Such rights exist by reason of Article 119, and are not dependent on implementation by statute, or through scheme amendment. Thus, if a member can show that, at any time since the date of *Defrenne II* (8 April 1976), any benefit has been

---

[54] 'It is not being argued that indirect discrimination law never imposes costs on employers: moving towards a more formal and objective recruitment system is likely to do so. What is suggested is that courts and tribunals are unlikely to require changes in fundamental patterns of work organisation when to make such changes will entail substantial cost.' R. Townsend-Smith, *Sex Discrimination and Employment* (Sweet & Maxwell, 1989), p. 88.

[55] 'since Article 119 appears in the context of the harmonisation of working conditions while the improvement is being maintained, the objection that the terms of this article may be observed in other ways than by raising the lowest salaries may be set aside.' Note 13 above, at p. 472.

offered to members of another sex on a more favourable basis, she or he has an entitlement to that higher benefit. (The relevant date may be later than this, given the ECJ's limitation on the retrospective effect of its ruling. See below.) Since equal pay requires every element of remuneration to be equal, members are entitled to compare their entitlement to each and every aspect of the pension scheme with that offered to the other sex, and if the other sex receives more favourable terms, to claim them. Thus, for example, if the scheme offers, or has offered, early retirement to women at age 55, and to men at age 60, men may retire at 55. If the scheme offers women augmented pensions if they retire after aged 60, men are now entitled to similar augmentation.

Levelling up requires that members immediately enjoy the better benefits offered to the other sex. It does not require those better rights to continue to be offered in future. Thus employers may react to *Barber* by imposing a unisex deferred pay cut: reducing the benefits paid to both sexes in the future. (See below.)

The need to level up has implications for the question as to against whom the right to equal benefits may be enforced. In the context of pension schemes, it is unclear whether it is the employer, or the trustees, who are burdened by these rights. Does Article 119 require merely that the employer compensate for payments made indirectly through third parties, so that there is no right of action against the third parties themselves? The advantages of this approach are that trustees can continue to administer the scheme according to its provisions, and insurance companies can rely on their contracts with the employer and the trustees. The drawback to this interpretation is that whilst the favoured sex enjoys rights that are backed by the security of the trust fund, the rights of the other sex are unsecured. Thus, equal pay is not achieved. If every element of remuneration has to be equal, then there should be equal security for the benefits of each sex, which requires Article 119 to create rights against the trustees and, on occasions, even against the insurance company. If Article 119 operates to create rights against trustees and insurance companies, then it can be expected to override the trust rules and the insurance contract. Article 119 is superior to domestic law, whether that domestic law takes the form of statute, trust, or contract.[56]

The problems created by extending Article 119 rights to third parties depend on the extent to which the judgment has retrospective effect, and the ability of the employer to take action to alter future rights. Both of these questions are looked at later in the chapter.

---

[56] In their legal opinion for the National Association of Pension Funds, Jeremy Levy QC and Nicholas Warren argue that rights against the trustees would suffer from intractable practical problems because the trustees would have no way of knowing whether unequal rights in the pension scheme were compensated for in some other part of the remuneration package. This argument overlooks the need for *every* separate element of remuneration to be equal.

III. THE EFFECTS OF *BARBER* AND *BILKA-KAUFHAUS* ON SCHEME PROVISIONS

The survey which follows looks at five kinds of pension rules and practices: age-limits for receipt of pensions and related benefits; survivors' benefits; actuarial assumptions; integrated and bridging pensions; and rights of access to pension schemes. The first three practices are examples of direct discrimination. The fifth constitutes indirect discrimination. The fourth practice has elements of both.

A. AGE-LIMITS

Following *Barber*, men can demand an unreduced pension when they retire at the earlier women's pension age. Where women earn pensions at an augmented rate for working past their pension age, men must receive the same augmentation, from the same age. The right to take an unreduced pension at the same age as women is the single most expensive change resulting from *Barber*.[57] But voluntary action already taken will reduce the cost of equal pension ages. Whilst in 1976 the OPB found that the great majority of schemes, covering most members, had a lower normal pension age for women than men,[58] a 1988 survey found that over half the schemes surveyed either had implemented equal pension ages, or were set to do so in the near future.[59] However, *Barber* may have rendered much of that voluntary action ineffective, since over half of these schemes equalized pension ages at 65, that is, they levelled down to the least valuable benefit.[60] If *Barber* is retrospective, and *Defrenne II* applies, the men in these schemes have a right to take their pension at 60, not 65.

Equal pension ages will have some advantages for women. Early retirement benefits are sometimes augmented to take account of prospective service, with the result that men receive greater credit than women on the basis that they would have retired later. Henceforth women must now receive the same credit for prospective service. This follows from a combination of the requirement to level up and the need to look at rules affecting the pension benefit separately. However, there is at least an argument for saying that *Barber* should be applied to all the elements in the pension scheme before assessing the right to any particular advantage. With this approach, once men

---

[57] For example the OPB, in its 1976 report on the status of men and women in pension schemes, found that whilst introducing unisex mortality tables only increased the cost of providing women's pensions by 10%, the combined effect of lower mortality and earlier retirement meant that the capital value of a woman's pension at age 60, was about twice the value of the same pension for a man paid from age 65. Note 5 above, at 4.4.   [58] Ibid.

[59] P. Tomkins, *Flexibility and Fairness: A Study in Equalisation of Pension Ages and Benefits* (Joseph Rowntree Memorial Trust, 1989), p. 67.   [60] Ibid.

no longer have to receive their pension at 65, women may not be able to claim a prospective service credit up to age 65.

B. SURVIVORS' BENEFITS

Survivors' benefits were originally seen as provision provided not as pay, but in response to need. Widows were assumed to be financially dependent on their husbands' pensions. In retirement, as in work, the husband was the breadwinner.[61] In recognition of this assumption, schemes have either failed to grant pensions to widowers, or have made those pensions subject to a test of dependency which is not applied to widows' pensions. Employers may argue that survivors' benefits are an *ex gratia* benefit, provided in response to need, rather than pay, and therefore outside Article 119. However, for the reasons which follow, this argument is unlikely to succeed.

There is no case which pronounces directly on the status of survivors' benefits. When the ECJ looked at survivors' pensions in *Razzouk and Beydoun* v. *EC Commission*,[62] they decided that different pension provision · for the survivors of men and women was contrary to the principle of equal treatment, but it did not express an opinion on whether they constituted pay, since the obligations of the European Community Commission as an employer went beyond Article 119.[63]

The fact that a benefit is voluntary, and not required under the contract of employment, does not put it outside the definition of pay under Article 119. In *Garland* v. *British Rail Engineering*[64] the ECJ held that a non-contractual travel facility provided for the wives and dependent children of male but not female retired employees, constituted unequal pay under Article 119. The question was, as the court confirmed in *Barber*: 'did the worker receive [the benefit] albeit indirectly, in respect of his employment from his employer?'[65]

Survivors' benefits come closest to pay where they are paid without proof of financial need. However, the fact that a provision paid to the members of an employee's family is based on need, does not prevent it from being part of that employee's remuneration. Consider, for example, the status of employer-provided family health insurance.

Under United Kingdom law, the only requirement was for schemes which were contracted-out to provide both widows and widowers with a pension equal to half the member's GMP on similar terms.[66] But if Article 119 applies to survivors' pensions, dependants of women members will be entitled to

---

[61] What the OPB in its 1976 report called 'the traditional view' (n. 5 above, at para. 4.21. For a discussion of the influence of such assumptions on the state scheme, see B. Able-Smith, 'Sex Equality and Social Security', in J. Lewis (ed.), *Women's Welfare, Women's Rights*, n. 2 above, p. 91.   [62] Joined Cases 75 and 117/82, (1984) ECR 1509.
[63] Ibid., at 1530.   [64] [1982] IRLR 111.
[65] *Garland*, ibid., at 115. *Barber* (n. 1 above), at p. 257. In *Barber* the ECJ accepted that voluntary redundancy payments were pay.
[66] Social Security and Pensions Act 1975, ss. 29 (2A). See F. Davidson, n. 4 above, at 322.

receive pensions of equal amount, under the same conditions, as those of men. Thus, if widows' pensions are paid without proof of dependency, widowers' pensions of the same amount must also be paid automatically. Where both pensions are discretionary, evidence that the discretion is unequally applied will provide grounds for challenging a denial of benefit.[67]

The cost to a particular scheme of offering survivors' benefits to women members on the same terms as men is not particularly great, at least when compared with the costs of equalizing pension ages.[68] And, as with unequal pension ages, the total cost of this reform for all occupational pension schemes has been reduced by voluntary action. The OPB found that in 1976, survivors' benefits were, in most schemes, paid only to widows and not to widowers, and if paid to widowers, were often subject to a test of dependency;[69] but the position has improved since. A 1988 survey[70] found that whilst 100 per cent of schemes provided widows's pensions, only slightly less, 98 per cent, provided widowers' benefits. Discriminatory use of a test of dependency had, with respect to the schemes surveyed, shown a similar reduction. Whilst 96 per cent of schemes provide automatic widows' pensions, 93 per cent of widowers' pensions were also provided without proof of dependency.[71]

C. ACTUARIAL ASSUMPTIONS

Actuarial judgments are involved when the benefits for men and women are valued. Unequal pension ages make the benefits of women more expensive than those of men, because they receive them earlier. This discrepancy will be removed by the requirement of equal pension ages. However, a further element of expense relates to the mortality and morbidity tables used to calculate benefits, which reflect the fact that women, on average, live longer than men.[72] These tables indicate that women will draw their pensions for longer than men, and that their pensions will therefore, *on average*, be more expensive. As a result, women who offer to commute part of their pension into a lump sum, or who take a transfer value, have usually received a higher capital value than men. On the other hand, when women purchase pensions,

---

[67] If statistical evidence of unequal distribution were forthcoming, the trustees would have to justify such prima-facie evidence of discrimination. See *Handels-og Kontorfunktionaerernes Forbund i Danmark* v. *Dansk Arbejdsgiverforening* (acting for Danfloss), n. 34 above and E. Szyszczak, n. 40 above.

[68] The cost of offering widowers' pensions is reduced by the assumption that women members will, on average, outlive their male partners.

[69] Note 5 above, at para. 3.5 (b).   [70] Note 59 above, at pp. 61–70.   [71] Ibid.

[72] The importance of actuarial factors, and the case for requiring the use of unisex tables, are discussed in D. Wilkie, 'Notes on Equal Treatment for Men and Women in Occupational Social Security Schemes', 111 Journal of the Institute of Actuaries (1984) 15; 'Report of the Working Party on Discrimination in Insurance and Pensions' (Institute of Actuaries and Faculty of Actuaries, 1988); and A. Goldrick, *Equal Treatment in Occupational Pension Schemes: A Research Report* (Equal Opportunities Commission, 1984).

they have to pay more than men. Thus, with money purchase schemes, women have to accumulate more contributions in order to secure an annuity which pays them the same rate of benefit as a man. And, when women purchase additional pensions from a final salary scheme, they have to pay more than men for the same increase in pension. Some final salary schemes apply the same principles to the basic pension, with women enjoying a lower rate of accrual, or having to pay a higher rate of contributions to enjoy the same rate of accrual.[73]

Since the effect of using different actuarial tables is that men and women receive different levels of benefit, different capital sums, and pay different contributions in exchange for equal benefits, the continued use of these tables is incompatible with the requirement in *Barber* that each element of pay must be equal, in order to facilitate comparisons.[74] The use of sex-based tables has been defended on the basis that their use increases the ability of an employer to pay men and women benefits of equal actuarial value.[75] While this may be true, the pursuit of actuarial accuracy must here, as in *Barber*, be sacrificed to facilitate the comparison of benefits paid to men and women.

Subject to the interpretation given to *Barber* on the question of retrospective effect, pension entitlements must now be calculated using the same tables for each sex, with respect to each element of benefit. This will undoubtedly increase the cost of these accrued benefits, since each sex will ask for their benefits to be calculated using the other sex's tables whenever this will result in their receiving more.[76]

1. Actuarial Assumptions and Additional Voluntary Contributions

Employers may argue for the right to continue to use different tables when calculating the benefits to be provided in respect of additional voluntary contributions ('AVCs'), on the basis that since these are financed entirely through the employee's own contributions, they should not be regarded as pay. However, where employers meet the administrative costs of offering AVCs,[77] this element of subsidy may be sufficient to justify treating AVCs as pay.

But even where employees are charged the full cost of AVCs, they still represent a benefit to the employee, since the cost of purchasing such benefits from an outside source is usually much higher.[78] The right to purchase an employer's goods at cost price is usually seen as a benefit in kind, which

---

[73] The OPB found only a few schemes which practised discrimination of this type. N. 5 above, at para. 3.10.   [74] See pp. 204–5.

[75] See the respondent's arguments in *Neath* v. *Hugh Steeper Ltd.* [1991] PLR 91 at 102.

[76] See e.g. the pleading of the applicant in *Neath* v. *Hugh Steeper Ltd.* (ibid.).

[77] Where they already meet the administrative costs of the main scheme, they are likely also to meet the costs of paying AVCs.

[78] Upwards of 20% of contributions to personal pensions go in administrative charges. The administrative costs of occupational pension schemes are only 10%. B. Davies, *Better Pensions for All* (Institute of Public Policy Research, 1993) pp. 16, 18.

forms part of the employees' remuneration. It is hard to see why the right to purchase a pension from the employer should be treated differently.

D. BRIDGING PENSIONS AND INTEGRATED SCHEMES

1. Integrated Pensions

So-called 'integrated schemes' reproduce the inequalities of the state pension scheme. These schemes offer a pension which 'tops up' the basic flat-rate state retirement pension to a given figure. To calculate what the scheme must pay, one must therefore take that figure and that subtract all or part of the basic state pension which the member receives, or is assumed to receive. Whilst treatment is equal when men and women are in receipt of the same state pensions, the schemes work differently when men retire between 60 and 65, since, unlike women of this age, they receive no state pension and consequently have no deduction in respect of it.

Where the integration is based on the assumption that basic state pension will be paid at the full rate, women suffer from the fact that, more often than men, their national insurance contribution record does not qualify them for a full pension.[79]

2. Bridging Pensions

These are often paid by ordinary schemes to members who retire before the state pension age.[80] They are intended to compensate these members for the fact that, until they reach state pension age, they cannot draw the basic state pension. They thus reduce the hardship of early retirement. Discrimination occurs when men retire between the ages of 60 and 65 years. During this period, women will be in receipt of a basic state pension while men are not, and therefore men receive extra remuneration from the pension scheme while women do not.

Do Bridging Pensions and Integrated Schemes Contravene Article 119?   Where women are in receipt of a full state pension, integration and bridging pensions allow men and women aged 60 to 64 to receive the same total level of benefits. However, while their total income is equal, their pay is not. The argument that all social security benefits paid with respect to employment should be treated as pay within Article 119 was considered and rejected by the ECJ in *Defrenne I*.[81] Only the occupational pension is pay, and it must be equal.

In consequence, within integrated schemes, the pension paid to women

---

[79] See Linda Luckhaus, 'Social Security: A Question of Difference?', 19 ILJ (1990) 48 at 52.

[80] A 1988 survey of 138 occupational pension schemes with an employed population of 2.2 million showed that 30% incorporated an element to compensate for non-payment of state pension prior to state pension age. See P. Tomkins, n. 59 above.

[81] Note 20 above.

aged 60 to 64 years should not be reduced to take account of the state pension. Where bridging pensions are paid to men, women can also claim them.[82]

Even when both sexes are in receipt of state pensions, integrated pensions which assume that both sexes receive a full flat-rate state retirement pension may indirectly discriminate against women. This is because fewer women than men manage to pay all the contributions required for the full basic state pension. On the other hand, integrated schemes which deduct only such of the basic state pension as is actually received, may discriminate indirectly against men, for the same reason.

There will also be problems in those schemes where, to compensate for taking the state pension into account, no contributions are charged, and no occupational pension earned, with respect to those earnings upon which the state pension is based, (the lower earnings limit). This disregard will affect lower-paid workers to a greater extent than higher-paid ones, and will have the effect of excluding the lowest-paid workers from any occupational pension whatsoever. Women tend to have lower earnings than men, and are therefore disproportionately affected by such rules. Unless the employer can show that the rule which disregards lower earnings is justified, this will amount to indirect discrimination.

E. ACCESS TO SCHEMES

Stipulating different entry conditions for each sex is contrary to the Social Security and Pensions Act 1973.[83] Regulations made under the Act[84] allow employers to stipulate different maximum ages for scheme entry, but these regulations will now fall foul of Article 119 on the basis that women and men who are the same age must have the same rights of access to pension schemes, or they will not enjoy the same rates of pay. Conditions of access which make no reference to a member's sex will still be open to challenge as indirect discrimination where they have an adverse impact on one sex. Restricting access by reference to an employee's hours of work, salary levels, years of service, or job description (whether by reference to trade, occupation, or more general categories such as 'staff' versus 'works' or 'manual' employees, or by having special top-up schemes for executive grades) can all be challenged where the effect of those restrictions is to exclude a larger proportion of one sex that another. The difference in impact required to

---

[82] This interpretation of Article 119 was accepted by the EAT in *Roberts* v. *Birds Eye* [1991] IRLR 19 with the result that the female appellant was entitled to receive a pension up to age 65 without any deduction in respect of her state pension.

[83] Section 53. Trustees and managers of schemes have a statutory duty to see that their schemes comply with this requirement, which the OPB enforces. The OPB can modify a scheme's rules whenever the scheme's own power of amendment seems inadequate for these purposes.   [84] Note 7 above.

sustain such a challenge will, on occasions, be very slight. In *Lea* v. *The Greater Manchester Police Health Authority*[85] the fact that 99.4 per cent of women, and only 93.4 per cent of men, could comply with a job condition, was held sufficient to uphold a finding of indirect discrimination under the Sex Discrimination Act 1975.

There are important forms of discrimination in the provision of pensions which lie beyond the reach of Article 119. It will be hard to challenge the exclusion of women from occupational schemes which results from their concentration in companies and industries which do not offer occupational pensions to their employees.[86] These women cannot point to another employee who, by reason of a pension, receives higher pay from their common employer.[87]

The ECJ has interpreted Article 119 to require equal pay for the same work, or 'for work to which equal value is attributed'.[88] Where pensions are offered to only some grades or occupations within a company, challenge cannot be based on the failure to provide equal pay for the same work, but must be based on the claim that each group of workers is doing work of equal value. In the absence of proof that different work is of equal value, the employer is free to provide unequal pay.[89] Unequal pay can take the form of different rates of current pay, or equal current pay but different access to fringe benefits such as pensions. Thus, where the employer discriminates in its pension provision between technical and clerical workers, or industrial and catering staff, challenging that discrimination under Article 119 will be made difficult by the need to show that the work of these different sectors is of equal value.

Part-timers have an advantage in challenging such practices. The division between part- and full-time work does not by itself encompass any difference in skills or qualifications. Both kinds of workers are assumed to be doing work of equal value.[90]

Once adverse impact is shown, the employer will, as discussed earlier, have to justify the rule in question. Whilst cost is no defence to a charge of direct discrimination, it can be used to show the necessity of continuing with a practice which has adverse impact. Administrative costs and indeed, administrative convenience have, in the context of challenges under the Sex

---

[85] [1991] PLR 81. EAT.

[86] 3.1 million male employees, as against 3.5 million female employees, work for employers who offer no pension scheme. This represents 51.6% of male employees and 77.7% of female employees. Note 3 above, table 5.3. For a discussion of women's segregation within the labour force, and the reasons for it, see J. Lewis, *Women in Britain Since 1945* (Blackwell, 1992), Ch 3.

[87] The Equal Pay Act, s. 6, allows comparison with workers employed by an 'associated employer'. Whilst Article 119 may also extend this far, it cannot be expected to require equal pay for work done for different independent employers.

[88] *Worringham & Humphries* v. *Lloyds Bank Ltd.*, n. 24 above, at 187.   [89] Ibid.

[90] 'The pay practice results in *different pay* (in a broad sense) for *identical work* carried out under different conditions (full or part-time).' A. G. Darmon in *Bilka-Kaufhaus* (1986) ECR 1607 at 1617.

Discrimination Act 1975, been accepted.[91] But administrative cost is not, by itself, a particularly strong argument. Extra administrative costs may justify giving someone a lower level of benefit, but they do not justify forfeiting the benefit altogether. A more equitable solution is to take account of the increased administrative costs by decreasing the value of the benefit, and only to remove the benefit altogether where its value is equalled or exceeded by the administrative costs involved.

Employers will be on stronger ground where they can argue that market conditions justify them in saving themselves not simply administrative costs, but the whole benefit. They can be expected to argue, as did the employer in *Bilka-Kaufhaus*, that there is no need to pay pensions to workers in particular categories of employment. However, before making such arguments, employers will need to look carefully at the constitution of both the included and the excluded groups. For example, it may seem plausible to argue that full-time workers require pensions while part-timers do not, but the argument is less convincing where the part-time workers include book-keepers and accountants and the full-time workers are manual labourers.

IV. EMPLOYERS' REACTIONS TO BARBER

A. RISING FUTURE COSTS

Whatever the outcome of the cases pending on the question of retrospection, the future costs of funding pensions are going to rise as a consequence of the need to comply with Article 119. As from 17 May 1990, the rights of men and women to pension benefits are equal under European Community law. Whatever that equality may finally come to mean, it is clear, as the last section has shown, that a large number of provisions which purport to grant one sex benefits on more advantageous terms will fail to have that effect. *Defrenne II*[92] indicates that levelling up is required, and both sexes must enjoy whichever terms are the more advantageous with respect to each element of the pension scheme.

The full costs of complying with Article 119 depend, in part, on the ability of employees to enforce their rights under Article 119. If the only means of enforcement is by actions before industrial tribunals or the Pensions Ombudsman, then employers can reckon on less than 100 per cent enforcement of the right to equal benefits. However, making employees fight to enforce their legal right to equal pensions may damage industrial relations and many, if not most employers, will prefer to avoid this.

If Article 119 operates to overrule the scheme's provisions, the implementation is harder to avoid. The trustees will be in breach of trust if they pay out benefits on an incorrect basis, or if they fail to ensure that the employer's

---

[91] *Rainey* v. *Greater Glasgow Health Board Eastern District* [1987] IRLR 26 (HL). See Hervey, n. 47 above, pp. 818–20.   [92] Note 13 above.

contribution is calculated on a post-*Barber* basis. Knowingly allowing a scheme to be funded on an incorrect basis, or paying out benefits that are known to be wrong, could both be considered to be examples of wilful default and therefore make the trustees personally liable.[93]

1. Reacting to Increased Costs

While some employers will react to *Barber* by hoping that their employees will never hear of their increased rights, or never enforce them if they do, the majority can be expected to make their pension schemes comply with Article 119.[94] They will therefore be looking to amend their schemes' provisions. But not all employers will wish to provide levelled-up benefits in future. Employers may wish to have equal pension ages above the current women's pension age, or to introduce a common basis for commutation of pension which is less generous than that currently given to men. Such amendments are likely to cause legal problems, both in contract and under the law of trusts. We shall look first at the problems in trust law.

2. Amending Trusts

Powers of amendment usually prohibit amendments which reduce the members' accrued rights.[95] Future service rights are usually seen as expectations rather than accrued rights, and therefore fall outside this prohibition. However, the power of amendment has to be exercised in accordance with the trustees' general duties to the beneficiaries. The highest of these duties, as described in Chapter 3, is to act in the best interests of the members. Thus trustees may not be able to use the power of amendments to reduce the effects of *Barber* simply because the employer requests this. There will be some pressure on them to demonstrate that the amendments are in the interests of the members. In effect, they are called upon to negotiate the

[93] For example, the legal opinion obtained by the National Association of Pension Funds (n. 56 above) advised that trustees whose pension schemes are discontinued as a consequence of *Barber* should seek the advice of the court on the value of benefits to be paid before implementing winding up.

[94] In a survey carried out for the NAPF after *Barber*, it was found that 37% of schemes had made changes in response. The resultant level of compliance with Article 119 appears to be quite high. Some 65% had equalized pension ages for all scheme members, whilst a further 18% had equalized pension ages for new and future scheme entrants. 56% had equalized the amounts by which early retirement pensions were reduced in respect of all service, a further 6% with respect to future service, and a further 16% in respect of new entrants. Commutation terms had been equalized in 55% of schemes for all service, and a further 3% of schemes in respect of future service. 30% of schemes had equalized the terms of additional voluntary contributions for all service, and a further 10% in respect of future contributions. But action to equalize benefits in respect of ex-employees seems much less. Of the 37% of companies who had taken action in response to *Barber*, just over one-fifth (21%) had not taken any action to equalize the benefits of the deferred or current pensioners. But note that there is some evidence that equalizing does not mean levelling up. For example, before *Barber* only 19% of schemes had a common pension age of 65. After *Barber* this rose to 43%, See 'Survey Reveals Dramatic Equalizing of Pension Ages', IRS Employment Trends, 7 June 1991, p. 2.

[95] Such a restriction may even be implied. See Inglis-Jones, *The Law of Occupational Pension Schemes* (Sweet & Maxwell, 1989), paras. 7–11.

amendments which should follow from *Barber* in a manner similar to that which has been previously adopted over the distribution of surpluses. In these negotiations the same factors will be brought to bear, that is, conflicts of interest, and the awareness that the employer, in the last instance, can wind up the scheme and leave the members without a pension scheme or substitute an inferior scheme in its place. The employer's ability to carry out this threat is affected by the terms of the winding-up clause (in particular, whether the trustees have an independent power to augment the benefits on winding up). There may be circumstances in which the employer's use of this threat could be seen as a breach of the duty to act in good faith, but, as Chapter 4 showed, it is extremely unclear what conduct is covered by this duty.

New entrants to the scheme are not current beneficiaries, and should be outside the duty of care and not covered by any restriction on the amendment power. As such, trustees who alter scheme rules to reduce the benefits offered to new entrants can be more sure that their actions will not be challenged. However, whilst new entrants are not beneficiaries, this does not mean that the trustees are free to reduce their benefits simply because the employer asks for this. The fact that current beneficiaries are not harmed by a reduction in the benefits of new entrants is not the point. Trustees have a duty to do their best for the current members,[96] not simply to avoid acts which harm them. If the employer wishes the trustees to alter the terms of the trust, it can be expected to grant some form of quid pro quo to the current members.[97]

Problems only arise in the law of contract if the current terms of the pension scheme are considered to be part of the contract of employment. As was shown in Chapter 2, one interpretation of the pension term in an employment contract is simply to allow the employee to be a member of whatever pension scheme exists on whatever terms it contains. On this basis, an amendment which was itself not a breach of trust could not give rise to a separate action in contract.[98] But if the current terms of the pension scheme are considered to form part of the contract of employment,[99] then an amendment which radically altered them could constitute a breach of contract. If an employee left in response to the breach, it might ground an action in unfair dismissal. An employee may prefer to stay on and apply to court for a declaration and injunction restraining the breach,[100] or damages.

---

[96] *Cowan* v. *Scargill* [1985] 1 Ch. 270.

[97] *Re Courage Group's Pension Schemes* [1987] 1 All ER 528 at 545.

[98] See *Cadoux* v. *Regional Council* (1986) IRLR 131 and *Beech* v. *Reed Corrugated Cases Ltd.* (1956) 1 WLR 807.

[99] See *Mihlenstedt* v. *Barclays Bank Ltd.* [1989] IRLR 124; *Imperial Group Pension Trust Ltd.* v. *Imperial Tobacco Limited* (Ch. d) [1991] 2 All ER 597; [1991] 1 WLR 589; and Chapter 2, pp. 54–63.

[100] Specific performance would be available if common law damages were felt to be an unsatisfactory remedy. The availability of an injunction and declaration for a contractual breaches arising in connection with pension schemes is acknowledged by Nourse LJ in *Mihlenstedt*, ibid., at 125.

Employees who take no action may continue to accrue rights on the basis of their previous contract of employment on the basis that they have worked on 'under protest'. To prevent this, it may be necessary to formally dismiss and retire each employee.[101]

Some employers may wish to undo the retrospective effects of *Barber* by offering members equal past service rights but without levelling up.[102] Restriction on a power of amendment may be circumvented by winding up the scheme and then giving the member a choice of equal levelled-up early leaver's benefits in the existing scheme, or lower equal benefits with the chance of future service benefits in the replacement scheme. While this might still give rise to an action for constructive dismissal, it is not expected that many such actions will be pursued. The feasibility of this plan depends on the terms of winding-up power, or the power of transfer, and the interpretation which is likely to be given to the general duty of care which applies to the exercise of such powers.[103] It is also unclear whether the ECJ will allow accrued Article 119 rights to be overridden by employers' actions in this manner. If Article 119 genuinely requires that male and female employees receive equal pay in respect of past service, the national courts are required to give effect to those rights *directly*. If the national law of contract or trusts can be manipulated to defeat those rights, European Community law may still require that the national courts find means to give them direct effect.[104]

But the employers' need to undo the retrospective effects of *Barber* depends on the extent to which the ruling has retrospective effect. And it is to this issue which we now turn.

V. HOW RETROSPECTIVE IS *BARBER*?[105]

The court exercised its power to take account of the serious difficulties which its ruling would have, and to restrict its application to events in the past. The particular difficulties of which it had been made aware were 'the serious financial consequences' which would follow if the judgment were applied immediately to UK schemes, given the number of workers who belonged to such schemes and the degree of discrimination practised by them, in

---

[101] See *Burdett-Coutts* v. *Herts County Council* (1984) IRLR 91 and *Rigby* v. *Ferodo* (1987) IRLR 516 (H of L). *Hogg* v. *Dover College* (1990) ICR 38.

[102] One computer company reacted to *Barber* by writing to all its female employees saying that, unless they signed an agreement to change their employment age to 65, they would be made redundant and re-employed on a new contract the following day. Talk given by Bill Day of the GMB to the Northern Independent Pensions Research Group, 13 October 1990.

[103] For the trustees' duties, see Chapter 3. For the employers' duty of good faith, see Chapter 4.

[104] *Marleasing SA* v. *La Comercial Internacional De Alimentacion SA* (Case c-106/89) [1992] 1 CMLR 305.

[105] See, generally, *The Encyclopedia of Labour Law*, paras. 1B-2618–1B-2622.

particular by providing for different pensionable ages.[106] This was not simply a question of expense. The court noted that the member states had been allowed to defer the equalization of pension ages within state pension schemes under the 1979 Directive on equal treatment in matters of social security, and that this exception had been incorporated into the 1986 Directive on equal treatment within occupational social security schemes:

In light of those provisions, the Member States and the parties were reasonably entitled to consider that Article 119 did not apply to pensions paid under contracted-out schemes and that derogations from the principle of equality between men and women still existed in that sphere.[107]

The court therefore ruled that Article 119 has no direct effect with respect to 'entitlement' to a pension with effect from a date prior to the judgment.

The court seemed unaware of the number of interpretations that could be given, within a pension scheme, to the idea of an 'entitlement', and of the widely different financial implications which these interpretations yield. There are at least five interpretations.

A. THE ACCRUALS BASIS

One interpretation of *Barber* is that it only relates to entitlements that were accrued through service after 16 May 1990. For example, in a scheme based on sixtieths, male employees will receive a pension of 1/60th of final salary from age 65 for each year of service before this date, and a pension of 1/60th of final salary payable at age 60 for each year of service thereafter. This interpretation removes almost all retrospective application of *Barber*. Only actions commenced before the *Barber* decision can affect benefits accrued for service before 17 May 1990. This interpretation minimizes the disruption caused by *Barber* to scheme funding.[108]

B. THE DATE OF FIRST PAYMENT

The second interpretation of *Barber* is that it only excludes pensions which have actually come into payment, or been the subject of a transfer value, before 17 May 1990. The word 'entitlement' is taken to mean an entitlement to receive money from the scheme. The value of members' accrued rights cannot be known before they leave the scheme. They cannot claim any

---

[106] The UK government has estimated the cost of implementing *Barber* to range from £40 to £50 million, depending on the assumptions used. See statement by Secretary of State for Social Security, 26 June 1991 HC 998.   [107] Note 1 above, p. 259.

[108] The latter interpretation was argued in counsel's opinion obtained by the National Association of Pension Funds, n. 56 above. It is based on the approach adopted in *Defrenne II* (n. 13 above), at p. 481, in which the ECJ stated that: 'The direct effect of Article 119 cannot be relied upon in order to support claims concerning pay periods prior to the date of this judgment.'

payment until they retire or leave the scheme (when they can ask for a transfer value). A survivor's entitlement to payment does not commence until the member dies.[109]

C. ALL FUTURE INSTALMENTS OF PENSION

There is a third interpretation. Each payment from the fund may be treated as a separate entitlement. This interpretation would improve the position of existing pensioners, who could ask for their future pensions to be adjusted to take account of any detriment suffered when the initial rate of pension was calculated. For example, a man who received a pension which was reduced because he retired between the ages of 60 and 65 could now ask that it be recalculated so that future payments could be on an unreduced basis.

D. ALL CURRENT EMPLOYEES' ENTITLEMENTS

A fourth interpretation, based on the reading of the judgment in French,[110] is that the court only intended to exclude claims by persons whose contract with the employer had terminated.[111] On this basis, pensioners and deferred pensioners would be excluded, whilst those who left a scheme without leaving employment would not, and the status of persons whose companies had been the subject of amalgamation would depend on whether reorganization of companies took place before or after the introduction of the Transfer of Undertaking (Protection of Employment) Regulations[112] (which preserve continuity of contract on transfer of business).

E. ALL BENEFITS EXCEPT THOSE PAYABLE UNDER THE WINDING-UP CLAUSE IF THE SCHEME HAD BEEN WOUND UP ON 16 MAY 1990

A fifth interpretation excludes such rights to benefit as a member had if the scheme had been wound up on 16 May 1990. This is like the accruals basis described before, except that, by calculating the part of the benefit excluded from *Barber* on the same basis as an early leaver, the effect of the exclusion is lessened.[113] The method is compatible with the idea of mimimum entitlements, since the only benefits members are sure to receive are their rights under the winding-up clause, to the extent that these have been properly funded.

---

[109] This interpretation was accepted by the industrial tribunal in *Roscoe* v. *Hick Hargreaves & Co. Ltd.* [1990] IRLR 240.

[110] Though the authoritative version was in English.

[111] See Pension Lawyer, June 1990, p. 10.

[112] SI 1981 No. 1794/1981. On the effect of these regulations, see generally J. McMullen, *Business Transfers and Employee Rights* (Butterworths, 1987).

[113] NAPF opinion, n. 56 above.

F. AND HOW FAR BACK?

Unless one interprets *Barber* to refer only to benefits accrued after 17 May 1990, the extent to which past accruals could be increased must also be considered. Would Article 119 cover benefits which were accrued before the European Community Act 1972? If men and women are to have the right to have their pensions calculated in the same manner, using the same rules, this will, with respect to long-serving employees, alter the value of benefits which accrued in respect of service before the United Kingdom joined the Community.[114] However, if the right is only to have those rules altered for the purpose of achieving equal deferred pay, and only for such period as equal pay was required by Article 119, then adjustments will only affect benefits which are attributable to service after 1976. The latter approach is in keeping with the ECJ's treatment of pension benefits in *Defrenne II*[115] where the right to claim equal pay was limited to periods of service after Article 119 became effective in Belgium.[116] However, the fact that the ECJ used different language from *Defrenne II* may indicate that a different time-limit was intended.[117]

G. CHOOSING THE RIGHT INTERPRETATION

The text of the judgment provides few clues as to which standard was intended. The reference to 'financial consequences' provides no indication of what level of cost might reasonably be born by occupational pension schemes, remembering that it was only in 1986 that the government introduced legislation aimed at curbing what it regarded as overfunding (surpluses) within UK funds.[118]

The judgment refers to:

overriding considerations of legal certainty [which] preclude legal situations which have exhausted all their effects in the past from being called in question where that might upset retrospectively the financial balance of many contracted-out schemes

The only situations where pensions have exhausted all their legal effects are where all the monies due to a member or her dependants have been paid. This is the third standard described above. However, if the judgment only protects schemes from claims by persons who have already received a transfer payment, or the estate of pensioners who have died, it will do little to prevent financial upset amongst schemes. At the other extreme, whilst applying

---

[114] Barber claimed for rights accruing under his pension scheme prior to the date when the UK joined the European Economic Community.   [115] Note 13 above.

[116] The end of the first transition period, 1 January 1973.

[117] See D. Curtin (n. 27 above), at 488.

[118] Finance Act 1986, Schedule 12, now Income and Corporation Taxes Act 1988, Schedule 22.

Barber only to those benefits accruing after 17 May 1990 will leave the schemes with no unexpected liabilities, it will also mean that men and women continue to receive unequal benefits until the last survivor of a member with pre-1991 service dies, which will be well into the twenty-first century. Such leniency serves neither the social nor economic aims of Article 119.[119] The social aims will be undermined by the time taken for the effects of discrimination to disappear. The economic aim of fair competition between companies employing different amounts of male and female labour will also be undermined, since those companies which have anticipated *Barber* will, under the non-retrospective ruling, have suffered a major competitive disadvantage compared with those who have been content to wait.

In the absence of any evidence as to the precise financial position of individual funds, method 5 has some merit. Because it treats all members as if the scheme was wound up on 16 May 1991, it can be justified on the basis that all properly funded schemes would have been able to meet their liabilities if they had been wound up on this date, in response to *Barber*. Schemes which did not wind up must be presumed to be able to afford this extra liability. On the other hand, if large numbers of schemes do wind up in response to the *Barber* ruling, that can hardly be anything other than a major upset to the equilibrium of British companies and industrial relations, even if the schemes prove to be solvent.

H. CONTRACTED-IN SCHEMES

The judgment only refers to contracted-out schemes, and therefore the temporal limitation is restricted to them also. But the rules of contracted-in schemes are likely also to breach Article 119, and they too relied upon the two Directives cited by the ECJ as reasons why contracted-out schemes could not have expected this liability. However, there are two factors which should be taken into account when deciding whether to treat contracted-in schemes with the same leniency. The first is the decision in *Defrenne I*,[120] and particularly the opinion of Advocate-General Dutheillet de Lamonthe, which indicated that schemes which pay benefits in addition to state schemes ('supplementary schemes') were within the scope of Article 119. Thus, contracted-in schemes were on notice, two years before the United Kingdom joined the European Economic Community, that their benefits were covered

---

[119] 'First, in the light of the different stages of development of social legislation in the Member States, the aim of Article 119 is to avoid a situation in which undertakings established in states which have actually implemented the principle of equal pay suffer a competitive disadvantage as compared with undertakings in states which have not yet eliminated discrimination against women workers as regards pay. Secondly, this provision forms part of the social objectives of the Community, which is not merely an economic union, but is at the same time intended, by common action, to ensure social progress and seek the constant improvement of the living and working conditions of their people, as emphasized by the Preamble to the Treaty.' *Defrenne II* (n. 13 above), at 472.   [120] Note 20 above.

by Article 119. The second factor is the decision in *Bilka-Kaufhaus*.[121] In this case, four years before *Barber*, and three months before the 1986 Directive on occupational social security, the ECJ positively ruled that supplementary schemes were subject to Article 119. This judgment gave no protection against retrospective liability.

I. THE ATTITUDE OF THE UNITED KINGDOM GOVERNMENT

The United Kingdom government will argue that *Barber* should not be applied to benefits referable to service before May 1990. In the meantime, it has increased the ability of funds to afford retrospective application of Article 119, by announcing that it will not implement the provisions of the Social Security Act 1990 which were to have required schemes to index pensions in payment by up to 5 per cent.[122] It has also been party to the addition of a protocol to the Maastricht Treaty[123] which will, if the treaty is ratified by all twelve member states, have the effect of limiting the application of Article 119 to occupational pension scheme benefits accruing as a result of service after 16 May 1990. The protocol[124] states that:

For the purposes of **Article 119** of this Treaty, benefits under occupational social security schemes shall not be considered as remuneration if and in so far as they are attributable to periods of employment prior to 17 May 1990, except in the case of workers or those claiming under them who have before that date initiated legal proceedings or introduced an equivalent claim under the applicable national law.

The protocol states that benefits accruing with respect to service before 17 May 1990 shall not be pay under Article 119. Employers will not need to provide such benefits on an equal basis. As such benefits will not be pay, there is no restriction on the form of inequality which may occur. Thus, they can be paid at different ages, calculated using different actuarial tables, or subject to different conditions. With respect to benefits accruing before 17 May 1990, all of the discriminatory practices outlined at the beginning of this chapter will become lawful under European Community Law.

J. FUTURE PROBLEMS WITH RETROSPECTION

Whatever the final decision on *Barber*, and whether or not Maastricht is finally ratified by all twelve member states, problems of retrospection will not disappear. Even after schemes have sorted out their liability for direct discrimination, claims based on indirect discrimination will continue to arise. Employees who can show that they have been unjustifiably excluded from pension schemes in the past, will have rights to past service pension benefits.

---

[121] Note 19 above.

[122] Statement by Tony Newton, Secretary of State for Social Security, 26 June 1991. HC 998.

[123] [1992] CMLR 573.

[124] Ibid., at 740.

If the application of Article 119 is limited to benefits accruing after 16 May 1990, the cost of providing such past service rights will be small at first but, as time passes, the retrospective costs of failing to anticipate European law in this area will steadily rise. Whilst this may cause the pensions industry some concern, it should be stressed that such retrospective liability is not simply a problem with pensions. Past service creates past liability for unequal pay, whether that pay be fringe benefits, wages, or pensions. The extent to which Article 119 rights can be defeated by domestic law on the limitation of actions has yet to be sorted out.[125]

VI. CONCLUSION

The application of Article 119 to pension schemes is likely to lead to considerable future litigation. There are many questions remaining to be answered and, given the importance of pension rights to retiring employees, and the opportunity for litigation presented by industrial tribunals, actions involving them will undoubtedly be brought. Uncertainty as to the boundaries of indirect discrimination will encourage scheme members to challenge rules of access, and basic pension formulas. Where the application of Article 119 is clear, as it is in most cases of direct discrimination, the government should not expect employees to enforce Article 119 through actions in the tribunals, but should introduce implementing legislation which provides for scheme rules to be overruled or modified to give effect to Article 119.

[125] The Limitation Act 1980 provides for a limitation period for actions in trust or contract of six years. There are at least two problems with this limit. First, the extent to which accrued Article 119 rights can be defeated by member states limitation legislation. In *Emmott* v. *Minister for Social Welfare and Attorney General* [1991] IRLR 387, the ECJ held that such Acts could not take effect until national implementing legislation was correctly applied. (But this was in an action brought against a public body, and the reasoning was equivalent to estoppel.) The Limitation Act 1980 would certainly have to be interpreted in such a way as not to defeat Article 119 rights, *Marleasing* (n. 104 above). Secondly, must actions to protect Article 119 rights be brought within six years of the date such rights accrue, or six years from when payment first commences, or six years from the receipt of a particular payment? Whatever the outcome of *Barber* on temporal limitation, the need to make Article 119 effective indicates that employees should be able to commence an action within six years of a date when they are likely to become aware of their rights. This indicates that payments, rather than accruals, should mark the commencement of the limitation period.

[10]
The Reform of Pensions Law

I. THE DIFFERENT PERSPECTIVES

Only when that issue [who owns the pension funds] has been settled can other important matters, such as which interests should be represented on the pension fund, and what weight should be given to each interest, be considered.[1]

The central concern of this book has been whether the current law of occupational pension schemes, which is based upon the law of trusts, provides adequate protection for the rights and expectations of scheme members. Identifying the law has been complicated by the need to take account of two opposing perspectives: are pension funds deferred pay, to be kept independent from the employer; or are they part of the employer's production costs, and necessarily under its control? These same two perspectives are fundamental to the process of reform. Without forming a view of what members are entitled to expect from their pension schemes, one cannot assess what constitutes abuse. Identifying abuse is a precondition to recommending and assessing proposals for reform.

Having decided what needs to be restrained, one must then assess the likely reaction of employers to restrictions on their freedom to draft and operate pension schemes in their own interests. Those who accept the legitimacy of members' claims may still decide that the price of reform, in terms of lower or different benefits, is too great.

The earlier chapters of this book have indicated the need for reform of the law of occupational pensions. For those who accept the viewpoint, articulated most fully in Chapter 2, that pension funds are members' pay, much of the current legal framework is unsatisfactory. The employers' ability to manipulate funding levels, discussed in Chapter 6, indicates the need either for minimum funding levels, or for some other restraint on the manner in which contribution levels are fixed and transfer payments calculated. The duties of trustees (Chapters 3 and 8) and employers (Chapter 4), will seem too uncertain and, given the problems which members face in securing access to information, and their inability to meet legal costs (Chapter 5), difficult to

[1] See Social Security Select Committee, second report, 'The Operation of Pension Funds', HC 61-II 1991/2, para. 284.

enforce through the courts. For those who consider that all of the pension fund belongs to the members, there are insufficient restraints on the employer's ability to benefit from surpluses (Chapter 7).

From a deferred pay perspective, there is clearly a need for reform. The second part of this chapter, which is written from this perspective, examines how pension law might be reformed to meet members' expectations. But we begin by considering the employers' attitude towards reform.

II. PROPOSALS FOR REFORM—FROM THE EMPLOYERS' PERSPECTIVE

A. THE EMPLOYERS' ATTITUDE TO REFORM

Employers do not require radical reforms to the current law of pensions. They value the fact that trust law allows them to draft a scheme's rules in whatever manner they see fit.[2] And where the rules of a particular scheme are inconvenient, they have greater ability to change those rules than do members.[3] Whilst trust law and the employer's duty of good faith undoubtedly restrain employers, there is no evidence that employers generally are so inconvenienced by such restrictions that they wish to see the present system radically changed.

To the employees' claim that the pension fund is their property, the employers' reply is essentially, 'Read the rules'. It is a variant of *caveat emptor*. Employers don't have to provide pensions, so why should employees object to the form in which they have been provided?[4] If employees have generally misunderstood the nature of trust law, and failed to realize that the rules of a pension scheme create a situation in which the pension fund is controlled by the employer, this is no fault of employers.

The pension promise is, from the employers' perspective, simply to pay the fixed benefits. These will be paid from the scheme, to the extent of the assets in the pension fund, and from the company, if the pension fund has insufficient assets. The pension fund, which secures the fixed benefits, is like a mortgage. The assets which exceed the amount necessary to secure the fixed benefits on winding up are the equivalent of the mortgagor's equity, with the employer as mortgagor. The Confederation of British Industry would like to see a statutory statement that:

[2] '. . . the employer must have the freedom of employers to write the constitution of a pension fund in its trust deed.' Confederation of British Industries' (CBI), evidence to the Pension Law Reform Committee ('the Goode Committee'), 'Occupational Pension Schemes: Securing the Future', p. 15. 'It is no more desirable that legislation should restrict [the employer's] freedom to provide pensions, and the terms on which they are provided, than it is for requirements to be made on any other element of the remuneration package, including pay'. KPMG Peat Marwick, 'The Future of Pensions: Proposals by a Group of Major UK Employers', November 1992, p. 7.

[3] By amending the scheme, or transferring assets from one scheme to another, or applying to the OPB for a modification order to allow refunds.

[4] 'It is illogical to restrict the terms on which an employer will provide benefits if there is no requirement that any benefits at all need be provided', KPMG, n. 2 above, p. 7.

a pension fund is not to be regarded as a conventional trust with the beneficiaries having an interest in the assets of the fund, but as a guarantee fund supporting the employer's promise.[5]

This does not mean that employers oppose all reform. Subject to a concern to avoid significant increases in administrative costs, employers will not object to being required to live up to 'good practice': being required to do what most employers do anyway, or being prohibited from doing what employers have no wish to do. Thus, for example, there was no outcry against the recent introduction of self-investment restrictions,[6] since this is a minority practice which the managements of most companies do not expect to carry out in future. However, restrictions on refunds, which are simply self-investment without any prospect of repayment, would be far more controversial.

The standard of 'good practice' will justify measures to restrain employers who break the law, with an inevitable emphasis in the context of the Maxwell scandal (in which £420 million went missing from pension schemes under the control of the late Robert Maxwell[7]), on the prevention of fraud. This will extend to employers who breach contractual rights by, for example, failing to pay contributions which have been recommended by the scheme actuaries or, with insured schemes, failing to pay insurance company premiums when these fall due.[8] Most employers will also recognize the need to regulate internal accounting and auditing procedures, so that trustees can know when the security of scheme benefits is threatened by non-payment or misfeasance.[9] There is even acceptance amongst some employers that member-appointed trustees should become mandatory, *provided that they remain a minority*.[10]

Regulations to make 'good practice' into a statutory requirement will increase the administrative costs of 'good' employers, if only through the need to take legal advice on whether their procedures comply with regulations. But in the context of the Maxwell scandal, these costs may be worthwhile, if only to reassure the members that their fixed benefits are adequately secured. Employers who fall below this standard of 'good practice' are likely to threaten to reduce or terminate the provision of pensions to their workforce if this standard becomes mandatory.

[5] CBI, n. 2 above, p. 14.

[6] Occupational Pension Schemes (Investment of Resources) Regulations 1992, SI 1992/246.

[7] For a description of the events leading up to the loss of this money, see n. 1 above, paras. 76–178.

[8] See the National Association of Pension Fund's (NAPF) submission to the Goode Committee, p. 59. [9] CBI, n. 2 above, p. 14.

[10] The Engineering Employers' Federation, who recognize member trusteeship as good practice, are concerned only that employers do not lose their right to appoint the majority of trustees. See their submission to the Goode Committee, p. 1. The NAPF went so far as to accept that members should have a mandatory right to appoint one member, or to agree with the employer for the appointment of an independent trustee. N. 8 above, p. 6. The CBI, who represent a large number of employers who do not appoint member trustees, were opposed to mandatory minority trustees. Ibid., p. 16.

If employers accept that the ignorance of employees, which leads them to regard the pension fund as their property, needs to be altered, they may support a requirement to provide employees with more information on scheme administration.[11] This represents a move from *caveat emptor*, to *informed caveat emptor*. In its starkest form, such a policy would necessitate employees receiving a document which contains the following 'health warnings':

The money put into this scheme will be used first to secure the deferred pension which you will receive if the scheme winds up. (A benefit fixed by reference to your salary on the date you leave the scheme indexed by the lower of RPI or 5 per cent p.a.). Any assets held in excess of this amount are not held for your benefit but may be used by the trustees/employer, at their absolute discretion, to reduce the employer's contribution rate, to pay a refund to the employer, or to increase benefits.

You should not expect to receive benefit increases whatever level of assets builds up in the pension scheme.[12]

B. ASSESSING THE RISK OF LOWER OR DIFFERENT PENSION PROVISION

If reform goes beyond requirements for disclosure, or measures designed to reduce the risk of fraud or the non-payment of contributions, there is a danger that large numbers of small employers, or even some of the larger employers, will reduce or alter the benefits offered. Some employers may cease to offer pensions altogether.

Against this, one should not readily assume that pension provision is something which can be replaced easily and cheaply by other forms of remuneration, such as increased current wages, or the provision of other 'fringe benefits'. As the Confederation of British Industry recognizes:

It . . . seems certain that the effects of demographic change and employee expectations mean that some sort of occupational pension provision will remain an important recruitment, retention or even motivational tool for many employers into the future.[13]

Some employers may prefer to move from final salary schemes into money purchase arrangements, in the belief that the latter are less complex and offer the prospect of a stable contribution rate. However, many of the supposed advantages and disadvantages of money purchase schemes depend on the assumption that these schemes will escape the process of reform. And when assessing what those reforms might be, one should not forget why final salary schemes are so popular with employers and employees.

---

[11] The Engineering Employers' Federation would accept a requirement to disclose the employer's powers. Ibid., p. 14.
[12] The CBI believes that pension documentation should spell out the nature of the pensions promise, and that members should not be entitled to discretionary increases simply because their 'expectations' exceed their rights. N. 2 above, p. 14.   [13] CBI, n. 2 above, p. 11.

Employees understand inflation, and know that pensions promised in pounds may be devalued. In order to plan for their retirement, they need to know how their pension will compare with their pre-retirement income. Final salary schemes contain such information in the benefit formula itself. Moving to money purchase schemes will not make employees lose interest in this vital information. They will demand projections as to the pensions likely to be funded by the assets held for them, and for those projections to be made in a form which they can understand and on which they can rely. One can envisage a future in which money purchase schemes have to produce periodic projections of the value of an individual's benefits, using standard actuarial methods, and a prescribed basis of presentation. Such regulations will erode the relative 'simplicity' of money purchase schemes.

If money purchase schemes were required to reveal the likely future value of their benefits, this might also erode their ability to operate on the basis of a fixed contribution rate. If the actuary's valuation revealed that the current contribution rate was unlikely to provide adequate pensions, the members would be expected to press for increased contributions. If the employer found that its current contribution rate was likely to produce money purchase benefits that were in excess of two-thirds of retirement salary, it might seek a reduction in the future contribution rate.

Employers may believe that by threatening to move to money purchase arrangements, they can resist employees' claims for disclosure and control. But if they actually move to money purchase arrangements, they will have much greater difficulty justifying their present controls over pension scheme administration and investment. If the employer has no legal obligation to fund a deficit, and if the value of the employees' benefits are directly determined by the value of the pension fund, the members' claim to control of the pension fund becomes far easier to make, and far harder to resist.

C. ASSESSING THE RISK OF LOWER FUNDING LEVELS

In response to proposals which are intended to ensure that surpluses are used solely for the members' benefit, employers have threatened to reduce future funding levels, so as to prevent surpluses from arising. The implications of this threat are that, if the members seek a right to benefit from surpluses, funding will fall, and there will be lower benefits or increased scheme failures in future. But is it so clear that restricting employers' access to surpluses will lower funding?

At present, any contribution made by the employer has to be viewed as a possible payment for its own benefit, which makes it hard for employees to appreciate the cost of their pension provision. Employees, or at least their trade union representatives, now know that funding above an actuarial minimum may simply lead to employer refunds or contribution holidays in future. In these circumstances, unless the legal framework is altered, they may prefer lower funding levels and higher current pay. To restore their acceptance of the need for prudent funding levels, the full benefit of such funding must be held solely for the members.[14] Such a reform may not only make prudent funding more acceptable, it will also make it easier to negotiate on the cost of pension provision. A system which genuinely alienates the employer from its contributions as they are made, makes it clear what part pensions play in the annual 'total remuneration package'.

III. PROPOSALS FOR REFORM—FROM A DEFERRED PAY PERSPECTIVE

In its strongest form, the claim that pensions are pay refers both to the benefits that employees have been promised and to the contributions which the employer makes to fund those benefits. The pension fund is seen as the members' property. If it is not to be managed directly by them, it must at least be managed in their sole interests.

From this perspective, the employer's promise takes the following form:

We are paying an amount that is certain to fund these benefits and will, if the investments do well, allow for benefit increases. The assets used to secure this promise are held in trust for your benefit.[15]

Under the current legal framework, the employer can renege on this promise. As we saw in Chapter 7, the investments can do well, and yet the employer may use the surplus for its own benefit. Worse still, in the absence of minimum funding standards and with the possibility of fraud, there is no guarantee that even the first part of the promise will be met: the pension scheme may be wound up with insufficient assets to pay even the fixed benefits.

The discussion which follows looks at various reforms[16] which may restrain the employer's ability to defeat this promise, beginning with those intended to meet the least radical of the members' demands (that schemes

---

[14] The Institute and Faculty of Actuaries, and the Association of Pension Lawyers, accept that some employers may wish to fund on this basis, and suggest that 'funding plans' be adopted which set out how surpluses will be used. See their respective submissions to the Goode Committee.

[15] Such a promise is analogous to a with-profit insurance policy, which 'guarantees' a defined benefit, plus an assurance of greater benefits if the policy's investments do at all well. No one suggests that insurance companies, who are unquestionably responsible for the 'deficit' which might arise in such contracts, should be able to renege on the agreement and claim all the 'surplus'.

[16] This is not intended to be a comprehensive review of all possible reforms. In particular, it does not examine whether employers should be forced to offer pension schemes, or required to offer only final salary schemes, or compelled to make all benefits fully indexed. Instead, it has looked at the scope for deferred-pay based reforms on the assumption that the provision of pension schemes and the choice of benefits will remain a voluntary matter.

have sufficient assets to pay fixed benefits), and ending with the most radical proposal (member control).

1. Safe Custody

The Maxwell scandal points to the need to examine procedures for the custody of scheme assets. As described in Chapter 8, the trustees have a general duty to be diligent, and can be expected to take action if they become aware of facts which indicate that the funds are at risk. Whilst this residual duty can be useful, it is undermined where a scheme's financial affairs are so organized that the trustees are not kept informed of the location of scheme assets or the payment of contributions. There is general consensus on the need for auditing and accounts procedures to be put in place which will ensure that the trustees can properly carry out their custodial and supervisory role.[17]

2. Prudent Funding Levels

If a scheme is to have sufficient assets to pay the fixed benefits, funding must be prudent. The present situation, in which members rely on the scheme actuary's judgment, may not be satisfactory. While members may think of actuaries as independent professionals, bound by professional standards to set funding rates which ensure the security of their benefits, the reality, as seen in Chapter 6, is quite different. Actuaries may alter the method of funding, or the assumptions used in connection with any method, and are not required to ensure that the scheme has sufficient assets to meet its obligations on winding up. There is a need to restrain the ability of actuaries to adopt imprudent funding levels. But there is a divergence of opinion on how to achieve this. In particular, should funding below a prescribed minimum be prohibited, or is it acceptable, provided that the relevant parties are informed?

Minimum Funding Levels These raise two major problems. First, in common with every proposal for the reform of pension law, there is a danger that employers who view compliance with this standard as an unacceptable cost will offer lower benefits, or move to money purchase arrangements, or simply cease to offer a pension scheme. Second, and more specifically, there is a danger that any minimum funding level will be set too low, creating a

---

[17] The CBI wanted custody of scheme assets to be handled by a custodial service or trustee which was regulated and separate from the fund manager. See their submission to the Goode Committee, n. 2 above, p. 8. They wanted trustees to be under a duty to report non-payment of contributions or premiums to the OPB. The NAPF, whose membership in the main excludes schemes which are fully insured, wanted insurance companies to be under a duty to report non-payment of premiums to a regulator. See their submission to the Goode Committee, n. 8 above, p. 59.

false sense of security amongst members, reduced funding by employers, and increased scheme failures in future.[18]

Increasing the Effectiveness of Disclosure   The disclosure regulations already require the scheme actuary to state periodically whether scheme assets are sufficient to meet the fixed benefits payable on winding up.[19] Such statements could be made more often, and there could be a standard basis for calculating the adequacy of assets for this purpose. But such measures fail to address the major weakness of disclosure as a form of protection: the members' general inability to rectify what is disclosed. At present, the employee's only remedy is to leave the pension scheme, and take a transfer value based on her right as an early leaver.[20]

3. A Compensation Fund

The security of fixed benefits could be increased by a statutory compensation scheme which undertook to meet out of a central fund any shortfall arising on winding up. But a scheme which guaranteed the payment of fixed benefits in all circumstances might encourage employers to lower funding levels or increase the riskiness of their investments. Without minimum funding levels or investment controls, the cost of the compensation fund could be very high. And if the fund had to be paid for by a levy on all pension schemes, it could result in the more prudent schemes subsidizing the less prudent ones.

Most of the complications and cross-subsidies caused by a compensation fund can be avoided by reducing its coverage to losses arising through fraud, leaving the risks associated with low funding or imprudent investment to be dealt with via other reforms.[21]

---

[18] It is also important to consider how to treat schemes which fall below the standard. If they had to be wound up, and their assets used to purchase immediate annuities for all members, this could impose substantial costs on the fund. Non-profit (i.e. guaranteed) annuities are a very expensive way of securing members' benefits. The amount required to secure benefits in this way could exceed the assets ordinarily considered sufficient to secure the members' accrued liabilities on an ongoing basis. Thus, a small drop below ongoing scheme funding standards might precipitate a large reduction in the members' benefits. If minimum funding levels were introduced, it might be better for large schemes to continue as closed schemes rather than wind up. A national body would need to take over the assets and liabilities of small schemes which fell below minimum funding standards. Such a body could be run like a large closed scheme, and secure the members' accrued liabilities without the need to purchase insurance annuities. See the Institute and Faculty of Actuaries submission to the Goode Committee.

[19] Occupational Pension Scheme (Disclosure of Information) Regulations 1986, SI 1986 No. 1046, Schedule 4.

[20] Adopting a standard basis for calculating the security of benefits on winding up would also repeat one of the major dangers of prescribed minimum standards (that all or most employers will drop their funding to the minimum), without assuring members that the minimum will actually be paid.

[21] Employers seem to be firmly against a compensation fund which covers risks other than fraud. The NAPF originally proposed a fund which covered loss of fixed benefits for any reason, but was forced by its membership (most of whom are employers) to favour compensation solely for losses due to fraud, theft, and criminal negligence. See the NAPF's submission to the Goode Committee, n. 8 above, p. 43.

B. THE LONG-TERM BENEFITS OF PRUDENT FUNDING—A RIGHT TO BENEFIT INCREASES

Prudent funding should make it is extremely unlikely that a scheme will fail to pay the members' fixed benefits. Conversely, where a scheme has been prudently funded, it is *more likely that not* that the scheme assets will exceed what is required to pay fixed benefits. So the call for benefit increases when investments do well is really a demand that members should benefit from the *expected* long-term effects of prudent funding. As we saw in Chapter 7, the employer may currently benefit from such surpluses through contribution reductions or holidays, and in some circumstances, through a refund.

1. Guaranteeing Discretionary Benefit Increases

One could introduce a regime similar to that used by the Inland Revenue to decide when a scheme is to suffer partial loss of approval.[22] Schemes which exceeded a solvency level identified through the use of a standard actuarial basis[23] could be required to take action to reduce the surplus by benefit increases.[24] This proposal would duplicate the major risk associated with the Inland Revenue's regime: that employers would cease to fund above this level, effectively establishing a maximum funding level, which might turn out to be too low.

C. CHANGING THE BALANCE OF POWER

It is impossible to devise a regulatory regime for pension schemes which will not leave the members' interests crucially affected by the exercise of discretions. Regulation cannot provide in detail for each and every aspect of pension administration. For example, if there was a rule requiring all funding in excess of a mandatory maximum to be absorbed through benefit increases, there would still be a need for a body to decide which group of members received benefits, and in which form. Where an employer used the excess to fund its redundancy programme through generous early retirement benefits, this might still, from the members' point of view, represent an unacceptable exploitation of their fund.

---

[22] See Chapter 6, pp. 136–8.

[23] Without a standard basis for such calculations, rules requiring surpluses to be used for benefit increases are open to avoidance. The actuary can delay a surplus from being declared by adopting a more prudent funding level. In the meantime, the employer may be able to introduce new members who have no, or less well-funded, pensions, and absorb the surplus, or eject members from the scheme so that they cannot participate in the benefit improvements. There is also a danger that surpluses will be identified and benefit improvements declared in schemes which are using low funding standards, increasing the likelihood that such schemes will fail.

[24] The beginnings of such an arrangement are contained in the Social Security Act 1990, Schedule 2, para. 3, which requires actuarial surpluses to be used to provide for the price indexation (up to 5% p.a.) of benefits accruing with respect to service before the appointed day. At the time of writing (March 1993), this provision had not been implemented.

As one cannot exclude all discretion, one needs to examine how discretions should be allocated and restrained. The first question to consider is whether trust law provides an appropriate framework for such discretions.

1. The Need to Retain Trust Law

The central idea of trust law, that of a fiduciary (a person acting on behalf of and in the interests of others),[25] should not, and indeed cannot, be abandoned. As long as there are discretions which need to be exercised on behalf of the members, one is reliant upon some kind of fiduciary relationship. There is no point in replacing trust law by another fiduciary relationship, such as that applied to agents or company directors,[26] unless this offers increased protection.

Agency and company law contain fiduciary duties similar to those operating within the law of trusts: to act in the best interests of the principal/company; and to avoid conflicts of interest. But these duties are generally expected to operate more strictly against trustees than against agents or company directors.[27] Abandoning trust law in favour of these other legal relationships may therefore result in the administrators of pension schemes having reduced fiduciary duties.

2. The Current Deficiencies of Trust Law

From the members' perspective, the problem is not trust law *per se*, but the freedom which trust law gives employers, subject only to the constraints of revenue practice and social security legislation, to draft the pension trust in whatever manner they see fit.

By their ability to appoint the trustees, employers can prevent persons who might take too robust a view of the members' entitlements from becoming trustees. This would not be so important if the standards applied to trustees were always strong and easy to follow. But, as we saw in Chapter 3, trustees are subject to a quite flexible system of review, in which different standards may be applied to their actions, depending on the wording of the scheme, and the court's view of what is appropriate. In the present climate, in which the

---

[25] See Chapter 1, pp. 11–12.

[26] The Social Security Select Committee favoured giving pension schemes a legal framework that was analogous to company law. Note 1 above, para. 74.

[27] Directors are both agents and trustees: trustees of the company's property, agents in the transactions which they enter into on behalf of the company. *G. E. Ry.* v. *Turner* (1872) LR 8 Ch. 149, 152. As trustees, 'their position differs considerably from that of ordinary trustees, and the strict rules applicable to such trustees do not apply in all respects to directors'. *Palmer's Company Law*, 25th edn. (Sweet & Maxwell, 1992), para. 8.403. The rule of prudence in investment is more relaxed, as is the right to hold offices in competing enterprises, see *Bell* v. *Lever Bros.* [1932] AC 161 at 195. (But cf. *Scottish Co-operative Wholesale Society Ltd.* v. *Meyer* [1959] AC 324, 366.) The general business practices of directors and agents may be impliedly authorized. See *Kelly* v. *Cooper* [1992] 3 WLR 937 at 941–3. Articles of Association commonly waive the conflict of interest rule, *Palmer*, para. 8.518. On the scope of Articles to exclude the rule against self-dealing, see *Motivex Ltd.* v. *Bullfield* [1988] BCLR 104.

employer's entitlement to benefit from the pension scheme is unclear, members cannot be sure that trust law will require their interests to be preferred over those of the employer. And even if the courts were to require trustees to act solely in the best interests of the members, the difficulties of obtaining information about the reasons for trustees' actions, and the risks of starting hostile actions (see Chapter 5), would severely undermine the members' ability to enforce this duty.

The employer's freedom to draft pension schemes means that it need not rely solely on its control over the appointment of trustees. It can reserve powers to veto benefit increases and wind up the scheme. With such powers held by the employer, there is no certainty that any of the assets in excess of those required to secure the members' benefits on winding up will be used to pay members' benefits. In its dealings with the trustees, such powers represent a trump card which can be played whenever trustees seek to exercise their discretions in a manner which the employer finds unacceptable.[28]

In addition, through its control over the appointment of the trustees, or through the reservation of express powers, the employer can ensure that the persons advising the trustees act in its interests. Thus, through its influence over the actuary, the employer can control the scheme's funding level. It can manipulate transfer payments, and alter the basis upon which its contribution rate is calculated. Similarly, through its control over the appointment of financial advisers, it can ensure that those persons responsible for formulating or carrying out investment policy act in its interests. As the Maxwell saga showed, this can even extend to having one of its own subsidiaries acting as the scheme's financial manager, with the consequent risk of large-scale fraud.[29]

By controlling the advice and services received by trustees, the employer effectively circumvents the protections offered by trust law. Trustees who follow the advice of experts, or rely on them to carry out the day-to-day management of the trust, will rarely be found guilty of a breach of trust. There is a general assumption, discussed in Chapter 8 in the context of investment, that trustees cannot be expected to second-guess the opinions of experts. Unless they can be shown to have failed to act diligently, they can expect to escape liability when they have relied on the advice and actions of the fund manager, actuary, and scheme administrators.

3. Supplementing Trust Law

What members need is a statutory framework which ensures that persons they trust are appointed as trustees, and that those persons have sufficient powers, duties, and abilities to protect the members' interests. The first thing

---

[28] 'In June 1991 a formal proposal to agree to the refund was put to the trustees with the employer indicating that if their agreement was not forthcoming the scheme would be wound up.' Case study presented by the Charter for Pension Fund Democracy in their submission to the Goode Committee, p. 31.   [29] Note 1 above, para. 128.

to consider is who the trustees should be. Should the current situation be replaced by one requiring the appointment of independent trustees, minority member-appointed trustees, or majority member-appointed trustees?

Independent Trustees   When employers speak of independent trustees, they usually refer to persons appointed by themselves who have no past or present contractual relationship with the employer. However, unless such persons agree to work unpaid, they do have a financial interest in acting on behalf of the party who has appointed them. Furthermore, whether paid or not, people appointed to this position are likely to hold views which are acceptable to the employer.

From the members' perspective, the good thing about the rising popularity of independent trustees is that they represent an acknowledgement that trust law cannot prevent employer-appointed tustees from preferring the employer's interests to those of the members. But is unclear why members should expect their interests to be as well protected by persons chosen by the employer, rather than by themselves.

Minority Member-Appointed Trustees   The appointment of a minority of member-appointed trustees is already considered to be good practice by the National Association of Pension Funds, and could be made compulsory without too hostile a reaction from employers.[30] It would overcome some of the problems which result from the members' lack of access to information, since the minority would be privy to the trustees' deliberations and could ask the majority to justify decisions with which they disagreed. But without access to independent legal advice and assistance, minority trustees would be unable to seek a review of the majority's actions or prevent a breach of trust. And even then, if the cost of such reviews and actions is not to be prohibitive, there would also be a need for a pensions tribunal.

Even with all these reforms, a system which requires a minority of member-appointed trustees is still likely to remain unacceptable to members. For in any situation where the law allows trustees to take different views as to what should be done, it will be the majority employer-appointed trustees whose votes carry the day. Thus, for example, if the member-appointed trustees preferred safer investments with less risk, it would still be open to employer-appointed trustees to seek higher returns at greater risk.

This problem goes to the heart of the nature of discretion. If there is only one course of action which could reasonably be in the beneficiaries' interests, then there is a sense in which trustees have no discretion: they are bound to act in that way. But if they are allowed to choose between a number of options, how should such choices be made? From the perspective of deferred pay, any decisions which are not dictated by legal duties should be taken by

---

[30] See p. 231 on employers' likely reaction to reform.

the persons appointed by the members themselves. To quote the Charter for Pension Fund Democracy (an organization which represents 3.5 million employees):

This reform [majority member-appointed trustees] is essential to ensure that pension fund assets are entirely separate from employer assets and that trustees act in the best interests of members. *The best judges of members' interests are the members themselves.* Increasingly, scheme members do not perceive employers as suitable guardians of their trust funds.[31]

Majority Member-Appointed Trustees   To the extent that the duty to act in the members' interests has substance and is enforceable, the actions of trustees should be the same under this proposal as they are at present. But to the extent that this duty is vague or otherwise unenforceable, it would be member-appointed trustees who had freedom to act, rather than employer-appointed ones as at present.[32]

If members appointed the majority of the trustees, many of the difficulties of enforcing trust law would no longer have the same importance. Much of the case for a pensions tribunal rests on the need to make trust law effective in restraining breach of trust by persons under the employer's control. With the transfer of control to the members, the importance of access to the courts is diminished.

Nevertheless, a tribunal may still be necessary to facilitate actions by members or by employers on behalf of members, where the member-appointed trustees act in breach of trust. It may also be useful to prevent connivance between an employer and corrupt member trustees, or to prevent trustees appointed by current members from sacrificing the interests of deferred or current pensioners. The interests of deferred and current pensioners could be further protected by giving these groups the right to appoint some of the trustees, and then giving those trustees a right to separate legal advice and assistance.

The Powers and Duties of Trustees   Giving members the power to appoint a majority of the trustees may ensure that the trustees are more willing to protect the members' interests, but it will not, without further reforms, ensure that they are able to do this. If such trustees are to act independently from the employer, they need to be able to appoint their own advisers who should not, ideally, act also for the employer. They also need to acquire and retain the confidence and competence that would enable them to act effectively on behalf of the members. This requires a programme of

---

[31] Submission to the Goode Committee by the Charter for Pension Fund Democracy, n. 28 above, para. 5.2. (emphasis added).

[32] This argument would also apply to the duty to act impartially as between different groups of members.

mandatory training, both initial and continuing, for all trustees. Member Trustees also need to have their employment protected, and to be given entitlements to time off in order to undertake their activities.

As noted in Chapter 3, accepting that the employer is a beneficiary undermines the ability of trustees to act solely in the members' interests. There is a need to confirm that the trustees' sole duty is to the members.[33] There is also a need to remove the ability of employees to threaten winding up, with its consequent loss of pension benefits and the likelihood of a refund to the employer. This could be done by removing the employer's right to the refund, or removing the employer's power to veto benefit increases on winding up, or simply by passing the power to wind up to the trustees.

Making Trustees More Accountable   Trustees are currently required to prepare an annual report which is available to members on request. The report will inform members of any non-payment of contributions, the degree of self-investment, and the year's financial transactions. Through such disclosure the members will learn, *up to twelve months after the end of the scheme's financial year*, whether events have occurred which imperil the security of their benefits.[34]

There is a case for more regular reporting, and reporting more quickly after the occurrence of events which may threaten the security of benefits. In addition, there is as yet no statutory requirement for trustees to keep or reveal records of the reasons why they have taken particular decisions. As we saw in Chapter 5, trustees are able to resist disclosing their reasons on the general basis that their deliberations are confidential. Whilst the Courts may be persuaded to narrow the trustees' right to refuse to account for their actions, mounting an action to force disclosure of information is likely to be expensive and the outcome uncertain. In these circumstances there is a case for requiring the trustees to keep minutes which should, unless the information contained therein is personal or price-sensitive, be disclosed to members on request.

Requiring trustees to disclose their reasons would assist members to judge whether the trustees were acting in their best interests. This would have obvious relevance where trustees were elected by the members, since any re-election would take place on an informed basis. It would also be even more useful if trustees continued to be appointed by the employer, since the general absence of information on the reasons for trustees' decisions makes it extremely difficult to obtain a review of their actions.

---

[33] The Association of Pension Lawyers' submission to the Goode Committee argues that employers must be considered beneficiaries of the scheme simply because they are affected by the trustees' actions. This definition would allow employers to argue that their interests should be considered even in those schemes where the employer is expressly prohibited from receiving any money from the scheme.   [34] Note 19 above, reg. 9.

The Final Bastion—Control over Funding and Benefits The deferred pay perspective requires members' fixed benefits to be paid, all the benefits of prudent funding to accrue to the members, and the scheme to be managed solely in their interests. This cannot be achieved within defined benefit schemes if control over funding and benefit increases is left with the employer. To give full effect to the deferred pay perspective, members need to exercise power over funding and benefit increases through their appointed representatives. Thus, the trustees should be given the power to decide what contribution rate is appropriate for the scheme, and what benefit increases it can afford, with a majority of those trustees appointed by the members.[35] This would prevent employers being able to decide unilaterally to retain the entire benefit of surpluses for themselves by vetoing benefit increases and reducing the contribution rate.

With these two powers, member trustees could ensure that money paid into the pension scheme was, so far as is possible, completely alienated from the employer. At every actuarial review, the trustees and the employer would decide whether they wished to continue with the present pension scheme. If the employer would not agree to pay the contribution rate thought appropriate by the trustees' actuary, the trustees should have the option of using the current assets to augment benefits and, if necessary, wind up the scheme. If the employer could persuade the members' trustees that it was in the members' interests to allow the scheme to continue with reduced contributions, then this could occur.

---

[35] There are international precedents for members having this degree of control.

In Spain, tax relief is restricted to schemes in which all the assets, including any surpluses, belong to the scheme members and their dependants. (Law 8/87 governing Pension Plans and Pension Funds. BOE 137, of 9.06.87, Art. 8.4, 8.7). To ensure that ownership and control go together, the law requires that representatives of the members are in the majority on two key committees: the pension plan control committee, and the pension funds control committee (Art. 7(3)). The pension plan control committee administers the scheme. Its functions include selecting the scheme actuary, supervising the rules, checking the rules are observed, and proposing modifications to the contributions and benefits based upon actuarial reviews. The pension funds control committee oversees the scheme's investments. Where a pension scheme has its own fund, this committee will consist of the same persons as the pension fund control committee. It operates with different personnel only when a number of schemes pool funds. With pooled funds, representatives of the various schemes' control committees are delegated to sit on the pension funds control committee. This committee appoints its own accountants and actuaries for annual audits. It also has the power to appoint and dismiss the fund manager.

In Australia, by 1995 all pension schemes with more than 200 members must provide for at least half the scheme trustees to be appointed by the members. See Occupational and Superannuation Standards Act 1987. The Australian government proposes further radical reforms to ensure a pension scheme's independence from the employer: requiring equal representation in schemes with more than forty-nine members, requiring equal representation or an independent trustee in schemes with five to forty-nine members, specifying the duties of trustees, restricting the employer's right to draft pension scheme rules which reduce the trustees' independence or effectiveness, and requiring trustees to keep minutes of their meetings which members may inspect. See 'Strengthening Super Security: New Prudential Arrangements for Superannuation', Statement by John Hawkins, MP, Treasurer of the Commonwealth of Australia, 21 October 1992.

This proposal would leave the employer with the power not to have a pension scheme, but with no legal powers over the scheme, and therefore no way of using such powers to benefit from past contributions. The only power which would remain with the employer would be the power to refuse to offer future service benefits. If the scheme is a good scheme, the trustees will wish for it to continue to operate. This ensures that the trustees will act reasonably when deciding whether or not to increase benefits.[36]

Under this proposal, the employer will be expected to pay an amount that is certain to fund the benefits set out in the rules, and then, if the investments do well, to negotiate with the trustees about the use of any monies left over. At present, similar negotiations are occurring within schemes over the refund of surpluses, but with the members represented by trustees appointed by the employer. Even worse, through their control of scheme actuaries, employers are able to set a scheme's funding level without negotiation. An employer's unilateral decision as to what it will pay into the pension scheme can be presented to the members, through the use of an actuary, as the 'appropriate' funding level for the scheme.[37]

Employers will argue that the loss of control represented by this proposal puts them in an impossible position. How can they be exposed to the risk of deficits within schemes over which they have no control? This objection could be met by repealing the Social Security Act 1990, Schedule 4, para. 2, which makes the employer liable for any shortfall arising on winding up. If this were done, the members would be exchanging what is at present a right to pursue an unsecured debt against an often bankrupt employer, for a legal structure which would give them control of their deferred pay.[38]

IV. CONCLUSION

Any body charged with the reform of pension schemes has to choose between making employers live up to the pension promise as it is understood by the members, and making members understand the lesser promise which employers claim to have made. One doubts the ability of this or any other government to convince members that the pension fund is not their property, and this may force employers to come to grips with a legal structure in which

---

[36] As Ferris J observed in *Aitken* v. *Christy Hunt PLC* [1991] PLR 1, when the employer attempted to argue that a balance of power such as this was unworkable.

[37] This proposal could be varied by giving the employer power to refuse to pay the contribution rate recommended by the trustees. This would introduce extra flexibility. If the employer had to contribute what the trustees recommended, the trustees might end up in a situation in which they had only two choices: to require a contribution rate which would lead to the employer withdrawing from the scheme, or to appear to endorse a contribution rate which they felt was too low. Allowing the scheme to continue with the employer paying less than trustees recommend could, in the right circumstances, be a valuable third option.

[38] Where the shortfall was due to fraud or another breach of trust by the employer, the members would still be able to sue for damages and seek to trace the lost assets.

the pension fund is less under their control than before. The changes necessary to achieve this will undoubtedly have cost implications, and the long-term consequences may be a reduction in the benefits offered by schemes, and a reduction in the number of employers offering pension schemes. But against this, one should not underestimate the degree to which confidence in pension provision has been undermined by employees learning that the pension fund is not their property, but has to be shared with their employer.[39] For confidence to be restored, the pension trust needs to be reformed to give effect to an understanding of pension rights as deferred pay.

[39] The Charter for Pension Fund Democracy, after holding a conference attended by 250 member trustees and pension representatives, and conducting a survey of member trustees, found: 'a widespread lack of confidence in the ability of employers to protect the interests of beneficiaries . . .'. See n. 28 above, para. 3.1.

Glossary

Accrued Rights Premium
State scheme premium payable when a scheme ceases to be contracted out. In exchange, the state relieves the scheme of the need to pay a Guaranteed Minimim Pension. The premium need not be paid if alternative arrangements are made to secure the Guaranteed Minimum Pension (e.g., through another contracted-out scheme).

Additional Component
An earnings related pension payable by the state. To be contrasted with Guaranteed Minimum Pensions, which are funded by the state (through lower national insurance contributions), but paid by a contracted-out occupational scheme.

Additional Voluntary Contributions
Extra contributions made by an individual employee in order to increase her pension provision. Some schemes credit members with extra years of pensionable service, whilst others offer money purchase benefits.

Aggregate Method
A method for fixing a scheme's contribution rate which takes account of all past and future liabilities. The contribution rate will aim to ensure that the assets of the scheme equal its liabilities by the end of the working lifetimes of the scheme current members.

Attained Age Method
A method for assessing the solvency of a pension scheme which assumes that the annual contribution will be sufficient to meet the average annual cost of future service liabilities. It is less prudent that the entry age method, which assumes that contributions will be insufficient to fund the future service liabilities. In practice, it is indistinguishable from the current unit method.

Automatic Resulting Trusts
A trust which arises by operation of law when the rules of an express trust fail to fully dispose of the trust property. The unexpended balance is held on resulting trust for the settlor.

Average Salary Scheme
These schemes offer benefits that are fixed by reference to the employees' average salary during their membership of the scheme.

Bona Vacantia
Unowned property held for the crown.

Bridging Pension
An additional pension paid by a scheme to a retired male member aged between 60 and 65 to compensate him for the fact that he will not receive the basic flat rate state retirement pension.

Bulk Transfer Payments
Payments made on behalf of a group of employees transferring into another pension scheme where the new scheme has taken over responsibility for their accrued benefits.

Cash Equivalent Method
A method for calculating bulk transfer payments based on the individual members' statutory right to a transfer payment: the estimated cost of funding accrued benefits, fixed by reference to salaries at the date of leaving service, on the assumption that those benefits would be indexed in accordance with the Social Security Acts.

Committee of Management
In some schemes this is simply another name for the trustees. In others it refers to a committee of trustees or other persons, to whom some of the trustees' functions have been delegated.

Contingent Benefits
Benefits payable on the occurrence of a defined event. For example, a current member's pension entitlement is a contingent benefit, since it will not be paid unless and until that member retires.

Contra Proferentum
The rule of construction which requires ambiguities in documents to be construed against the interests of the party who drafted them.

Contracted-in scheme
A scheme which offers benefits as additions to (rather than substitutes for) the additional component payable under the State Earnings Related Pensions Scheme. The employer and employees pay the full national insurance rate.

Contracted-out scheme
A scheme which offers its benefits as substitutes for the additional component payable under the State Earnings Related Pension Scheme. In return, the employer and employees pay a lower rate of national insurance contribution.

Contributory Scheme
A scheme which requires the employees to contribute towards the cost of their benefits.

Current Unit Credit Method
A method for assessing the solvency of a pension fund by comparing the scheme's assets with its accrued liabilities, but ignoring the increase in the value of those benefits likely to be brought about by future salary increases.

Deferred Pension
A pension earned by a person who is no longer a member of a scheme, who has not yet retired.

Defined Benefit Scheme
A scheme in which the benefits are fixed (usually by reference to the employee's salary) and the employer undertakes to make whatever contributions are necessary to pay these benefits.

Defined Contribution Scheme
Another name for a money purchase scheme (see below).

Discretionary Trusts
A trust in which the interests of beneficiaries are determined through the exercise of powers held by the trustees.

Early Leaver Method
Another name for the cash equivalent method, see above.

Entry Age Method
A method for assessing the solvency of a pension scheme. The actuary must compare the past and future service liability with accrued assets plus the value of an assumed low future contribution rate, (based on the cost of providing the benefits of new entrants to the scheme).

Family Trust
A trust used to settle property on members of a family.

Final Salary Scheme
A defined benefit scheme in which the benefits are calculated by reference to the salaries paid to individual members at or around the date on which they leave the scheme, and their total years of membership.

Fixed Trust
A trust in which the interests of beneficiaries are set out in the trust, and do not depend on the exercise of powers held by the trustees.

Fraud on a Power (Doctrine of)
The rule that persons who are given a power over property must use that power in accordance with its purpose.

Funded Scheme
A scheme in which the benefits are secured by a fund of assets.

Guaranteed Minimum Pension
The benefit paid by a contracted-out scheme as a substitute for the additional component payable under the State Earnings Related Pension Scheme. It is the minimum benefit a contracted-out scheme must provide.

Integrated Scheme
A scheme in which the pensions are reduced to take account of the basic flat rate state retirement pension.

Irrevocable Trust
A trust which contains no power of revocation.

Mere Power
A power which the holder has no duty to exercise.

Money Purchase Scheme
A scheme in which the employer's contributions on behalf of each employee are fixed, and the scheme undertakes to pay whatever benefits can be met through such accumulated contributions.

Non-Contributory Scheme
A scheme in which employees are not required to pay contributions.

Past Service Reserve
A method for calculating transfer payments based on the accrued benefits of the transferring members, increased to take account of expected increases in their salaries prior to their retirement.

Pension Schemes Office
The Inland Revenue Branch which deals with the approval of pension schemes, formerly known as the Superannuation Funds Office.

Pensionable Service
An employee's years of scheme membership.

Pensions Ombudsman
The person appointed to investigate and determine any dispute of fact or

law, or any complaint of maladministration, which arises between a member, past member or their widow or surviving dependant, and the managers or trustees of an occupational or personal pension scheme or the employer. The ombudsman provides an alternative to an action in the courts.

Personal Pension Scheme
A money purchase scheme arranged for an individual employee through an insurance company, bank, or building society.

Power of Appointment
A power, usually held by a trustee, to decide who may enjoy rights to the income or capital of a property.

Preservation Requirements
The necessity to provide a deferred pension to scheme leavers with more than 2 years pensionable service. This pension must be calculated on the same basis, and subject to the same conditions, as the pensions provided to those who remain with the scheme.

Projected Unit Method
A method for assessing the solvency of a pension scheme which requires the actuary to calculate the scheme's accrued liabilities by reference to projected future salaries and compare this figure with the value of the scheme's assets.

Resulting Trust
See Automatic Resulting Trusts, above.

State Earnings Related Pension Scheme
The state scheme for paying an earnings related contributory pension in addition to the basic flat rate retirement pension. The pension may be received direct from the state, or indirectly through a contracted-out pension scheme.

Superannuation Funds Office
The former name of the Pension Schemes Office.

Total Service Reserve Method
A method for calculating a transfer payment. The transfer payment should aim to ensure that the future contribution rate of both the transferring and receiving scheme will be equal for the remaining working lives of the current scheme members.

Transfer Payment
A payment made by an occupational scheme to another occupational scheme

or personal pension scheme which has undertaken to take over the transferring scheme's liability for a member's accrued rights.

Trust Power
A power which the holder has a duty to exercise.

Unfunded Scheme
A scheme in which the benefits are not secured by a fund of assets.

Index